Decolonizing Law

This volume brings together Indigenous, Third World and Settler perspectives on the theory and practice of decolonizing law.

Colonialism, imperialism and settler colonialism continue to affect the lives of racialized communities and Indigenous Peoples around the world. Law, in its many iterations, has played an active role in the dispossession and disenfranchisement of colonized peoples. Law and its various institutions are the means by which colonial, imperial and settler colonial programs and policies continue to be reinforced and sustained. There are, however, recent and historical examples in which law has played a significant role in dismantling colonial and imperial structures set up during the process of colonization. This volume combines usually distinct Indigenous, Third World and Settler perspectives in order to take up the effort of decolonizing law, both in practice and in the concern to distance and to liberate the foundational theories of legal knowledge and academic engagement from the manifestations of colonialism, imperialism and settler colonialism.

Including work by scholars from the Global South and North, this volume will be of interest to academics, students and others interested in the legacy of colonial and settler law and its overcoming.

Sujith Xavier is Associate Professor at the Faculty of Law, University of Windsor, Canada.

Beverley Jacobs is Associate Professor and Associate Dean (Academic) at the Faculty of Law, University of Windsor, Canada.

Valarie Waboose is Assistant Professor at the Faculty of Law, University of Windsor, Canada.

Jeffery G. Hewitt is Assistant Professor at the Osgoode Hall Law School, York University, Canada.

Amar Bhatia is Associate Professor at the Osgoode Hall Law School, York University, Canada.

Part of the Indigenous Peoples and the Law series
series editors: Dr Mark A. Harris
University of British Columbia, Canada
Professor Denise Ferreira da Silva
University of British Columbia, Canada
Dr Claire Charters
University of Auckland, New Zealand
Dr Glen Coulthard
University of British Columbia, Canada

for information about the series and details of previous and forthcoming titles, see www.routledge.com/law/series/INDPPL

A GlassHouse book

Decolonizing Law

Indigenous, Third World and Settler Perspectives

Edited by Sujith Xavier, Beverley Jacobs, Valarie Waboose, Jeffery G. Hewitt and Amar Bhatia

Routledge
Taylor & Francis Group
www.routledge.com
a GlassHouse book

First published 2021
by Routledge
2 Park Square, Milton Park, Abingdon, Oxon OX14 4RN

and by Routledge
605 Third Avenue, New York, NY 10158

A GlassHouse book

Routledge is an imprint of the Taylor & Francis Group, an informa business

British Library Cataloguing-in-Publication Data
A catalogue record for this book is available from the British Library

Library of Congress Cataloging-in-Publication Data
Names: Xavier, Sujith, 1977- editor. | Jacobs, Beverley, editor, author. | Waboose, Valarie, editor, author. | Hewitt, Jeffery G., editor. | Bhatia, Amar, editor, author.
Title: Decolonizing law : Indigenous, third world and settler perspectives / edited by Sujith Xavier, Beverley Jacobs, Valarie Waboose, Jeffery G. Hewitt and Amar Bhatia.
Description: Milton Park, Abingdon, Oxon ; New York, NY : Routledge, 2021. | Series: Indigenous peoples and the law | Includes bibliographical references and index.
Identifiers: LCCN 2020055913 (print) | LCCN 2020055914 (ebook) | ISBN 9780367751876 (hardback) | ISBN 9780367751883 (paperback) | ISBN 9781003161387 (ebook)
Subjects: LCSH: Decolonization. | Indigenous peoples—Legal status, laws, etc.
Classification: LCC KZ1269 .D436 2021 (print) | LCC KZ1269 (ebook) | DDC 342.08/72—dc23
LC record available at https://lccn.loc.gov/2020055913
LC ebook record available at https://lccn.loc.gov/2020055914

ISBN: 978-0-367-75187-6 (hbk)
ISBN: 978-0-367-75188-3 (pbk)
ISBN: 978-1-003-16138-7 (ebk)

Typeset in Galliard
by Apex CoVantage, LLC

Contents

Acknowledgements

The long journey in completing this project has been enriched by many people.

This project started out as an idea to gather handful of scholars together in conversation about different and intersecting approaches that peoples from the Global South and Indigenous Peoples from the Global South and Global North adopt in writing and working against colonialism and imperialism. As we refined and nurtured this idea, we decided to expand it to a larger conference. The Decolonizing Law: Strategies, Tactics and Methods conference took place in April 2018. The conference would not have been possible without many minds and in particular the leadership of Dr. Amaya Alvez Marin, University of Concepción, Chile. We are also grateful to Dr. Signa A. Daum Shanks and Professor Karen Drake for sharing their insights during the early stages of the conference planning. The conference greatly benefited from the guidance of two Elders from Walpole First Nation, Myrna Kicknosway and Bryan Loucks. The conference would not be possible without Katie Bartleds, Michelle Nadhee and Marcie Demmans along with the research and administrative support of the student researchers, Karly Lyons and Cheyenne Arnold-Cunningham. We are grateful to the hands that prepared the food that nourished us and indebted to those who participated in the conference in sharing their knowledge, wisdom and kindness. We are grateful to the generous support of the various funders that made this event possible, including Faculty of Law, University of Windsor, Vice-President, Research and Innovation Office, University of Windsor, Water Research Centre for Agriculture and Mining, Universidad de Concepción, Chile, Osgoode Hall Law School, York University & Politics of Sexual Violence Initiative, The City College of New York.

This volume would not be possible without the research assistance of Shantal Beckford and Mikal Daniel. Their editorial and reference help was invaluable in completing the volume this past summer. We are deeply indebted to the contributors for their work and their enduring patience.

Like all research and writing endeavors, this project would not have been possible without the strength, kindness and love we have received from our loved ones – the families we are born into and the ones we make. We are also grateful for the friendship that we share, and we hope that this project adds to the existing knowledge in decolonization and law in a meaningful way.

Introduction

Decolonizing law in the Global North and South: expanding the circle

Sujith Xavier and Jeffery G. Hewitt

Our starting point(s)

Colonialism, imperialism and settler colonialism continue to affect the lives of communities of colour and Indigenous Peoples around the world. 'Law',[1] in its many iterations, has played an active role in the dispossession and disenfranchisement of colonized peoples. Law and its various institutions are the means by which colonial, imperial and settler colonial programs and policies continue to be reinforced and sustained. In the same vein, if conceptualized and deployed correctly, law may have the potential to 'decolonize'[2] our respective communities and societies. There are recent and historical examples in which law has played a significant role in dismantling colonial and imperial structures set up during the process of colonization. For example, Third World scholars have chronicled the ways in which law has allowed for decolonization that allegedly brought about freedom to former colonies.[3] We suggest that it is alleged because of the very nature of decolonization that was proposed and because law was used as the handmaiden of domination and control.[4] The relics of the past continue to remain within the law and the legal architecture created since the legal process of decolonization initiated with article 22 of the Covenant of the League of Nations. Nevertheless, law has not been successful in completing the decolonial processes and many 'former' colonized peoples continue to search for their freedoms.[5]

1 We use the moniker 'law' to describe Western notions of law, legal authority and legitimacy.

2 We are cautious about the use of the terms decolonial, decolonization and decolonize; see E. Tuck & K. W. Yang, "Decolonization Is Not a Metaphor" (2012) 1 *Decolonization: Indigeneity, Education & Society* 1.

3 R. P. Anand, *New States and International Law* (New Delhi: Vikas, 1972); Antony Anghie and B. S. Chimni, "Third World Approaches to International and Individual Responsibility in Internal Conflicts" (2003) 2:1 *Chinese J Intl L Law* 71; George Galindo, "Splitting TWAIL" (2016) 33:2 *Windsor YB Access Just* 37.

4 See for example Sundhya Pahuja, *Decolonising International Law: Development, Economic Growth and the Politics of Universality* (Cambridge: Cambridge University Press, 2011); Mark Mazower, *No Enchanted Palace: The End of Empire and the Ideological Origins of the United Nations* (Princeton: Princeton University Press, 2009).

5 Haunani-Kay Trask, *From a Native Daughter: Colonialism and Sovereignty in Hawaii*, Revised ed. (Honolulu: Latitude 20, 1999); Antony Anghie, *Imperialism, Sovereignty and the Making*

This volume is especially important today as there is a greater emphasis on attempting to decolonize various academic disciplines. There are sincere efforts to distance and or liberate the foundational theories of knowledge and academic engagement from the manifestations of colonialism, imperialism and settler colonialism.[6] Law schools, universities and the broader educational communities have embarked on the journey of decolonizing their curriculum while Indigenous Peoples and formerly colonized peoples continue to reel from the effects of colonialism.[7] We want to add our voices to this ongoing conversation. The voices included in this compilation gathered together during the Decolonizing Law: Strategies, Tactics and Methods conference held in Windsor, Canada (April 2–3, 2018). The conference attracted more than 80 scholars, activists and writers to the University of Windsor, which sits on the traditional territories of the Three Fires Confederacy of First Nations, comprising the Ojibway, the Odawa and the Potawatomie.

In this compilation, we invited together scholars from the Global North and South working on decolonizing law, knowledge and knowledge production, with a focus on Indigenous communities and communities of colour.[8] The gathering of these scholars within a single collection is unique, as we have tended to engage with our own respective communities and disciplinary fields. For example, legal scholars writing under the auspices of Third World Approaches to International Law (TWAIL) did not always fully engage with the settler colonial realities of Indigenous Peoples on Turtle Island.[9]

Scholars writing about Indigenous Peoples and scholars writing about the lived experience of the peoples of the Global South have created collective but insular spaces of engagement. These efforts to build community have meant that we have not built bridges between our communities reeling from the ongoing onslaught of colonialism, imperialism and settler colonialism. By bringing

---

of International Law (Cambridge: Cambridge University Press, 2005); Irene Watson, *Aboriginal Peoples, Colonialism and International Law: Raw Law* (New York: Routledge, 2015).

6 Raewyn Connell, *Southern Theory* (Cambridge: Polity Press, 2007); Gurminder K. Bhambra, *Connected Sociologies* (London: Bloomsbury, 2014); Boaventura de Sousa Santos, *Epistemologies of the South: Justice against Epistemicide* (London: Paradigm, 2014); Daniel Bonilla Maldonado, "Introduction" in Daniel Bonilla Maldonado, ed., *Constitutionalism of the Global South* (Cambridge: Cambridge University Press, 2013); Maile Arvin, Eve Tuck & Angie Morrill, "Decolonizing Feminism: Challenging Connections between Settler Colonialism and Heteropatriarchy" (2013) 25:1 *Feminist Formations* 8; Sanjay Subrahmanyam, "Connected Histories: Notes towards a Reconfiguration of Early Modern Eurasia" (1997) 31:3 *Mod Asian Stud* 735.

7 Jeffery G. Hewitt, "Decolonizing and Indigenizing: Some Considerations for Law Schools" (2016) 36:1 *Windsor YB Access Just* 85; Karen Drake, "Finding a Path to Reconciliation: Mandatory Indigenous Law, Anishinaabe Pedagogy, and Academic Freedom" (2017) 95 *Can B Rev* 9.

8 There are multiple volumes that tackle the issue of decolonization and law in various languages, especially in Spanish. See as an example Roger Merino & Areli Valencia, *Descolonizar El Derecho: Pueblos indígenas, derechos humanos y Estado Plurinacional* (Lima: Palestra, 2018).

9 For a reminder to TWAIL scholars, see for example Sujith Xavier, "Loving, Working, and Living on Stolen Land: People of Colour, Settler Colonialism & White Supremacy" (Reconciliation Syllabus, 8 December 2018).

scholars from racialized and Indigenous communities from the Global North and South writing in solidarity together, our volume seeks to transcend disciplinary and thematic borders. With this volume, we seek to sound our voices in the space between our respective community-based projects within Indigenous communities and communities of colour from the Global North and South, while still challenging the white supremacist practices wrought by colonialism, imperialism and settler colonialism in the Global North.

The editors of this volume are in relationships with various communities from the Global North and the Global South. For example, Valarie Waboose (Anishinaabe), Beverley Jacobs (Haudenosaunee/Mohawk) and Jeffery G. Hewitt (Cree) are from their respective nations from Turtle Island. Sujith Xavier is a queer refugee settler of colour and Amar Bhatia is a second-generation immigrant settler of colour. The final two editors are working under the auspices of the TWAIL network on the territories of the First Peoples of what is now known as Canada. All of the editors are committed to engaging in intellectual praxis that unsettles and challenges settler and colonial narratives within their respective universities and local communities. As such, our experiences in ongoing and unfolding global dialogues relating to decolonization are framed and nuanced within our own particular experiences. We also recognize that there are multiple engagements in decolonization that currently sit outside of our individual frameworks.

Our conference in April 2018 posed the following question to the participants: how do Third World and Indigenous Peoples' movements approach decolonization in the face of neo-colonial and settler colonial laws? These laws take the appealing shapes of constitutions, rights and reconciliation while at the same time maintaining (for example) economic domination, water contamination and Indigenous incarceration. During the first plenary panel of the conference with Anishinaabe legal scholar John Borrows and TWAIL scholar Usha Natarajan, we asked two questions: Based on your scholarship and your lived experience, how would you characterize decolonization? What are the strategies and tactics you have deployed in decolonizing law? Both speakers (Borrows in particular) characterized two strands of thought that are essential in the process of decolonizing: building relations and reflective/reflexive practice.

Picking up from Professor John Borrows, we are committed to building better relations within our communities, with each other and with the lands, waters and nature that are part of our daily lives. We also firmly believe that reflective and reflexive practice, especially as it relates to our own positionality within colonial, imperial and settler colonial processes, is essential to any attempts to move beyond merely existing in oppressive societal structures. We are also committed to designing and developing processes that will help us not just decolonize but rather deprogram[10] our minds and our hearts and in effect shift the way in which we build relationships with each other.

10 Amar Bhatia Dialogue with Beverly Jacobs, Sylvia McAdam and Jeffery G. Hewitt, *TWAIL Review* (forthcoming).

In the following sections, we build on these two critical strands of building relations and reflexive practice. Before delving into these two aspects, however, we wish to add our voices to the debates about decolonization, decolonizing and decolonial thinking.

Decolonizing law? Everyone wants to decolonize something, at some point!

If we take the perspective that a settler colonial place is one where enslaved peoples have been forced to go to, and fled to, where refugees have been forced to go to, and fled to, and where immigrants have been coerced or chosen to go to, then these spaces are also gathering places. In the Anishinaabe gathering place, where the conference was held, we sought to bring together a diverse collection of peoples, who are learning about each other, each other's struggles, ways of knowing and experiences of different kinds of law. The book is necessarily shaped by this context and emphasizes these connections and perspectives. Attempts to resist the colonial, imperial and settler colonial impetus of European empires can be traced all the way back to the 'discovery' of non-Europeans around the world.[11] These moments of first contact between Europeans and the newly discovered 'savages'[12] can be viewed as the first instance and the starting point of decolonial thinking. More importantly, this moment is the starting point of the resistance to the arrival of what Irene Watson has described as the 'muldari' (or the demon spirits) on the traditional territories of Indigenous Peoples and communities of colour around the world.[13] There is of course ample evidence of resistance to settler and colonizer incursions into the traditional territories of non-Europeans across the globe.[14]

Indigenous scholars have long chronicled the various ways in which their respective communities have responded to the arrival of the European colonizers and settlers.[15] People of colour have also storied their resistance to the invaders

11 Truth and Reconciliation Commission, *The Final Report of the Truth and Reconciliation Commission of Canada* (Montreal: McGill-Queen's University Press, 2015) at 45–46; Ibram X. Kendi, *Stamped from the Beginning: The Definitive History of Racist Ideas in America* (New York: Nations Books, 2018) at 31–46; A. Loomba, *Colonialism/Postcolonialism* (New York: Routledge, 1998); and Howard Adams, *Tortured People: The Politics of Colonization* (Penticton, BC: Theytus Books, 1999).

12 For a full discussion of the invention of savage, see Robert A. Williams, *Savage Anxieties: The Invention of Western Civilization* (New York: St. Martin's Press, 2012); and Makau W. Matua, "Savages, Saviors and Victims: The Metaphor of Human Rights" (2001) *Harv Intl LJ* 221.

13 Watson, *supra* note 5 at 2–4.

14 See for example Nira Wickramasinhe, *Sri Lanka in the Modern Age: A History* (Oxford: Oxford University Press, 2014); Sujit Sivasundraram, *Islanded: British, Sri Lanka and the Bounds of an Indian Ocean Colony* (Chicago: University of Chicago Press, 2013); Bonita Lawrence, "Rewriting Histories of the Law: Colonization and Indigenous Resistance in Eastern Canada" in Sherene Razack, ed., *Race, Space and the Law* (Toronto: Between the Lines, 2002) at 21–46.

15 Lawrence, *supra* note 14 at 21–46.

and those that sought to 'trade'.[16] Notwithstanding these discussions on the origins of decolonial thinking within academic spaces, decolonization has specific etymologies and outcomes. For example, international lawyers from the newly freed colonies conceptualized decolonization as emancipation from colonial rule.[17] Yet, this process of decolonization in the Global South brought with it a whole host of problems that are intrinsically tied to the Westphalian nation-state model[18] and the relics of colonialism and imperialism that continue to be imbedded within, for example, Western legal systems.[19]

Various scholarly disciplines too have engaged with the topic of decolonial thinking and decolonization. Scholars in education,[20] sociology,[21] literary theory[22] and history,[23] for example, have spilled much ink in thinking and theorizing the meaning and scope of decolonization. Indigenous scholars and scholars of colour have sought to trouble the ways in which the scholarly debates about decolonization have unfolded and have been co-opted by white supremacist thinking.[24] Some have sought to challenge the ways in which research and scholarship is undertaken,[25] while others have asked related questions about the meaning and scope of decolonization.[26] The literature on decolonial thinking and decolonization is vast and has many different modes of engagement.

16 See for example Bill Ashcroft, Gareth Griffiths and Helen Tiffin, eds., *Postcolonial Studies: The Key Concepts*, 3rd ed. (London: Routledge, 2013).

17 Anghie & BS Chimni, *supra* note 3; Anand, *supra* note 3.

18 Obiora C. Okafor, "Re-defining Legitimacy: International Law, Multilateral Institutions and the Problem of Socio-cultural Fragmentation within Established African States" (PhD thesis, UBC, Faculty of Law, 1998), online: <http://law.library.ubc.ca/abstracts/#1998>.

19 Uppendra Baxi, "Modelling 'Optimal' Constitutional Design for Government Structures: Some Debutant Remarks" in Sunil Khilnai et al., eds., *Comparative Constitutionalism in South Asia* (New Delhi: Oxford University Press, 2013) at 23–44; Sujith Xavier, "False Western Universalism in Constitutionalism? The 1867 Canadian Constitution & the Legacies of the Residential Schools" in Richard Albert, Paul Daly & Vanessa MacDonnell, eds., *The Canadian Constitution in Transition* (Toronto: University of Toronto Press, 2018).

20 Marie Battiste, *Decolonizing Education: Nourishing the Learning Spirit* (Saskatoon: Purich, 2013).

21 Aníbal Quijano, "Coloniality and Modernity/Rationality" (2005) 21:2–3 *Cultural Studies*.

22 Walter Mignolo, "Delinking: The Rhetoric of Modernity, the Logic of Coloniality and the Grammar of De-coloniality" (2007) 21:2–3 *Cultural Studies* 449; Walter Mignolo, "Geopolitics of Sensing and Knowing: On (De)coloniality, Border Thinking and Epistemic Disobedience" (2011) 14:3 *Postcolonial Studies* 273; Walter Mignolo, "Citizenship, Knowledge, and the Limits of Humanity" (2006) 18:2 *American Literary History* 312; Nelson Maldonado-Torres, "On the Coloniality of Being: Contributions to the Development of a Concept" (2007), 21:2 *Cultural Studies* 240; Tuck & Yang, *supra* note 2.

23 John Darwin, *Britain and Decolonisation: The Retreat from Empire in the Post-War World* (New York: St. Martin's Press, 1988); Tuck & Yang, *supra* note 2.

24 Tuck & Yang, *supra* note 2.

25 Linda Tuhiwai Smith, *Decolonizing Methodologies: Research and Indigenous Peoples* (London: Zed Books, 2012); Clelia O. Rodríguez, *Decolonizing Academia: Poverty, Oppression and Pain* (Winnipeg: Fernwood, 2018).

26 Jeffery G. Hewitt, "Decolonizing and Indigenizing: Some Considerations for Law Schools" (2016) 33:1 *Windsor YB Access Just* 64.

Turning back to our own discipline of law, public law and international law have been the central spaces in which thinking about decolonization has unfolded most frequently. The aspirations of colonized peoples and Indigenous Peoples can be situated within international law's respective provisions of the League of Nations Covenant[27] and its successor, the United Nations Charter.[28] The general narrative is that the provisions within these legal documents, along with the creation of the 'post'-colonial world order, have set in motion some theorizing about 'decolonizing international law'. In this engagement, the literature has tended to focus on the nature of the laws that led to decolonization from the mid-1800s[29] to the decolonization of the Class A, B and C mandates[30] (except for Palestine).

Within the domestic spaces in settler colonial places such as Australia, Canada, Israel, South Africa, New Zealand and the United States, Indigenous Peoples have struggled for some form of decolonization. While the claims have been framed within the vernacular of sovereignty[31] and self-determination,[32] they have often relied on public law as a means to challenge the colonial and settler colonial apparatus that was constructed around them.[33]

Notwithstanding these developments, for us, as two lawyers, legal academics and survivors who have devoted our time and energy to thinking about the emancipation of our respective communities and studying the effects of settler and colonial laws, we are interested in traversing the limitations of Western legal thought. We want to turn to non-Western sites of knowledge production,[34] beyond the pale of citing to and regurgitating outdated Western canons. We are interested in thinking about decolonizing law not as a political project that will lead to a pluralistic society that respects our differences. We are not interested in having our differences mediated by whiteness and settler colonial courts[35] as the arbitrators of oppression Olympics.[36] Rather we are interested in thinking beyond law, beyond Western institutions of governance and surveillance and beyond Western notions of knowledge.

27 Mazower, *supra* note 4 at 28–65.
28 *Ibid.*
29 Darwin, *supra* note 23 at 6.
30 Article 22 of the League of Nation; Provisions of the UN Charter; see also Mazower, *supra* note 4.
31 Heidi Kiiwetinepinesiik Stark, "Nenabozho's Smart Berries: Rethinking Tribal Sovereignty and Accountability" (2014) 2013 *Mich St L Rev* 339.
32 Darlene Johnston, "Self-Determination for the Six Nations Confederacy" (1986) 44 *UT Fac L Rev* 1; Catherine J. Iorns, "Indigenous Peoples and Self-Determination: Challenging State Sovereignty" (1993) 24 *Case W Res J Int'l L* 199.
33 See for example Mazen Masri, *The Dynamics of Exclusionary Constitutionalism: Israel as a Jewish and Democratic State* (Oxford: Hart, 2017).
34 Sujith Xavier, "Theorising Global Governance From Below? Learning from the Global South through Ethnographies and Critical Reflections" (2016) 32:3 *Windsor YB Access to Just* 229.
35 Glen Sean Coulthard, *Red Skins White Masks: Rejecting the Colonial Projects of Recognition* (Minneapolis: University of Minnesota Press, 2014).
36 Xavier, *supra* note 9.

Building bridges, connecting communities

One of the animating themes that brought the conference organizers (and subsequently the volume editors) together was the need and desire to build bridges between various marginalized communities. We draw from our own lived experience as members of these communities to build our scholarship and our research agendas. But within our respective fields of research, we note a tendency to be insular in how we address and challenge colonialism, imperialism and settler colonialism and the ongoing effects of these process. TWAIL scholars have actively gathered and formed a network only as recently as 1997 under the TWAIL moniker.[37] Even though former colonized peoples have engaged in multiple forms of resistance to invasion, domination and occupation, the legal techniques used to achieve these endeavours were not fully challenged as a critique of international law and its institutions. TWAIL scholars have then sought to dismantle the existing racial hierarchies and push for new forms of governance. Before the creation of this coalitionary movement, some Third World scholars believed that international law could lead to the emancipation of Third World peoples and sought to utilize international law for this purpose.[38]

Most often, TWAIL scholars cite both critical race theory and feminist approaches to law as inspirations.[39] While TWAIL scholars initially relied heavily on the techniques used by these two other theoretical approaches, the conversations between TWAIL and, for example, critical race theory are growing.[40] In this light, TWAIL has also engaged in critical reflexivity in thinking through some of the gaps apparent within the existing scholarship. As noted by two of the contributors to this volume, Amar Bhatia and Usha Natarajan, TWAIL has not 'foregrounded' the struggles of Indigenous Peoples in the Global South and the Global North.[41] More importantly, TWAIL scholars who have settled on stolen land (e.g. in the settler colonies of what are now known as Australia, the United States of America and Canada) did not fully engage with their own complicity in the processes of genocide of Indigenous Peoples.[42] The editorial group of this volume consists of both Indigenous scholars in what is currently known as Canada with those who have sought asylum here, or a better life, and have collectively generated relationships with one another in order to, as this chapter title says, expand the circle.

Indigenous communities have also been continuously resisting the onslaught of colonialism, imperialism and settler colonialism. Understandably the focus has

37 Usha Natarajan et al., *Third World Approaches to International Law: On Praxis and the Intellectual* (Abingdon: Routledge Press, 2018).

38 James Gathii, "TWAIL: A Brief History of Its Origins, Its Decentralized Network, and a Tentative Bibliography" (2011) 3:1 *Trade, L & Development* 26.

39 *Ibid.*

40 See Critical Race Special Issue in *Villanova Law Review*, Ruth Gordon, "Critical Race Theory and International Law: Convergence and Divergence" (2000) 45 *Vill L Rev* 827.

41 Amar Bhatia, "The South of the North: Building on Critical Approaches to International Law with Lessons from the Fourth World" (2012) 14 *Or Rev Intl L* 131; Natarajan, *supra* note 37.

42 Xavier, *supra* note 9; Michael Fakhri, "Third World Sovereignty, Indigenous Sovereignty, and Food Sovereignty: Living with Sovereignty Despite the Map" (2019) 9:3/4 *Transnational Legal Theory* 218.

been on pushing against the various violent techniques of surveillance, oppression and genocide.[43] We hope, with this volume, to add to the ongoing work of others in generating deeper relationships in the Global North and South.

By privileging and centring the voices of Indigenous Peoples and people of colour from the Global North and Global South, we set out to build relations between our relatives from various parts of the world through the conference in April 2018. In this volume, we continue with this tradition by making space and place for scholars from these communities and their allies to come together to make a substantive contribution to the academic literature on decolonizing law. Rather than focusing solely on our respective communities, we found it enriching and rewarding to turn to each other and our collaborators to listen to, learn from and battle alongside one another. In our efforts to deprogram and transcend the existing legal structures of oppression and genocide, we believe that allyship and community with each other and our relations are vital for our survival.

We would be remiss if we did not mention the lack of focus in our volume on the experiences of former enslaved peoples in, for example, North America, as well as those who are situated and writing about lived realities in various parts of the African continent. Our conference did intend to include participants from these communities, including South Africa. Unfortunately, and as happens all too often when conferences are held in the Global North, the settler colonial state of Canada did not grant the required visa to our colleague from South Africa, who was thus unable to attend the conference. We also hoped to receive chapters from various colleagues and collaborators focusing on these perspectives from North and South American settings. Given life circumstances and demands of their academic institutions, we were unable to receive contributions that spoke to these experiences that we could include in our volume. Nonetheless, there are robust and important contributions that signal to the existing bridge-building between Indigenous communities and communities of the descendants of enslaved peoples,[44] as well as decolonial thinking in (for example) South Africa,[45] Ghana[46] and Nigeria.[47] We

43 National Inquiry Into Missing and Murdered Indigenous Women and Girls (Final Report), *Reclaiming Power and Place*.

44 Zainab Amadahy & Bonita Lawrence, "Indigenous Peoples and Black People in Canada: Settlers or Allies?" in Arlo Kempf, ed., *Breaching the Colonial Contract: Anti-colonialism in the US and Canada* (Dordrecht: Springer, 2010) at 105; Tapji Garba & Sara-Maria Sorentino, "Slavery Is a Metaphor: A Critical Commentary on Eve Tuck and K. Wayne Yang's "Decolonization Is Not a Metaphor" (2020) 52:3 *Antipode* 765.

45 Tshepo Madlingozi, "Social Justice in a Time of Neo-apartheid Constitutionalism: Critiquing the Anti-black Economy of Recognition, Incorporation and Distribution" (2017) 28:1 *Stell L Rev* 123; Tshepo Madlingozi, "Decolonising 'Decolonisation' with Mphahlele" (1 November 2018) *New Frame*, online: <www.newframe.com/decolonising-decolonisation-mphahlele/>.

46 Kwasi Wiredu, "Toward Decolonizing African Philosophy and Religion" (1998) 1:4 *Afr Stud Q* 17.

47 Foluke Ifejola Adebisi, "Decolonising Education in Africa: Implementing the Right to Education by Re-appropriating Culture and Indigeneity" (2016) 67:4 *N Ir Leg Q* 433; Ogba Adejoh Sylvester & Okpanachi Idoko Anthony, "Decolonization in Africa and Pan-Africanism" (2014) 12:23 *Yönetim Bilimleri Dergisi* 7.

hope to expand our circle in the future to include these important voices into our conversations.

Reflective and reflexive practice

In order to build bridges and create and foster nurturing relationships, we saw the need to engage in reflective and reflexive practices that seek to decolonize our hearts, minds and bodies. For example, while we gathered in the Art Gallery of Windsor, overlooking the giant skyscrapers of what is now known as Detroit, Michigan, we were reminded to marvel at the beauty and resilience of the lands and waters around us – *waaiiatonong ziibi* (Anishinaabemowin for 'where the river bends') – rather than the stark splendour of the capitalist structures and towers that have been forced on top of the land. In her opening address, Anishinaabe Elder Myrna Kicknosway asked the conference participants to give thanks to the land and the waters. She asked them to begin their journey of reconciliation by locating and reimagining our relationship to the water, the land, the planet and the universe, and by engaging in the reflective and reflexive practice of situating ourselves within the larger project of settler colonialism and our complicity in the ongoing colonization of Indigenous Peoples and the territory of the Three Fires Confederacy.

This journey is one that must be predicated on reflective practice that seeks to unlearn colonial and imperial ways of knowing and reconnecting (e.g. with the land that we are on). For us, reflectivity must be in conjunction with reflexive practice. The former is a meditation on the past while the latter seeks to ground us 'in the moment' while moving forward.[48] We borrow this framing from Western critical feminist social scientists, who have sought to challenge orthodox practices of research rooted in objectivity and neutrality.[49] This type of reflexive inquiry seeks to ground the researcher, lawyer and activist within their environment while noting their relationship to others and the land. We seek to recalibrate it to our own purpose of deprogramming our surroundings, our institutions and ourselves.

There are pressing problems of how to teach with, and research against, Western laws, and how to do so in allyship with one another across Indigenous and Third World networks. The chapters in this volume seek to answer some of these questions from inter- and transdisciplinary perspectives across the Global North and South. While the conference focused on Third and Fourth World movements, our final contributions ended up emphasizing Indigenous movements in the Global North and South.

Organization and themes of the collection

The volume comprises this introduction and 13 chapters that trace these questions of decolonization of law from the Global North to the Global South and back again. The emphasis is on the decolonization of law for Indigenous and racialized communities in the Global North and South through ways of knowing,

48 We are grateful to Tyler Dunham for this formulation predicated on Ellyn Lyle, *Of Books, Barns, and Boardrooms: Exploring Praxis through Reflexive Inquiry* (Rotterdam: Sense, 2017).
49 *Ibid.* at vii–xi.

knowledge production and legal systems. For instance, contributors to this volume examine the need to fundamentally reframe how we define, articulate and compare laws in the Global North and the Global South. This reframing pertains directly to relationships with people, land, water and law, as well as how resurgent Indigenous legal orders inform the governance of these components of revitalized nationhood. This volume opens and closes with the voices of Anishinaabe women. In addition to the conference being located on Anishinaabe lands, we also sought to complete an intellectual and relational circle by substantively and methodologically drawing the last chapter back to the first.

A key component of our approach is the understanding that, while decolonization needs to be more than metaphorical (e.g. Tuck and Yang), it must also occur across the wide range of spaces and scales occupied by colonization and settler colonialism. We have organized the collection in and around three major groupings: Challenging Limitations of Settler Colonialism, Perspectives from the Global North and South, and Decolonizing through Indigenous Worldviews.

The contributions in our volume are emblematic of the lived experiences of different colonial contexts across the world. They represent the glimmer of hope that encapsulates why we do what we do and why we do it now, in this place and time.[50] These interventions help us to educate ourselves and student learners about the lived experiences of the peoples from our various territories, lands and nations. For us, the conference and this volume serve as further starting points of decolonization: *listening and learning, before acting or reacting.*

By bringing all of the contributions in this volume to the forefront, we hope to transcend the limitations of TWAIL and its inability to shed the shackles of Law/law in whatever iteration conceptualized through Western universalism.[51] We hope to build on the scholarship of those who have helped us identify the problems with Law's demands for recognition[52] and the possibilities of refusals.[53] In doing so, we also hope to listen and learn from each other as a way of constituting conceptions of legal normativity that are based on our own normative, real, embodied experiences.

This volume begins with Challenging Limitations of Settler Colonialism, with Anishinaabeg perspectives on law and research methodologies. Opening the volume in this way echoes the ceremonial opening of the conference by Elder

50 Natarajan, *supra* note 37 at 4–7.

51 For limitations, Ruth Buchanan, "Writing Resistance into International Law" (2008) 10 *Intl Community L Rev* 445; Mohsen al Attar, TWAIL: A Paradox within a Paradox (Draft, available online on Academia.edu); Luis Eslava and Sundhya Pahuja, "Between Resistance and Reform: TWAIL and the Universality of International Law" (2012) 3:1 *Trade, L & Development* 103; Sundhya Pahuja, *Decolonising International Law: Development, Economic Growth and the Politics of Universality* (Cambridge: Cambridge University Press, 2011); see also Sundhya Pahuja, *Decolonising International Law: Development, Economic Growth and the Politics of Universality* (Cambridge: Cambridge University Press, 2011).

52 Coulthard, *supra* note 35.

53 Audra Simpson, *Mohawk Interruptus: Political Life across the Borders of Setter States* (Durham: Duke University Press, 2014).

Kicknosway, who reminded us to breathe and see what is around us to better locate ourselves at *waaiiatonong ziibi* (where the river bends). The placement of this contribution as the first chapter provides readers with a guide to navigate the conceptualization of law and its sources, such as water and land. Craft, McGregor, Seymour-Hourie and Chiblow challenge the "dominant colonial narrative that aims to supersede community-based views on responsibilities and obligations that relate to ethical water relationships".[54] As with the opening ceremony of the conference, this chapter centres the role of water and language in the worldview of Anishinaabeg peoples and seeks to shift how we think about relationships to law and knowledge.

Bhatia's contribution reflects on limitations of the Westphalian nation-state through the doctrine of statehood in international law: permanent population, defined territory, government/laws and international relations. In this instance, he shows how an international law doctrine was implemented within the Canadian context while simultaneously denying sovereignty to the First Peoples of the territory. He interrogates some complicities of international and Canadian law in relation to Indigenous peoples. Bhatia examines Western legal mythology that assumes Crown sovereignty while literally setting aside Indigenous laws, treaties and peoples. The hegemony of this legal orthodoxy does damage to building Indigenous-immigrant relations where non-Indigenous peoples must rely on this sovereignty, shorn of treaties, to legitimize their status and presence on Indigenous lands.

Natarajan, one of our plenary speakers, draws upon a key theme from the conference in her chapter, which calls for building and rebuilding relationships across the Global North and Global South. In this chapter, Natarajan draws out aspects of hope when reflecting on the theme of Third and so-called Fourth World decolonization in the context of solidarity and sustainability. As with the first two chapters, Natarajan considers the meaning and power of recognition of sovereignty, independence and self-determination, and recognition of peoples. This chapter leads us into the second section, Perspectives from the Global North and South.

Bahdi and Kassis offer a cross-cutting comparison that thematically continues with building and rebuilding relationships across the Global North and South. The authors remind us that relationships are not always positive. As an example of a reflexive practice, this chapter centres its critique on Global North aid, in particular the Canadian aid agency's international work in Palestine. However, like Natarajan, the authors offer hope when reflecting on the theme of Third and Fourth World decolonization in the context of solidarity and sustainability.

Continuing with a comparative analysis and international law, the next chapter offers a critique of researching and teaching international law through a colonial academic structure that leans away from centring a Latin American context.

54 A. Craft, D. McGregor, R. Seymour-Hourie & S. Chiblow, "Decolonizing Anishnaabe *Nibi Inaakonigewin* and *Gikendaasowin* Research: Reinscribing Anishnaabe Approaches to Law and Knowledge" [in this volume].

Authors Acosta-Alvarado, Álvez Marín, Betancur-Restrepo, Prieto-Ríos, Rivas-Ramírez and Veçoso emphasize the distance still remaining for generating decolonized research and teaching spaces. Continuing to draw the thread of hope forward from other chapters, the authors interrogate some of the ways in which to decolonize international legal education. This decolonization of disciplinary divides and knowledge production is important as the same European crowns that 'discovered' Indigenous lands and ignored Indigenous laws. It also shaped the founding of comparative and public international law fields that have not fully reflected on their colonial pasts and continuing presence in the minds of students and domestic and international legal institutions.

Building on direct conversations with affected Indigenous peoples, Libardi de Souza and da Costa Oliveira offer a case study in the complexities of Indigenous responses to state-ordered resettlement of Indigenous families for a hydroelectric project. The authors demonstrate the possibilities from political mobilization of Indigenous peoples and law's response(s). These possibilities also afford opportunities to share knowledge and experiences with other Indigenous nations, including those in the Global North, who also struggle to defend lands and waters in the face of encroachment by public and private actors.

Van Wagner and Bargh consider the structure of relations in the context of environmental law and mining in Aotearoa New Zealand. The authors critique the use of assumed colonial authority to govern lands, resources and people-place relationships. Like others, the authors offer hope that such relationships may be positively reshaped through a deeper engagement with Māori law to decolonize the state-structured legal framework for mining in Aotearoa New Zealand.

Alvez, Inatani and Infantino consider the 'epistemologies of ignorance' in Latin America and offer a case study of how the Constitutional Court of Chile seeks to render Indigenous claims invisible. Through a framework of comparative law, the authors reflect on the 15th-century 'civilizing' mission of Spanish imperialism and trace its trajectory in modern-day constitutional adjudication in relation to Indigenous claims. This chapter demonstrates how the desire to decolonize law must address both knowledge production and formal legal systems in order to break the loop between these (and other) aspects of society that construct and hold colonialism in place.

Eberts outlines some of the hurdles yet to be surpassed facing the reception of Indigenous laws in Canadian courts. Through a doctrinal examination, the author illustrates the exercise of assuming Crown sovereignty and how it has shaped the relationship between the state and Indigenous peoples. This chapter underscores how the default and dominant settler law approaches remain far from the spirit and practice of Indigenous laws and methodologies.

Mitchell, Arseneau, Aylwin and Thomas examines resource extraction in the North and South through a comparison of Canadian and Chilean state responses to the principle of free, prior and informed consent in the United Nations Declaration on the Rights of Indigenous Peoples. The similarities between the state responses in the Global North and Global South are striking in their methods of preserving colonialism and the limitations constructed against the rights of

Indigenous peoples. The authors of this chapter have built bridges with one another and opened a path for these communities to learn from their respective experiences while reflecting how state and corporate interests engage in systemic attacks that warrant a systemic, solidarist response.

The chapters in this section examine state responses in relation to land, resources, legal education, international law and domestic doctrine as levers of control over Indigenous peoples. Taken together, they critique the master narrative and interrogate state assertions of sovereignty and control of Indigenous peoples. They also examine the role of law and legal education in upholding state storytelling. This leads us to the final section, Decolonizing through Indigenous Worldviews, comprising three chapters.

By setting out the stark data skewed against Indigenous women in Canada's prison system, demonstrating a reflexive practice, Jacobs calls for a complete transformation of the prison-industrial complex in what is now known as Canada. Engaging in conversation with Yvonne Johnson and Joey Twins, both Indigenous peoples who have been incarcerated, on the particular impacts of Canada's prison system on Indigenous women, the author critiques the correctional system from voices within and offers a pathway forward.

Lindberg returns us to land and the laws of *nêhiyaw* (Cree). The author considers the role of stories in constituting laws and the colonial interruption of nêhiyaw constitutionalism. Weaving together nêhiyaw land-based stories and the stories of colonialism as told through federal legislation and case law, Lindberg returns us to land stories (reflective of the conference opening) as a means of healing and reorganizing the imposition of colonial legal structures. The author reminds us that listening to understand is a necessary component in (re)constitutional dialogues.

The volume closes with a reconnection of the opening chapter on water, law, responsibility and methodology with the sound of an Anishinaabeg waterdrum. Waboose's chapter focuses on developing research from an Anishinaabeg lens in the context of Indian Residential School survivors. The author emphasizes the multifaceted Anishnaabeg law components of the waterdrum as a method of research, teaching and resilience. Waboose closes this volume in a befitting way that summarizes not only the author's work but ours as well, when we held the conference in Windsor, Canada: "the Light-skinned Race will be given a choice between two roads. If they choose the right road, then the Seventh Fire will light the Eighth and Final Fire – an eternal Fire of peace, love, brotherhood and sisterhood".[55]

We offer this volume with the many hopes expressed by the authors that it contributes toward choosing the right road and expanding the circle.

55 V. Waboose, "Conducting Research from an Indigenous Lens" [in this volume].

Challenging limitations of settler colonialism

1 Decolonizing Anishinaabe *nibi inaakonigewin* and *gikendaasowin* research

Reinscribing Anishinaabe approaches to law and knowledge

Aimée Craft, Deborah McGregor, Rayanna Seymour-Hourie and Sue Chiblow

Notes on *Anishinaabemowin* terminology

Aki: earth or creation
Anishinaabe (pl. Anishinaabek or Anishinaabeg): a person or the people, also in reference to Ojibwe, Chippewa, etc.
Anishinaabemowin: the language
Anishinaabekweg: Anishinaabe women
Gikendaasowin: knowledge(s)
Inaakonigewin: law
Minobimaadiziwin: the good life
Nibi: water
Waazhusk: muskrat

Introduction

This chapter emanates from a series of discussions, some in person and others electronically, that have evolved over the last several years. Some of these discussions have taken place on the land and water, overseas in Aotearoa (or New Zealand) and at the annual Nibi Gathering in the Whiteshell, at a sacred petroform site called Manito Api (or Bannock Point) in Treaty 3 territory. Brought together through a common passion for the water, deep community accountability and engagement in research through spirit, each of us reflects on key questions of importance to us as Anishinaabe *ikwewag* (women) researchers and our traditional roles as "keepers of the water".[1] This role as keepers results from our sacred

1 Kate Cave & Shianne McKay, "Nibi Song: Indigenous Women and Nibi" (2012) 7:6 *Solutions J* 64–73; Kim Anderson, *Aboriginal Women, Water and Health: Reflections from Eleven First Nations, Inuit, and Metis Grandmothers* (Halifax and Winnipeg: Atlantic Centre of Excellence for Women's Health & Prairie Women's Health Centre of Excellence, 2010); Deb Danard, "Be the Water" (2015) 30:2/3 *Canadian Woman Studies* 115; Sheri Longboat, "First Nation Water Security: Security for Mother Earth" (2015) 30:2/3 *Canadian Woman Studies.*

connection to the spirit of water. Our ability to bear children through the birth water we carry raises "particular responsibilities to protect and nurture water".[2]

The work of ikwewag reclaiming their roles as keepers of the water is evident through the Mother Earth Water Walks, led by Grandmother Josephine Mandamin.[3] The Water Walks' intent is to teach others the importance of nibi. The Walks began at Lake Superior in 2003 and have journeyed to each of the Great Lakes, the St. Lawrence and through the four directions of ocean water, covering distances of over 1,000 km at a time.[4] The goals of the Walks were to raise awareness of nibi by changing the perception of nibi as a resource to the acknowledgement of it as a spiritual entity.[5] Each of us has walked and/or worked for the water.

This brings us to Indigenous research and particularly the two areas of research each of us works with: inaakonigewin and gikendaasowin research relating to water. Research relating to Indigenous legal traditions and knowledge continues to be very much a colonial practice, reinscribing power imbalances between the academy and Indigenous communities and peoples through continued control over knowledge production, access and mobilization. Through our practice and scholarship, we explicitly challenge the dominant colonial narrative that aims to supersede community-based views on responsibilities and obligations that relate to ethical water relationships.

Collectively, we advocate for the utilization of an Anishinaabe research paradigm and methodologies, a distinct research approach rooted in Indigenous ontology, epistemology, axiology and knowledge systems. More specifically, we engage with Anishinaabeg theory and modes of inquiry, which emphasize responsibility-based research ethics practice. We argue this approach is ideally suited for working with *Anishinaabeg nibi inaakonigewin* (Anishinaabeg water law) at the community level.

Through our journeys, each of us has worked alongside Elders and knowledge holders, and have worked for nibi, by walking for nibi and by participating in other forms of ceremony or through our participation in organizing water events (such as the Nibi Gathering) or through the development of laws and policy. Each of us incorporates our personal practice into our research pursuits, governed always in relational systems of accountability and responsibility. While none amongst us is a fluent language speaker, we know that Anishinaabe inaakonigewin and gikendaasowin flow directly from the language. Each of us is attempting

2 See Aimée Craft, "Giving and Receiving Life from Anishinaabe Nibi Inaakonigewin (Our Water Law) Research" in Jocelyn Thorpe et al., eds., *Methodological Challenges in Nature-Culture and Environmental History Research* (New York: Routledge, 2016) at 109 [Craft, "Life"]; Cave & McKay, *supra* note 1; Kim Anderson, Barbara Clow & Margaret Haworth-Brockman, "Carriers of Water: Aboriginal Women's Experiences, Relationships and Reflections" (2013) 60 *J of Cleaner Prod* 11.

3 See Deborah McGregor, "Indigenous Women, Water Justice and Zaagidowin (Love)" (2015) 30:2/3 *Canadian Woman Studies* 71 [McGregor, "Zaagidowin"].

4 *Ibid.* at 2, 3, 71–78.

5 *Ibid.*

to reclaim language as an important source and method of Anishinaabe inaakonigewin and gikendaasowin. We also appreciate the role of ceremony and spirit in guiding not only the research we do, but also the ongoing obligations that we have with respect to nibi and all of creation.

We approached this chapter by identifying three areas to begin the conversation on decolonizing laws to better reflect Anishinaabeg understanding of inaakonigewin, namely: language, land and Western influence on Indigenous values and structures. The topics covered below relate our winding journey(s) through our own Anishinaabe inaakonigewin and gikendaasowin reclamation.

We are of the view that thinking about inaakonigewin and gikendaasowin from an Anishinaabe perspective requires a critical reflection on our assumptions and the colonial baggage we import from our other sources of knowledge or training. In short, we are working to re-inscribe ourselves in the process of understanding our relationship with nibi. Correspondingly, we are aiming to provide pathways for decolonizing law and knowledge as it relates to water. This requires continuous self-reflection and an approach to the work we do with the spirit of humility, reciprocity and service to our nations and to nibi itself.

How important is it to understand and speak Anishinaabemowin (our language) while working with Anishinaabe nibi inaakonigewin?

RAYANNA: Language is part of the Anishinaabe way of life,[6] and learning how to understand and speak *anishinaabemowin* contributes to our decolonization.[7] Anishinaabemowin holds a key to understanding our legal traditions more deeply. We are taught that the language safe-keeps "older ideas and narratives",[8] it embeds our history, and it encompasses our collective memory as Anishinaabe.[9]

Elders say the language is "crucial" to a greater understanding of inaakonigewin, our laws and knowledge.[10] The work (or "research") for nibi incorporates

6 Tobasonakwut Kinew, "'Let Them Burn the Sky': Overcoming Repression of the Sacred Use of Anishinaabe Lands" in Niigaanwewidam James Sinclair and Warren Cariou, eds., *Manitowapow: Aboriginal Writings from the Land and Nibi* (Winnipeg: HighWater Press, 2011) 142 at 145.

7 Brock Pitawanakwat, "Strategies and Methods for Anishinaabemowin Revitalization" (2018) 74:3 *Can Modern Language Rev* 461 at 461. Pitawanakwat uses "mitigate colonial affects" rather than decolonization.

8 Margaret Noori, "*Beshaabiiag G'gikenmaaigowag:* Comets of Knowledge" in Jill Doerfler, Niigaanwewidam James Sinclair & Heidi Kiiwetinepinesiik Stark, eds., *Centering Anishinaabeg Studies: Understanding the World through Stories* (East Lansing: Michigan State University Press, 2013) 35 at 36 [*Centering Anishinaabeg Studies*].

9 Lindsay Keegitah Borrows, *Otter's Journey through Indigenous Language and Law* (Vancouver: UBC Press, 2018) at 127.

10 Basil Johnston, as cited in Roger Spielmann, *'You're So Fat': Exploring Ojibwe Discourse* (Toronto: University of Toronto Press, 1998) at 234.

language practice and contributes to revitalization organically. For example, opportunities to gather on the land with Elders and community members who are knowledgeable in the language and our stories is at the foundation of this journey.[11]

Learning anishinaabemowin is an individual choice, since we all have "been given our own agency".[12] We continue to be "the translators of the knowledge of our grandmothers"[13] as we continue to learn and spread the teachings as Anishinaabekweg and as scholars.

AIMÉE: Blackfoot scholar Leroy Little Bear tells us that the Blackfoot language allows us to "think Blackfoot".[14] Many of the Elders I have worked with throughout my life (including Anishinaabe, Cree, Dakota, Dene, Blackfoot and others) have said similar things. Elder D'Arcy Linklater (Nisichiwayasik Cree Nation) said to me many years ago that "the law is in the language".[15] Elder Sherry Copenace (Ojibways of Onigaming) reminds me often that we should not seek to translate Anishinaabe words or concepts into English because they do not translate the intent or spirit that the Anishinaabemowin language expresses.[16] Elder Harry Bone reminds us that there are four levels of language including the language expressed through conversation, ceremony/prayer, spirit and dreams.[17]

Many of the instructions on how to live inaakonigewin (to live according to relationships meant to foster *mino-biimaadiziiwin*, or collective well-being) are contained in the language. We cannot undertake a deep exercise of Anishinaabe law without addressing linguistic and cultural disconnections. This is also why, in the Anishinaabe nibi inaakonigewin research and nibi gatherings, Elders have been engaged as a Faculty of Elders and knowledge holders,[18] who are versed in

11 See Aimée Craft, *Anishinaabe Nibi Inaakonigewin Report:* Reflecting the Water Laws Research Gathering conducted with Anishinaabe Elders June 20–23, 2013 at Roseau River, Manitoba (CHRR/PILC, 2014) [Craft, "Nibi Report"]. Examples of gathering on the land include the "Nibi Gathering" that started in 2013 and continue annually in the spring; and the Gikendaasowin Gatherings held July 2017 to January 2018.

12 Keegitah Borrows, *supra* note 9 at 27.

13 Lee Maracle, *I Am Woman: A Native Perspective on Sociology and Feminism* (Vancouver: Press Gang, 1996) at 40.

14 Leroy Little Bear, "Jagged Worldviews Colliding" in Marie Battiste, ed., *Reclaiming Indigenous Voice and Vision* (Vancouver: UBC Press, 2000) at 77.

15 D'Arcy Linklater, *Harry Bone, and the Treaty & Dakota Elders of Manitoba with Contributions by the AMC Council of Elders, KA'ESI WAHKOTUMAHK ASKI, Our Relations with the Land: Treaty Elders' Teachings*, Vol. 2 (Winnipeg: Treaty Relations Commission of Manitoba & Assembly of Manitoba Chiefs Secretariat, 2014) at 11.

16 Personal Communication with Sherry Copenace, Elder from Ojibways of Onigaming (n.d.) at Winnipeg, MB.

17 Personal Communication with Harry Bone, Elder from Keeseekoowenin First Nation (n.d.) at Winnipeg, MB.

18 Craft, "Nibi Report" *supra* note 11.

language, ceremony, culture and Anishinaabe way of life. The Faculty of Elders have the ability to transmit that knowledge to the people who engage in the *wiigwaam* teaching lodge of the nibi gatherings.

Younger generations that have not been raised in the language and who are not fluent display a gap in understanding. This is not necessarily of our own doing (see colonization, residential schools, assimilation, dislocation, discrimination, colonialism and racism); however, we are part of a generation that can reclaim the language. These acts of reclamation can be through technology, pedagogy and relationship, all of which are connected to reclamation of our laws. With active learning and immersion (doing the work), the concepts, teachings, values, norms and laws are within our grasp. This requires commitment on our part. While we become fluent again, ceremony and song help fill the void and help ensure our spiritual, emotional, physical and intellectual well-being.

SUE: I have heard numerous times from Elders and Anishinaabemowin speakers the importance of learning our language. These Elders and speakers have stated that mino-bimaadiziwin is embedded in Anishinaabemowin. Learning Anishinaabemowin allows us to simultaneously learn a new way of looking at the world.[19]

Recently, Elder/language speaker Linda Toulouse explained that everything is alive in the language and understanding that gives us the understanding of our responsibilities.[20] Mary Ann Corbiere declares that Anishinaabemowin is descriptive and action based.[21] She also explains how there are several complexities in translating Anishinaabemowin into the English language, such as "in the types of connotations words convey".[22] The fact that translation proves difficult and concepts are lost through translation makes gikendaasowin unique to the language speakers and learners. Without the benefit of knowing the language, scholars cannot get the heart and soul and spirit of a culture to truly understand Anishinaabe perceptions and interpretations.[23] It is therefore important to have at minimum a basic understanding of the language in order to understand our legal traditions.

I have heard language speakers state that gikendaasowin is in the language and comes from the land, meaning it is place based. For example, regional dialects exist because "vocabulary varies as you go from region to region".[24] While

19 Patricia Ningewance, *Talking Gookom's Language: Learning Ojibwe* (Winnipeg: Mazinaate Press, 2007) at xvii.

20 Personal communication with Linda Toulouse, Elder from Anishinabek of Sagamok (28 November 2018) at Traditional Ecological Knowledge Elders Gathering in Sagamok, ON.

21 Mary Ann Corbiere, "Aanish go naa gaa-nendmaanh" in Alan Corbiere, Deborah McGregor & Crystal Migwans, eds., *Anishinaabwin Niizh: Culture movements, Critical Moments* (M'Chigeeng: Ojibwe Cultural Foundation, 2011) 67 at 76.

22 *Ibid.* at 78.

23 Basil Johnston, "Is That All There Is? Tribal Literature" in Doerfler, Sinclair & Stark, eds., "Centering Anishinaabeg Studies" *supra* note 8, 3 at 5.

24 Ningewance, *supra* note 19 at xvii.

hosting Gikendaasowin Gatherings, Elders and other participants spoke in the language to explain relationships and responsibilities to the lands. Without a basic understanding of the language, these stories and teachings would not be understood.

DEBORAH: Indigenous laws are held in different places/spaces, as well as in our language.[25] In other words, language is not the only place where legal orders are held and manifested. Indigenous languages, such as Anishinaabemowin indeed, provide profound insights into what the legal orders mean. Every concept has layers and different meaning depending on the context. Direct translation does not serve Indigenous languages such as Anishinaabemowin well.

The importance of language cannot be underestimated. When working with Elders or knowledge keepers, we see that unspoken language matters as well. For example, there is the knowledge of the land/waters "as living entit[ies] providing the central underpinnings for all life, the understanding of interconnected relationships".[26] There is the knowledge that is conveyed in ceremony and other communal experiences in which all are silent. All beings in Creation speak a language, and it may not be a human language, but it exists. Silence and listening is as critical as speaking as evident in our Creation story:

> Thought itself, in our creation, is what creates everything. The One, whoever that was in the darkness, who heard that sound, that energy-sound in that in-between place, the One from whom the first thought came. . . . all of Creation emerged from that very first thought that arose from the that in-between place where that energy-sound came from. From out of thought-consciousness emerge.[27]

The same heartbeat that pulsed out from the centre of the Universe in the beginning (the Creator's heartbeat) is the same rhythm, the same pulse, the same heartbeat that is given to the Anishinaabe.[28]

The Creator also gifted Anishinaabeg the breath of life and in doing so gave us spirit. Every time our heart beats, every time we take a breath, we are speaking the

25 See generally, John Borrows, *Canada's Indigenous Constitution* (Toronto: University of Toronto Press, 2010); Craft, "Nibi Report" *supra* note 11.

26 In this sense, knowledge and laws can come directly from the Land and Waters (and by this I mean all of Creation). As expressed by Indigenous scholar Sandra Styres & Dawn Zinga, "The Community-First Land-Centred Theoretical Framework: Bringing a 'Good Mind' to Indigenous Education Research? Sharing Our Journey" (2013) 36:2 *Canadian Journal of Education* 284 at 62.

27 Jim Dumont, *Indigenous Intelligence* (Sudbury: University of Sudbury, 2006) at 5.

28 *Ibid*. at 7.

language of Creation. One can argue the language of nibi is held in our bodies, our blood, tears, sweat and womb. It is held in our spirit. Indeed, we may well be limited by lacking the ability to speak Anishinaabemowin, but there are other senses that also convey language and understanding. It is just as important to think about language as more than the spoken word, but held in every heartbeat, every breath, every body.

What is the importance of connection to land (and land-based practices) in understanding Anishinaabe inaakonigewin?

DEBORAH: To be Anishinaabeg is to be of the land. The Creation story conveys that "People are not only shaped by the land, but were also created from the land", which means there is no separation of Anishinaabeg "from the land, identity, sense of place, and history".[29] The human person is then "of the earth and from the earth".[30] Thus, because Anishinaabeg literally come from the land, "we are all relatives because we have the same mother".[31] Edward Benton-Banai adds, "She is called Mother Earth because from her come all living things. Water is her life blood. It flows through her, nourishes her, and purifies her".[32]

It is essential that Anishinaabeg live and practice Anishinaabeg legal traditions and recognize that "the whole of creation are relatives to the human being".[33] In other words, Anishinaabeg legal traditions guide these relationships to live harmoniously with each other.[34] Furthermore, it may in fact not be entirely correct to think of all laws that govern our relationships to the land/waters as Anishinaabeg (our tendency to be human-centric), but of the Earth itself.[35] It is not possible to understand or practice Anishinaabeg laws without a connection to the Earth (as Dumont describes her), as we are the law itself. One of the most powerful characteristics of the ontology of Anishinaabeg legal orders is that it dissolves the binary between human/nature or environment. All beings/entities and humans make up the whole of Creation.

29 *Ibid.* at 36.
30 *Ibid.*
31 *Ibid.* at 12.
32 Edward Benton-Banai, *The Mishomis Book: The Voice of the Ojibway* (Hayward: Indian Country Communications, 1988) at 2.
33 Dumont, *supra* note 27 at 12.
34 See Borrows, *supra* note 25; Craft "Nibi Report" *supra* note 11; McGregor, "Zaagidowin" *supra* note 3.
35 Earth in this sense, in a similar vein to Styres and Zinga, according to Dumont, *supra* note 27 at 12, to think of our relationship to the Earth as "The Universe is said to be a family – Grandfather Creator, Grandmother Moon, Mother Earth. . . . The world is permeated with life-force, spiritual energy and with conscious purposeful beings. The human being is personally related to the environment, the landscape and the forces all around". The Earth herself is living, breathing, conscious being, complete with heart/feeling, soul/spirit, and physical/organic life, as it is with all the relatives of Creation".

SUE: One version of the Anishinaabe Creation story describes how humans were created last and all other beings created are our older brothers and sisters that guide and sustain us as the babies of Creation. This directly links us to the lands in which we were born, making legal traditions based from the lands.

Many laws come from the land by teaching us behaviours, which is a form of governance. One component of Anishinaabe governance is based on the clan system directly linking us to the lands.[36] Our Anishinaabeg ancestors relied on the lands to survive. They had to observe everything happening on the lands, and this connection provided them with gikendaasowin about legal traditions. Kathleen (Minogiizhigokwe) Absolon explains that gikendaasowin lives in the animals, birds, land, plants, trees and Creation, who happen to be our original teachers, which makes our philosophies earth centred.[37]

In many ceremonies, I have been given visions or shown things without any language exchange. These visions are a connection to the land as they give me knowledge on relationships to the lands. Traditional knowledge keepers have advised that the connection to the lands comes also from ceremony.

Once, I participated in a sunrise ceremony where it was reiterated that everything we need is given to us by the lands, the waters, the sky world and the animals. Learning to *bizindam* (listen) to all of life's beings is key to understanding and gaining gikendaasowin about legal traditions. Whether I am paddling on the water, harvesting from the lands or simply visiting the bush, I am constantly familiarizing myself with "and listening deeply to the language of the land".[38] It is the earth and the sky world that has provided Anishinaabe with teachings; it is the clan system that has provided us with gikendaasowin about our relationships with the lands and all life.

I remember hearing an Elder state that the land is the law and Anishinaabeg are the land, so therefore Anishinaabeg are the law.

RAYANNA: Connection with land is key to understanding legal traditions. Embodying our teachings includes working with Elders on our homelands,[39] as there is no separation between the land, Anishinaabe identity, sense of place and history.[40]

36 The clan system linking us as Anishinaabeg to the lands comes from many ceremony teachings. See for example: Quill Christie-Peters, "Anishinaabe art-making as falling in love: Reflections on artistic programming for urban Indigenous youth." (MA Thesis, University of Victoria, 2017).

37 Kathleen (Minogiizhigokwe) Absolon, *Kaandossiwin: How We Come to Know* (Halifax & Winnipeg: Fernwood, 2011) at 31.

38 Melissa Nelson, "The Hydromythology of the Anishinaabeg" in Doerfler, Sinclair & Stark, eds., "Centering Anishinaabeg Studies" *supra* note 8, 213 at 216.

39 Leanne Betasamosake Simpson, "Land as Pedagogy: Nishnaabeg Intelligence and Rebellious Transformation" (2014) 3:3 *Decolonization: Indigeneity, Education & Society* at 17 [*Land as Pedagogy*].

40 Dumont, *supra* note 27 at 36; See also Joshua K. Tobias & Chantelle A. M. Richmond, "That Land Means Everything to Us as Anishinaabe. . .": Environmental Dispossession and Resilience on the North Shore of Lake Superior" (2014) 29 *Health & Place* 26 at 26;

Connecting to land is essential in understanding legal traditions, which is illustrated through our Nibi Gatherings. Participating in kinship, relationship making, sitting with the sacred fire, visiting by and with the river, listening and witnessing the thunderbirds (*binesiiyag*) above us, while also sounding our voices to honour the land and nibi is *practicing* our legal traditions. Removing ourselves from the intellectual traditions we learned in Western education is done by connecting with land in this way because gathering on the land is in "an Indigenous context using Indigenous processes".[41]

On both an individual and community level, striving for strong connections to our lands contributes to our well-being in the "physical, social, cultural, environmental, emotional, and spiritual" senses.[42] Unfortunately, due to settler colonialism, not everyone is connected to their homelands. Yet, everyone is connected to some form of Indigenous land and territory. This means connecting to land in order to understand legal traditions can happen on territories that are not one's homelands.

Thus, although connecting to one's homelands in order to understand one's own legal traditions is essential, starting (or continuing) the learning journey in building relationship with Mother Earth can be achieved anywhere. Building relationship can be done in a variety of ways. For example, learning some of the local Indigenous peoples' stories, learning words from the local languages to describe their landscape and waterways, gathering in community and connecting with other Indigenous relatives are all good ways to strengthen relationship with the land one is visiting on and living off of.

AIMÉE: To begin, I want to problematize the distinction between land and water.[43] Often we hear teachings that identify the earth as our mother, the waterways as her veins that carry her sacred life blood. These types of reflections are often invoked in the context of contesting natural resource extraction and industrialization that is impacting lands and waters. They artificially divide land and water as two parts of creation with whom we have particular relationships, rather than considering creation as a whole.[44] This reinforces the Western compartmentalization of resources (timber, minerals, petroleum) and allows for the purchase and exploitation of them, despite impacts on other parts of creation (including what are regarded to be lands and waters). I view this as pragmatic re-visioning of teachings that were originally

---

Helen L. Berry et al., "Mind, Body, Spirit: Co-benefits for Mental Health from Climate Change Adaptation and Caring for Country in Remote Aboriginal Communities" (2010) 21:6 *N.S.W. Pub Health Bull* 139.

41 Simpson, "Land as Pedagogy" *supra* note 39 at 9.

42 Tobias, *supra* note 40 at 26.

43 Aimée Craft, "Navigating Our Ongoing Sacred Legal Relationship with Nibi (Water)" in Jennifer Goyder et al., eds., *UNDRIP Implementation: More Reflections on the Braiding of International, Domestic and Indigenous Laws Special Report* (Saskatoon: Centre for International Governance Innovation & Wiyasiwewin Mikiwahp, 2018) 53 [Craft "Navigating"].

44 *Ibid.* (UNDRIP Special Report).

intended to illustrate that we should be in relationships with all of creation. These relationships are multidimensional and provide for our well-being. Water and land as part of that creation are not separate but rather part of one whole, one creation:

> The Great Spirit instructed us to honor all of life and to respect all of Creation. He gave us laws that govern all our relationships, to live in harmony with Creation and with humankind. We are spiritually and culturally obliged to have in our interest, the total well being of this Earth, this Creation, and the people.[45]

I will use clay pots that our ancestors used to make as an illustration of this intimate interconnection between land and water and ourselves.[46] Over an extended period of time, the water pounded rocks to break them down into clay form. We then used that clay to build pots. We dried and heated those pots at high temperatures to remove all water from them to return them to a solid form (pottery firing). We then filled them with water and food and cooked over a fire to feed ourselves. We buried them in the earth of locations we would return to, so that they would not freeze and crack. When the pots broke, we returned them to the earth and the water as an offering.

In anishinaabemowin, the word for clay is *waszhish'ke*.[47] Clay thus recognizes and remembers the role of waazhusk (the muskrat)[48] in Anishinaabe creation stories. Waazhusk sacrificed her/himself and dove down in the water after the Great Flood to grab a small handful of clay to help rebuild the land.[49] While the muskrat lives primarily in the water, it also lives on land, which deepens its connection to both.

Collaborative learning relationships between non-human beings and humans have resulted in customary law, developed over generations and centuries between us and the rest of creation (including animals, the land and the water). There are many things we can learn being on, in and with water and land. By observing interactions between other beings amongst themselves and all of creation, we

45 Jim Dumont, "Seven Principles of Anishinaabe First Nationhood, Anishinaabe Izhichigaywin" in Lea Foushee and Renee Gurneau, eds., *Sacred Water: Water for Life* (Lake Elmo: North American Water Office, 2010) at 15 [Dumont, "Seven Principles"].

46 With many thanks to my friend KC Adams (visual artist), who has taught me about traditional clay methods and who has brought those teachings to all people at the annual Nibi Gathering. See further "Clay-KC Adams" (24 March 2018) *YouTube*, online: <www.youtube.com/watch?v=aVwowDT4j54>.

47 Personal communications, Allan White, Elder from Noatkamegwanning First Nation, ON at Winnipeg, MB; and Sherry Copenace, Elder from Ojibways of Onigaming First Nation, ON at Winnipeg, MB.

48 *Ibid.* (Allan & Sherry personal communication), where they shared *waszhish'ke* for *waazhusk* (muskrat) and *aki* (earth or creation).

49 Benton-Benai, *supra* note 32 at 32–33; Basil Johnston, *Honour Earth Mother: Mino-audjaudauh Mizzu-kummik-quae* (Cape Croker Reserve: Kegedonce Press, 2003) at 5.

have learned to model our relationships. These deeply intimate and interconnected relationships between parts of creation include the earth and water and cannot be compartmentalized as easily as they may be in a colonial context.

When working with Indigenous legal traditions, we risk replicating Western legal values and structures. How do you avoid that when working with Anishinaabe nibi inaakonigewin?

AIMÉE: First I would ask: *What is Anishinaabe law?* In response, we can easily find ourselves drawing comparisons with Western legal traditions. It is often easier, or tidier, to be aligned with what is *identifiable* as law from a Western perspective, where sources are written, codified and reported. In Western legal systems, even convention makes its way into historical documentation and common knowledge.

In the classroom, it is often easier to revert to teaching Indigenous laws through contrasting, comparing and building on Western legal theories with accessible materials. Often, this proved to be the fastest and less turbulent route to having law students understand Indigenous normative values as law.[50] While it may allow us to more easily explain Anishinaabe concepts, structures, processes and normative obligations to those who do not live and breathe that law, there is a risk of replicating values and structures that are not inherent to Anishinaabe law. In turn, this can impact and distort the form and substance of Anishinaabe law. The same is true for other Indigenous legal traditions, framed, modeled, contrasted and integrated into Western modes of thinking, conceptualizing and analyzing.

Thinking of Western legal orders as a point of direct comparison is problematic because Indigenous laws are derived from different sources and are framed through profoundly different structures. They are also meant to achieve very different goals. For example, what we describe in Anishinaabemowin (the Anishinaabe language) as inaakonigewin is not a set of rules but rather an illustration of what is available to us, what may be taken up as responsibilities in order to live well together in relationship with one another. This includes not only the relationships and well-being of human beings but with all beings that are part of Creation. These relationships exist between all beings that are part of creation, in a variety of permutations and according to a system of generalized reciprocity.[51]

I have often told the story that led to my Anishinaabe legal "a-ha" moment. It's the story of my Mishomis guiding my father and me (and our boat) into a rock on the Winnipeg River. By pointing towards a rock, my father directed the

50 See Aaron Mills, "The Lifeworlds of Law: On Revitalizing Indigenous Legal Orders Today" (2016) 61:4 *RD McGill* 847.

51 See Aimée Craft, *Breathing Life into the Stone Fort Treaty: An Anishinaabe Understanding of Treaty One* (Saskatoon: Purich, 2013) [Craft, "Breathing Life"].

boat into/over it. My Mishomis later explained his action of pointing as indicating what was there, rather than telling us to go there.[52] Rather than an act of interference with my father's agency, he was enabling him to make informed decisions for our collective well-being.

This non-interfering framework of relationality, deeply respectful of individual autonomy and agency, is exactly what I fear we might lose sight of (at least in part) by framing Indigenous laws in Western legal spheres of rights and obligations aimed at preserving individual interests that are related to the protection of private property. Western systems tell us what to do. They do not accept that, as humans, we are often not the final decision makers in the legal reasoning world. Whereas Anishinaabe inaakonigewin often requires placing trust in relationships with others, including trust in Kije-Manito or spirits to determine outcomes. We are often dependent on our natural environment and other beings in creation to show us law, which help us reflect on how we must replicate those responsibilities in our human relationships.[53]

I often think to that day on the river, and that rock, and how something greater than my Mishomis, my father or myself was at work. This experience led me to my understanding of what Anishinaabe inaakonigewin ultimately offers us, which I attempt to understand and live on a daily basis.

DEBORAH: There is very much a risk that by engaging in and conducting research in relation to Indigenous legal traditions, that we replicate Western colonial legal systems. The main challenge many scholars have, both Indigenous and non-Indigenous, is that the majority of their formal training is in Western legal systems and *then* they decide to research Indigenous legal traditions. Their grounding in Indigenous legal traditions is not within an Indigenous context until later in life. In fact, many learn by reading about Indigenous laws rather than experiencing and learning from the practitioners. The frame of reference remains firmly entrenched in Western legal systems, not Indigenous systems. As an emerging area of scholarship in the academic sense, there is an overwhelming inclination to make Indigenous legal traditions palatable to the more powerful, institutionally and politically legal systems. This is best expressed by Mohawk Professor Emeritus Marlene Brant Castellano in commenting about the distance between academia and lived experience in Indigenous intellectual traditions:

> What aboriginal and non-Aboriginal writers have in common is a degree of distance from the everyday practices or an oral culture. They are also insulated from the discipline imposed on purveyors of knowledge in an oral culture – that is – from the collective analysis and judgement of a community, each of whose members share equal authority to interpret

52 Craft, "Nibi Report" *supra* note 11.
53 Craft, "Navigating" *supra* note 43 at 54.

reality. Immunity from corrective influence renders suspect any outsider interpreting insider knowledge and, indeed any writer whether a member of the community or not. Writing things up gives authority to a particular view and a particular writer.[54]

We need to ask different questions of Indigenous laws and not the same kinds of questions that would be asked of Western legal orders. The effect is to literally "box in" Indigenous legal traditions into preconceived legal paradigms. There is a failure to recognize that Indigenous legal orders may indeed be of a qualitatively different order and were intended to serve Indigenous societies and their kin (water, animals, plants, etc.) and have done so for thousands of years.

One of the greatest challenges is that non-Indigenous systems of understanding law exclude the non-human. It is people who hold court, argue cases, research law and so forth. Indigenous legal traditions recognize the agency of other beings/teachings/relatives in generating, practicing and adjudicating law.[55] This constitutes a major worldview and ontological difference. Not all legal orders are meant to be shared broadly (e.g. spiritual laws). There are of course risks of romanticizing Indigenous legal traditions and freezing them in time (the "good old days") despite the indications that they were adaptive, transformative and continually deliberated.[56]

RAYANNA: Due to the laws and policies meant to diminish our relationship with the land and water (either directly or indirectly),[57] what is left is this lasting residue of trauma which calls for a journey to healing.[58] When learning inaakonigewin (our stories, songs and protocols), it is an act of resistance, part

54 Marlene Brant Castellano, "Updating Aboriginal Traditions of Knowledge" in George Dei, Budd Hall & Dorothy Golden Rosenberg, eds., *Indigenous Knowledges in Global Contexts* (Toronto: University of Toronto Press, 2000) 21 at 32. Her observation is clearly evident in contemporary Indigenous scholarship, in which problematic ideologies dominate the intellectual landscape without any debate, discussion and dissention (dissention can also be productive). Castellano points out the "corrective influence" necessary for rigor is absent.

55 Robin W. Kimmerer, "The Fortress, the River and the Garden: A New Metaphor for Cultivating Mutualistic Relationship between Scientific and Traditional Ecological Knowledge" in Kelley Young & Dan Longboat, eds., *Contemporary Studies in Environmental and Indigenous Pedagogies: A Curricula of Stories and Places* (Rotterdam: Sense, 2013); Kyle Whyte, "Indigenous Climate Change Studies: Indigenizing Futures, Decolonizing the Anthropocene" (2017) 55:1/2 *English Language Notes* 153.

56 See further Val Napoleon, "Thinking about Indigenous Legal Orders," Research paper prepared for the National Centre for First Nations Governance (2007); John Borrows, *Canada's Indigenous Constitution* (Toronto: University of Toronto Press, 2010).

57 Brock Pitawanakwat, "Anishinaabeg Studies: Creative, Critical, Ethical, and Reflexive" in Doerfler, Sinclair & Stark, eds., "Centering Anishinaabeg Studies" *supra* note 8, 363 at 368.

58 See generally, Renee Linklater, *Decolonizing Trauma Work: Indigenous Stories and Strategies* (Winnipeg: Fernwood, 2014).

of our decolonization and healing process as it strengthens our relationships with ourselves, nibi, our Elders, each other and all of creation.

In our work, we resist compartmentalization; instead we view everything (including our work, life, culture, bodies and lands) as a whole.[59] We recognize that working with our legal traditions is not simply an "intellectualizing project",[60] but it is "a way of life".[61] It is a way of life that has shown us that we are "not only shaped *by* the land, but we [are] also created *for* the land"[62] and "of the land".[63] There stems an obligation to have a good relationship with nibi and contribute to nibi's healing (which ultimately contributes to our own healing).

I recognized the power nibi had in my own healing in my first year of law school. I struggled with the realization that my inherent rights as Anishinaabe were being defined, infringed and justifiably extinguished by non-Indigenous peoples.[64] I sought and maintained my balance, my mino-bimaadiziwin, by strengthening my relationship with nibi through seeking out our stories, songs and language.

Thus, the goal as learners (rather than researchers), when learning Anishinaabe nibi inaakonigewin, is to, in Elder Allan White's words: "embed these ideas instead of (simply) writing everything down".[65] Ultimately, there is no separation between our research, our Anishinaabe communities and our lives. Viewing everything as a whole ensures that we are strengthening our laws by continuing to live our mino-bimaadiziwin.

SUE: In all things that we do as Anishinaabeg peoples, offerings come first. An offering is a gift, an act of responsibility and a gesture of relationship between people and other entities, given in the interest of creating ties, honoring them or asking for assistance and direction.[66] To avoid replicating Western legal systems values and structures, Anishinaabeg can follow the footsteps of our ancestors by remembering that offerings come first.

Settler cultures have been less attentive to the relationship between humans and nibi and mainstream society typically sees nibi as a resource or a commodity,[67] in

59 Christie-Peters, *supra* note 36.

60 Brent Debassige, "Re-conceptualizing Anishinaabe Mino-Bimaadiziwin (the Good Life) as Research Methodology: A Spirit-Centered Way in Anishinaabe Research" (2010) 33:1 *CJNE* 11 at 16.

61 Craft, "Nibi Report" *supra* note 11 at 8 (quoting Nawaa'kamigowinini).

62 Dumont, "Seven Principles" *supra* note 45 at 36.

63 Craft, "Breathing Life" *supra* note 51 at 94.

64 See for example, *R v Sparrow*, [1990] 1 SCR 1075.

65 Craft, "Nibi Report" *supra* note 11 at 7.

66 Jill Doerfler, Niigaanwewidam James Sinclair & Heid Kiiwetinepinesiik Stark, "Bagijige: Making an Offering" in Doerfler, Sinclair & Stark, eds., "Centering Anishinaabeg Studies" *supra* note 8, xv.

67 Maude Barlow, "10 Water Commons Principles: A Co-creative Approach for Protecting the Plant's Future" (11 July 2012) *On the Commons: Water* (magazine), online: <www.onthecommons.org/work/10-water-commons-principles#sthash.gacjO80a.dpbs>; Karen Bakker,

stark contrast to its treatment in Anishinaabeg law. Understanding the differences in two worldviews allows individuals to be consistent with Anishinaabeg laws, principles and process. Western legal systems values and structures are based on control and ownership contrasting Anishinaabe nibi inaakonigewin, which is based on five Rs: relationship, respect, reciprocity, responsibility and reflection.[68]

The Oxford Dictionary defines water (nibi) as "a colorless transparent odourless tasteless liquid compound of oxygen and hydrogen".[69] Linton explains that "H_2O consists of an oxide of hydrogen H_2O or $(H_2O)_x$ in the proportion of 2 atoms of hydrogen to one atom of oxygen and is an odourless, tasteless" compound.[70] These definitions and understandings flow against Anishinaabe gikendaasowin, as nibi is alive with responsibilities to life. This is the basic difference between colonial ontology and Anishinaabe ontology, as Blackstock (2001) explains: "water is a meditative medium, a purifier, a source of power and most importantly has a spirit".[71] McGregor (2001) reinforces the Anishinabek ontology by reiterating that "water is life" and is considered "a living-entity".[72] Several articles also state that the nibi is life; the nibi is sacred; nibi is alive with a spirit.[73] The difference between colonial ontology and Anishinaabe ontology is

---

"Commons versus Commodities: Political Ecologies of Water Privatization" in Richard Peet, Paul Robbins & Michael Watts, eds., *Global Political Ecology* (London: Routledge, 2010) 345.

68 See generally, Robin Wall Kimmerer, *Braiding Sweetgrass: Indigenous Wisdom, Scientific Knowledge and the Teachings of Plants* (Minneapolis: Milkweed Editions, 2013); Jo-Anne Archibald, *Indigenous Storywork: Educating the Heart, Mind, Body, and Spirit* (Vancouver, UBC Press, 2008); Nicole Bell, "Anishinaabe Bimmaadiziwin: Living Spiritually with Respect, Relationship, Reciprocity, and Responsibility" in A. Kulnieks, D. R. Longboat & K. Young, eds., *Contemporary Studies in Environmental and Indigenous Pedagogies* (Rotterdam: Sense, 2013); Doerfler, Sinclair & Stark, "Bagijige: Making an Offering" *supra* note 67; Craft, "Nibi Report" *supra* note 11; Aimée Craft, "Nibi onje biimaadiiziiwin" (March/April 2017) 17:2 *Water Canada: The Complete Water Magazine* 16 at 16 [Craft, "Nibi onje biimaadiiziiwin"].

69 A. Bisset, *Oxford Canadian Dictionary* (Toronto: Oxford University Press, 2004) at 17.

70 Jamie Linton, *What Is Water? The History of a Modern Abstraction* (Vancouver: UBC Press, 2010) at 20.

71 Michael Blackstock, "Water: A First Nations' Spiritual and Ecological Perspective" (2001) 1:1 *J of Ecosystems and Management* 2 at 21.

72 Chiefs of Ontario, "Drinking Water in Ontario First Nation Communities: Present Challenges and Future Directions for On-Reserve Water Treatment in the Province of Ontario" in Deborah McGregor et al., eds., *Part II Submissions to the Walkerton Inquiry Commission* (2001) at 21, online: <www.archives.gov.on.ca/en/e_records/walkerton/part2info/may15/index.html> [COO, "Walkerton Inquiry"].

73 See further, Blackstock, *supra* note 72; Anderson, *supra* note 2; Deborah McGregor, "Traditional Knowledge: Considerations for Protecting Water in Ontario" (2012) 3:3 *Intl J Policy J* 1; Cave & McKay, *supra* note 1; Karletta Chief, Alison Meadow & Kyle Whyte, "Engaging Southwestern Tribes in Sustainable Water Resources Topics and Management" (2016) 8:350 *Water* 1; Whyte, *supra* note 56; Craft, "Nibi Report" *supra* note 11; "Indigenous Peoples Kyoto Water Declaration" (Declaration delivered at the Third World Water Forum, Kyoto, Japan, 2013); Nadia Joe, "Our Water, Our Life: A New Model for Water Resource Management in the Aishihik Drainage" (Toronto: Walter & Gordon Duncan Foundation, 2012); Joyce Tekahnawiiaks King, "The Value of Water and the Meaning of Water Law for

understanding what nibi is, the basis of how peoples manage, understand and exist with nibi. Yazzie and Baldy (2018) reiterate that nibi is not a resource to be used by corporations but is a relative[74] adding to Anishinaabe ontology. Daigle (2018) discusses the need for regenerating nibi relations, confirming that nibi is a relative to Indigenous peoples.[75] The colonial understanding of what "water" is stands in opposition to Anishinaabe understandings. Anishinaabe know that nibi can manage itself, contrasting the colonial position that humans can manage nibi.

Conclusion

While Western legal thought might equate this responsibility to jurisdiction, Anishinaabe inaakonigewin encourages us to reflect on responsibilities as diffused in a web of multiple legal interactions, some of which we are aware of, some not, and through which we are all somehow affected. This allows us to think and act according to multiple senses, including spirited knowledge. It also allows us to value gendered pedagogies as relevant to teaching and learning about responsibilities to nibi.

Such gendered pedagogies relating to our responsibilities to nibi include the Water Declaration of the Anishinaabe[g], Mushegowuk and Onkwehonwe in Ontario, which states that "the Anishinaabe[g], Mushegowuk and Onkwehonwe women are keepers of nibi as women bring babies into the world carried on by the breaking of the water".[76] The Water Walks have raised this awareness of women's special relationship with nibi and the responsibility to nibi.[77] Craft (2014) and Anderson (2010) have quoted Elders who reiterate women have a special connection to nibi, as women have the ability to give birth through the waters.[78] McGregor (2001) also explains the responsibility women have to the waters by sharing information about the "Akii Kwe: Anishinaabe women who speak for the water".[79] The Chiefs of Ontario Report on the First Nations Water Policy Forum (2008a) has several quotes from participants stating that women have a special

the Native Americans Known as the Haudenosaunee" (2007) 16:3 *Cornell J of Law and Public Policy* 449; William E. Marks, *Water Voices from around the World* (Edgartown: William E. Marks, 2007).

74 See further, Melanie K. Yazzie & Kutcha Risling Baldy, "Introduction: Indigenous Peoples and the Politics of Water" (2010) 7 *Decolonization: Indigeneity, Education & Society* 1.

75 See further Michelle Diagle, "Resurging through Kishiichiwan: The Spatial Politics of Indigenous Water Relations" (2018) 7:1 *Decolonization: Indigeneity, Education & Society* 159.

76 Chiefs of Ontario, Media Release, "Water Declaration of the Anshinabek, Mushkegowuk and Onkwehonwe" (October 2008) *COO* at 1, online: <www.chiefs-of-ontario.org/sites/default/files/files/COO%20water%20declaration%20revised%20march%202010.pdf> [COO Water Declaration].

77 Josephine Mandamin, "Foreword: Water Is Life" in Dayna Nadine Scott, ed., *Our Chemical Selves: Gender, Toxics, and Environmental Health* (Vancouver: UBC Press, 2015) xi at xiii.

78 McGregor, "Zaagidowin" *supra* note 3; Craft, "Nibi Report" *supra* note 11.

79 COO, "Walkerton Inquiry" *supra* note 73 at 18. See further Anderson, *supra* note 1; Craft "Nibi Report" *supra* note 11; McGregor, "Zaagidowin" *supra* note 3.

responsibility to nibi and are the "water keepers.[80] This special relationship that ikweyag have with nibi needs to be transmitted to the world as more women are picking up their responsibilities and protecting nibi.

While men also carry responsibilities and are responsible to look after our mothers, we are becoming the next generation of mothers and grandmothers that will give effect to those sacred responsibilities. We, as Anishinaabekweyag, are engaged in honouring nibi because it is part of our individual and collective wholeness, which in turn brings us balance and healing.[81] Recognizing our role as ikweyag in healing nibi centres around "call[ing] better futures into being".[82] We want our nieces, daughters, sisters and granddaughters to know their responsibility to nibi and nibi's responsibility to each of them as a reciprocal relationship that necessitates caring. The work will continue for years to come and will take many forms over time. Ultimately, this movement of caring for and being in relationship with water (as gifted to us through our inaakonigewin and responsibilities) is meant to build strong communities for ourselves, our families and for future generations[83] while also contributing to nibi's sustainability.[84]

80 COO Water Declaration, *supra* note 76.
81 Dumont, "Seven Principles" *supra* note 45 at 34–35.
82 Danika Medak-Saltzman, "Coming to You from the Indigenous Future: Native Women, Speculative Film Shorts, and the Art of the Possible" (2017) 29:1 *Studies in Amer Indian Lit* 139 at 164.
83 Debassige, *supra* note 60 at 12.
84 Deborah McGregor, "Traditional Knowledge and Nibi Governance: The Ethic of Responsibility" (2014) 10:5 *Alternative: An Intl J of Indigenous Peoples* 493 at 496.

2 Statehood, Canadian sovereignty, and the attempted domestication of Indigenous legal relations

Amar Bhatia

Introduction

This chapter lays out how the Canadian state attempts to displace the wealth of Indigenous legal relations in what is currently known as Canada. This attempted displacement is particularly galling given the necessity of Indigenous laws, including treaties, in order to legitimate the presence of Canada. As noted by Cree international law scholar Sharon Venne:

> The simple fact is that, without the treaty, no one other than Indigenous Peoples has the right to live in our land. The International Court of Justice in the Western Sahara case stated that the only way for non-indigenous people to live in the lands of Indigenous Peoples is through a treaty. . . . Without the treaties, what legitimate law can the colonizers use to occupy our lands? If Canada gets rid of the treaties, what happens to the treaty rights of the non-indigenous people?[1]

Notwithstanding the necessity of these treaty relations, Canada has sought to 'domesticate' Indigenous peoples and laws and realize its own statehood through their erasure. This chapter starts by examining an inter-state international law definition of statehood before turning to the mechanisms of Canadian law deployed in the attempt to realize that definition on these lands. These mechanisms include Canadian constitutional law and especially Canadian Aboriginal law. The latter includes the historical treaties, the Indian Act, the common law of Aboriginal title, and the negotiation of modern treaties (among other areas). I mainly focus here on the domestication of the historical treaties and the use of the Indian Act to consolidate Canadian statehood and its sovereignty at the direct expense of Indigenous laws and self-determination. Conventional markers of statehood and state sovereignty interrupt the revitalization of Indigenous modes of making and maintaining relations through treaties and adoption.

1 Sharon Venne, "Treaties Made in Good Faith" in Paul W. DePasquale, ed., *Natives & Settlers, Now & Then: Historical Issues and Current Perspectives on Treaties and Land Claims in Canada* (Edmonton: University of Alberta Press, 2007) at 5, 10.

Statehood and state sovereignty

A working definition of statehood and state sovereignty

How did settler colonialism and state sovereignty displace Indigenous peoples and the authority of their laws and legal systems? Following European colonization and settlement, these Indigenous laws and systems were severely repressed during the establishment of Canadian statehood and state sovereignty. Although not developed in accordance with Indigenous laws, statehood and sovereignty overlaps with key functions like population powers and treaty-making. The Montevideo Convention on the Rights and Duties of States (1933) is a convenient shorthand for comparing these powers. Article 1 of the Convention defines statehood as follows. The state as a person of international law should possess the following qualifications: (a) a permanent population, (b) a defined territory, (c) government, and (d) capacity to enter into relations with other states.[2]

Clearly, statehood, and the incident of sovereignty, may not be useful or appropriate concepts for articulating the demands of Indigenous peoples and nations, either generally or in the context of treaty relations. Some have referred to them as inappropriate concepts that are, in many ways, rotten to their core.[3] But statehood and sovereignty can be useful as comparative aids to understand minimum factors that allow a political community to exist and reproduce itself in seeming perpetuity.[4] Time plays an important part here, including the emphasis in international law (most of the time) on the permanence of a population, the stability

2 Convention on the Rights of and Duties of States, Montevideo, 26 December 1993, 165 LNTS 19, online: <www.oas.org/juridico/english/treaties/a-40.html>. See also, for example, James Crawford, *The Creation of States in International Law* (Oxford: Clarendon, 2007) [Crawford 2007]; James Crawford, *Brownlie's Principles of Public International Law*, 8th ed. (Oxford: Oxford University Press, 2012) at 127–142 [Crawford 2012]. Note that these 'qualifications' for statehood do not generally include a minimum population, do not always require the territory to be clearly defined at all times, can accommodate more than one government at a time, and are subject to much debate on the aspects of 'the capacity to enter into relations with other states' (and the declarative versus constitutive aspects of independence) (Crawford 2012 at 127–142).

3 See, e.g., Makau W. Mutua, "Why Redraw the Map of Africa: A Moral and Legal Inquiry" (1995) 16 *Mich J Intl L* 1113; Sujith Xavier, "For the Purposes of the Rome Statute" (draft paper on file with author); Rose Parfitt, "Theorizing Recognition and International Personality" in Florian Hoffman & Anne Orford, eds., *The Oxford Handbook of International Legal Theory* (Oxford: Oxford University Press, 2016) [Parfitt]; Taiaike Alfred, *Peace, Power, Righteousness: An Indigenous Manifesto* (Don Mills, ON: Oxford University Press, 1999) at 78–81 [Alfred]. On recognition and the politics of refusal, see also Audra Simpson, *Mohawk Interruptus: Political Life across the Borders of Settler States* (London: Duke University Press, 2014) [Simpson]; Heidi Kiiwetinepinesiik Stark, "Nenabozho's Smart Berries: Rethinking Tribal Sovereignty and Accountability" 2013 *Mich St L Rev* 339, online: <https://digitalcommons.law.msu.edu/lr/vol2013/iss2/6)>.

4 See, e.g., Heidi Kiiwetinepinesiik Stark & Kekek Jason Stark, "Nenabozho Goes Fishing: A Sovereignty Story" (2018) 147:2 *Daedalus J Am Academy Arts & Sciences* 17–26 [Stark & Stark]; Michael Fakhri (2018) "Third World Sovereignty, Indigenous Sovereignty, and Food Sovereignty: Living with Sovereignty Despite the Map" (2018) 9:3–4 *Transnat'l Leg Theory* 218.

of the political community, and the definition of territories through clear borders and frontiers.[5] I am thus using the attributes of statehood and the incident of sovereignty here as a heuristic to compare what Canada has accumulated in order to maintain itself over time and in contrast to what it has taken or negotiated away from Indigenous nations to their continuing detriment. To put it differently, and as asserted by then Chief Justice Lamer of the Supreme Court of Canada (SCC): "we are all here to stay".[6] But how exactly is a nation here to stay?[7] Lands and people are necessary parts of the answer, but settler societies have taken, and continue to take, both aspects from Indigenous nations.[8] In a landmark UN study on treaties, Special Rapporteur Martinez noted that Indigenous peoples

> have been deprived of (or saw greatly reduced) three of the four essential attributes on which their original status as sovereign nations was grounded, *namely their territory, their recognized capacity to enter into international agreements, and their specific forms of government. Not to mention the substantial reduction of their respective populations* . . . due to a number of factors, including assimilationist policies.[9]

In the sections that follow, I look briefly at aspects of the statist reduction and occupation of these attributes that are necessary for Indigenous continuity: treaty relations, territory, and people. In other work, I argue that the return or expansion of these attributes turns on the revitalization of Indigenous laws for making and maintaining relations through treaties and adoption.[10] If we are truly all treaty people, then the permanence of Canadian presence and its immigrant future is tied to the permanence of the treaties and Indigenous peoples and nations.[11]

5 Crawford 2012, *supra* note 2 at 128–129.

6 *Delgamuukw v. British Columbia* [1997] 3 S.C.R. 1010 at para 186 [*Delgamuukw*]. See also Tsilhqot'in Nation v. British Columbia, 2014 SCC 44 (CanLII), online: <http://canlii.ca/t/g7mt9> at para. 82 [*Tsilhqot'in Nation*].

7 See Michael Asch, *On Being Here to Stay: Treaties and Aboriginal Rights in Canada* (Toronto: University of Toronto Press, 2014). See also Christopher Tomlins, *Freedom Bound: Law, Labor, and Civic Identity in Colonizing English America, 1580–1865* (New York: Cambridge University Press, 2010) [Tomlins] (on 'manning, planting, & keeping' territory over time).

8 See, e.g., Martha Stiegman, *Honour Your Word* (Montreal: Productions Multi-Monde, 2013) [Stiegman] – documentary showing the Algonquins of Barriere Lake's resistance and Marylynn Poucachiche's words.

9 Miguel Alfonso Martinez, *Study on Treaties, Agreements and Other Constructive Arrangements between States and Indigenous Populations: Final Report by Miguel Alfonso Martinez, Special Rapporteur.* UN Doc. E/CN.4/Sub.2/1999/20, online: UN OHCHR <https://documents-dds-ny.un.org/doc/UNDOC/GEN/G99/137/73/PDF/G9913773.pdf?OpenElement> at para. 105 (emphasis added) [Martinez 1999].

10 See Amar Bhatia, "Re-peopling in a Settler-Colonial Context: The Intersection of Indigenous Laws of Adoption with Canadian Immigration Law" (2018) 14:4 *AlterNative: Intl J Indigenous Peoples* 343 [Bhatia 2018].

11 Amar Bhatia, "We Are All Here to Stay? Indigeneity, Migration, and 'Decolonizing' the Treaty Right to Be Here" (2013) 13:2 *Windsor YB Access Just* 39 [Bhatia 2013].

The capacity to enter into international relations

How did treaties go from regulating relations within, between, and beyond Indigenous nations to "grey law",[12] seen as having no force at international law? In short, they were "domesticated" by the empires and states seeking to benefit from them. Domestication entails efforts by the Canadian state and society to reduce ongoing, nation-to-nation treaty relations guided by Indigenous laws to one-time land cessions interpreted solely by state laws and policies.[13]

In this vein, historian Jim Miller set out three main types of treaty-making traditions with settlers:[14] (1) early commercial compacts between Indigenous peoples and chartered corporations that had been granted monopolies and exclusive trade rights (e.g. the fur trade) from the 17th century onwards; (2) treaties of peace, friendship, and alliance, situated within "rival networks" of imperial European powers, from the late 17th century and especially the 18th century; and (3) territorial treaties governing settlers' "access to and use of" Indigenous lands, from the later 18th century to the early 20th century, along with the related but distinct formal agreements pursued from the 1970s to now (the so-called modern treaties).[15]

By starting with the early commercial compacts, Miller marks the beginning of time somewhat earlier than most accounts. Other examples usually proceed from the Maritime treaties of peace, friendship, and alliance; to the pre-Confederation treaties in Upper Canada; to the post-Confederation numbered treaties in the Prairies and beyond (from 1871 to 1923); to the so-called modern treaties of comprehensive land claims agreements (e.g. 1975 James Bay and Northern Quebec Agreement and following).[16] Most accounts do not mention the rich history of inter-Indigenous treaty-making.[17] Aboriginal Affairs and Northern Development Canada (currently Crown-Indigenous Relations and Northern Affairs

12 See, e.g., Ben Saul, *Indigenous Peoples and Human Rights: International and Regional Jurisprudence* (Portland, OR: Hart, 2016) [Saul] at 19–21.

13 See, e.g., Isabelle Schulte-Tenckhoff, "Reassessing the Paradigm of Domestication: The Problematic of Indigenous Treaties" (1998) 4:2 *Rev Const Stud* 239 [Schulte-Tenckhoff 1998]; John Borrows, "Domesticating Doctrines: Aboriginal Peoples after the Royal Commission" (2001) 46:3 *McGill LJ* 615 [Borrows 2001]. See also Martinez 1999, *supra* note 9 at paras 191–194; Aimée Craft, *Breathing Life into the Stone Fort Treaty: An Anishinabe Understanding of Treaty One* (Saskatoon: Purich, 2013) at 14 [Craft 2013].

14 J. R. Miller, *Compact, Contract, Covenant: Aboriginal Treaty-Making in Canada* (Toronto: University of Toronto Press, 2009) at 4–5.

15 Note Janna Promislow's criticism of Miller's typology for excluding epoch-crossing events and adhesions that took place after the 1923 Williams treaties and before the 1975 James Bay Northern Quebec Agreement (e.g. Treaty 6 and Treaty 9 adhesions), see Janna Promislow, "Treaties in History and Law" (2014) 47 *UBCLR* 1085–1183 at para 41 (QL) [Promislow].

16 See, e.g., Aboriginal Affairs and Northern Development Canada, Treaty-Making in Canada, "Summaries of Pre-1975 Treaties," online: INAC <www.aadnc-aandc.gc.ca/eng/1370362690208/1370362747827>.

17 For some examples, see references in Amar Bhatia, "The South of the North: Building on Critical Approaches to International Law with Lessons from the Fourth World" (2012) 14 *Or Rev Intl L* 131–175 [Bhatia 2012a].

Canada) uses a map entirely devoid of these relationships.[18] Historian Ken Coates tracks the standard trajectory of domestication across all three of the main treaty types.[19] From being seen as "accords between nations", they turned to agreements "formalizing the subordination" of Indigenous peoples to colonial powers that also 'clear the way' for settlers and their states.[20] As noted by Manitoba historian Jean Friesen, "The negotiators viewed the treaties as finalizing, once and for all, the clearing of title while, for the Anishinabe, it was 'the beginning of a continuing relation of mutual obligation'".[21]

The implications of this divergence are far-reaching. At Saskatchewan's Office of the Treaty Commissioner, Justice David Arnot set out the key points of contrast in two perspectives on treaties: from covenantal oral agreements governing every aspect of relations with the Crown and all non-First Nations peoples, including consent to share territories, versus written text merely obtaining First Nations' consent to settling territories by European populations.[22]

The covenantal, permanent, and sharing approach outlined in holistic treaties with political, legal, and sacred status stands in stark contrast to an approach predicated on the Crown privileging written texts and grudging developments in Canadian common law. Certainly, it is not in keeping with the Federation of Saskatchewan Indian Nations' (FSIN; now Federation of Sovereign Indigenous Nations) important response to the Office of the Treaty Commissioner's (OTC) 2007 report on treaty implementation.

Questions of sovereignty and perpetuity were brought up by the FSIN directly,[23] which contested the capture of treaties by state sovereignty as much as it re-asserted the treaties' *international* stature and that First Nations' sovereignty *will continue forever*.[24] Specifically, the FSIN response to the treaty

18 See "Pre-1975 Treaties and Treaty First Nations in Canada Infographic," *Aboriginal Affairs and Northern Development Canada*, online: INAC <www.aadnc-aandc.gc.ca/eng/1380223988016/1380224163492>.

19 Ken S. Coates, *A Global History of Indigenous Peoples: Struggle and Survival* (New York: Palgrave Macmillan, 2004) at 173.

20 *Ibid*.

21 Craft 2013, *supra* note 13 at 22, citing Jean Friesen, "Magnificent Gifts: The Treaties of Canada with the Indians of the Northwest, 1869–76" (1986) 5:1 *Transactions of the Royal Society of Canada* 41 at 49 [Friesen]. See also Friesen at 50 ("The new settlers who flooded in over the next couple of decades . . . survived their pioneer years because the Indians permitted them access to the fish and game resources.").

22 David Arnot, *Treaty Implementation: Fulfilling the Covenant* (Saskatoon: Office of the Treaty Commissioner, 2007) at 4–5 (notes omitted) [Arnot]. *Cf.* Federation of Saskatchewan Indian Nations, *Response to the Recommendations in Treaty Implementation: Fulfilling the Covenant Report* (Saskatoon: FSIN 2007) [FSIN 2007].

23 This is one example among many, though the Federation and its articulation of treaty peoplehood is a very influential one. See also Harold Cardinal & Walter Hildebrandt, *Treaty Elders of Saskatchewan: Our Dream Is That Our Peoples Will One Day Be Clearly Recognized as Nations* (Calgary: University of Calgary Press, 2000).

24 FSIN 2007, *supra* note 22.

commissioner's recommendations and vision, that treaties "find their rightful place in the Canadian state", was that this vision was "inconsistent with First Nations' assertion of sovereignty" and one that they did not accept.[25] Instead, the FSIN Treaty Implementation Principles contemplate *a different kind of sovereignty*, visualized through a tree. This sovereign tree is characterized by a relationship with Mother Earth; sovereign occupation of North America with their own laws and jurisdiction; permanent sovereignty, including the power to enter into international treaties with other nations; the greater validity of the spirit and intent of treaties over their written text; and Canada's ongoing obligation to fulfil this spirit and intent.[26] While not premised on independent statehood, these principles reflect the attributes of land, laws, government, people, and independent international relations mentioned above. They also add other important factors like stewardship of the land and oral traditions. This vision ultimately connects Indigenous lands and laws to the maintenance of their sovereignty. The reduction of these treaties to internal Canadian matters subject to Canadian laws and courts thus strikes at the heart of Indigenous survival and the institutional bias pitted against that survival.[27] The process of domestication remains hugely contested and forms one of the biggest challenges to treaty interpretation and broader reconciliation today.

Systemic biases exist across the various treaty types but, following Borrows, I briefly mention a few examples here of institutional bias with respect to treaties of peace and friendship, the numbered treaties, and modern treaties. For instance, a Canadian court notoriously pronounced in 1929 that

> the Indians were never regarded as an independent power . . . [and the 1752 Treaty between the British and the Mi'kmaq] *is not a treaty at all and is not to be treated as such*; it is at best a mere agreement made by the Governor and council with a handful of Indians giving them in return for good behaviour food, presents, and the right to hunt and fish as usual.[28]

In relation to a later interpretation of treaties of peace and friendship in New Brunswick, Borrows argues that "the status quo is preserved and the Crown is not disturbed in its use or possession of land, even though it has not legally justified its assumed pre-eminent position".[29] However, these "values and assumptions

25 *Ibid.* at 4 (of 18).

26 *Ibid.* at ii, 1 (of 18).

27 Schulte-Tenckhoff 1998, *supra* note 13 at 257.

28 *Rex v. Syliboy* [1929] 1 D.L.R. 307 (Co. Ct.) at 313–314 (Patteson J., emphasis added) [*Syliboy*]. See also *Attorney-General of Ontario v Attorney-General of Canada: Re Indian Claims* [1897] A.C. 199 (P.C.).

29 Borrows 2001, *supra* note 13 (contrasting these examples with the 1996 recommendations of the landmark Royal Commission on Aboriginal Peoples (RCAP) and at 625 (in reference to *R v Peter Paul* (1998), (*Sub nom. R. v. Paul*) 158 D.LR. (4th) 231, [1998] 3 C.N.L.R. 221 (N.B.C.A.)).

of imperial treaty makers"[30] remain unquestioned, such that Indigenous "rights under treaties are ***domesticated*** and placed in a subordinate position relative to the Crown".[31] Similar domesticating constraints are evident in the interpretation of the sacred numbered treaties "that cover most of northern and western Ontario, the three prairie provinces, and the newly realigned Northwest Territories".[32] These treaties are open to state interpretations that subordinate Indigenous treaty rights (like using land for hunting or spiritual purposes) to wider Canadian objectives, including settlement and "visible non-Aboriginal development".[33]

Beyond adjudication, this subordination also occurs at the political level, where Indigenous peoples "view peace and friendship treaties as creating bilateral relationships" in contrast to "non-Aboriginal governments or courts [that assume] the power to determine ultimate allocations of lands and resources".[34] The so-called modern treaties are no less subordinated, subject as they are to Canadian constitutional law, courts, and doctrine. The Nisga'a Final Agreement is just one example, with (1) its introduction of fee simple lands that may be alienated in the future (in contrast to the communal, inalienable nature of Aboriginal title lands); (2) the conversion and replacement of traditional House governance with a new government; (3) the paramountcy of provincial and federal laws over Nisga'a laws; (4) the jurisdiction of Canadian courts over Nisga'a institutions and interpretive disputes arising from the Final Agreement; and (5) the collection of individual Nisga'a taxes towards general Canadian revenues.[35] The Nisga'a Final Agreement also stipulates that its citizenship provisions do not impact Canadian immigration law or Indian Act status.[36] The combination of historical treaties interpreted to "significantly erode the land base" with new treaties largely bound to "non-Aboriginal structures, values, and processes"[37] does not bode well for countering the process of domestication.

In addition to treaty relations, similar domestication took place with Indigenous standing (at international fora) and with Indigenous lands and governance systems.[38] As with their Confederacy and Great Law (Kaianerekowa), the Haudenosaunee provide one of the most well-known examples here, too.

30 *Ibid.* (citing Canada, *Report of the Royal Commission on Aboriginal Peoples, Vol. 2: Restructuring the Relationship* (Ottawa: Supply and Services, 1996) [RCAP]).
31 *Ibid.* (emphasis added).
32 *Ibid.*
33 *Ibid.* at 630–631 (citing *R. v. Horseman*, [1990] 1 S.C.R. 901; *R. v. Badger*, [1996] 1 S.C.R. 771).
34 *Ibid.* at 630.
35 *Ibid.* at 636 (referring to *Nisga'a Final Agreement* (4 August 1998) [*NFA*]).
36 *NFA* at 39–40 (Nisga'a Citizenship).
37 Borrows 2001, *supra* note 13 at 640.
38 See for example Amar Bhatia, "The South of the North: Building on Critical Approaches to International Law with Lessons from the Fourth World" (2012) 14 *Or Rev Intl L* 131 (references to Levi General (Deskaheh) and the Haudenosaunee (Six Nations) Confederacy's 1920s quest for status at the League of Nations, foiled by Canada and Great Britain) [Bhatia 2012b]. See also the trio of international arbitration decisions in the 1920s and '30s relating to domestication in and out of treaty relations in James Anaya, *Indigenous Peoples in International Law* (Oxford: Oxford University Press, 1996) at 23 [Anaya 1996].

Government

It is impossible to succinctly recount how Canada replaced Indigenous governance and took Indigenous lands in order to cement its own statehood and sovereignty. It is equally impossible to separate discussions of land and territory from questions of population and government; these 'qualifications' for establishing Canadian statehood and dismantling Indigenous nations are necessarily interwoven across the different sections of this chapter.[39] However, one story that encapsulates many of these elements took place right at the same time that Canada was seeking to assert its sovereign international status, "which before 1919 had in no sense existed".[40]

The Haudenosaunee Confederacy has had a 'Two Row Wampum' treaty with imperial and colonial governments for over 400 years. The first treaty was with Dutch settlers in 1613 and was followed by a Covenant Chain treaty with the British in 1677. The Two Row and Covenant Chain treaties served as key frameworks for all of the treaties that were to follow, including the 1764 Wampum at Niagara that sanctioned the Royal Proclamation of 1763.[41] The Two Row Wampum symbolizes the agreement that neither the Haudenosaunee nor the British "will make compulsory laws or interfere in the internal affairs of the other".[42] The Six Nations' long alliance with the imperial British included some of their member Nations fighting on their side during the war with the colonies. It also included the 1784 Haldimand Treaty negotiating land for the Six Nations on the banks of the Grand River (purchased from the Mississaugas).[43] Unfortunately, through questionable sales and cessions to the Crown, some of these lands were used for British settlers, with the subsequent trust funds lost in a failed investment without Six Nations consent.[44]

In the sunset of the military aspects of their alliance, the Haudenosaunee Confederacy found itself subject to the colonial pretensions of Canadian jurisdiction

39 See Crawford 2012, *supra* note 2 at 128–129 (population: to be used 'in association' with territory; defined territory: a 'reasonably stable political community . . . in control of a certain area'; and, government: 'a stable political community supporting a legal order to the exclusion of others in a given area').

40 Richard Veatch, *Canada and the League of Nations* (Toronto: University of Toronto Press, 1975) at 10 [Veatch]. This time also overlapped with the moment that international law, thanks to the League of Nations, became more than "simply a European law" (see Mohammed Bedjaoui, *Towards a New International Economic Order* (New York: Holmes & Meier, 1979) at 50 [Bedjaoui]). This section of the chapter draws on Bhatia 2012a, *supra* note 17.

41 See generally, John Borrows, "Wampum at Niagara: The Royal Proclamation, Canadian Legal History, and Self-Government" in Michael Asch, ed., *Aboriginal and Treaty Rights in Canada: Essays on Law, Equity, and Respect for Difference* (Vancouver: UBC Press, 1997) [Borrows 1997].

42 See Tehanetorens, *Wampum Belts* (Ohsweken, ON: Iroqrafts, 1983) at 11. See also Ruth Koleszar-Green, "Understanding Your Education: Onkwehonwe and Guests Responsibilities to Peace, Friendship and Mutual Respect" (PhD thesis, OISE/University of Toronto, 2016).

43 Bhatia 2012b, *supra* note 38 at 163 (and references therein).

44 *Ibid.*

under the British North America Act of 1867.[45] Section 91(24) placed "Indians and lands reserved for Indians" under federal jurisdiction and provided the mandate for the successive Indian Acts aimed at their "civilization and assimilation".[46] Among many other things, the Indian Act provided for (1) the creation of Indian Act status and highly gendered exceptions to entitlement; (2) Crown management of Indian lands and resources; (3) voluntary and then compulsory Indian enfranchisement and, thus, forced removal of Indian Act status and reserve land; (4) enforcement of penal liquor laws and imprisonment; and (5) the imposition of an elected band council government (subject to a Canadian "Indian Agent") to replace traditional governance established under Indigenous laws.[47]

Before the elected council was imposed, Levi General was installed as a new hereditary chief (Deskaheh) of the Cayuga Nation of the Six Nations in 1917 by Louise Miller (matron of the Young Bear Clan).[48] In relation to earlier grievances including the mishandling of trust funds from lands that were taken, Deskaheh was chosen as the Speaker and deputy for the hereditary Council when it sought aid from the imperial government. Although Deskaheh petitioned King George V in August 1921, then Colonial Secretary Winston Churchill rebuffed this attempt in a reply to the Governor General of Canada: "the matters submitted within the petition lie within the exclusive competency of the Canadian Government".[49] While the Confederacy wanted to press the question of Six Nations' status politically in Ottawa, "the door was closed in [their] faces".[50] The SCC was also blocked to the Six Nations due to the need to seek leave from the Governor General's office, which in turn deferred to a Department of Indian Affairs decision based on a negative opinion from the Department of Justice.[51] While subsequent negotiations sought out an impartial tribunal to examine the question of Six Nations' sovereignty, Canada only offered up judges from (first) the Ontario Supreme Court and (later) any British subject.[52] In combination with a raid by the Royal Canadian Mounted Police (RCMP), spurious liquor violation arrests, and the establishment of an RCMP garrison on site, Deskaheh and the Six Nations sought out international (non-imperial) recourse in Geneva at the League of Nations.[53]

45 *Constitution Act, 1867*, 30 & 31 Vict, c 3, s. 91(24).

46 *Ibid.* For the Act devolving imperial authority to the colonial government, see *An Act Respecting the Management of Indian Lands and Property*, S.C. 1860, c. 151.

47 See Bhatia 2012b, *supra* note 38 at 163–165 (and related references).

48 Donald B. Smith, "Deskaheh (Levi General)" (2005) 15 *The Dictionary of Canadian Biography* 1921–1930, online: DCB <www.biographi.ca/en/bio/deskaheh_15E.html>.

49 Douglas Sanders, "Aboriginal Rights: The Search for Recognition in International Law" in Menno Boldt, J. Anthony Long & Leroy Little Bear, eds., *The Quest for Justice: Aboriginal Peoples and Aboriginal Rights* (Toronto: University of Toronto Press, 1985) at 292–304 [Sanders 1985].

50 Deskaheh, "Last Speech of Deskaheh – Address on WHAM Radio in Rochester, N.Y. (Mar. 10, 1925)" in *Basic Call to Consciousness* (Mohawk Nation via Rooseveltown, NY: Akwesasne Notes, 1978) at 25–33.

51 Bhatia 2012b, *supra* note 38 at 164.

52 *Ibid.* (in part to exclude Deskaheh's American lawyer, George Decker).

53 Bhatia 2012b, *supra* note 38 at 165–166.

The appeal from Six Nations sought to place a number of items on the League Council's agenda, including recognition of their independent right of home rule according to their treaties, a just accounting of misappropriated trust funds, and freedom of transit for the Six Nations across Canadian territory to and from international waters.[54] On the basis of their centuries-old Two Row Wampum relationship with Dutch settlers, Deskaheh was successful in having the Netherlands forward the petition to the secretary general of the League. Unfortunately, and despite Deskaheh's wider efforts with the public in Geneva, the Six Nations' petition for sovereign status was never formally placed on the League Council's agenda. The British Foreign Office criticized the Netherlands for its "uncalled for interference in [the] internal affairs of Canada".[55] The acting secretary general agreed to "'enterrer' [bury] the matter", in large part due to Canada's vehement denial of League jurisdiction.[56] Among other charges, Canada noted that the Six Nations were not self-governing peoples and that discussing treaties with them would be like talking of "a treaty alliance with the Jews in Duke Street or with the French emigrants who have settled in England".[57]

The official response also noted that the recognition of the independent or sovereign status of Indians in treaties of cession, not used by the Dominion of Canada in the international law sense, would mean "the entire Dominion would be dotted with independent or quasi-independent Indian States 'allied with but not subject to the British Crown'. . . . such a condition would be untenable and inconceivable".[58] By way of an Order-in-Council on September 17, 1924, the Canadian government also mandated that an elected band council be imposed at Six Nations pursuant to the Indian Act. The Six Nations' hereditary council was deposed, and "free elections" were held under armed guard and the dark cloud of a large boycott, where fewer than 30 ballots were cast on the most densely populated reserve in Canada.[59] In part motivated by Canadian disdain for the hereditary council and the matriarchal role in selecting chiefs, the election had the added effect of "depriving Deskaheh of his right to speak for the confederacy, at least according to Canadian law".[60] Criminalized in Canada, Deskaheh was

54 See Deskaheh, *The Redman's Appeal for Justice* (6 August 1923) online: <http://law.lib.buffalo.edu/collections/berman/pdfs/Redmanappeal.pdf> at 1, 13, 20 (this last point related to Jay Treaty rights secured under that treaty in 1796).

55 Veatch, *supra* note 40 at 94.

56 *Ibid.*

57 See Statement of Government of Canada respecting the "Appeal of the 'Six Nations' to the League" (June 1924) 5 *League of Nations Official Journal* 829 [27 December 1923]. This statement was written by Duncan Campbell Scott (see E. Brian Titley, *A Narrow Vision: Duncan Campbell Scott and the Administration of Indian Affairs in Canada* (Vancouver: UBC Press, 1986) at 132).

58 *Ibid.*

59 Carl Carmer, *Dark Trees to the Wind: A Cycle of York State Years* (New York: W. Sloane Associates, 1949) at 110–111 [Carmer]; Grace Li Xiu Woo, "Canada's Forgotten Founders: The Modern Significance of the Haudenosaunee (Iroquois) Application for Membership in the League of Nations" (2003) *L Soc Just & Global Dev J*, online: LSJGDJ <http://elj.warwick.ac.uk /global/03-1/woo.html>; Titley, *supra* note 57 at 132.

60 Sanders 1985, *supra* note 49 at 300.

forced to take refuge in the United States with Tuscarora chief Clinton Rickard until his death in 1925.[61]

The story of the Six Nations' quest for status ranges from colonial Ottawa to imperial London to nascent inter-state international law in Geneva. The Haudenosaunee Confederacy were hampered at every turn by the notion that their "grievances were a domestic concern of Canada and hence outside the League's [or London's] competency".[62] At the same time, they were then forced to split community energies and allegiances between an elected, funded council and the unfunded hereditary one. All of this took place on an ever-shrinking land base subject to the Indian Act and its draconian provisions for extinguishing Indian Act status.

Having momentarily domesticated the Six Nations' claims, Canada then left them without recourse to Canadian courts or counsel. The Canadian government amended the Indian Act in 1927 to make it "an offence to solicit or receive funds from any Indian for the purpose of prosecuting an Indian claim".[63] This amendment "effectively chilled any legal initiatives to advance the Indian land claim movement" until the amendment was finally repealed in 1951.[64] But by then, it would already be much too late. From 1896–1914, Canada "was admitting more immigrants than in any preceding or subsequent eighteen year period".[65] By 1912, "Canada's total population [had] increased by almost thirty-five per cent [and] a million immigrants flooded the three prairie provinces and British Columbia".[66] By 1921, immigration "had successfully

61 Carmer, *supra* note 59 at 114–115. Note that the Six Nations did not stop their attempts to draw international attention to question of their sovereignty and self-determination. See Darlene M. Johnston, "The Quest of the Six Nations Confederacy for Self-Determination" (1986) 44 *UTFLR* 8 at 23; Sanders, *supra* note 49 at 487 and following. See also Sid Hill, "My Six Nation Haudenosaunee Passport Is Not a 'Fantasy Document'" (30 October 2015) *The Guardian*, online: <www.theguardian.com/commentisfree/2015/oct/30/my-six-nation-haudenosaunee-passport-not-fantasy-document-indigenous-nations>.

62 Anaya 1996, *supra* note 38 at 57. See also Titley, *supra* note 57 at 134 (". . . a permanent police presence at Grand River, the replacement of the hereditary council by a compliant elective one, and the use of informers all ensured a degree of official control at the reserve level. On the international front, the services of the British diplomatic corps were effectively employed to intimidate governments sympathetic to the Indians").

63 See *The Revised Indian Act*, R.S.C. 1927, c. 98, s. 149A. Although protection of Indians from unscrupulous lawyers was the purported reason, the Royal Commission noted: "The effect of this provision was not only to harass and intimidate national Indian leaders, but also to impede Indians all across Canada from acquiring legal assistance in prosecuting claims until this clause was repealed in 1951." Canada: Royal Commission on Aboriginal Peoples, *Report of the Royal Commission on Aboriginal Peoples*, Vol. 1: *Looking Forward, Looking Back* (Chapter 9 – the Indian Act), online: LAC <www.collectionscanada.gc.ca/webarchives/20071207032318/http://www.ainc-inac.gc.ca/ch/rcap/sg/sg25_e.html#89>.

64 See Michael Jackson, "A Model of Scholarship" (2005) 38 *UBC L Rev* 315 at 317.

65 Ninette Kelley & Michael Trebilcock, *The Making of the Mosaic: A History of Canadian Immigration Policy*, 2nd ed. (Toronto: University of Toronto Press, 2010) at 163 [Kelley & Trebilcock].

66 See John Leslie & Ron Maguire, eds., *The Historical Development of the Indian Act*, 2nd ed. (Ottawa: Treaties and Historical Research Centre, INAC, 1978) at 105–106 (the impact of immigration and WWI) [Leslie & Maguire].

populated the country".[67] Indigenous attempts to press land claims and treaty rights would have to contend with settlers' "insatiable"[68] demands for land and all of the "visible non-Aboriginal development"[69] that came with them. If the Western conception of government meant "a stable political community supporting a legal order to the exclusion of others in a given area",[70] then this is exactly what Canada sought to accomplish for itself through Confederation and beyond. Although inaccurate then and now, the settler colonial contention that Indigenous nations lacked these attributes was part of Canada's work to make it so and keep it that way.

A defined territory and a permanent population for Canada

Canada's approach to the treaties first recognized and then later renounced Indigenous laws about making and maintaining relations. This treaty two-step allowed the nascent state to pursue its tripartite Indian policy: the control of lands, government, and children.[71] In turn, this policy served the larger goals of Confederation and nation-building, namely, territorial expansion, agricultural settlement, and the construction of a national railway.[72] Having discussed the domestication of treaties, the foreclosure of international advocacy, and the replacement of Indigenous government, this section turns to two other attributes of statehood: the establishment and maintenance of a permanent population and a defined territory for Canada. The domesticated treaties facilitated the establishment of the permanent population and defined territory necessary to ensure Canadian statehood. At the same time, Canada also fostered the precarity of Indigenous populations amidst shrinking territories through its asserted sovereignty over both.

Lands

How did the treaties dispossess?[73] Comprehensive studies have been conducted from the perspectives of Canadian history and Indigenous legal history, including attempts to compare these competing sets of views.[74] These treaties emerge

67 David Scott FitzGerald and David Cook-Martin, *Culling the Masses: The Democratic Origins of Racist Immigration Policy in the Americas* (Cambridge, MA: Harvard University Press, 2014) at 159 [FitzGerald & Cook-Martin].

68 Leslie & Maguire, *supra* note 66 at 105.

69 Borrows 2001, *supra* note 13 at 631.

70 Crawford 2012, *supra* note 2 at 129.

71 See, e.g., Jean Barman, *The West Beyond the West: A History of British Columbia*, 3rd ed. (Toronto: University of Toronto Press, 2007) at 169 and following [Barman 2007]; Darlene Johnston, *The Taking of Indian Lands in Canada: Consent or Coercion?* (Saskatoon: University of Saskatchewan Native Law Centre, 1989) at 90–91 [Johnston 1989].

72 See, e.g., *Daniels v. Canada (Indian Affairs and Northern Development)*, 2016 SCC 12 at paras 25–26.

73 See also Cole Harris, "How Did Colonialism Dispossess? Comments from an Edge of Empire" (2004) 94:1 *Ann Association Am Geographers* at 165–182.

74 See Miller, *supra* note 14. See also Richard T. Price, ed., *The Spirit of Alberta Indian Treaties*, 3rd ed. (Edmonton: University of Alberta Press, 1999); John S. Long, *Treaty No. 9:*

against the backdrop of the Royal Proclamation of 1763 (October 7, 1763),[75] which has sometimes been called the 'Indian Magna Carta' or 'Indian Bill of Rights'. In the aftermath of the Treaty of Paris and Pontiac's uprising, it set out a lands policy meant to restrain settlers, with the 'ultimate safeguard' for unceded lands lying in a purchase procedure requiring "Crown monopoly over the acquisition of Indian lands . . . and the consent of the Indians concerned".[76] However, the Royal Proclamation only gained legitimacy and authority with Indigenous nations following the 1764 Treaty or Wampum at Niagara. This massive gathering of chiefs, Nations, and the imperial Crown signified Indigenous assent to proceed with treaty-making under Indigenous legal systems and principles, including those of the Two-Row Wampum.[77] The process of domestication excised this wampum constitutionalism[78] of Niagara and left only the textual guarantees from the Royal Proclamation. These guarantees paled in the face of imperial devolution and colonial settlement. As noted above, responsibility for Indigenous peoples was transferred from imperial to local governments following the decline of Indigenous military and demographic power. In turn, local governments from the Maritimes to Quebec to Upper Canada were either hard-pressed or solicitous with squatters to ignore or allow settlements contrary to the Proclamation. These settlements were then legitimized afterwards through inaction and local (as opposed to imperial) government legislation.[79] When compliant with the Proclamation, if not the Treaty at Niagara, the initial treaties alienated traditional lands and pushed Indigenous peoples to "remote regions".[80] Later treaties were then used to acquire or reduce the remaining reserve lands to which Indigenous peoples had been pushed. Despite the Proclamation showing that "territorial rights akin to those asserted by sovereign Princes are recognized as belonging to the Indians", the commissioners appointed to look in to Indian affairs in 1856 were told to do so "without impeding the settlement of the

Making the Agreement to Share the Land in Far Northern Ontario in 1905 (Montreal: McGill-Queen's University Press, 2010); Arthur Ray, Jim Miller & Frank Tough, eds., *Bounty and Benevolence: A History of Saskatchewan Treaties* (Montreal: McGill-Queen's University Press, 2000).

75 *Royal Proclamation of 1763*, reprinted in R.S.C. 1985, App. II, No. 1, 1 [*Royal Proclamation, 1763*].

76 See Johnston 1989, *supra* note 71 at 6–7 (emphasis added). On the 'Indian Bill of Rights' label, see *St. Catharines Milling and Lumber Company v The Queen* (1887), 13 S.C.R. 577 at 652, 2 C.N.L.C. 441 at 516, per Gwynne J.

77 See, e.g., Borrows 1997, *supra* note 41.

78 See Alan Corbiere, Wampum Belts presentation to Osgoode Hall Law School; see also Heidi Libesman, "In Search of a Postcolonial Theory of Normative Integration: Reflections on A. C. Cairns' Theory of 'Citizens Plus'" (2005) 38:4 *Can J Poli Sci* at 955–976.

79 Johnston 1989, *supra* note 71 at 15–16 ("But the Royal Proclamation of 1763 has long since been forgotten and the imperial authorities had long since abdicated their responsibility for the Indians to the local government."). See also Alain Beaulieu, "The Acquisition of Aboriginal Land in Canada: The Genealogy of an Ambivalent System (1600–1867)" in Saliha Belmessous, ed., *Empire by Treaty: Negotiating European Expansion, 1600–1900* (Oxford: Oxford University Press, 2015).

80 Johnston 1989, *supra* note 71 at 48–51.

country".[81] As Johnston notes, the prioritization of white settlement "inevitably meant the diminution of the territorial rights of Indians".[82]

Given this tight relationship between the taking of Indian lands and white settlement of those lands, and since they coincided with the peak of immigration to Canada, I turn now to the 11 post-Confederation numbered treaties negotiated from 1871 to 1923. The vast prairie lands relevant to the numbered treaties are visible in light green in a government map.[83] The preamble to Treaty One from 1871 (the Stone Fort Treaty) states that "*it is the desire of Her Majesty to open up to settlement and immigration a tract of country bounded and described as hereinafter mentioned*".[84] The emphasized language serves as the boilerplate of settler colonialism in the text of all of the other numbered treaties. While the 1871 Treaty Two (Manitoba Post) contains the exact same language, Treaty Three (North-West Angle) expands the language to the following: "that it is the desire of Her Majesty *to open up for settlement, immigration, and such other purposes as to Her Majesty may seem meet*, a tract of country bounded and described as hereinafter mentioned".[85] In 1874, Treaty Four (the Qu'appelle Treaty) adds "trade" as one of the stated purposes in this clause.[86] Treaty Five in 1875 (the Lake Winnipeg Treaty) and Treaty Six in 1876 (Forts Carlton and Pitt) both use the same language as Treaty Three ("settlement, immigration, and such other purposes").[87] Treaty Seven in 1877 (Blackfoot Treaty) has its own variant on this formula: "that it is the desire of Her Majesty to open up for settlement, and such other purposes as to Her Majesty may seem meet".[88] Concluded in 1899, Treaty Eight uses even broader language: "it is Her desire *to open for settlement, immigration, trade, travel, mining, lumbering, and such other purposes* as to Her Majesty may seem meet a tract of country bounded and described".[89] Treaties Nine (1905 James Bay Treaty), Ten (1906), and Eleven (1921) all use the same preamble language as in Treaty Eight.[90]

81 *Ibid.* at 52–53 (quoting "Report of the Special Commissioners appointed to Investigate Indian Affairs in Canada," Journals of the Legislative Assembly of Canada, 1858, App. No. 21, Part III).

82 *Ibid.* Johnston also speculates here that the commissioners' despair at protecting reserve lands from encroachment may have been "calculated to make regulated settlement seem like the only alternative to unregulated dispossession" (53).

83 See INAC, Maps of Treaty-Making in Canada, Pre-1975 Treaties of Canada, online: INAC <www.aadnc-aandc.gc.ca/DAM/DAM-INTER-HQ/STAGING/texte-text/htoc_1100100032308_eng.pdf>.

84 Alexander Morris, *The Treaties of Canada with the Indians of Manitoba and the North-West Territories, Including the Negotiations on Which They Were Based, and Other Information Relating Thereto* (Toronto: Coles, 1971) [1880] at 313 [Morris] (emphasis added).

85 *Ibid.* at 321 (emphasis added).

86 *Ibid.* at 330 (emphasis added).

87 *Ibid.* at 343, 351.

88 *Ibid.* at 368.

89 Robert A. Reiter, *The Law of Canadian Indian Treaties* (Edmonton: Juris Analytica, 1995) at 137–138 (emphasis added).

90 *Ibid.* at 170.

These shifting preambles stemmed from the need to fulfil the promise of a transcontinental railroad (exchanged for British Columbia's entry to Confederation) and to pursue settlement goals. In relation to Treaty One, Morris noted that Indigenous peoples in Manitoba were "full of uneasiness" at the settler influx and had obstructed settlers and surveyors, leading Indian Commissioner Simpson to conclude "that it was desirable to secure the extinction of the Indian title".[91] Lieutenant-Governor Archibald's report from July 29, 1871, also underscored this pressure:

> We told them that *whether they wished it or not, immigration would come in and fill up the country*; that every year from this one twice as many in number as their whole people there assembled would pour into the Province . . . and that now was the time for them to come to an arrangement that would secure homes and annuities for themselves and their children.[92]

Similarly, Commissioner Simpson's report from May 3, 1871, mentions this push-pull pressure and the anxiety of Indigenous nations for treaty negotiations combined with settlers' uneasiness at being warned by Indigenous people that settlers were mere squatters on the land.[93]

This 'uneasy feeling' amongst the squatting settlers prompted an editorial in the *Manitoban* at the time:

> The Indians are confident that now a permanent treaty is to be made, and are ready to make it. . . . Why keep the Settlement in suspense; why place the lives of the people in jeopardy by such tardiness; and why leave the great impediment to immigration removed?[94]

Settler jeopardy and the desire for closure (to "have done with it") have resonated through the centuries, from the pre-Confederation treaties to the numbered treaties up to our current context. As noted by Indian Affairs, settlement was accompanied by "massive construction" of railways, roads, cities, and towns; "insatiable demand for agriculture land"; and the encroachment by 1906 on "formerly isolated reserves" such that the Department had modified its policies protecting undeveloped reserves by 1908.[95]

91 Morris, *supra* note 84 at 25–26 (see also at 33, citing Archibald's report on the contested authority of the Indigenous signatories to the earlier Selkirk Treaty).

92 *Ibid.* at 34 (emphasis added).

93 *Ibid.* at 37 (emphasis added). On the wealth of the lands and waters, their fertility, and how the 'settlers from the Provinces in Canada and elsewhere are pushing their way beyond the limits of the Province of Manitoba', see Morris, *supra* note 84 at 42–43 (citing Commissioner Simpson's report of 3 May 1871).

94 Craft 2013, *supra* note 13 at 44 (quoting the Manitoban 1871 at 1).

95 Leslie & Maguire, *supra* note 66 at 105–106 (emphasis added). See also Johnston 1989, *supra* note 71 at 93 (on deterioration of consent to alienation of reserve lands and expansion of 'public interest' expropriation).

This encroachment shows the direct connections between treaty negotiation, the entry of settlers, the domestication of the treaties, and the corresponding diminishment of associated treaty rights. As noted above:

> Between 1896 and 1914, more than 3 million people emigrated to Canada (many from central and southern Europe), and dramatic growth was experienced in agricultural, manufacturing, and service industries. Cities mushroomed across the country, and the population of the prairies increased by close to 1 million in the first decade of the century.[96]

This combination of lands and people that Canada accomplished through the treaties was also made possible by its immigration and Indian acts.

People

While the British North America (BNA) Act brought "Indians and lands reserved for Indians" under federal jurisdiction with Confederation in 1867, it also gave the federal government exclusive jurisdiction over "Naturalization and Aliens". The BNA Act gave the federal government concurrent jurisdiction with provincial governments over immigration and agriculture, with federal authority trumping the provinces in cases of conflict.[97] Early immigration legislation was characterized by "permissiveness" before turning to exclusion in later statutes.[98] The first post-Confederation Immigration Act (of 1869) was less concerned with keeping people out than with providing procedural and transportation safeguards for those emigrating to Canada.[99] "Aliens" also made their appearance in statute, such that they were allowed to naturalize "as local British subjects after three years of residence in Canada".[100] Relatively open immigration following Confederation meant "few entry prohibitions" and incentives like travel assistance, affordable settler homesteads, no removal after landing, and naturalization as a British subject after three years of residency.[101] After initial failures to attract settlers in the desired numbers,[102]

96 See, e.g., Kelley & Trebilcock 2010, *supra* note 65 at 12.

97 The Constitution Act, 1867, 30 & 31 Vict, C 3, ss. 91(25), 95.

98 For example, see Law Union of Ontario, *The Immigrant's Handbook: A Critical Guide* (Montreal: Black Rose Books, 1981) at 17–27 [LUO]; Jamie Chai Yun Liew & Donald Galloway, *Immigration Law*, 2nd ed. (Toronto: Irwin Law, 2015) at 13–14 [Liew & Galloway]; Kelley & Trebilcock 2010, *supra* note 65 at 62–66. See also Valerie Knowles, *Strangers at Our Gates: Canadian Immigration and Immigration Policy, 1540–2015*, rev. ed. (Toronto: Dundurn Press, 2007) [Knowles].

99 See *An Act Respecting Immigration and Immigrants*, SC 1868, c. 10. The 1869 Immigration Act sets out these protections en route and also after arrival, along with recognition of provincial powers to 'determine their policy concerning the settlement and colonization of uncultivated lands, as bearing on immigration' (preamble).

100 See Liew & Galloway, *supra* note 98 at 14 (citing *Aliens and Naturalization Act*, SC 1868, c 66).

101 Kelley & Trebilcock, *supra* note 65 at 107.

102 Emigration (largely to the United States) exceeded immigration in the first 30 years after Confederation, notwithstanding the looser legislative approach (see generally Knowles,

offers of free land under the 1872 Dominion Lands (Homesteading) Act[103] led immigration levels to historic highs, with the aforementioned millions arriving between 1896–1914.[104] This increase also benefited from the completion of the transcontinental railroad with the labour of Chinese railroad workers (prior to the head tax and their later exclusion).[105] In addition to settling colonists, the profits of steamship and railways companies were integral, too. These companies benefited from the transportation of Chinese railroad workers across the Pacific, the passage of European settlers across the Atlantic and then over their railways, and then from selling "Crown" land granted along those railroads to the same settlers.[106]

From the general openness of the 1869 immigration legislation, there was a shift in 1872 to include "the identification of prohibited classes – frequently defined in vague, value-laden, and vituperative terms – [becoming] a central element and defining characteristic of Canadian immigration law".[107] The general introduction of such prohibited classes was expanded in subsequent immigration acts, from the innovation of deportation in 1906 to the 1910 prohibition of the landing "of immigrants belonging to any race unsuited to the climate or requirements of Canada".[108] The selectivity and exclusivity of these changes were followed by the flexible framing of various Orders-in-Council in 1911 to the 1919 Act[109] and the 1923 Order-in-Council.[110] The latter Order-in-Council prohibited

> the entry of all immigrants except for six narrowly defined classes . . . "agriculturalists" with sufficient means to begin farming; farm labourers

---

supra note 98; Kelley & Trebilcock, *supra* note 65; FitzGerald & Cook-Martín, *supra* note 67). See also Shin Imai, *Canadian Immigration Law and Policy: 1867–1935* (LLM thesis, York University, 1983) at 30 [Imai 1983] – noting that, at that time, it was Canada's privilege for immigrants to come here.

103 See, e.g., Daniel Francis, *Selling Canada: Three Propaganda Campaigns That Shaped the Nation* (Vancouver: Stanton Atkins & Dosil, 2011) [Francis]; LUO, *supra* note 98 at 20.

104 See Knowles, *supra* note 98; Kelley & Trebilcock, *supra* note 65; FitzGerald & Cook-Martin, *supra* note 67.

105 See, e.g., Francis, *supra* note 103 at 7–66; Patrick Dunae, "Promoting the Dominion: Records and the Canadian Immigration Campaign, 1872–1915" (Winter 1984–1985) *Archivaria* 19. More generally, see Norman Macdonald, *Canada: Immigration and Colonization, 1841–1903* (Toronto: Macmillan of Canada, 1966).

106 *Ibid.* See also LUO, *supra* note 98 at 23–24. Sifton concluded secret incentive agreements with shipping companies to increase settler traffic to Canada as well.

107 See Liew & Galloway, *supra* note 98 at 14 (citing *An Act to Amend the Immigration Act of 1869*, SC 1872, c. 28).

108 *Immigration Act, 1910*, S.C. 1910, c. 27, s. 38 (see LUO, *supra* note 98 at 27, noting provision not removed until 1978, but ostensible deracialization with removal of race in 1962 and 1967 points system (except for family sponsorship: Liew & Galloway, *supra* note 98 at 24)). *Cf.* FitzGerald & Cook-Martin, *supra* note 67 at 141–185 (challenging cause but not necessarily effect of deracialization, along lines of Cold War Civil Rights thesis).

109 Note that the 1919 Act allowed family sponsorship and encouraged family reunification, explicitly allowing admission of those who did not meet literacy requirements if they were related to people already in Canada: *An Act to amend the Immigration Act*, SC 1919, c. 25, s. 3(t) (see Liew & Galloway, *supra* note 98 at 21).

110 PC 1923–183 (1923) C Gaz II 4106.

> with arranged employment; female domestic servants; wives and children under eighteen of those resident in Canada; citizens of the United States "whose labour is required"; and British subjects with sufficient means for self-maintenance.[111]

Confirming the key features noted above, Liew and Galloway observe that immigration law in Canada changed "from a generally permissive regime, with admittedly broad and undefined exceptions, to an exclusionary regime with narrow and well-defined exceptions".[112] These measures and reflections are echoed generally in global, regional, and comparative approaches to the topic as well.[113] The confluence of framework legislation with a gradual shift from seemingly 'wide-open' immigration to selective immigration, restricted naturalization, and increased removal and deportation[114] operated concurrently with targeted racist immigration laws and policies. But the racist selectivity and exclusionary immigration law to follow only took place *after* completion of massive European migration accompanying the numbered treaties. As noted above, immigration "had successfully populated the country".[115] This successful settlement of a permanent population (a stable political community) on a defined territory (the given area of government and a legal order to the exclusion of others) provides the qualifications for Canadian statehood and the circular rationale for Canadian sovereignty to perpetuate that statehood. In order to do so, the Canadian state must continue to undercut Indigenous self-determination and sovereignties, including the *keeping* of Indigenous lands that were taken and the *taking* of Indigenous peoples, including Indigenous children.

A precarious Indigenous population

In summary, Canada was able to realize the necessary attributes of statehood and the incidents of sovereignty through negotiation with, and then the coercion and domestication of, Indigenous peoples and their legal systems of making relations. By negotiating the treaties, Canada was given access to vast lands and the ability to

111 *Ibid.* Liew & Galloway, *supra* note 98 at 21 (See also Liew & Galloway at 22, citing Dirks that "officials were not interested in why people came but what they could offer in terms of labour market needs, capital supply and know-how to create jobs, or simply settle the land").

112 See Liew & Galloway, *supra* note 98 at 21–22.

113 See, e.g., Adam M. McKeown, *Melancholy Order: Asian Migration and the Globalization of Borders* (New York: Columbia University Press, 2008); Donna R. Gabaccia, "Migration History in the Americas" in Steven J. Gold and Stephanie J. Nawyn, eds., *Routledge International Handbook of Migration Studies* (New York: Routledge, 2013) at 65–70.

114 Introduced in 1906 Act (see LUO, *supra* note 98 at 20). See also *Attorney General for the Dominion of Canada v Everett E. Cain and James Raymond Gilhula (Ontario)* [1906] UKPC 55 (27 July 1906) (confirming the Dominion Parliament's authority to deport aliens) [*Cain & Gilhula*]. See generally Shin Imai, "Deportation in the Depression" (1981) 7:1 *Queen's LJ* 66 [Imai 1981].

115 FitzGerald & Cook-Martin, *supra* note 67 at 159.

settle massive numbers of people upon those lands. The duo of domesticated treaties and Canada's constitution paved the way for Canadian sovereignty to consolidate and maintain state control over Indian lands, governments, and people through the Indian Act. As seen with the example of the Six Nations of the Grand River above, dispute resolution was successfully restricted to Canadian courts and laws. The Indian Act was then amended to cut off access to counsel and the courts. The Act also dictated all aspects of reserve life and undercut Indigenous self-government through the band council and Indian Agent system.[116] In the same period that lands were being taken through treaties and immigration reached levels of hyper- or explosive colonization,[117] the government fostered the development of church-run residential schools to remove and assimilate Indigenous children. Indian Act regulations were adopted in the 1880s, allowing Indian agents to order Indian children to attend residential schools if the agent thought they were "not being properly cared for or educated".[118] The Act was later amended in 1920 to let the government "compel *any* First Nations child to attend residential school".[119] Three graphs tellingly illustrate the coincidence of the negotiation of numbered treaties (from Treaty One in 1871 to Treaty Eleven in 1921), the influx of settlers (with millions arriving between 1896 and 1914), and the rise of residential schools (with thousands of Indigenous children being forced to attend from 1869 onwards).[120]

The nexus of these processes set Canada on its way to achieving and maintaining the necessary attributes of statehood (permanent population, defined territory, government and laws, and the capacity to enter international relations) and the accompanying sovereignty that reproduces these attributes on a daily basis.

For the same reasons, these interrelated processes set Indigenous peoples on a path of domestication that they have resisted ever since. The dispossession of their lands, repression of traditional governments and laws, and the removal of their capacities to enter into relations have all been detailed above. The other major component of Canada's genocide targeted the permanent populations of Indigenous peoples.[121] As detailed in the Final Report of the Truth and Reconciliation

116 See, e.g., Truth and Reconciliation Canada, *Honouring the Truth, Reconciling for the Future: Summary of the Final Report of the Truth and Reconciliation Commission of Canada* (Winnipeg: Truth and Reconciliation Commission of Canada, 2015), online: TRC <www.trc.ca/websites/trcinstitution/File/2015/Honouring_the_Truth_Reconciling_for_the_Future_July_23_2015.pdf> [TRC Executive Summary].

117 The exponential rise in immigration has been called 'explosive' or 'hyper'-colonization by some (e.g. James Belich, *Replenishing the Earth: The Settler Revolution and the Rise of the Anglo-World, 1783–1939* (Oxford: Oxford University Press, 2009); Barman 2007, *supra* note 71).

118 TRC Executive Summary, *supra* note 116 at 60.

119 *Ibid.* at 62 (emphasis added).

120 See "Numbered Treaties" in *Canadian Encyclopedia*, online: <www.thecanadianencyclopedia.ca/en/article/numbered-treaties/>; TRC Executive Summary, *supra* note 116 at 64; StatsCan, "150 Years of Immigration in Canada," online: <www.statcan.gc.ca/pub/11-630-x/11-630-x2016006-eng.htm>.

121 TRC Executive Summary, *supra* note 116 at 1; see also Reclaiming Power and Place: Executive Summary of the Final Report (National Inquiry into Missing and Murdered Indigenous Women and Girls) (2019) at 4.

Commission (TRC) into Indian Residential Schools, hundreds of thousands of children were forced to attend residential, day, and industrial schools from before Confederation up to the 20th century.[122] However, the Indian Act also comprised various other assaults on the future and identity of Indigenous peoples. Contrary to Indigenous laws and respectful treaty relations, the Indian Act created individual Indian status while emphasizing rules of patrilineal descent, pseudo-blood quantum, and enfranchisement leading to the loss of status and reserve lands.[123] From the Royal Proclamation of 1763[124] ("the several Nations or Tribes of Indians, with whom We are connected, and who live under Our Protection") to all of the statutes from the 1850s onwards, the creation, revocation, and revision of persons deemed to be or not to be "Indians" has been constant and punishing. These revisions have been determined by various markers, including government-defined blood, status contingent upon "marrying-in" and "marrying-out" of communities, voluntary and involuntary enfranchisement, residence on certain lands, and membership in particular bands.[125] The impact of these changes over time has been especially pernicious for Indigenous women. Sharon McIvor's decades-long quest to reform the Indian Act to allow perpetual transmission of status, singly, by both fathers *and* mothers is a testament to this harm.[126]

As noted by ethnographer Scott Lauria Morgensen,

> in its definition of over six hundred "First nations" whose members received "Indian status" by state decree, the Act also separated myriad communities of common nationality, radically reduced land bases (if any remained), and enabled the state to determine the fact or erasure of their existence.[127]

122 TRC Executive Summary, *supra* note 116.

123 Truth and Reconciliation Canada, *Canada's Residential Schools: The History, Part 1 (Origins to 1939)*, Vol. 1 (Montreal & Kingston: McGill Queen's University Press, 2015) online: NCTR <http://nctr.ca/assets/reports/Final%20Reports/Volume_1_History_Part_1_English_Web.pdf> at 106, 108 [TRC Vol. 1].

124 Reprinted in R.S.C. 1985, App. II, No. 1.

125 For a relatively succinct summary of the various changes, see Canada, Royal Commission on Aboriginal Peoples, *Report of the Royal Commission on Aboriginal Peoples*, Vol. 4 (Ottawa: Canada Communication Group, 1996) at 24–49 (on gendered impact) and Vol. 1 at 258–318 (on more general history and impact of the Indian Act) [RCAP Vol. 4, RCAP Vol. 1]. See also Bonita Lawrence, *"Real" Indians and Others: Mixed-Blood Urban Native Peoples and Indigenous Nationhood* (Vancouver: University of British Columbia Press, 2004) [Lawrence].

126 See, e.g., Statement by Sharon McIvor (22 June 2016), online: <http://fafia-afai.org/wp-content/uploads/2016/06/2016Statement-of-Sharon-McIvor-Engfinal.pdf> (calling for Indian Act reforms prior to launch of MMIWG Inquiry and criticizing Canada's attempt to suspend McIvor's UN petition). See also Mary Eberts, "Victoria's Secret: How to Make a Population of Prey" in Joyce Green, ed., *Indivisible: Indigenous Human Rights* (Winnipeg: Fernwood, 2014) [Eberts]; *Gehl v. Canada (Attorney General)*, 2017 ONCA 319 online: CanLII <http://canlii.ca/t/h38cq> [*Gehl*].

127 Scott Lauria Morgensen, "The Biopolitics of Settler Colonialism: Right Here, Right Now" (2011) 1:1 *Settler Colonial Stud* 52–76 at 62 [Morgensen]. On the role of accounting in this

Indeed, the statutes governing entitlement to registration were "amended for 150 years" with "many amendments [being] bold attempts at reducing the Aboriginal population of a province or the whole country".[128] The point of reduction is emphasized in the context of the fiscal burden of Indigenous peoples at the federal level.[129] This view accords with the historical record, demographic projections, recent SCC case law, and legal, political, and socio-legal critiques of the legislation:[130] "Indian Affairs continues to control land and resources required to accommodate these members and Canada will differentiate between band members' registration status".[131] As recognized by the late Mocreebec chief Randy Kapashesit in a presentation to the Royal Commission on Aboriginal Peoples (RCAP),[132] an emphasis on wider territorial confederations and inter-nation relations ruptures membership bound to Indian Act bands:

> But, they've always been in the interest of the state to have treaties and to have arrangements and agreements. *We've never had the opportunity to work out our relationship with each other, within families, as individuals, between communities and beyond communities, nation-to-nation.*[133]

Emphasis on the wider definitions and relations matters where mere proof of ancestry might suffice instead of the quasi-blood quantum required by various versions of the Indian Act.[134] Plains Cree Indigenous studies scholar Robert Innes (Cowessess First Nation) further complicates the simplistic, essentialized picture painted by the Indian Act. He notes:

---

process, see also: Dean Neu & Cameron Graham, "The Birth of a Nation: Accounting and Canada's First Nations, 1860–1900" (2006) 31 *Accounting, Org Soc'y* 47–76 [Neu & Graham].

128 Larry Gilbert, *Entitlement to Indian Status and Membership Codes in Canada* (Scarborough, ON: Carswell, 1996) at 12 [Gilbert].

129 See RCAP Vol. 1, *supra* note 125 at 304 (federal government self-interest in the Indian Act's diminishing definition of Indian (relegation to provincial responsibility)); Pamela Palmater, *Beyond Blood: Rethinking Indigenous Identity* (Saskatoon: Purich, 2011) at 45–46 [Palmater] (on the related point of infringement and recolonization).

130 See various references, *supra* notes 127–129. See also: Sebastien Grammond, *Identity Captured by Law: Membership in Canada's Indigenous Peoples and Linguistic Minorities* (Montreal: McGill-Queen's University Press, 2009) [Grammond]; Val Napoleon, "Extinction by Number: Colonialism Made Easy" (2001) 16:1 *CJLS* 111 (Napoleon).

131 Gilbert, *supra* note 128 at 13.

132 Palmater notes the spectrum of statuses, from Indian Act status and band citizenship, to treaty rolls, to Metis scrip, to modern treaty citizenship, to Indigenous nationhood (Palmater, *supra* note 129 at 125).

133 Canada. Royal Commission on Aboriginal Peoples. Transcripts of Public Hearings and Round Table Discussions, 1992–1993. Presentation by Chief Randy Kapashesit (9 June 1992) in University of Saskatchewan Archives, Native Law Centre fonds, RCAP Vol. 30 (Box 4), part of Volume 2A (Moosonee) 368–380, online: University of Saskatchewan Archives <http://scaa.sk.ca/ourlegacy/permalink/29378> [Kapashesit].

134 Gilbert, *supra* note 128 at 14; Grammond 2009, *supra* note 130 at 71–73.

> most Aboriginal bands in the northern plains of Saskatchewan were kin-based and multicultural. Plains Cree, Saulteaux (also known as Chippewa or Western/Plains Ojibwe/Ojibwa), Assiniboine, and Métis individuals shared *similar cultural kinship practices that allowed them to integrate others into their bands.*[135]

A core feature of Indigenous legal systems is the ability to integrate other individuals and nations into existing webs of relations. Nonetheless, in line with the notorious statement by Duncan Campbell Scott (deputy director of the Department of Indian Affairs), the Indian Act was geared to "a time when 'there is not a single Indian in Canada that has not been absorbed into the body politic, and there is no Indian question'".[136]

Indian Act changes and definitions did not impact Indigenous peoples equally. Instead, as noted by Nellie Carlson, they had a very calculated gendered impact which disproportionately affected women:

> Historically the Indian Act has thoroughly brainwashed us. Since 1869 Indian women already were legislated as to who she should be. Six times the Indian Act changed on Indian women. But each time she lost a little bit of her rights as an Indian.[137]

While the first statutory language from the 1850 legislation (in Lower Canada) was wide and inclusive,[138] it was amended in 1851 to exclude from status (among others) "non-Indian men who married Indian women" while still allowing "non-Indian women who married Indian men" the right to Indian status.[139] As noted by the RCAP: "For the first time, Indian status began to be associated with the male line of descent".[140] The ability of Indian men to transfer Indian status by

135 Robert Alexander Innes, "Multicultural Bands on the Northern Plains and the Notion of 'Tribal' Histories" in Jarvis Brownlie and Valerie Korinek, eds., *Finding a Way to the Heart: Feminist Writings on Aboriginal and Women's History in Canada* (Winnipeg: University of Manitoba Press, 2012) [Innes 2012] at 124 (emphasis added) and at 139–140 (on multicultural bands versus tribal hegemony/exclusivity, and importance of kinship determinations regardless of tribe/band; see also Patricia A. McCormack, "'A World We Have Lost': The Plural Society of Fort Chipewyan" in the same volume). See also Grammond 2009, *supra* note 130 at 77–80 (also making reference to Plains/Prairie Cree and James Smith First Nation).

136 Morgensen 2011, *supra* note 127 at 62–63 (citing Duncan Campbell Scott in J. R. Miller, *Skyscrapers Hide the Heavens: A History of Indian-White Relations in Canada* (Toronto: University of Toronto Press, 1989) at 207.

137 Nellie Carlson, Indian Rights for Indian Women, Edmonton, Alberta, 11 June 1992 (in RCAP, Vol. 4, *supra* note 125 at 25). See *ibid.* at 24–49 (summarizing gendered impact).

138 See *An Act for the Better Protection of the Lands and Property of the Indians in Lower Canada*, S. Prov. C. 1850, c. 42. s 5 [*Lands and Property Act*].

139 See RCAP Vol. 4, *supra* note 125 at 25.

140 *Ibid.* at 25 (notes omitted). See the 1851 amendment: "*All women, now or hereafter to be lawfully married* to any of the persons included in the several classes hereinbefore designated; the children issued of such marriages, and their descendants" (emphasis added).

marriage to non-Indian women, without any such ability for Indian women to transfer status by marriage to non-Indian men, mirrored the rise of dependent nationality in the broader, still very much gendered context of colonial and imperial legislation.[141]

While the 1861 Act Respecting Indians and Indian Lands still defined Indians "as those with Indian blood *reputed* to belong to a tribe, all those intermarried among them, and their descendants", the notions of blood and belonging would soon narrow in the subsequent acts.[142] With respect to kinship connections, in 1869, further changes went beyond the former inability of women's non-Indian spouses to 'marry in' and enshrined the loss of status for Indian women 'marrying out' and their inability to transmit status to any children of such a union.[143]

This provision carried through to the very first consolidated Indian Act of 1876, which defined the term 'Indian' through men, their 'blood', and male descent:

> The term 'Indian' means
>
> First. Any male person of Indian blood reputed to belong to a particular band;
> Secondly. Any child of such person;
> Thirdly. Any woman who is or was lawfully married to such person: . . .
>
> (c) Provided that any Indian woman marrying any other than an Indian or a non-treaty Indian shall cease to be an Indian in any respect within the meaning of this Act.[144]

Given federal Indian policy's tripartite focus on the control of lands, government, and children,[145] the loss of status for Indian women 'marrying out' to non-Indian men or non-status Indians has been one of the most devastating and long-lasting

141 See, e.g., Philip Girard, "'If Two Ride a Horse, One Must Ride in Front': Married Women's Nationality and the Law in Canada 1880–1950" (2013) 94:1 *Can Hist Rev* 28–54 [Girard]; Helen Irving, *Citizenship, Alienage, and the Modern Constitutional State: A Gendered History* (New York: Cambridge University Press, 2016) [Irving].

142 Palmater, *supra* note 129 at 40–41 (citing *An Act Respecting Indians and Indian Lands*, C.S.L.C. 1861, c. 14 at s. 11) (emphasis added).

143 *An Act for the Gradual Enfranchisement of Indians, the Better Management of Indian Affairs, and to Extend the Provisions of the Act 31st Victoria, Chapter 42*. S.C. 1869, c. 6 (32–33 Vict.), s. 6. See also Leslie & Maguire, *supra* note 66 at 66; Palmater, *supra* note 129 at 41; Allyson Stevenson, "The Adoption of Francis T: Blood, Belonging, and Aboriginal Transracial Adoption in Twentieth Century Canada" (2015) 50.3 *Canadian Journal of History* 470–491 at 484–486 and notes 47–49; and the *Indian Act*, R.S.C. 1951, c. 29. s. 12 (involuntary enfranchisement & marrying out) [*Indian Act*].

144 *An Act to Amend and Consolidate the Laws Respecting Indians*, S.C. 1876, c. 18 (39 Vict), s. 3. The Act also provided for exclusion of 'illegitimate' children and for a woman's status to potentially transfer to her spouse.

145 See, e.g., Barman, *supra* note 71 at 169 and following.

tactics in the larger colonial strategy.[146] As summarized by the RCAP, a whole host of detrimental effects for Indian women sprang from their excision from status, including the inability to vote in band elections, loss of membership in home communities, loss of Indian status, and loss of the right to transmit Indian status to their children (among others).[147]

The state's emphasis on 'patrilineal descent' also ran counter to both the "predominant principle of [bilateral] descent among the tribes . . . traced equally through both the mother's and the father's relatives" and the next most common principle of matrilineal descent.[148] Patrilineal descent also coincided with the state undermining matriarchal authority generally and in the context of particular communities' political and legal systems. The example of the Six Nations of the Grand River is pertinent here, too, given colonial distrust of clan mothers' powers to hold title and select the Confederacy's chiefs.[149] Restriction through male lineage was made worse by the reductive policies of voluntary and involuntary enfranchisement.[150] The introduction of enfranchisement to further assimilate Indigenous peoples arose in an 1857 statute applicable to Upper and Lower Canada, providing rights to vote and own individual property in exchange for giving up Indian status and residency rights on reserve.[151] The role of enfranchisement was confirmed in the consolidated 1876 Indian Act,[152] which also included the forced replacement of traditional governance systems with elected band councils acting as local governments under the Indian Agent.[153] The examples of

146 In addition, see also Eberts, *supra* note 126 at 144–165.

147 RCAP Vol. 4, *supra* note 125 at 28 (note omitted).

148 RCAP Vol. 4, *supra* note 125 at note 19 (citing Sally Weaver, "First Nations Women and Government Policy 1970–92: Discrimination and Conflict" in Lorraine Code and Lindsay Dorney, eds., *Changing Patterns: Women in Canada*, 2nd ed. (Toronto: McClelland and Stewart, 1993) at 98.

149 On this point, in the context of Six Nations of the Grand River and the Haudenosaunee Confederacy, see related references at Bhatia 2012b, *supra* note 38 at 166–169.

150 See, e.g., RCAP Vol. 4, *supra* note 125 at ch. 2; Megan Furi & Jill Wherrett, *Indian Status and Band Membership Issues* (Ottawa: Political and Social Affairs Division, Parliamentary Research Branch, Library of Parliament, 2003) [Furi & Wherrett]; Heidi Bohaker and Franca Iacovetta, "Making Aboriginal People 'Immigrants Too': A Comparison of Citizenship Programs for Newcomers and Indigenous Peoples in Postwar Canada, 1940s–1960s" (September 2009) 90:3 *Canadian Historical Review* 427–461 [Bohaker & Iacovetta].

151 RCAP Vol. 4, *supra* note 125 at 25–26 (citing *Act to Encourage the Gradual Civilization of the Indian Tribes in this Province, and to Amend the Laws Respecting Indians*, S. Prov. C. 1857, c. 26, s. 3. See also Michael Posluns, *Speaking with Authority: The Emergence of the Vocabulary of First Nations' Self-Government* (New York: Routledge, 2007) at 11, 60–61, and 66 [Posluns].

152 *An Act to Amend and Consolidate the Laws Respecting Indians*, S.C. 1876, c. 18 (39 Vict), s. 5, 86, 87 [*Indian Act 1876*].

153 In addition to the example at Six Nations, see more recently Shiri Pasternak, *Grounded Authority: The Algonquins of Barriere Lake against the State* (Minnesota: University of Minnesota Press, 2017) [Pasternak]. Section 74 of the Indian Act was used to impose an elected band council at Rapid Lake Reserve by mail-in ballot after multiple unsuccessful attempts.

'marrying out', enfranchisement, and band councils illustrate the *weaponization* of race, gender, class, and democracy within Canadian Indian policy. This legal cocktail also highlights the near-lethal consequences of the Indian Act and Indian status for Indigenous self-determination under Indigenous legal and political systems. As noted by Saulteau and Gitksan legal scholar Val Napoleon, cataloguing Indigenous peoples per the Indian Act disconnected First Nations from their territories and allowed the federal government to "reduce the number of Indians requiring reserve land or federal resources . . . [nullifying] First Nations cultural systems for determining citizenship".[154]

In contrast to this conspiracy of legislated identity, Mi'kmaq legal scholar Pamela Palmater argues that "Indigenous nations have inherent jurisdiction to determine citizenship rules for themselves, though this might practically emerge only through negotiated self-government agreements or modern treaties".[155] In the absence of this full-blown self-determination approach to identity, Palmater notes that assimilation will continue because traditional communal identity will be reduced to band membership belonging that is determined by the recognized identity of the Indian Status registry.[156] In contrast to the reductive definitions of the Indian Act, the definition of Aboriginal peoples from the eponymous Royal Commission is much broader: "organic, political, and cultural entities that stem historically from the original peoples of North America" (and not collections of individuals united by so-called racial characteristics).[157] The RCAP definition of Aboriginal nation is likewise wider than the current Indian Act definition of band: "sizeable body of Aboriginal people who possess a shared sense of national identity and constitute the predominant population in a certain territory or collection of territories".[158] As with Indigenous treaties, territories, and governments, the process of domestication operates to shrink and isolate what would otherwise be dynamic Indigenous nations with relationships to the Crown to "individual Indians" regulated by Canada.[159]

154 See Napoleon 2001, *supra* note 130 at 118, 122.

155 Palmater, *supra* note 129 at 30. Various scholars differ on these points, see, e.g., Pamela Palmater, "Justifying Blood Quantum as Sui Generis State Law," book review of Kirsty Gover, *Tribal Constitutionalism: States, Tribes, and the Governance of Membership* (New York: Oxford University Press, 2011) (2012) 17:1 *Rev Const Stud* 135–145 [Palmater 2012]; Douglas Sanderson, "Book Review: *Beyond Blood: Rethinking Indigenous Identity* (P. Palmater) and *Tribal Constitutionalism: States, Tribes and the Governance of Membership* (K. Gover)" (2013) 63:3 *UTLJ* 511–515. See also Grammond 2009, *supra* note 130.

156 Palmater, *supra* note 129 at 30. The key distinction in the Act between the 'fuller' s. 6(1) and the 'lesser' s. 6(2) registrants has to do with transmission and the inability of 6(2) registrants "to pass on Indian status to children in their own right" (with attendant distinctions between 6(1) registrants as well, such as those reinstated, sometimes under duress, through Bill C-31) (at 34). See also John Borrows, "Physical Philosophy: Mobility and the Future of Indigenous Rights" in Benjamin J. Richardson, Shin Imai & Kent McNeil, eds., *Indigenous Peoples and the Law: Comparative and Critical Perspectives* (Oregon: Hart, 2009).

157 Palmater, *supra* note 129 at 36.

158 *Ibid.* at 36.

159 *Ibid.* at 37.

These domesticating developments are all-important because they dishonour sacred treaty relations and foreclose the self-determination and continuity of Indigenous peoples. At the same time, they also guarantee essential attributes of Canadian statehood and the sovereign capacity to maintain these attributes in seeming perpetuity.

Conclusion

This chapter has shown how domesticated versions of the treaties were used to consolidate the attributes of statehood through the establishment of a defined Canadian territory, the immigration and settlement of a permanent population, and a corresponding government. This consolidation allowed the Canadian government to exercise its sovereignty to bring about the Indian Act, which further transformed Indigenous relations with both the state and one another through the introduction of band councils, Indian Act status, and residential schools. As I have discussed in other recent work, the hard, cutting edges of this state sovereignty persevere at the intersection of Indigenous, Aboriginal and immigration law when it comes to Indigenous ways of making and maintaining relations through treaties and adoptions.[160]

160 Bhatia 2018, *supra* note 10.

3 Decolonization in Third and Fourth Worlds

Synergy, solidarity, and sustainability through international law

Usha Natarajan

Recognition

The Australian Prime Minister made the following statement as part of his address in December 1992 to launch the International Year of the World's Indigenous Peoples:

> It begins, I think, with that act of recognition. Recognition that it was we who did the dispossessing. We took the traditional lands and smashed the traditional way of life. We brought the diseases. The alcohol. We committed the murders. We took the children from their mothers. We practiced discrimination and exclusion. It was our ignorance and our prejudice. And our failure to imagine these things being done to us. With some noble exceptions, we failed to make the most basic human response and enter into their hearts and minds. We failed to ask how would I feel if this were done to me? . . . it might help us if we non-Aboriginal Australians imagined ourselves dispossessed of land we had lived on for fifty thousand years and then imagined ourselves told that it had never been ours. Imagine if ours was the oldest culture in the world and we were told that it was worthless. Imagine if we had resisted this settlement, suffered and died in the defense of our land, and then were told in history books that we had given up without a fight. Imagine if non-Aboriginal Australians had served their country in peace and war and were then ignored in history books. Imagine if our feats on sporting fields had inspired admiration and patriotism and yet did nothing to diminish prejudice. Imagine if our spiritual life was denied and ridiculed. Imagine if we had suffered the injustice and then were blamed for it. It seems to me that if we can imagine the injustice we can imagine its opposite. . . . We cannot imagine that the descendants of people whose genius and resilience maintained a culture here through fifty thousand years or more, through cataclysmic changes to the climate and environment, and who then survived two centuries of dispossession and abuse, will be denied their place.[1]

1 Paul Keating, *Redfern Address*, Sydney, 10 December 1992 [Keating].

Six months earlier, the High Court of Australia had delivered the momentous *Mabo* judgment.[2] *Mabo* is significant for international lawyers because it considers how title is acquired over territory, in this case examining the international law doctrine of *terra nullius*, permitting empty lands to be settled. Australia was considered terra nullius by European colonists because, although it was populated, its peoples were considered by Europeans to be too primitive and lawless to signify. Hence, despite extensive warfare between colonists and Indigenous peoples, European title over Australia was asserted through settlement rather than conquest. The distinction between settlement and conquest has legal implications. Settlement allows settlers to determine the applicable legal system. Conquest recognizes the pre-existence of native legal systems and potential sovereign entities that must be dealt with in accordance with international laws on warfare and conquest. *Mabo* recognized for the first time that Australia was not terra nullius. Hence, European settlement of Australia did not commence with a legally clean slate after all. Indigenous peoples and their laws must be recognized, including consideration of which of these laws survived European conquest into the present day, such as those laws which grant native title over territory. Alongside *Mabo*'s legal recognition that Indigenous peoples existed at the time of European conquest, the Redfern Address recognized the efforts colonists made to eliminate them. Terra nullius was the foundation upon which colonial legal systems evolved in Australia for more than 200 years, and many of these laws and policies attempted to make real the imagined empty land through enabling genocide, apartheid, racial discrimination, and forced cultural assimilation.

Third World Approaches to International Law (TWAIL) is a movement that unpacks the Western colonial legacies of international law, demands decolonization, and advocates for a discipline that is genuinely international. For TWAIL, the relationship between international law and Indigenous and Tribal peoples raises several challenges. The above extract is a selected abridgement of a longer address, but for our purposes, it is worth mentioning that the last sentence of the extract ends as follows:

> We cannot imagine that the descendants of people whose genius and resilience maintained a culture here through fifty thousand years or more, through cataclysmic changes to the climate and environment, and who then survived two centuries of dispossession and abuse, will be denied their place *in the modern Australian nation.*[3]

While an Australian Prime Minister is unlikely to end such a sentence in any other way, therein lies the rub for Indigenous and Tribal peoples. Denying the sovereignty, independence, and self-determination of Indigenous and Tribal peoples also poses fundamental challenges for international law and for TWAIL.

2 *Mabo and Others v Queensland (No 2)* (1992) 175 CLR 1 [*Mabo*].

3 Keating, *supra* note 1 (emphasis added).

Sovereign statehood is the fundamental building block of international law, so it is unsurprising that the disciplinary criteria for sovereign statehood have been a central subject of TWAIL's anti-imperial critique.[4] To what extent has such critique been helpful for addressing the predicament of Indigenous and Tribal peoples? Could TWAIL do better? Or are Third World approaches destined to be problematic for Indigenous or Fourth World approaches? This chapter argues that TWAIL should operate in synergy and solidarity with Fourth World approaches to promote justice and self-awareness. It concludes that such a stance is particularly indispensable to evolving adequate responses to epochal environmental change and achieving sustainable development.

It may help to begin with recognition that the questions explored in this chapter stem from my own journey as an international lawyer. I have been part of TWAIL for many years and, although the colonial experience is central to TWAIL, I did not think seriously about the plight of those still colonized until recently – this despite being from two countries, India and Australia, deeply implicated in the dispossession and oppression of Indigenous and Tribal peoples. Born in India, I was raised with a keen awareness of the evils of the caste system and racial discrimination, yet I never thought about Tribal peoples. That they existed at all never entered my urban life or daily politics. My parents moved to Australia when I was a teenager. At school, we were not taught that our homes and school were on land sacred to others who had been massacred. Attempted genocide by colonists in the early to mid-1800s had decimated Indigenous populations in Victoria, where I grew up. While the peoples who previously lived where I lived had in some sense been wiped off the map, they were still present in the soil on which we grew and learned, our homes, and our schools, some of which I later learned were burial grounds. I had never to my knowledge met an Indigenous or Tribal person during my school years, but they haunted us in the violence and ignorance we were inheriting and passing on.

An interest in global justice eventually drew me to international law and TWAIL, but I focused on the postcolonial dilemmas of the peoples of the Global South – which spoke most closely to my own life experience – and the need to combat contemporary forms of imperialism. In 2012, Amar Bhatia wrote an influential article about what TWAIL could learn from Indigenous and Fourth World approaches.[5] Three years later, Amar, John Reynolds, Sujith Xavier, and I organized the first TWAIL conference in the Global South in Cairo. That it had taken so long to meet in the South was due to the political, financial, and administrative

4 The canonical TWAIL text is Antony Anghie's, *Imperialism, Sovereignty, and the Making of International Law* (New York: Cambridge University Press, 2005) [Anghie 2005]. Other influential works include R. P. Anand, *New States and International Law* (New Delhi: Vikas, 1972) [Anand 1972a] and Siba N'Zatioula Grovogui, *Sovereigns, Quasi-Sovereigns, and Africans: Race and Self-Determination in International Law* (Minneapolis: University of Minnesota Press, 1996) [Grovogui].

5 A. Bhatia, "The South of the North: Building on Critical Approaches to International Law with Lessons from the Fourth World" (2012) 14 *Or Rev Intl L* 131 [Bhatia].

barriers to organizing large-scale events here. The conference theme was praxis, a fitting reminder for us to address TWAIL's blind spots; yet ultimately, we failed to draw significant Indigenous participation to Cairo, whether from the Global South or North. Barriers that prevented regular TWAIL meetings in the South were present to a much greater degree for Indigenous and Tribal scholars. Those who overcame systemic barriers to their participation in knowledge production then faced disproportionate demands on their time and energy, strains on health and finances, macro- and microaggressions, and inadequate infrastructure and support systems. That is to say, they face the consequences of structural violence that many peoples in the Global South are familiar with, but in much more intensified and protracted forms because they remain colonized.

The conference commemorated in this edited collection was the first to explicitly unite in conversation scholars of Third and Fourth World approaches. Organized by Sujith Xavier, Valarie Waboose, Jeffery G. Hewitt, Amar Bhatia, and Amaya Álvez Marín at Windsor, Canada, in April 2018, the conference was titled Decolonizing Law: Methods, Strategies, Tactics. Rather than discussing how to decolonize law, Indigenous scholars instead showed how it is done through living, enacting, and performing diverse Indigenous legal orders that are alive, present, and functioning. Many of these orders are grounded in knowledges missing or lost to contemporary international law: life as profoundly interconnected, respect for self and others, and wisdom and dignity in the face of immense suffering. Indigenous legal traditions often spoke directly and indirectly to challenges in international investment law, economic law, migration law, environmental law, human rights law, and so on that we regularly encounter in mainstream international law conferences. They provide much more than a path to law reform, showing new ways of understanding law, our role in society as the producers of legal knowledge, and what example we set. As a TWAIL scholar, all I had to offer was my attention. The following sections contemplate ways in which TWAIL could operate in synergy and solidarity with Indigenous legal orders. It concludes by considering what the stakes are at a time of environmental change.

Synergy

International law is Eurocentric in its origins and evolution, and Western biases persist in its contemporary operations.[6] In attempting to change this discipline into something truly international, TWAIL is contending with a philosophy and discourse structured to either assimilate or destroy that which is foreign to Western thought.[7] Hence, transformation is a taxing endeavor requiring careful

6 B. S. Chimni, "Third World Approaches to International Law: A Manifesto" (2006) 8 *Intl Community L Rev* 3; James Thuo Gathii, "TWAIL: A Brief History of Its Origins, Its Decentralized Network and Tentative Bibliography" (2011) 3 *Trade L Dev* 26.

7 Antony Anghie, *Imperialism, Sovereignty and the Making of International Law* (Cambridge: Cambridge University Press, 2003) [Anghie 2003]; Peter Fitzpatrick, *Modernism and the Grounds of Law* (Cambridge: Cambridge University Press, 2001) [Fitzpatrick].

strategies. Long before TWAIL was established in 1997, international lawyers from the Global South sought to introduce alternative legal philosophies, concepts, and languages into the discipline.[8] This was particularly the case after many Southern states gained their independence from colonial rule. Against overwhelming odds, they achieved a measure of success,[9] but much work remains to be done for those of us who stand on their shoulders. Against this background, and given the even more arduous struggles faced by Indigenous and Tribal peoples, is it mutually beneficial for the two groups to ally themselves? When it is a challenge to create and maintain solidarity within each of these large transnational groups, is it worthwhile simultaneously striving for solidarity across them, given that the trials of those who remain colonized are different in many ways to those of the postcolonial world? This chapter argues that such an alliance can be mutually beneficial. What is more, for TWAIL, supporting Indigenous and Tribal approaches is indispensable for the sake of justice, self-awareness, and achieving TWAIL's own goals.

TWAIL's raison d'être is to resist colonialism and imperialism. As such, independence and self-determination for Indigenous and Tribal peoples, as well as others who remain colonized, is imperative to our aims. Moreover, synergy with Fourth World approaches may help TWAIL better understand and negotiate some of the challenges and pitfalls of the past and shape tactics based on greater self-awareness. Past endeavors evidence that postcolonial efforts to transform international law may have unintended consequences. After the Second World War, many states in the Global South gained their independence. Alliances across the Global South, such as the G-77 and the Non-Aligned Movement, were used to introduce new legal concepts into international law through, among other things, southern states' majority in the United Nations

8 See for example R. P. Anand, ed., *Asian States and the Development of International Law* (New Delhi: Vikas, 1972) [Anand 1972b]; Christopher Weeramantry, *Islamic Jurisprudence: An International Perspective* (Basingstoke: Macmillan, 1988) [Weeramantry]; S. P. Sinha, *Legal Polycentricity and International Law* (Durham: Carolina Academic Press, 1996) [Sinha]; Yasuaki Onuma, "When Was the Law of International Society Born? An Inquiry of the History of International Law from an Intercivilisational Perspective" (2000) 2 *J Hist Intl L* 1 [Onuma]; C. H. Alexandrowicz, *An Introduction to the History of the Law of Nations in the East Indies (16th, 17th, 18th Centuries)* (Oxford: Clarendon Press, 1967) [Alexandrowicz]; R. P. Anand, *The Legal Regime of the Sea Bed and the Developing Countries* (New Delhi: Thomson, 1975) [Anand 1975]; K. Krishna Rao, "The Legal Regime of the Sea-Bed and Ocean Floor" (1969) 9 *Indian J Intl L* 1 [Rao]; A. O. Adede, "The Group of 77 and the Establishment of the International Sea-Bed Authority" (1979) 7 *Ocean Dev & Intl L* 31 [Adede]; Kamal Hossain & Subrata Roy Chowdhury, eds., *Permanent Sovereignty over Natural Resources in International Law: Principle and Practice* (London: Frances Pinter, 1984) [Hossain & Chowdhury]; Nico Schrijver, *Sovereignty over Natural Resources: Balancing Rights and Duties* (New York: Cambridge University Press, 1997) [Schrijver].

9 For a description, see Antony Anghie & B. S. Chimni, "Third World Approaches to International Law and Individual Responsibility in Internal Armed Conflicts" (2003) 2 *Chinese J Intl L* 77 [Chimni].

General Assembly.[10] These reform efforts were grounded on the sovereign equality of new states and their right to participate as equals with existing states in international lawmaking. These interventions, many of which took place in the 1960s and 1970s, were intended to benefit the peoples of the Global South. However, ultimately, many of them served to strengthen the power of southern ruling elites, including unrepresentative authoritarian elites who benefited at the expense of the peoples of the South.[11]

The establishment of TWAIL in 1997 was a reaction to these outcomes, demanding a type of Third World critique that would empower the poor masses of the South against the exploitation of transnational elites.[12] To more fully understand why past Third World efforts to participate in international law did not meet with the anticipated success, TWAIL scholars from the 1990s onwards scrutinized above all the route that enabled their participation, namely sovereign statehood. They uncovered the structural violence the postcolonial world inherited through the medium of the sovereign state, a violence embedded in and universalized through international law. Sovereign statehood constrained the choices of postcolonial societies in innumerable ways, including their governance and development pathways,[13] their relationship to the natural environment,[14] their relationship with neighboring communities,[15] and so on. For the purposes of this chapter, the characteristic to note is that the suffering of Indigenous and Tribal peoples is a founding element in the violence of the sovereign state.

There is a commonality of experience for Indigenous and Tribal peoples across the Global North and South in terms of dispossession of their culture, land, and dignity. This is not a coincidence but, among other things, the inevitable and systemic product of the sovereign state system. This chapter commenced with one of the starkest examples, the doctrine of terra nullius as applied in Australia that declared the continent uninhabited before European settlement. The peoples living across the Australian continent represent the greatest cultural and linguistic diversity in the

10 The success of this strategy was limited since UN General Assembly resolutions were relegated to the category of 'soft law' by Western states because they did not satisfy positivist legal requirements. See Anghie 2003, *supra* note 7, ch. 4.

11 Usha Natarajan, "TWAIL and Environment: The State of Nature, the Nature of the State, and the Arab Spring" (2012) 14 *Or Rev Intl L* 177 [Natarajan 2012].

12 See generally Anghie & Chimni, *supra* note 9.

13 Gilbert Rist, *The History of Development: From Western Origins to Global Faith* (London: Zed Books, 2002) [Rist]; Sundhya Pahuja, *Decolonizing International Law: Development, Economic Growth, and the Politics of Universality* (New York: Cambridge University Press, 2011) [Pahuja].

14 Natarajan 2012, *supra* note 11.

15 Obiora Chinedu Okafor, *Re-Defining Legitimate Statehood: International Law and State Fragmentation in Africa* (Hague: Kluwer Law International, 2000) [Okafor]; Makau W. Mutua, "Why Redraw the Map of Africa: A Moral and Legal Inquiry" (1995) 16 *Mich J Intl L* 1113 [Mutua]; Usha Natarajan, "Creating and Recreating Iraq: Legacies of the Mandate System in Contemporary Understandings of Third World Sovereignty" (2011) 24:4 *Leiden J Intl L* 799 [Natarajan 2011].

world, a precious and irreplaceable part of the cultural heritage of humanity.[16] Yet their erasure was the foundation on which Australian sovereign statehood was built.

When compared with the British settler colonies of the Global North such as Australia, New Zealand, Canada, and the United States, the experiences of Indigenous and Tribal peoples across the Global South have been much more diverse but no less devastating in final effect. One of the framing doctrines of sovereign statehood in the global South is that of *uti posseditis juris*, requiring that colonial frontiers be preserved as a condition of independence.[17] The transformation of diverse governance and territorial arrangements, first through colonial rule and consequently into sovereign states, threatened those cultures that straddled multiple state territories as well as those habituated to modes of governance and law not accommodated by the modern state.

Alongside borders and political structures that were determined by Europeans, sovereign statehood in the Global South also required commitment to developmentalism and the continual pursuit of economic growth. Cultures that were not committed to the commodification of nature in the Western sense were considered primitive, undeserving of sovereignty, and requiring transformation. Across the world, international law played its part in universalizing Western understandings of progress: development as industrialization, nature as a natural resource, earth as property, humans as atomistic individuals in sovereign states, and the world as a collection of states committed to economic growth. Cultures that understood life and progress differently, including most Indigenous and Tribal communities across the Global South and North, were encompassed within state systems designed to assimilate citizens into the developmental mainstream and eradicate incommensurate worldviews.[18]

The dynamics of imposing a culturally incongruous Western state system across the world are anything but straightforward. It was not simply that the Third World reluctantly accepted the concept of the sovereign state. The psychology of colonization to some extent indoctrinated the colonized into wanting the attributes of the colonizer, as this was usually the means to freedom and independence. To overcome the operation of such psychology, independence leaders such as Mahatma Gandhi and Frantz Fanon pointed out that the move to independence need not logically conclude with the establishment of yet another sovereign state. Gandhi warned that modern statehood contained structural violence: "We want the English rule without the Englishman. You want the tiger's nature but not the tiger".[19] These cautions have since proved prescient across

16 James Fearon, "Ethnic and Cultural Diversity by Country" (2003) 8 *J Econ Growth* 195 [Fearon]; *1972 UNESCO Convention Concerning the Protection of the World Cultural and Natural Heritage* [UNESCO 1972].

17 Roughly translates as "you will have sovereignty over those territories you possess as of law". See *Frontier Dispute (Burkina Faso v Republic of Mali)* [1986] ICJ Rep 554 [*Frontier Dispute*]; Antonio Cassese, *International Law* (Oxford: Oxford University Press, 2001) at 57.

18 Natarajan 2011, *supra* note 11.

19 As quoted in Leela Gandhi, *Postcolonial Theory: A Critical Introduction* (New York: Columbia University Press, 1998) at 20–22 [Gandhi].

many parts of the Global South. For instance, across the Arab world the ongoing uprisings over the last decade show how sovereign independence alone cannot provide freedom from imperialism and that the postcolonial state is an effective vehicle of this imperialism.

That violence against Indigenous and Tribal peoples is embedded in state structures has several implications for Third and Fourth World approaches. As Anghie and Chimni observe, contemporary strategies need to keep in mind that reform attempts that strengthen the power of sovereign states may occur at the expense of people power.[20] With this in mind, Indigenous and Tribal demands for sovereignty and self-determination cannot be understood as merely wanting membership within the club of sovereign states, but rather as a contestation of this homogenizing system through insisting on recognition of different, and hopefully less violent and harmful, modes of collective organization and structures of governance. That is to say, decolonization and sovereign independence is fundamental and crucial for the Fourth World, but it must be on their own terms in order to stand a chance of not replicating the violence of colonialism. In the Global South, there has to be recognition that, as in the Global North, the postcolonial state and its non-Indigenous citizens are also complicit in the oppression and colonization of Indigenous and Tribal peoples. For peoples of the Global South, it requires understanding the violence we inherited through the experience of colonization and decolonization, and the innumerable ways in which this violence is reproduced and proliferated through modern institutions, cultures, and citizenship. Such understandings will hopefully produce a commitment to finding ways to transcend this violence through an openness to and respect for Indigenous and Tribal sovereignty and worldviews.

When it comes to the TWAIL movement, though much of our scholarly attention is devoted to analyzing the dilemmas of the postcolonial state and the persistence of imperialism, we have not usually foregrounded Indigenous and Tribal struggles for decolonization across the Global South and North. Such struggles speak directly to TWAIL's anticolonial and anti-imperial commitments yet remain systemically neglected, notwithstanding calls to attention from Bhatia and some increase in notice over the last decade.[21] TWAIL is not alone in this quandary. Critical movements more generally, particularly those dedicated to postcolonialism and antiracism, have long been called on to take Indigenous and Tribal decolonization seriously and have struggled to do so.[22] When considering

20 Anghie & Chimni, *supra* note 9.

21 Bhatia, *supra* note 5; Prabhakar Singh, "Indian International Law: From a Colonised Apologist to a Subaltern Protagonist" (2010) 23 *Leiden J Intl L* 1 [Singh]; Rajshree Chandra, "Understanding Change with(in) Law: The Niyamgiri Case" (2016) 50:2 *Contributions Indian Sociol* 137 [Chandra]; Roger Merino Acuna, "An Alternative to 'Alternative Development'?: *Buen Vivir* and Human Development in Andean Countries" (2016) 44:3 *Oxford Dev Stud* 271 [Acuna].

22 Boaventura De Sousa Santos asked in *Toward a New Common Sense: Law, Science and Politics in the Paradigmatic Transition* (1995), "what can we learn from the Indigenous peoples who, in a sense, are the South of the South?" On the struggle to respond effectively to such

the way in which TWAIL scholarship has understood the relationship between Indigenous and Tribal peoples and international law, while there seems an openness to learning from Indigenous and Tribal experiences in selective ways, particularly in a historical context, there are fewer examples of TWAIL scholarship that take contemporary Indigenous and Tribal legal approaches and demands for self-determination seriously.[23] Building on Bhatia's study of the contemporary implications of settler colonialism in North America for Indigenous peoples and international law, listening to and taking into account the experiences and stories of Indigenous and Tribal peoples across the Global South as well would help develop a more self-reflexive movement in conscious synergy with Indigenous calls for self-determination within postcolonial states.[24]

TWAIL scholars such as Anghie and Porras have foregrounded that colonizing Indigenous territory was central to the creation and evolution of international law. Their scrutiny of disciplinary origins reveals the colonial encounter to be formative for the European founding fathers of international law, from Vitoria with regard to Spanish conquest of the Americas[25] to Grotius defending Dutch corporations in the East Indies.[26] Through a close reading of Vitoria's texts, both Anghie and Porras identify the origins of disciplinary archetypes that emerged from European encounters with the Americas. Anghie traces the disciplinary technique for eradicating cultural difference through either assimilation or destruction. Porras points to the commodification of nature in putative service of the providential design doctrine of international commerce (commerce understood as a consensual, reciprocal, mutually beneficial exchange that builds amity among separated peoples). Both scholars trace the harmful contemporary operations of

calls, see Bonita Lawrence & Enakshi Dua, "Decolonizing Antiracism" (2005) 32:4 *Soc Just* 120 at 127–136 [Lawrence & Dua].

23 For examples that address contemporary Indigenous concerns, see note 21. Bhatia advocates recovering the historic and contemporary participation of Indigenous peoples in international law as independent sovereigns. He examines particularly the Six Nations Appeal, put forward under article 17 of the *Covenant of the League of Nations* for disputes between member states and non-member states, whereby the Six Nations Confederacy alleged "a menace to international peace" and requested recognition of their independent right of home rule, an account of their trust funds and interest from the imperial government, and freedom of transit for the Six Nations to and from international waters. Singh considers TWAIL and the history of Indian contributions to international law, adding a crucial but forgotten 'tribal tale' to the existing canon. Chandra also considers tribal struggles in India, looking particularly at the *Niyamgiri* judgment in the Supreme Court – a situation where local tribal government rejected the mining project put forward by the state and transnational corporation – as an interruption of the dominant development paradigm and more importantly as inaugurating a particular form of lawful relations for Indigeneity. Merino studies the appropriation of Indigenous legal concepts by other actors to serve their own agendas (such as environmentalists and state representatives), the resultant mutation of concepts and multiplicity of meanings, and the strategic re-appropriation of these terms by Indigenous peoples.

24 *Ibid.*

25 Anghie 2003, *supra* note 7.

26 Ileana Porras, "Appropriating Nature: Commerce, Property and the Commodification of Nature in the Law of Nations" (2014) 27:3 *Leiden J Intl L* 641–660 [Porras 2014].

these enduring disciplinary archetypes. Porras points out that contemporary difficulties with moving towards sustainable development can be at least partially attributed to long-standing disciplinary dedication to protecting commercial interests.[27] Both scholars have also drawn parallels between excluding Native Americans from legal protection in the early 20th century because of their allegedly lawless and uncivilized character, and the exclusion of suspected terrorists from legal protection in the early 21st century by the same reasoning.[28] Indeed, these interconnections reveal themselves in more recent spaces of violence, with North American soldiers in Vietnam and peacekeepers in Somalia both referring to the places they occupied as 'Indian country'.[29] Anghie and Porras have been formative and influential in the TWAIL movement and, by building on their insights, TWAIL scholarship could also address the complexity of contemporary Indigenous and Tribal struggles and their relationship with other historical and contemporary struggles across the South. Beyond a historical phenomenon that helps shed light on how international law treats the non-European world, the suffering of Indigenous and Tribal peoples is an ongoing protracted assertion of sovereignty and self-determination to which TWAIL owes its allegiance.

The parallels Anghie and Porras draw between the treatment of Native Americans in the 'Wild West' and suspected terrorists in 'outlaw states' – that they are both perceived to behave lawlessly and hence undeserving of legal protection and cast outside the ambit of the law – has resonance with the state of exception as understood by Agamben and Schmitt.[30] Mbembe and others have pointed out, in the same vein as Anghie and Porras, that state of exception powers became entrenched in European legal systems through colonial projects for eliminating Indigenous nations.[31] The state of exception is a powerful enactment of sovereign power,[32] and Dafnos examines its use and evolution in the Canadian context to assert executive power in attempts to eradicate competing sovereignties from Indigenous nations.[33] Dafnos goes on to show how, in the past, the state of

27 *Ibid.*

28 Anghie 2003, *supra* note 7. See also Ileana Porras, "On Terrorism: Reflections on Violence and the Outlaw" in Dan Danielsen & Karen Engle, eds., *After Identity: A Reader in Law and Culture* (London: Routledge, 1995) at 294–313 [Porras 1995].

29 Sherene Razack, *Dark Threats and White Knights: The Somalia Affair, Peacekeeping, and the New Imperialism* (Toronto: University of Toronto Press, 2004) at 17.

30 Giorgio Agamben, *State of Exception* (Chicago: University of Chicago Press, 2005) at 12 [Agamben 2005].

31 Achille Mbembe, "Necropolitics" (2003) 15:1 *Public Culture* 11 [Mbembe]; Mark Rifkin, "Indigenizing Agamben: Rethinking Sovereignty in Light of the 'Peculiar' Status of Native Peoples" (2009) 73 *Cultural Critique* 88 [Rifkin]; Scott Lauria Morgensen, "The Biopolitics of Settler Colonialism: Right Here, Right Now" (2011) 1:1 *Settler Colonial Stud* 52 [Morgensen].

32 Giorgio Agamben, *Homo Sacer: Sovereign Power and Bare Life* (Stanford: Stanford University Press, 1998) [Agamben 1998].

33 Tia Dafnos, "The Enduring Settler-Colonial Emergency: Indian Affairs and Contemporary Emergency Management in Canada" (2018) *Settler Colonial Stud* 1, DOI: <10.1080/2201473X.2018.1491157> at 3 [Dafnos].

exception was more easily observable because it operated in the context of war, conquest, and declarations of martial law. However, today, operations of the state of exception can be much more obscured, although the same reasoning underlies the way the state engages in social pacification through quotidian repressive and eliminatory practices against Indigenous and Tribal peoples as well as others who protest against and resist state power.[34] Dafnos attributes this obfuscation to, among other things, a gradual process of "discursive liberalization of legal doctrine".[35] While Dafnos focuses on the North American context, the same trends are observable in how many postcolonial states subdue their Indigenous and Tribal populations.[36]

Third World states assert their 'post'-coloniality only through ignoring Indigenous and Tribal sovereignty. Postcolonialist movements such as TWAIL have often been complicit in this neglect because, even when we extend our observations about the ongoing operations of imperialism to the situation of Indigenous and Tribal peoples in the Global South and North, it is rarely in the context of recognizing contemporary Indigenous sovereignty. If Indigenous and Tribal peoples only enter TWAIL as history, then we are participants in their erasure and the myth of terra nullius. For these reasons, some scholars contend that postcolonial movements can never be in solidarity with Indigenous movements.[37] When we see how South-South extractivism thrives upon the exploitation of Indigenous lands across the Global South, it is not hard to understand why. From state enticement of extractive industries that are swarming to mine the mineral-rich transnational Tribal belt across South Asia[38] to Chinese investment

34 *Ibid.*

35 *Ibid.* at 4.

36 See, for example, recently in India, "Dalits in India Hold Protests against 'Dilution' of SC/ST Act" (2 April 2018) *Al Jazeera*, online: <www.aljazeera.com/news/2018/04/dalits-india-hold-protests-dilution-scst-act-180402082213061.html>. In Indonesia, "West Papuans Demand Independence at Indonesia rally" (1 December 2018) *Associated Press*, online: <www.apnews.com/fac1e5cac8814e3585e195fe1c65584e>; Rob Attwell, "Massacre in Nduga: Indonesia's Papuan Insurgency" (24 December 2018) *The Diplomat*, online: <https://thediplomat.com/2018/12/massacre-in-nduga-indonesias-papuan-insurgency/>. In China, "Thousands of Tibetans Protest on 60th Anniversary of Uprising against China, as State Media Defend Beijing's Rule" (11 March 2019) *Associated Press*, online: <www.scmp.com/news/china/politics/article/2189464/thousands-tibetans-protest-60th-anniversary-uprising-against>; Emily Feng, "Crackdown in Xinjiang: Where Have All the People Gone?" (5 August 2018) *Financial Times*, online: <www.ft.com/content/ac0ffb2e-8b36-11e8-b18d-0181731a0340>.

37 In the TWAIL context, see Valerie Phillips, "Indigenous Peoples and the Role of the Nation-State" (2007) 101 *Proceedings* of the *ASIL Annual Meeting* 319, as discussed and contrasted with other scholars in Bhatia, *supra* note 5 at 157–158. More generally, see Clare Land, *Decolonizing Solidarity: Dilemmas and Directions for Supporters of Indigenous Struggles* (London: Zed Books, 2003) [Land].

38 Sumedha Pal, "Dantewada Tribal Protest Enters Fifth Day against Adani Mining on Hill" (11 June 2019) *Newsclick*, online: <www.newsclick.in/dantewada-tribal-protest-enters-fifth-day-against-adani-mining-hill>; Franz J. Marty, "Project to Exploit Afghanistan's Giant Copper Deposit Languishes" (25 April 2018) *China Dialogue*, online: <www.chinadialogue.net/article/show/single/en/10577-Project-to-exploit-Afghanistan-s-giant-copper-deposit-languishes>;

in exploiting Indigenous lands in Africa and Latin America,[39] Indigenous and Tribal lands across the Global South are not the target of Western exploitation alone. Often situated on the last remaining pockets of valuable natural resources, Indigenous and Tribal communities across the South are targets of powerful extractive industries from all over the world that ruthlessly compete for access regardless of provenance. In such a context, it is all the more crucial for TWAIL to strategize in synergy with Indigenous and Tribal approaches, to end our complicity in the diverse operations of imperialism and work together to dismantle imperial structures.

Solidarity

What does it mean for TWAIL to be in solidarity with Indigenous and Tribal peoples? As discussed in the previous section, everywhere the postcolonial state has contributed to marginalizing Indigenous and Tribal cultures and traditions in different ways and degrees. The diversity of experiences of Indigenous and Tribal communities across the global South needs to be kept in mind. Experiences across Central and South America where Indigenous populations are in the majority in some areas are significantly different to those facing Tribal minorities in India, China, and Indonesia; which are different again to communities across Melanesia and Polynesia; and different again in South Africa, West Africa, among Tribal communities in the Arab world, and so on. Within each of these regions itself, the diversity of experiences is staggering. But recognizing the complicity of the postcolonial state in the suffering of Indigenous and Tribal peoples is a commonality and a starting point for solidarity. However, solidarity entails more than a rhetorical acknowledgement of complicity. If we admit that, as in the Global North, postcolonial states and peoples have also oppressed Indigenous and Tribal cultures and stolen their land and resources, what follows is the task of putting an end to oppressive practices in political and personal spheres. For TWAIL, this entails framing arguments in ways that disrupt the hierarchies that lie at the foundations of the postcolonial state. Achieving greater participation for the Global South in international law will be insufficient unless this is leveraged to

"Order Evicting Over a Million Indian Forest Dwellers Sparks Protests" (25 February 2019) *TRT World*, online: <www.trtworld.com/asia/order-evicting-over-a-million-indian-forest-dwellers-sparks-protests-24485>; Felix Padel & Samarendra Das, "Cultural Genocide and the Rhetoric of Sustainable Mining in East India" (2010) 18:3 *Contemporary South Asia* 333, DOI: <10.1080/09584935.2010.503871>.

39 See, e.g., Ruben Gonzalez-Vicente, "Mapping Chinese Mining Investment in Latin America: Politics or Market?" (March 2012) 209 *China Q* 35 as part of special issue "From the Great Wall to the New World: China and Latin America in the 21st Century"; Neil Renwick, Jing Gu & Song Hong, "China and African Governance in the Extractive Industries" (2018) 10:1 *Intl Dev Pol'y*, DOI: <10.4000/poldev.2547>; Jennifer C. Li, "China's Rising Demand for Minerals and Emerging Global Norms and Practices in the Mining Industry" (2006) Foundation for Environmental Security and Security (FESS) Working Paper No. 2.

reshape an inherently imperial discipline, so that the nature of sovereignty is itself transformed to recognize the sovereignty of Indigenous and Tribal peoples and others who remain under colonial oppression. Unless TWAIL centers contemporary independence struggles and directly confronts colonial violence as it exists in the world today, we strengthen those disciplinary powers that made colonialism possible in the first place.

In attempts to show support, solidarity, and alliance, there is a temptation to make the easy move towards inclusiveness and pluralism. When postcolonial movements endeavor to bring ongoing colonization into the conversation, the tendency is to encompass contemporary decolonization struggles within a broad framework where decolonization is one component of a larger struggle across the Global South that incorporates dimensions of race, gender, sexuality, class, caste, and other identity-based movements. Pluralism and inclusivity of this type marginalizes Indigenous and Tribal peoples and obscures the complex ways in which peoples of the Global South have participated in projects of colonization.[40] Rather than one among many concerns of interest to TWAIL, ongoing colonization and the decolonization struggles it has given rise to speak to the central aim of TWAIL. Solidarity does not require every postcolonial scholar and activist to become an expert in Indigenous and Tribal laws or focus exclusively or extensively on these matters. Rather, when speaking of colonialism and imperialism as we regularly do, an explicit awareness and articulation of the intersection with Indigenous and Tribal concerns and others who are still colonized is helpful.[41] In this way, the nuances of how colonial structures operate – their persistence, reproduction, and proliferation – may be better understood. Through discussions with Indigenous and Tribal scholars and activists, we could frame claims about the Global South in ways that do not disempower Indigenous and Tribal peoples.[42] Unless TWAIL engages with Indigenous and Tribal struggles on their own terms, we are false to our anti-imperial commitments and undercut our ability to see and address the full violence of the postcolonial state, including our own participation in this violence.

Extrapolating from Lawrence and Dua's analysis of the relationship between antiracism movements and Indigenous and Tribal struggles, an important step for postcolonial movements showing solidarity with Indigenous and Tribal peoples is explicit recognition of and respect for Indigenous and Tribal sovereignty, self-determination, and legal systems. It is profoundly unsettling to the state and its dominant cultures – whether in the Global South or North – to remap traditional territories through recovering earlier names, boundaries, cosmologies, mythologies, and laws.[43] TWAIL can participate in recognizing the inherent sovereignty of Indigenous and Tribal nations as peoples that have occupied specific

40 Lawrence & Dua, *supra* note 22 at 131.
41 *Ibid.* at 136.
42 *Ibid.* at 137.
43 *Ibid.* at 128.

territories, permanent populations, forms of governance and law, and in many instances have entered into legal relationships with other sovereigns.[44]

Recognition of Indigenous and Tribal sovereignty underpins Tuck and Yang's exhortation that "decolonization is not a metaphor", which raises several issues with regard to solidarity.[45] Tuck and Yang write against the increasing tendency to dilute and co-opt the term 'decolonization' by using it signify any struggle against oppression, as well as the philanthropic process of privileged people ostensibly 'helping' those who in actuality underwrite their privilege. From 'decolonizing methodologies', 'decolonizing wealth', and 'decolonizing the mind' to 'decolonizing the university', 'decolonizing the curriculum', and 'decolonizing the syllabus',[46] the term has been stretched to encompass any social justice struggle. Tuck and Yang point out that "decolonization is not a metonym for social justice".[47] Crucially, decolonization requires the repatriation of land. Social justice efforts dedicated to fighting racism, sexism, classism, and so on may be commendable, but calling them decolonization can also entail "moves to innocence – diversions, distractions, which relieve . . . feelings of guilt or responsibility, and conceal the need to give up land or power or privilege".[48]

The importance of Tuck and Yang's observations for TWAIL lies not so much in their calls against diluting the seriousness, meaning, and promise of actual decolonization but in its metaphorical extensions. While this is a crucial point, it is an argument readily understandable for peoples across the Global South given our own independence struggles. Despite all the failings of the postcolonial state, it is infinitely preferable to alien rule, and respecting the ongoing relevance of the original meaning of the term 'decolonization' is presumably a stance most TWAILers would easily get behind and support. Even more helpful for TWAIL is their analysis of how the ostensible pursuit of critical consciousness and social justice can itself serve as a means of holding on to privilege while obfuscating its operations. Tuck and Yang explain this by taking Jacobs's concept of "white harm reduction models" applied in the context of antiracism struggles in North America and extending it to colonizers.[49] If the goal of white harm reduction models is to reduce the harm that white supremacy has had on white people, the "colonizer harm reduction model" is to reduce the harm that colonization has on the colonizer. The latter is how Tuck and Yang understand the pedagogical project of critical consciousness and its attempts to resuscitate non-Western ontologies.[50] In 2012 they presciently observed that, in a world of increasing environmental and

44 *Montevideo Convention on the Rights and Duties of States.*

45 E. Tuck & K.W. Yang, "Decolonization Is Not a Metaphor" (2012) 1 *Decolonization: Indigeneity, Education & Society* 1 [Tuck & Yang].

46 The top six Google auto-suggestions when searching 'decolonizing' (accessed 17 June 2019).

47 Tuck & Yang, *supra* note 45 at 21.

48 *Ibid.*

49 A. Jacobs, "Undoing the Harm of White Supremacy" (Master's thesis, The Gallatin School, New York University, 2009) as quoted in Tuck & Yang, *supra* note 45 at 21.

50 *Ibid.*

economic injustice where inequality and violence proliferates, those in positions of power and wealth have an acute need for harm reduction models so they can retain their positions of privilege. Indeed, in this decade, the metonymic use of decolonization has proliferated, and momentum continues to grow.[51] Tuck and Yang warn that such models function as stopgaps and do not inherently offer any pathways that lead to decolonization.[52] The point is particularly helpful given the comparatively elite context of academic life and the opportunities it offers for accumulating privilege and wealth, both for TWAIL's own awareness of privilege and for how we understand and relate tactically to other critical movements.

To illustrate the two different understandings and uses of decolonization in the world today, Tuck and Yank compare the approaches of Césaire and Fanon with that of Freire. In Freire's most celebrated work, *Pedagogy of the Oppressed*, the categories of the oppressed and oppressor are abstracted to the extent that it is not always clear who exactly the people are who constitute each category. Additionally, throughout the text, "an innocent third category of enlightened human" is inferred,[53] who is described thus by Freire in the opening dedication: "those who suffer with [the oppressed] and fight at their side".[54] Tuck and Yang point out that it is only through making such an inference that the critical scholar is able to indulge in a "fantasy of mutuality based on sympathy and suffering".[55]

Freire situates the work of liberation in the minds of the oppressed.[56] Undoubtedly colonization transforms not only territories and bodies but also minds. However, it is only by reducing colonization to 'mental colonization' that critical scholars turn decolonization into a metaphor for any oppression, opening the way to a lack of specificity about who exactly the oppressed and oppressors are. Tuck and Yang warn that this logically leads to the misleading proposition "decolonize your mind and the rest will follow",[57] allowing critique to conveniently sidestep political demands for sovereignty. In contrast, Césaire asks: "The essential thing is to see clearly, to think clearly – that is, dangerously and to answer clearly the innocent first question: what, fundamentally, is colonization?"[58] He then points out what decolonization is not: "Neither evangelization, nor a philanthropic enterprise, nor a desire to push back the frontiers of ignorance, disease, and tyranny".[59] Césaire and Fanon recognize that colonization must be understood specifically with attention to *colonial structures* that order relationships between peoples and the world. These structures differ from place to place, and the specificity of such structures must be understood and addressed alongside the global

51 See note 46.
52 Tuck & Yang, *supra* note 45 at 21.
53 *Ibid.* at 29.
54 Paolo Freire, *Pedagogy of the Oppressed* (New York: Continuum, 2000) at 42 [Freire].
55 Tuck & Yang, *supra* note 45 at 29.
56 Freire, *supra* note 54.
57 Tuck & Yang, *supra* note 45 at 20.
58 Aimé Césaire, *Discourse on Colonialism* (New York: Monthly Review Press, 2000) at 32 [Césaire].
59 *Ibid.*

and historical patterns of colonial relations.[60] And in considering these structures, Fanon was unambiguous about the identity of the oppressed and the oppressors – the colonized and colonizers – without admittance of an innocent third category.[61] This allowed him to predict that decolonization would be chaotic and that no clean break was possible.[62] He was under no illusions à la Freire that a free mind could produce ultimate liberation for both oppressed and oppressor. Again, this is not to denigrate the value and importance of mental freedom, but rather to make the point that liberation of the mind is not the same as decolonization and does not necessarily provide a pathway to decolonization – it is necessary but not sufficient and can be used by the privileged as a harm reduction model so as to preserve their privilege and distract from actual decolonization. For TWAIL, this observation provides a warning that critical intellectuals who metaphorize decolonization may be hybridizing decolonial thought with Western critical traditions, allowing them to adopt a stance simultaneously superior to both Third World intellectuals and Western theorists. Tuck and Yang compare such intellectuals with James Fenimore Cooper's Hawkeye from *The Last of the Mohicans*: "With his critical hawk-eye, he again sees the critique better than anyone and sees the world from a loftier station. It is a fiction, just as Cooper's Hawkeye".[63]

With these caveats in mind, it is apparent that genuine solidarity with Indigenous and Tribal peoples entails a long journey of self-awareness, humility, transformation, and sacrifice, not to be lightly undertaken. Solidarity across the Third and Fourth Worlds is not a new idea. Bhatia identifies in his prologue the political and personal ties between Indigenous activists in North America and African leaders and diplomats that together helped shape the notion of the Fourth World.[64] In pointing to the desire for solidarity among oppressed peoples, Bhatia quotes Deloria, that such ambitions somehow attributed "to people of foreign lands a sophisticated knowledge of North American affairs that they did not have or feel".[65] Yet this has not stopped transnational solidarity movements throughout the 20th and 21st centuries from regularly extrapolating in precisely this way. For instance, commonalities across the Global South – some of which were undoubtedly imagined or aspirational – underlie among other things the Non-Aligned Movement, the G-77, and also TWAIL.

Taking a more recent example, the environmental justice movement has built bridges from its beginnings in poor African American communities in the United States towards declaring global solidarity among all poor peoples of color.[66] These

60 *Ibid.*; Frantz Fanon, *The Wretched of the Earth* (New York: Grove Press, 1963) [Fanon]; see discussion in Tuck & Yang, *supra* note 45 at 20.

61 Fanon, *supra* note 60.

62 *Ibid.*

63 Tuck & Yang, *supra* note 45 at 16.

64 Bhatia, *supra* note 5 at 131–134.

65 Vine Deloria, "Foreword" to George Manuel & Michael Posluns, *The Fourth World: An Indian Reality* (1974) at 5–6, as quoted in Bhatia, *supra* note 5 at 136.

66 People of Color Environmental Leadership Summit, *Principles of Environmental Justice*, 24–27 October 1991, Washington DC, online: <www.ejnet.org/ej/principles.html> (accessed 12 September 2018).

links go beyond strategic support and strength and are founded on an awareness of genuine commonalities. Given the origins of environmental justice in the heartlands of the long-industrialized United States, with its particularities of race and class, at first glance such transnational links may seem surprising. However, the connections become evident when considering the US development pathway and its indivisibility from the exploitation of labor and resources worldwide. US particularities of race and class were produced by centuries of settler colonialism, genocide of Indigenous populations, slavery and forced labor, apartheid, access to labor and resources across the globe, and environmental degradation. Hence, when the People of Color Environmental Leadership Summit formulated their Principles of Environmental Justice in 1991, they explicitly acknowledged this historical and geographical link, stating that they are

> gathered together . . . to build a national and *international movement of all peoples of color* to fight the destruction and taking of our lands and communities . . . to respect and celebrate each of our cultures, languages and beliefs about the natural world and our roles in healing ourselves . . . and, *to secure our political, economic and cultural liberation that has been denied for over 500 years of colonization and oppression*, resulting in the poisoning of our communities and land and the genocide of our peoples.[67]

That is to say, environmental justice did not begin only in the United States. It stems from centuries of environmental degradation as a result of colonization and the oppression of communities of color worldwide – communities everywhere that carried the burden of Western industrialization through loss of land, livelihood, and life so that elites could profit.[68]

Deloria correctly observes that some alliances imply a familiarity with each other that belies the truth, but that is not to say that underlying commonalities are non-existent. Thus, Bhatia deduces that "while the relationship between the Third and Fourth World and their projects should not be either assumed or rejected outright, it is similar to international law in that there is no escaping from it".[69] Uncovering potential intersections requires learning more about contradictions and mutual concerns in specific Third and Fourth World sites of struggle. Bhatia addresses intersections between TWAIL and Indigenous struggles in the global North. Dua points out how, for postcolonialists, basic curiosity can play a role in learning about the South of the North: "In India, people wondered of another place where people were also called Indian".[70] In the Global South, in

67 *Ibid.* (emphasis added).
68 Usha Natarajan, "Environmental Justice in the Global South" in S. Atapattu, C. Gonzales & S. Seck, eds., *Cambridge Handbook on Environmental Justice* (New York: Cambridge University Press, forthcoming 2020).
69 Bhatia, *supra* note 5 at 159.
70 Lawrence & Dua, *supra* note 22 at 122.

most of the world, freedom from European rule did not produce postcoloniality for many Tribal peoples, and TWAIL scholars such as Chandra and Singh examine the relationship between international law and Tribal struggles across South Asia.[71] Examples of productive alliances in the Global South between Indigenous and other communities include environmental justice movements across Southeast Asia in the 1990s. These movements united in opposition to mega-dam and other mega-infrastructure projects financed by the World Bank in Indonesia, Thailand, and the Philippines. Solidarity among peasants, workers, and Indigenous and Tribal peoples not only put an end to projects but ended up pushing towards more representative governance.[72] Many Indigenous and Tribal struggles for sovereignty continue across Southeast Asia, as do worker and peasant struggles, so the assertion here is not that these alliances culminated in ultimate success for any of the movements involved, but rather that together they achieved certain tactical goals that they may not have achieved otherwise and this was mutually beneficial.

Sustainability

Postcolonial movements that articulate culture and race without taking Indigenous and Tribal suffering into account preclude an accurate and sophisticated analysis of how culture, identity, hybridity, diaspora, and so on are shaped.[73] Similarly, for TWAIL, failing to take contemporary anticolonial struggles seriously undermines our understanding of contemporary forms of cultural differentiation, racism, and xenophobia and the ways in which these phenomena play out in various fields of international endeavor such as migration, climate change, sustainable development, and economic inequality, among other things. Indigenous and Tribal laws often shed light on how to better respond to pressing contemporary international legal issues. This chapter concludes by considering the issue of environmental change on a planetary scale, which poses governance challenges to which international law has been unable to adequately respond, arguing that insights from Indigenous and Tribal legal systems could provide productive pathways towards resolving disciplinary dilemmas.

Environmental change at the scale we are witnessing today – amid the sixth mass extinction, a changing climate, deforestation, desertification, and increasing pollution and toxicity of the air, water, and land – is uncontainable by national borders. These are global concerns and need international cooperation for adequate response. So far, international lawyers have not been able to provide solutions. Since the 1970s, an increasingly specialized field of international environmental law has been brought to bear on the aforementioned concerns,

71 See note 21.

72 M. Ford, ed., *Social Activism in Southeast Asia* (London: Routledge, 2013) [Ford]; A. Kalland & G. Persoon, eds., *Environmental Movements in Asia* (Richmond: Curzon Press, 1998) [Kalland & Persoon].

73 Lawrence & Dua, *supra* note 22 at 130.

yet each continues to steadily deteriorate.[74] International lawyers are unable to produce viable solutions to either environmental destruction or increasing inequalities of wealth and power, the two outcomes of the dominant global economic model. The discipline remains trapped in the seemingly inescapable orbit of industrial development, globalized capitalism, and myths of economic progress. While experts routinely call for a post-capitalist future, international efforts to take steps together in this direction have not worked. Rather than systemic change, environmental lawyers instead look towards the 'green economy' and 'green growth' to solve environmental crises,[75] as though capitalism could simultaneously solve the problems it creates. So-called green solutions, from biofuels to electric vehicles, from carbon offsets to carbon trading, are creative ways to fuel economic growth but do not stand up to scrutiny when it comes to environmental protection.[76]

A significant barrier to creating economic development models that are more ecologically and socially sustainable is that the rich and powerful have vested interests in preserving the status quo. The wealthy few refuse to capitulate their privilege to provide economic and environmental justice to the masses. The current development model has its origins in the European Enlightenment and is founded on limitless commodification and exploitation of the natural environment.[77] Hence, natural limits for ecosystem repair and renewal are inevitably exceeded, creating environmental crises. Lawyers, economists, and politicians all play roles in creating, maintaining, and changing economic systems. A world of increasing inequality, rapid environmental change, and widespread injustice and unrest provides the opportunity to mobilize for change if sustainable alternatives can be imagined. We have not been able to articulate such alternatives effectively, and it may be helpful to consider some of the underlying reasons for this fruitlessness.

One of the reasons international law (and other social sciences) has been unable to tackle environmental problems is that it has conceptualized the environment in a manner that is inaccurate and hubristic. The environment cannot be understood solely as the object of legal regulation. Nature provides the basis for life

74 To take the best known examples of climate change and biodiversity loss, despite these two crises being the focus of sustained international law attention since the 1990s, half of all greenhouse gases currently in the atmosphere were emitted in the last 30 years (Peter Frumhoff, "Global Warming Fact" (15 December 2014) *Union of Concerned Scientists*, online: <https://blog.ucsusa.org/peter-frumhoff/global-warming-fact-co2-emissions-since-1988-764>) and one million species are now at risk of extinction (Intergovernmental Science-Policy Platform on Biodiversity and Ecosystem Services (IPBES) Media Release (10 May 2019), online: <www.ipbes.net/news/Media-Release-Global-Assessment>.

75 See for example, under the *United Nations Framework Convention on Climate Change (UNFCCC)*, Clean Development Mechanisms and carbon trading falling under the flexible and joint-implementation mechanisms of the *Kyoto Protocol to the UNFCCC*, and REDD+ developed by UNFCCC state parties.

76 J. Hickel & G. Kallis, "Is Green Growth Possible?" (2019) *New Political Economy* 1.

77 Rist, *supra* note 13.

and underlies all knowledge. While international lawyers cannot physically separate ourselves from the environment, we nevertheless assert our occupation of a conceptual position outside it, from which we putatively observe and govern it. Instead of producing regulatory solutions, the law's ability to conceptually isolate itself from the natural world has helped create environmental catastrophes. The environment cannot be merely the subject of a discrete disciplinary specialization. Understandings about the natural world underpin and organize the entire international legal order – and indeed all other social sciences – and these assumptions need to be identified, unpacked, and radically reworked if we are to think our way out of destructive development patterns and ecological crises. International law in its entirety structures and enables environmental degradation and, without radical disciplinary change, a sub-speciality dedicated to environmental protection is doomed to failure.[78]

Contemporary disciplinary understandings of economic development and the natural environment are an inherent part of Western modernity and its antecedents in the European Enlightenment.[79] This worldview was gradually universalized through the process of European colonization and the conditions of decolonization and normalized through, among other things, international law and international institutions. The belief that everything is knowable, classifiable, and governable – all of nature within the grasp of the human hand and mind – has helped transform a unified planet into discrete sovereign territories, converted nature into exchangeable property, turned interconnected ecosystems into realms of infinite commodification and exchange, and extracted and conceptually separated an atomized human individual from the intertwined mesh of life. Modern law not only enables environmental destruction but understands the natural environment in a manner that ensures the impossibility of remedy. Hence, remedy requires an exit from the confines of Western modernity.[80]

The environment and environmentalism as understood today within international law reconfirms Western modernity as the determinant of acceptable meanings, but the extant failures of international environmental law demand alternatives. A genuinely international solution to environmental problems requires an openness to other philosophical and theoretical understandings of the relationship between nature and law. Disciplinary willingness to take seriously those understandings of nature that gauge more accurately the parameters of our ability to govern it offers us a pathway to address environmental crises and towards more sustainable ways of life. Indigenous and Tribal communities are among the most sustainable societies in the world. Additionally, Bhatia points out

78 U. Natarajan & K. Khoday, "Locating Nature: Making and Unmaking International Law" (2014) 27 *Leiden Journal of International Law* 573.

79 Rist, *supra* note 13; V. Argyrou, *The Logic of Environmentalism: Anthropology, Ecology and Postcoloniality* (New York: Berghahn, 2005) [Argyrou].

80 U. Natarajan & J. Dehm, "Where Is the Environment? Locating Nature in International Law" (2019) 3 *TWAILR Reflections*, online: <https://twailr.com/where-is-the-environment-locating-nature-in-international-law/>.

that the complexity of Indigenous peoples' relationship to international law "registers at multiple scales and defies any easy distinctions between public, private, national, domestic, foreign, and international". This complexity is particularly helpful when it comes to identifying how environmental problems are systemically embedded within the law because it undoes the presumed innateness of these distinctions and reveals how environmental destruction is enabled through particular legal constructions and configurations of public/private, national/foreign, and domestic/international distinctions.

Indigenous understandings of the relationship between nature and law challenge and stretch legal systems everywhere. Laws recognizing the rights of Mother Earth in Bolivia,[81] the legal personality of non-human entities in New Zealand,[82] the rights of Indigenous and tribal peoples to hunt protected species in the Arctic,[83] climate justice demands of sinking small island developing states,[84] international rights of nature tribunals,[85] and Mother Earth summits held alongside international environmental law summits[86] are just some examples where Indigenous and Tribal legal systems are challenging the fundamental tenets of dominant legal systems. Targeting powerful entrenched transnational and global structures of violence that have long maintained inequality and environmental degradation, the high stakes are evidenced most starkly in the increasing murder of environmental defenders worldwide.[87] Despite these risks, movements continue to grow, necessitated by environmental change looming large and inescapable.

Indigenous and Tribal laws are not always easily articulated within mainstream legal discourse or incorporable into existing systems. Oftentimes, in challenging entrenched wealth and privilege and requiring paradigmatic change they can provoke deep resistance. In the 1980s, Dianne Otto observed that international law is incommensurable with difference[88] and is more capable and comfortable with

81 *Ley de Derechos de la Madre Tierra*, online: <https://bolivia.infoleyes.com/norma/2689/ley-de-derechos-de-la-madre-tierra-071>.

82 *Te Awa Tupua (Whanganui River Claims Settlement) Act 2017*, online: <www.legislation.govt.nz/act/public/2017/0007/latest/whole.html>.

83 European Union, *Trade in Seal Products: Scope of the EU Seal Ban*, online: <http://ec.europa.eu/environment/biodiversity/animal_welfare/seals/seal_hunting.htm>.

84 Louise van Schaik, Stefano Sarris & Tobias von Lossow, "Fighting an Existential Threat: Policy Brief Small Island States Bringing Climate Change to the UN Security Council" (March 2018) *Planetary Security Initiative Policy Brief*, online: <www.clingendael.org/sites/default/files/2018-03/PSI_PB_Small_Island_States_Climate_Change_UNSC.pdf>.

85 Rights of Nature Tribunals often occur alongside major international summits: online: <http://therightsofnature.org/rights-of-nature-tribunal/>.

86 *World People's Conference on Climate Change and the Rights of Mother Earth: Building the People's World Movement for Mother Earth*, online: <https://pwccc.wordpress.com/>; Peoples' Summit on Climate Change COP20 (27 September 2014), online: <http://rio20.net/en/iniciativas/peoples%E2%80%99-summit-on-climate-change-cop20/>.

87 Global Witness, *At What Cost? Defenders Annual Report 2017*, online: <www.globalwitness.org/en-gb/campaigns/environmental-activists/>.

88 Dianne Otto, "Subalternity and International Law: The Problems of Global Community and the Incommensurability of Difference" (1996) 5:3 *Soc & Leg Stud* 337 [Otto].

understanding the world through order – homogeneous classifications, universal truths, and other trappings and reassurances of knowability. Argyrou describes environmentalism in the Western sense as one such ordering move – in fact the ultimate ordering move – involving casting the net of knowledge over all of existence ('the environment') and subjecting it to the orderly discipline of Western thought.[89] The recalcitrance of law to accommodate different worldviews is shared across the humanities and social sciences and stems from a particular culture and history in the West about how the world can be understood and knowledge produced.

In Tuck and Yang's comparison of Freire with Fanon, they also identify the same worldview and its potential limitations.[90] For Freire, because liberation can be gained through mental effort, it is available to both oppressed and oppressor by virtue of the human mind. Tuck and Yang point out that Freire is able to attribute this kind of liberative power to the human mind and to critical consciousness only because he writes without history, without reference to specific oppressors or oppressed, only abstract categories. In contrast, Fanon recognized the postcolonial condition "as already over determined by the violence of the colonizer and unresolved in its possible futures".[91] Eerily prescient about the aftermath of liberation struggles across the Global South, he knew that this liberation could be incomplete and open ended. Tuck and Yang point out that these two approaches stem from two different worldviews. Freire's understanding of liberation is an inheritance of Plato's Cave, from which the thinking man emerges alone from the dark cave of ignorance into the light of critical consciousness,[92] whereas Fanon is more closely allied with a tradition in postcolonial, critical race, and black feminist thought that looks for freedom within the darkness itself. Tuck and Yang allude to the nature of this darkness through Audre Lorde's evocative portrayal of this enigmatic yet inexplicably familiar place:

> These places of possibility within ourselves are dark because they are ancient and hidden; they have survived and grown strong through darkness. Within these deep places, each one of us holds an incredible reserve of creativity and power, of unexamined and unrecorded emotion and feeling. The woman's place of power within each of us is neither white nor surface; it is dark, it is ancient, and it is deep.[93]
>
> . . . The white fathers told us, I think therefore I am; and the black mothers in each of us – the poet – whispers in our dreams, I feel therefore I can be free.[94]

89 Argyrou, *supra* note 79.
90 Tuck & Yang, *supra* note 45 at 20.
91 *Ibid.*
92 *Ibid.*
93 Audre Lorde, *Sister Outsider: Essays and Speeches* (Trumansburg, NY: Crossing Press, 1984) at 36–37 [Lorde].
94 *Ibid.* at 38.

For Lorde, knowledge production need not be an act of control over the world. Freedom is not something that all human minds can generate through critical consciousness. Rather, it is felt and particular to experience, not a truth to be grasped but a hidden and unknowable depth to be noticed.

International law is shaped by its European antecedents, but other worldviews may understand the sources and means through which knowledge is created differently, thus producing very different understandings of law and its functions. John Borrows provides an example in 'Earthbound', in which he describes, builds on, and consciously shapes an evolving legal tradition that both directly and indirectly addresses the role of law in understanding and responding to environmental change. Borrows points out that an ethic of care and reconciliation with the earth, and acknowledgement of inherent limits of the natural world, permeates the laws, sciences, myths, and stories of many Indigenous and Tribal cultures.[95] From this background and context, he is able to find in the laws of nature analogous sources for human laws and policies, looking to the sun, the river, and the grass, among other things. The sun, as the source of all life and growth, provides ceaseless and reliable bounty and benefit without discrimination. It is revivifying and shows us sustainability.[96] The river collects and channels nutrients and provides a free flow of support to all that surrounds it, creating deltas where abundance and richness of life gather. When analogized to human action, the river is love, as a binding legal obligation to create conditions for others to gather and thrive in their social ecosystems.[97] The grass shows us the potentiality and fulfillment of the life force, providing lessons of mindfulness and purpose beyond the immediate struggle of people with their surroundings.[98] Borrows points out that the experience of dire poverty, with all of its suffering and misfortune, may also have the virtue of bringing people closer to the earth, exposing them to the elements, revealing the existence of natural laws that humans cannot control. Through displacing humans from the jurisprudential center of the universe, it is possible to more fully sense and learn from the natural environment, our place as part of it, and the laws that govern it.[99]

Contemporary environmental crises are the consequence of industrial development and globalized capitalism as well as the colonialism, genocide, slavery, apartheid, and racial discrimination that underpin them. These crises confront international lawyers with the systemic environmental and social injustice we help create and maintain. They demand an acceptance that we were mistaken in thinking we could control the natural environment. They necessitate that we transcend the confines of Western modernity and embrace instead other narratives about our relationship with the natural world that are less destructive and

95 John Borrows, "Earthbound: Indigenous Resurgence and Environmental Reconciliation" (publication forthcoming, on file with author) at 1–3.

96 *Ibid.* at 5–6.

97 *Ibid.* at 6–7.

98 *Ibid.* at 7–8.

99 *Ibid.* at 9–11.

more accurately estimate human ability to regulate it. We need to make disciplinary space and learn to be comfortable with the different, the unknown, and the unknowable. A consideration of how to live sustainably with each other and with nature takes us back to the beginning, to recognition. First, recognition that peoples across the Global South and North caused and continue to be complicit in the suffering of Indigenous and Tribal peoples. Second, to stop participating in and reproducing this suffering requires working in synergy with Indigenous and Tribal communities to dismantle structures of violence including the modern state. Third, such a dismantling entails recognition of Indigenous and Tribal sovereignty and self-determination claims on their own terms. Finally, environmental crises provoke a recognition of our own failure to understand the world and our place in it, necessitating a turn to some of the most sustainable cultures in the world – targets of our fear and oppression and survivors of some of the most extreme forms of racism, impoverishment, and disenfranchisement – in search of knowledge.

Perspectives from the Global North and South

Part 1

International

4 Mastery and gratitude

Development aid and the colonial condition in Palestine

*Reem Bahdi and Mudar Kassis**

Introduction

Mastery and gratitude are elements of a scheme which follows a certain logic of inversion where "[s]ocial-symbolic violence at its purest appears as its opposite . . .".[1] Development aid replaces international legal obligations as the matrix through which the Global North's relationships with Palestine are understood and practiced. Instead of respecting Palestinian's equal rights to freedom, self-determination, and security, northern states give Palestine development aid. In the process, Palestine and Palestinians are posited as recipients of charity rather than bearers of rights, and the debt relationship or the question of who owes whom what and why is inverted. Palestinians are perceived less and less as a people living under occupation who can claim rights which impose obligations on the international community. Instead, Palestinians come to be perceived as a people who should be grateful to northern states for their generosity. In the process, through a toolset of "[a]dministrative procedures . . . [which] are the very material sites in which international disciplines are at work",[2] northern development agencies that dispense and manage aid assume control over Palestinian priorities and decision-making even as aid policy and aid practitioners insist that they value and promote local control and leadership.

* We are grateful to Suzanne McMurphy, Jamey Essex, Sujith Xavier, Jeffrey G. Hewitt, Jeremy Wildeman, Claire Mummé, and Christopher Waters for helpful comments and discussions. We are also grateful to participants at the Law and Society meeting in 2018 and the International Studies Association in 2019 who also offered helpful comments and suggestions. We have written about the decolonizing potential of aid programming and remain committed to the possibility that aid can have positive impacts if it is understood as a form of solidarity rather than charity. Other facets of our experiences with Karamah are laid out in Reem Bahdi & Mudar Kassis, "Decolonization, Dignity and Development Aid: A Judicial Education Experience in Palestine" (2016) 37:11 *Third World Q* [Bahdi & Kassis: Decolonization], and Bahdi & Kassis, "Institutional Trustworthiness, Transformative Judicial Education and Transitional Justice: A Palestinian Experience" in Quinn et al., eds., *The Preconditions of Transitional Justice* (Cham, Switzerland: Palgrave, 2020) 185–215 [Bahdi & Kassis: Trustworthiness].

1 Salvoj Žižek, *Violence: Six Sideways Reflections* (New York: Picador, 2008) at 36 [Žižek].

2 Luis Eslava & Sundhya Pahuja, "Between Resistance and Reform: TWAIL and the Universality of International Law" (2011) 3:1 *Trade, L & Development* 103 at 109 [Eslava & Pahuja].

Palestinians have come to rely heavily on aid donations from northern states. This aid, the very thing that was supposed to help them build a state and improve their living standards, has contributed to ongoing Palestinian oppression. Aid has overtaken international law as the main paradigm through which donor states engage with Palestine and Palestinians. Drawing in part on our experiences as co-directors of Karamah, a judicial education initiative in Palestine supported by the Canadian International Development Agency (CIDA), we outline the material and symbolic consequences of aid and identify the techniques embedded in aid structures that have helped produce the present state of affairs. When it was introduced in 2005, Karamah was Canada's largest CIDA-supported judicial education project in the world and the largest of any CIDA-supported project in the Middle East.[3]

Our goal is to demonstrate how imperial actors can navigate international institutions, how colonial impulses are driven through international relations, and why decolonization of international institutions and relations remain significant aspects of the global struggle for dignity and equality. We analyze donor coordination of Palestinian aid priorities alongside the day-to-day management of aid projects implementation through the logic model as two sites that facilitate control over Palestinians without producing sustainable results to the benefit the Palestinian people. Both sites give a glimpse into the minute techniques embedded in development aid that have advanced the political and economic interests of Israel and donor states at the expense of Palestinian rights. We situate this work within TWAIL praxis which calls for an examination of the ways in which international law, both in its presence and its silences, "unfolds on the mundane and quotidian plane through sites and objects which appear unrelated to the international".[4]

Aid to Palestine from northern states

Palestinians have become one of the most aid-dependent people in the world. Over the last 25 years, donations from donor countries to the West Bank and Gaza grew and formed an economic pattern (see Figure 4.1 below): standing at $79 per capita in 1993; jumping to $200 per capita in 1994; averaging $411 per capita during the years 1994–2017, with a peak of $767 per capita in 2009; and decreasing to $451 per capita in 2017. Development aid constituted around one-fifth of the gross domestic product (GDP) per capita, averaging $1,904 over the years 1994–2017.[5]

Donors dispense development aid to help address humanitarian needs, build Palestinian state institutions, advance access to justice, improve living conditions,

3 This project ran from 2005 to 2013 and had a budget of approximately $8 million with just over half contributed by CIDA and the rest representing cash and in-kind contributions from project participants.

4 Eslava & Pahuja, *supra* note 3 at 109.

5 World Bank, "West Bank and Gaza" (2018) *World Bank*, online: <https://data.worldbank.org/country/west-bank-and-gaza> [World Bank].

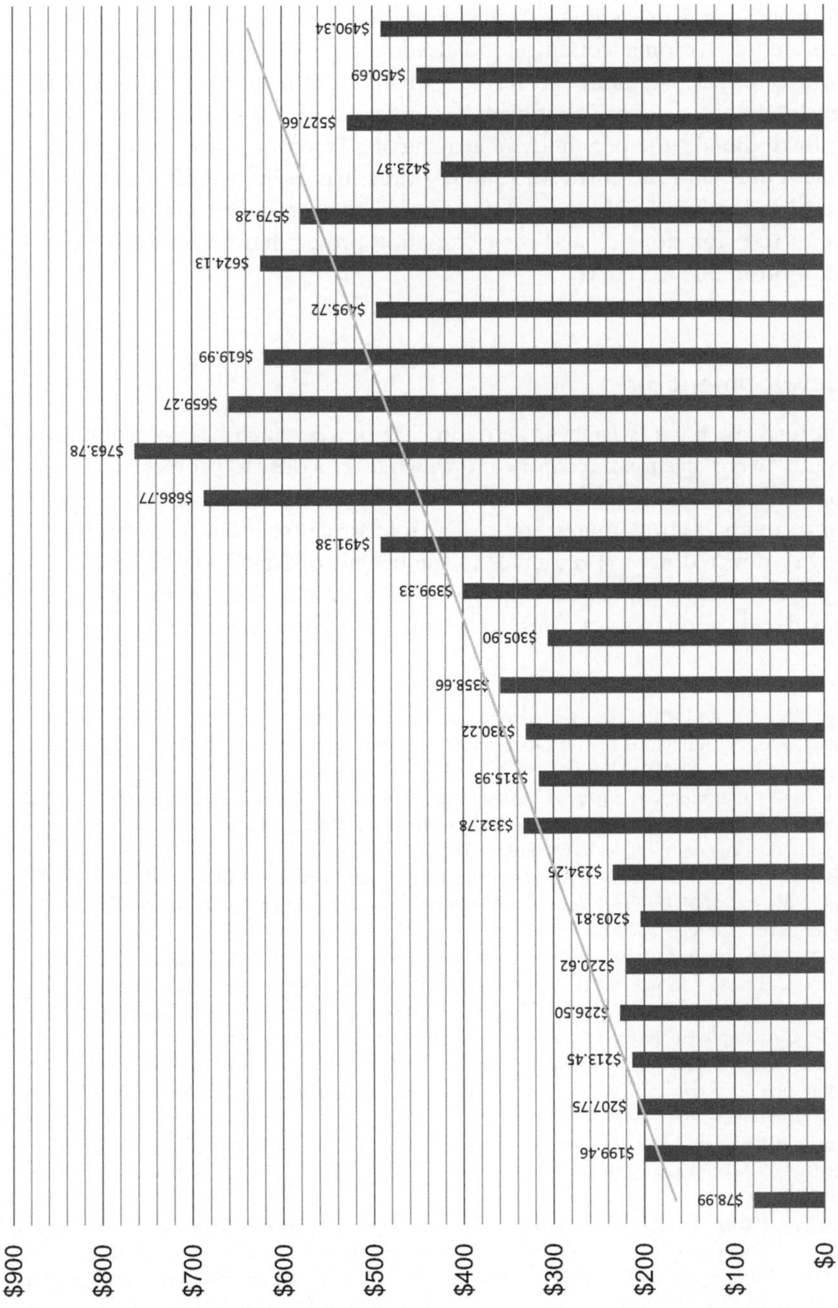

Figure 4.1 West Bank and Gaza net Official Development Assistance received per capita (current US$)

Data source: World Bank Group, 2020.

ensure security, encourage economic prosperity, and promote human rights – all important goals purportedly aimed at helping Palestinians build better lives and advancing peace with Israel.[6] However, foreign aid has not achieved its promise of assisting Palestinians to live better lives or advancing peace. Development aid has furthered the colonial condition in Palestine, a state of affairs marked by foreign control of people, land, and resources to the detriment of local prosperity and development. As aid to Palestinians has increased, their living conditions have drastically declined,[7] the possibility of arriving at a Palestinian state is decreasing, and Israel's hold on Palestinian land and resources has tightened.[8] Further, Palestinian civil and political rights have deteriorated,[9] social cohesion within Palestine has begun to break down,[10] and the occupation project has become less expensive if not profitable for Israel.[11]

International law, peace through negotiations, and development aid

International law regards Israel as an occupying power which has control but no sovereignty over Palestinian territory and which owes a duty to protect the civilian population. Israel, however, flouts those duties. It exercises control over Palestinian lives through its army, courts, and civilian infrastructure.[12] Israel has disproportionately re-directed natural resources to the benefit of Israelis over Palestinians. It has contributed to the de-development of Palestine in part by thwarting the Palestinian education system,[13] undermining Palestinian entrepreneurship and

6 Sahar Taghdisi Rad, "Political Economy of Aid in Conflict: An Analysis of Pre- and Post-Intifada Donor Behaviour in the Occupied Palestinian Territories" (2015) *Stability: Intl J Security & Dev* 1, DOI: <10.5334/sta.fl> at 11 [Taghdisi Rad].

7 OCHA, " Fragmented Lives: Humanitarian Overview 2015" (June 2016) *United Nations Office for the Coordination of Humanitarian Affairs*, online: <www.ochaopt.org/humanitarian-overview-2015> [OCHA 2016].

8 UNGA, "Situation of Human Rights in the Palestinian Territories Occupied since 1967" (16 October 2016) *OHCHR*, online: <www.ohchr.org/Documents/Countries/PS/A_71_554_en.pdf> [UNGA 2016].

9 *Ibid.* See also Amnesty International, *Israel and Occupied Palestinian Territories 2015/2016* (London: Press Report, n.d.), *Amnesty International*, online: <www.amnesty.org/en/countries/middle-east-and-north-africa/israel-and-occupied-palestinian-territories/report-israel-and-occupied-palestinian-territories/> [Amnesty International].

10 Waleed Al-Modallal, "Transforming Conflict and Building Cohesion through Identity Conference" in *Identity Conflict and Its Impact on Social Cohesion, Palestine Model* (Kyoto: Al-Modallal WH, 2013) [Al-Modallal].

11 Liora Sion, "The Problem with International Aid to Palestine" (20 March 2018), *+972*, online: <https://972mag.com/the-problem-with-international-aid-to-palestine/133930/> [Sion].

12 B'Tselem, 2016b, "Reality Check: Almost Fifty Years of Occupation" (5 June 2016) *B'Tselem*, online: <www.btselem.org/publications/201606_reality_check> [B'Tselem 2016b].

13 UNDP, "Development for Empowerment: The 2014 Palestine Human Development Report" (2015) *UNDP*, online: <www.undp.org/content/dam/papp/docs/Publications/UNDP-papp-research-PHDR2015Education.pdf> [UNDP].

economic development through the control of movement of people and goods within and outside of Palestinian centres,[14] and assuming direct and/or de facto control over Palestinian holy sites and tourist attractions.[15] The Israeli government routinely violates Palestinian individual and collective rights by imposing a sophisticated pass system and series of checkpoints or road blocks[16] and arbitrarily detaining and/or torturing Palestinians.[17] It has subjected Palestinians to military violence that has included the use of chemical and explosive weaponry on civilian populations.[18] It has frustrated Palestinian attempts to claim their own state by building a series of roads, settlements, walls, and enclosures that divide Palestinians from each other and make it virtually impossible to carve out contiguous borders necessary for statehood[19] and expropriating resources.[20] Moreover, the Israeli military exercises jurisdiction over Palestinian daily life through Israeli military orders, and Israel's civil administrative infrastructure directly or indirectly regulates all manners of Palestinian existence including, *inter alia*, family life, freedom of movement, and access to water and other vital resources while limiting Palestinian judicial jurisdiction[21] Israel, in short, acts as a typical colonizer, expanding into coveted territories, taking resources, and exploiting or oppressing people whom it considers outsiders or foreigners to its own body politic.[22]

Israel has pursued its colonial policies notwithstanding the fact that it entered into peace negotiations with the Palestine Liberation Organization (PLO) in 1993. This agreement led to a series of accords that were supposed to lead to two

14 Sara Roy, "Palestinian Society and Economy: The Continued Denial of Possibility" (2001) *J Palestine Stud.*, online: <www.jstor.org/stable/10.1525/jps.2001.30.4.5?seq=1#page_scan_tab_contents> [Roy].

15 Rami Kassis, "Tourism and Human Rights in Palestine" (2013) *Tourism Watch*, online: <www.tourism-watch.de/node/2028> [Kassis].

16 B'Tselem, "Restrictions on Movement" (11 November 2017) *B'Tselem*, online: <www.btselem.org/freedom_of_movement> [B'Tselem 2017].

17 Amnesty International, *supra* note 10. See also Human Rights Watch, "Palestine: Israeli Police Abusing Detained Children" (2016) *Human Rights Watch Organization Website*, online: <www.hrw.org/news/2016/04/11/palestine-israeli-police-abusing-detained-children> [Human Rights Watch].

18 UNGA, "Report of the United Nations Fact-Finding Mission on the Gaza Conflict" (22 September 2009) *OHCHR*, online: <www2.ohchr.org/english/bodies/hrcouncil/docs/12session/A-HRC-12-48.pdf> [UNGA 2009]. See also Reem Bahdi, "Phosphorus and Stone: Operation Cast Lead, Israeli Military Courts and International Law as Denial-Maintenance" (2014) *Criminal Just Intl Soc'y* 21 [Bahdi 2014].

19 Mehran Kamrava, *The Impossibility of Palestine: History, Geography, and the Road Ahead* (New Haven: Yale University Press, 2016) [Kamrava].

20 Ibrahim Matar, "The Quiet War: Land Expropriation in the Occupied Territories" (1997) *Palestine – Israel J Politics, Economics & Culture*, online: <www.pij.org/details.php?id=476> [Matar].

21 Sharon Weill, "The Judicial Arm of the Occupation: The Israeli Military Courts in the Occupied Territories" (2007) 89:866 *Intl Rev Red Cross* 395, online: <www.icrc.org/en/doc/assets/files/other/irrc_866_weill.pdf> [Weill].

22 Elia Zureik, *Israel's Colonial Project in Palestine: Brutal Pursuit* (New York: Routledge, 2016) [Zureik]. See also Ania Loomba, *Colonialism/Postcolonialism* (New York: Routledge, 2015) [Loomba].

states, Israel and Palestine, living together side by side in peace. Over 25 years later, it has become increasingly clear that this peace process will not bear fruit. One of the main barriers has been Israel's insistence that the negotiations should be defined by "the situation on the ground". The following exchange between Israeli and Palestinian negotiators (UD and SA, respectively) took place at a 2008 meeting over territory.

UD: As you know, our guiding principles are UNSC Res. 242, the need for boundaries that can provide security for Israel, and we're talking about the situation on the ground, as per Pres. Bush's letter.
SA: Do you mean the situation as it was then, or now?
UD: Reality now. . . . But we're not going to argue. We can't change reality on the ground. We don't see the 1967 border as a reference, first because we don't even know exactly where the line is.
SA: We have all the maps that were signed by *you*.
UD: But that wasn't exactly the line on the ground.
SA: If not the 1967 line, then what is your reference?
UD: We said already, the situation on the ground.[23]

Given its already almost total control and ability to disrupt Palestinian land, people, and resources, Israel has had virtually unfettered discretion to define "the situation on the ground" and has been dedicated to creating facts altering this "situation". Consider, for example, the statements made by Teddy Kolleck, former mayor of Jerusalem, in describing his time in office. Kolleck, a mayor who professed commitment to fairness and multiculturalism, makes clear that Arabs and Jews would be treated differently for a political purpose:

> We said things without meaning them, and we didn't carry them out, we said over and over that we would equalize the rights of the Arabs to the rights of the Jews in the city-empty talk. . . . Never have we given them a feeling of being equal before the law. [As mayor of Jerusalem, I] nurtured nothing and built nothing [for the Arabs]. For Jewish Jerusalem I did something in the past 25 years. For [Arab] East Jerusalem? Nothing! What did I do? Nothing! Sidewalks? Nothing. Cultural Institutions? Not one. Yes, we installed a sewage system for them and improved the water supply. Do you know why? Do you think it was for their good, for their welfare? Forget it! There were some cases of cholera there, and the Jews were afraid that they would catch it, so we installed [a] sewage and a water system against cholera.[24]

23 *The Palestine Papers Meeting Minutes: 1st Meeting on Territory* (West Jerusalem: Palestine Papers, 2008), online: Al Jazeera Investigations <www.ajtransparency.com/en/projects/thepalestinepapers/201218231827437381.html> at 2–3 of the document.

24 Ardi Imseis, "Facts on the Ground: An Examination of Israeli Municipal Policy in East Jerusalem" (2000) 15:5 *Am U Intl L Rev* 1039 at 1040 [Imseis].

Ardi Imseis chronicles how Israel pursued a policy of creating "facts on the ground" to ensure that negotiations over the status of Jerusalem favoured Israel. Facts on the ground would "be presented in the future negotiations as a geographic fact"[25] to define the baselines for negotiation and effectively render certain topics unnegotiable because the facts would declare them a *fait accompli*.

In similar fashion, the Israeli government set upon a path of appropriating Palestinian land located within the 1967 borders, also known as "the Green Line", through a series of measures including, inter alia, building the wall, moving settlers into Palestinian lands, funding settlements, and creating an elaborate network of roads and rail systems that connect settlements and settlers to Israel while simultaneously excluding and dividing Palestinians.[26] As of 2017, a total of more than 620,000 Israeli citizens reside in the West Bank[27] in settlements that constitute some 10% of the West Bank area.[28]

The current situation features a prolonged Israeli occupation, together with Israeli plans to annex more territory, further divide Palestinians from each other, and "legalize" the illegal annexation of East Jerusalem and the Golan Heights to Israel. Palestinians do not have much left with which to negotiate, and their circumstances are hindered even further by the Trump administration throwing its full political support behind Israel. Steps undertaken recently by this administration include supporting Israeli plans of annexation and recognizing Jerusalem as the capital of Israel while ignoring Palestinian claims to that city. On December 6, 2017, President Trump announced:

> today we finally acknowledge the obvious: that Jerusalem is Israel's capital. . . . This is nothing more or less than a recognition of reality. It is also the right thing to do. It's something that has to be done.[29]

Trump's announcement relied explicitly on the "situation on the ground" as justification for the controversial move.

Trying to counter Israel's imperialism and its ability to create the "situation on the ground", Palestinians have appealed to international law through bodies such as the International Criminal Court, the General Assembly, the Security Council, and various United Nations agencies and bodies to recognize Palestinian statehood and help limit Israeli and, more recently, American violations

25 *Ibid.* at 1049.

26 B'Tselem 2016a, "'The [Green] Line Is Long Gone': Gilo to Be Expanded, Creating Annexable Bloc That Includes Cremisan Valley and Extends to Har Gilo" (5 January 2016) *B'Tselem*, online: <www.btselem.org/jerusalem/20150105_expansion_of_gilo_settlement> [B'Tselem 2016a].

27 B'Tselem, 2019b, "Statistics on Settlements and Settler Population" (16 January 2019) *B'Tselem*, online: <www.btselem.org/settlements/statistics> [B'Tselem 2019b].

28 B'Tselem, 2019a, "Settlements" (16 January 2019) *B'Tselem*, online: <www.btselem.org/settlements> [B'Tselem 2019a].

29 Mark Landler, "Trump Recognizes Jerusalem as Israel's Capital and Orders U.S. Embassy to Move" (6 December 2017) *New York Times*, online: <www.nytimes.com/2017/12/06/world/middleeast/trump-jerusalem-israel-capital.html> [Landler].

against Palestinian collective and individual rights.[30] For Palestinians, the appeal to international law and international institutions is not an alternative to foreign aid. On the contrary, foreign aid and appeals to the international community to recognize Palestinian rights represent complementary, equitable, and necessary strategies.

On this view, Palestinians require liberation, and liberation is not a status to be negotiated with Israel, the very country that benefits most from Palestine's continued economic, political, and military subjugation. Aid, for its part, represents a fiduciary duty or, alternatively, a necessary evil, extended to Palestinians by the international community while Palestinians continue to endure an occupation that has been tolerated and sometimes supported by northern States. Israel's conduct, including its violent military campaigns, have forced Palestinians to seek protection from international institutions.

A 2016 report by the State of Palestine outlined the Palestinian view on aid, international institutions, and negotiations towards a two-state solution. It stressed that Palestinians are forced by Israel's creation of facts on the ground to go outside of the negotiation framework and seek international recognition of Palestinian sovereignty. The report also stressed that Palestinians need aid only because they are forced to live under occupation, colonialism, and limits on their right to self-determination, a situation that the international community has tolerated:

> At a certain point, the threshold for a viable two-state solution will be breached, potentially giving way to an apartheid solution where millions of Palestinians live without basic human and democratic rights. To avert such a catastrophe, we need to replace Israel's "facts on the ground" with the Palestinian State as a "fact on the international stage". This is the path forward that would transform vicious into virtuous circles. If sufficient international pressure were applied, the consequent of the Israeli occupation would not only unleash rapid economic growth and a jobs boom throughout Palestine but bring a swift end to aid dependency. These multiple challenges cannot be met by Palestine alone. If the two-state solution is to remain viable, concerted international action is required to reverse colonial Israel's annexation agenda and, together with the Palestinian Government, restore fiscal stability.[31]

30 On 28 September 2018, Palestine instituted proceedings at the International Court of Justice against the United States in response to President Donald Trump's announcement that his administration would recognize Jerusalem as the capital of Israel. The court is currently considering the issue of its jurisdiction and the admissibility of Palestine's application. Updates on the proceedings can be found on the court's website. See International Court of Justice, *Relocation of the United States Embassy to Jerusalem (Palestine v. United States of America)*, Latest Developments, online: <www.icj-cij.org/en/case/176>.

31 State of Palestine, "AHLC Report" (September 2016) *Local Aid Coordination Secretariat*, online: <www.lacs.ps/documentsShow.aspx?ATT_ID=29904> [State of Palestine 2016].

When negotiations between Palestinians and Israelis broke down in 2009, Palestinians stepped up their appeals to international institutions. The United Nations commissioned reports in 2009 and 2014 to investigate violations of international law in the Gaza Strip by Israel and Hamas. In 2012, the General Assembly raised Palestine's status to "Non-member Observer State", which led to Palestine's recognition of the jurisdiction of the International Criminal Court and vice versa.[32] In 2016, the Palestinian Authority (PA) advised donors that "Palestine's drive to enlist international support and increase pressure on Israel will intensify".[33]

For their part, northern states such as the United States and Canada met Palestine's international campaign with disapproval. In 2009, for example, American officials placed direct diplomatic and financial pressure on United Nations officials to refrain from criticizing Israel or advancing Palestinian self-determination.[34] Then, the United States stopped paying its share to the United Nations Relief and Works Agency for Palestine Refugees in the Near East and, eventually, halted all funding to Palestinian government and civil society organizations. When UNESCO admitted Palestine as a full member state in 2011, the Obama administration responded by withholding its financial contributions to the agency, thereby depriving it of 22% of its total budget.[35] The US administration has also

32 Office of the Prosecutor, International Criminal Court, "Report on Preliminary Examination Activities" (2015) *Office of the Prosecutor, International Criminal Court*, online: <www.icc-cpi.int//Pages/item.aspx?name=otp-rep-pe-activities-2015> [Office of the Prosecutor]. See also State of Palestine, "Declaration Accepting the Jurisdiction of the International Criminal Court" (31 December 2014), online: <www.icc-cpi.int/iccdocs/PIDS/press/Palestine_A_12-3.pdf> [State of Palestine 2014] and Rome Statute of the International Criminal Court (17 July 1998), *Rome: International Criminal Court*, online: <www.icc-cpi.int/nr/rdonlyres/ea9aeff7-5752-4f84-be94-0a655eb30e16/0/rome_statute_english.pdf> [*Rome Statute* 1998]: "On 1 January 2015, the Government of Palestine lodged a declaration under article 12(3) of the Rome Statute accepting the jurisdiction of the International Criminal Court (ICC) over alleged crimes committed "in the occupied Palestinian territory, including East Jerusalem, since June 13, 2014". On 2 January 2015, the Government of Palestine acceded to the Rome Statute by depositing its instrument of accession with the UN Secretary-General. The Rome Statute entered into force on 1 April 2015. Most recently, the ICC-Pre-Trial Chamber 1 issued an order setting the procedure and schedule relating to the submission of observations about the court's territorial jurisdiction. See International Criminal Court, Press Release: ICC Pre-trial Chamber Invites Palestine, Israel, Interested States and Others to Submit Observations (28 January 2020), online: <www.icc-cpi.int/Pages/item.aspx?name=pr1512>.

33 State of Palestine 2016, *supra* note 32.

34 Wikileaks, "Ambassador Rice's May 4 Telecons with Secretary General on Gaza Board of Inquiry Report" (25 May) *Wikileaks*, online: <https://wikileaks.org/plusd/cables/09USUNNEWYORK460_a.html> [Ambassador Rice].

35 Colum Lynch, "UNESCO Votes to Admit Palestine: US Cuts Off Funding" Press Report (2011) *Washington Post*, online: <www.washingtonpost.com/world/national-security/unesco-votes-to-admit-palestine-over-us-objections/2011/10/31/gIQAMleYZM_story.html?utm_term=.c02740135547> [Lynch]. See also Julian Pecquet, "Kerry Enlists Netanyahu in Congressional Fight Over UNESCO Funding" (2015) *Al-Monitor*, online: <www.al-monitor.com/pulse/originals/2015/12/kerry-netanyahu-congress-fight-unesco-funding.html> [Pecquet].

vetoed relevant Security Council resolutions with the exception of SC Resolution 2334, which passed on December 23, 2016, and threatened other international bodies with reprisals should they follow UNESCO in recognizing Palestinian sovereignty. A handful of other states – mostly northern – voted against similar General Assembly resolutions and some boycotted the 2014 meeting of High Contracting Parties to the Geneva Convention.[36]

At the same time that they have disapproved of Palestinian appeals to international law and bodies, northern donors have backed Israel's insistence that Palestinian sovereignty is to be achieved through negotiations, not by seeking international recognition. In other words, Palestinians must negotiate their rights and freedoms with Israel, the very country that is responsible for their violation, rather than seek recognition of it through traditional legal and international mechanisms.[37] Palestinian liberation, self-determination, security, and equality are thus conditioned on "convincing" the Israeli government of its value through a negotiation process that has not only given Israel the opportunity to further Palestinian's colonial condition but that, in reality, has ceased to exist.

These attempts have failed to end Palestinian appeals to international law and bodies.[38] After all, the Palestinian pursuit of self-determination dates back at least to World War I. It is not easy to quell a century-long struggle, particularly when the Palestinian people generally enjoy political and diplomatic support from states of the Global South which, given their history, understand colonialism all too well, can empathize with the collective quest for statehood, and recognize the social, political, economic, and personal costs of living under occupation.[39]

Attempting to cut Palestinians off from the international community legally and institutionally while offering aid constructs and declares a particular discursive

36 Matthew Happold, "The Conference of High Contracting Parties to the Fourth Geneva Convention" (2001) *YB Intl Humanitarian L* 4, DOI: <10.1017/S138913590000091X> [Happold]. See also Global Affairs Canada, "Canada Strongly Opposes Decision to Convene Anti-Israel Conference in Geneva" Press Report (2014) *Global Affairs Canada*, online: <www.international.gc.ca/media/aff/news-communiques/2014/12/16b.aspx?lang=eng> [Global Affairs Canada 2014] and Mission of the United States Geneva Switzerland, "U.S. Statement on the Conference of High Contracting Parties to the Fourth Geneva Convention" (17 December 2014), *U.S. Mission to International Organizations in Geneva* [Mission of the United States Geneva Switzerland].

37 Office of the United Nations Special Coordinator for the Middle East Peace Process, "Report to the Ad-Hoc Liaison Committee" (2016), online: <www.lacs.ps/documentsShow.aspx?ATT_ID=29843> [Office of the UN]. For example, on 1 July 2016, the Middle East Quartet issued its report outlining key threats to the two-state solution and offering recommendations for creating the conditions for an eventual return to meaningful negotiations. The report reiterated that a negotiated two-state outcome is the only way to achieve an enduring peace that meets Israeli security needs and Palestinian aspirations for statehood and sovereignty, ends the occupation that began in 1967, and resolves all permanent status issues.

38 Wikileaks, "U.S. Congress Officially Confirms Blocking Palestinian Aid, Explains Reasoning" (4 October) *Wikileaks*, online: <https://wikileaks.org/gifiles/docs/44/4408402_-os-us-pna-israel-gv-econ-u-s-congress-officially-confirms.html> [U.S. Congress].

39 Luis Eslava, Michael Fakhri & Vasuki Nesiah, eds., *Bandung: Global History, and International Law, Critical Pasts and Pending Futures* (New York: Cambridge University Press, 2017) [Eslava et al.].

landscape which fundamentally recasts the relationship between northern donor states and Palestine. When viewed through the lens of international law, northern states owe Palestinians significant duties. These duties are rooted in various sources, including international humanitarian law, and their precise range is the subject of significant scholarly analysis. Then, the International Court of Justice clarified the nature and extent of the duties owed to Palestinians by states to the 1949 Geneva Convention Relative to the Protection of Civilian Persons in Time of War. On July 9, 2004, the court determined by majority vote that the wall built by Israel cut deep into Palestinian territory in violation of international law and outlined the basic obligation of all states in response to Israel's violations.[40] The court indicated that all states must not "recognize the illegal situation created by the wall", refrain from rendering "aid or assistance in maintaining the situation" created by the construction of the wall, ensure that impediments to Palestinians' self-determination created by the wall is brought to an end, and ensure that Israel respects its full range of obligations under the Geneva Convention.

However, northern states do not consider their obligations as High Contracting Parties when they deliver their aid programming to Palestine. Instead, they have reconfigured themselves and their relationship to Palestine through the lens of development aid. Through this recasting, northern states allow themselves the illusion that they are charitable actors who extended generosity to Palestine rather than High Contracting Parties that owe duties to a nation under occupation. As a corollary, the charity paradigm perpetuates an image of Palestine and Palestinians as a backwards people in need of technical assistance rather than liberation. Mitt Romney's famous declaration that culture and providence explain the difference between Israeli GDP and Palestinian GDP reflects the enduring negative stereotypes of Palestinians and recalls the importance of imagination in the colonial projects of the Global North.[41] This image has become – or, more accurately, continues to be – a myth that assumes away occupation and its well-documented, devastating impacts on Palestinians, including their economy. Occupation's erasure explains Palestinian economic and other limitations as essential, fatal, and inherent flaws and also further the narrative of the master's generosity to an economically and culturally backwards people.

This generosity narrative constitutes part of a larger story about development aid from the Global North to the Global South which has helped justify and hide the exploitation that marks the relationship between richer and poorer nations in this world. As anthropologist Jason Hickel puts it:

> In the mainstream narrative of international development peddled by institutions from the World Bank to the UK's Department of International Development, the history of colonialism is routinely erased. According to the

40 *Legal Consequences of the Constructions of a Wall in the Occupied Palestinian Territory*, Advisory Opinion, [2004] ICJ Rep 136.

41 Brett LoGiurato, "Palestinians Are Calling Mitt Romney a 'Racist' over His Latest Overseas Gaffe" (2012) *Business Insider*, online: <www.businessinsider.com/mitt-romney-israel-economy-culture-racism-2012-7> [LoGiurato].

> official story, developing countries are poor because of their own internal problems, while western countries are rich because they worked hard, and upheld the right values and policies. And because the west happens to be further ahead, its countries generously reach out across the chasm to give "aid" to the rest – just a little something to help them along.[42]

This "little something to help them along" plays a powerful role in perpetuating hierarchies and shaping understandings of who owes what to whom as between North and South and shaping northern perceptions of the other's ontological significance. Imagination thus intertwines with denial and structural inequality to turn oppression into debt and generate expectations of gratitude by the generous party from the gift recipient. David Graeber's profound analysis demonstrates that a gift given in the context of hierarchal relationships can create its own dynamic of moral and social superiority.[43] Recent reparations movements have challenged the northern generosity narrative by bringing colonialism back into analysis of North-South aid relationships.[44] Against this context, an expanding circle of advocates and commentators have begun talking about the need for colonial powers to give reparations, not aid.[45] The turn from aid to reparations relies on overcoming historic amnesia and emphasizing colonialism's impact on both North and South.

In Palestine, however, the reverse trend has taken hold. Aid policies, institutions, and mechanisms function as an instrument of erasure, positioning Palestine as a nation in need of development reform while increasingly eliminating from view Palestine as the site of occupation and a space from which people can make moral and legal claims against Israel and the "international community". Aid serves as a site of normative struggle where assertions of mastery and expectations of gratitude exert themselves at various points through the aid relationship. As the next section of this chapter sets out, mastery becomes institutionalized through the aid relationship at the macro level through donor coordination mechanisms and at the micro level through project administration requirements.

Mastery through donor coordination

In its first connotation, "mastery" refers to having become expert or someone who excels at something, as in a master painter, a master furniture maker, or a master chef. In its second connotation, mastery relates to a hierarchical relationship, one marked by inequality and arbitrariness in which one party is presumed

42 Jason Hickel, "Forget about Aid; Let's Talk about Reparations" (27 November 2015) *Guardian*, online: <www.theguardian.com/global-development-professionals-network/2015/nov/27/enough-of-aid-lets-talk-reparations> [Hickel].

43 David Graeber, *Debt: The First 5,000 Years* (Brooklyn: Melville House, 2011) [Graeber].

44 *Ibid.*

45 Ricardo Rene Laremont, "Political versus Legal Strategies for the African Slavery Reparations Movement" (1998) *Afr Stud Q*, online: <https://asq.africa.ufl.edu/laremont_99/> [Laremont].

to have the authority to demand something, including gratitude, and to act upon the other from another by virtue of that hierarchy. Both connotations of mastery turn on control. One who has mastered a subject controls that subject. One who masters others controls them. The master painter controls the brush, the master furniture maker controls the tools and the master controls a subordinate. Slavoj Žižek's succinctly locates the source of "mastery". The complexity of reasons for and against gives rise to "the Master" who, imbued with discretion, transforms complexity "into a simple, decisive Yes or No".[46] Mastery can be manufactured by excluding others, suppressing those things that need to be understood in order for a situation to be fully appreciated, and by cultivating the discretion to announce a result without having to take other positions or views into account. Masters, then, are those who assume the authority to make the "decisive gesture which can never be fully grounded in reasons".[47]

Mastery in both its connotations relates to development aid; one meaning declares the basis for the aid relationship while the other develops from the aid relationship. Mastery as expertise forms the core of aid and aid programming. Northern states grant Palestine technical assistance and access to experts because they lay claims to superior knowledge, expertise, and experience that is mostly missing by Palestinians. This form of mastery is explicitly invoked to justify the aid relationship.[48] By its other connotation, mastery means cultivating control over the other. This form of mastery is integral to aid practices but is not declared. Hidden from view, mastery as hierarchical relationship is made possible through the banishment of international law, institutions, and obligations and the creation of new institutions that are packaged as politically neutral and practically necessary to the aid enterprise. In fact, these purportedly neutral, necessary, and non-normative structures pack a powerful political punch because they define priorities for Palestinians, remove them from decision-making, insert Israeli narratives and priorities, and render decisions according to arbitrary frameworks that move discretion into the hands of aid givers and aid workers. Mastery is cultivated at both the macro and micro levels within the aid relationship.

As northern aid to Palestinians began to flow more steadily, donors created mechanisms to coordinate that aid. The reasons, in theory, prove innocuous enough. Individual donors needed to know about each other's plans to help ensure aid effectiveness.[49] Which country was going to cover which "sectors"? How much funding was needed? Where and who would provide it? Ostensibly

46 Žižek, *supra* note 2 at 34.

47 *Ibid.* at 36.

48 Karamah's project with CIDA, for example, was created through a contribution agreement that noted that Canada was well placed to provide judicial education programming because Canada is respected worldwide for its human rights record and Canadian judges are cited by jurisdictions around the world.

49 See generally Jeremy Wildeman, "Donor Aid Effectiveness and Do No Harm in the Occupied Palestinian Territories" (10 December 2018), online: <www.academia.edu/37951770/Donor_Aid_Effectiveness_and_Do_No_Harm_in_the_Occupied_Palestinian_Territories_An_Oral_and_Document_Analysis_of_Western_Donor_perceptions_of_development_and_

politically neutral, donor coordination in fact became deeply normative. Through their coordination efforts, donors have set Palestinian priorities, defined aspirations, shaped the political system, reformulated the relationship between the public and private spheres, and defined lifestyles for aid recipients, all without concern for popular legitimacy. Donor coordination has also further concealed occupation from policy view. Given the central role of aid in the Palestinian economy, the reach and significance of donor coordination cannot be underestimated.

Two bodies play a particularly important coordinating role. Established in 1993, the Ad Hoc Liaison Committee "serves as the principal policy-level coordination mechanism for development assistance to the Palestinian people" and "seeks to promote dialogue between donors, the PA and the Government of Israel". Chaired by Norway and co-sponsored by the EU and the United States, the Committee brings together "a high level political group of key donors".[50] Its membership consists of Palestine, Israel, Canada, Egypt, the International Monetary Fund (IMF), Japan, Jordan, the United Nations, Russia, Saudi Arabia, and Tunisia. The World Bank acts as secretariat. Having met 22 times between 2005 and 2018, the Committee has become neither ad hoc nor simply a coordinating mechanism.

In 2005, the United States created the office of the US Security Coordinator (USSC), headquartered in Tel Aviv, commanded by US Department of Defense officials and comprising a "multinational team that consists of military and civilian personnel from Canada, the United Kingdom, Turkey and the Netherlands; as well as other international partners from Germany, Finland, Denmark, and Greece who provide technical training experts and advisors". The USSC is tasked with encouraging "coordination on security matters between Israel and the Palestinian Authority" and building "the security capacity of the Palestinian Authority in the West Bank".[51]

Donor coordination in Palestine reveals the overarching regulation of internal and external political relations and national priorities without regard to their popular legitimacy. Instead, new regulatory frameworks stemming from power relations that are external and largely unknown or inaccessible to the Palestinian people substitute for popular legitimacy and local knowledge. Neither the Ad Hoc Liaison Committee nor the USSC shows any particular concern for popular legitimacy or Palestinian priorities in its decision-making. Palestinians stress the importance of ending the occupation as a prerequisite to building justice both within an imagined Palestinian state and between Israelis and Palestinians,

---

peacebuilding_in_their_Palestinian_aid_programming> [Wildeman] for an overview of the principle of aid effectiveness in international development.

50 Rex Brynen, Hisham Awartani & Clare Woodcraft, "The Palestinian Territories" in Shepard Forman & Stewart Patrick, eds., *Good Intentions: Pledges of Aid for Postconflict Recovery* (Boulder, CO: Rienner, 2000) at 211 [Brynen et al.].

51 National Defence and the Canadian Armed Forces, "Operation PROTEUS" Press Report (2016) *National Defence and the Canadian Armed Force Website*, online: <www.forces.gc.ca/en/operations-abroad-current/op-proteus.page> [National Defence].

consistently maintaining that self-determination and justice go hand in hand. A 2015 survey of youth aged 15 to 29 found that 79.4% consider "ending the occupation and the building of Palestine" as a top priority for the Palestinian people, followed by improving the standard of living, which garnered 7.3% of respondents. The overwhelming emphasis on ending the occupation was consistent across the West Bank and Gaza and across genders.[52]

However, both the Liaison Committee and the USSC systematically exclude popular priorities or participation. They also dilute the priorities presented by the PA, which reiterates the popular refrain, advanced from within and outside Palestine, that occupation must end before Palestinians can have a fair chance at development.[53] Both coordinating bodies lack mechanisms to include Palestinian civil society in their decisions. These coordination mechanisms also lack platforms to encourage reporting back, let alone accountability, to the Palestinian people.

Sahar Taghdisi Rad argues that donors generally fail to understand the dynamics of conflict on political economies partially because of their unwillingness "to take effective account of the conflict stemming from their political, strategic and ideological interests and alliances in the conflict".[54] Rather than incorporate Palestinian experiences and insights into the decision-making process, donor coordination renders them even less intelligible. The structures are designed so that the needs and aspirations of Palestinians disappear, and those who are already disenfranchised in the current Palestinian political structures, such as youth, become even more distanced from and invisible within the structures that produce national priorities.

Palestinian civil society organizations have attempted to influence priorities communicated by the PA to the Ad Hoc Liaison Committee. A civil society consortium met over several months under the auspices of Karamah and prepared a vision document for the justice sector.[55] The latest report by the State of Palestine to the Committee emphasizes that it has attempted to enhance consultations.[56] Nevertheless, it remains unclear whether or how such initiatives and consultations have influenced the Committee and its decisions.

Disconnects between popular Palestinian aspirations and donor coordination mechanisms can be glimpsed through the reports prepared for the Ad Hoc Liaison Committee and the procedures adopted by the Committee. The

52 Palestinian Central Bureau of Statistics, "Palestinian Youth Survey, 2015: Main Findings" (2015) *Palestinian Central Bureau of Statistics*, online: <www.pcbs.gov.ps/portals/_pcbs/PressRelease/Press_En_YouthSurvPal2015E.pdf> [Palesinian Central Bureau of Statistics].

53 Brigitte Herremans, "The EU's Self-Defeating Aid Policy towards Palestine" (2016) 343:10 *Center for European Policy Studies Policy Brief*, online: <www.ceps.eu/system/files/PB343%20Herremans%20Aid%20to%20OPT.pdf> [Herremans]. See also State of Palestine 2016, *supra* note 32 at 4.

54 Taghdisi Rad, *supra* note 7 at 2.

55 Initiative on Judicial Independence and Human Dignity, "The View Point of Palestinian Civil Society on the Justice Sector" (May 2009) *Local Development Forum*, online: <www.lacs.ps/documentsShow.aspx?ATT_ID=1910> [Initiative on Judicial Independence].

56 State of Palestine 2016, *supra* note 32 at 4.

PA's report references occupation 13 times, emphasizing its negative impact on human rights, justice, and economic growth in no uncertain terms.[57] IMF and World Bank (2016) reports submitted in anticipation of a September 19, 2016, Committee meeting, for example, disregard the occupation altogether while the Quartet report mentions occupation only once.[58]

Norway chairs the Ad Hoc Liaison Committee meetings, which are held outside Palestine and information about the Committee's protocols, rules of procedure, minutes, decisions, or reports prove difficult to find. Some Committee reports are made publicly available online, usually in English, and major meetings are sometimes followed by press conferences. However, the Committee meetings remain closed.

Moreover, Palestinian development priorities must be negotiated through the Ad Hoc Liaison Committee with Israel's full participation. In the end, activities aimed at ending the occupation or holding the Israeli government to account for policies such as settlements expansion – policies that have been disavowed by the American government in international fora – do not figure in coordination efforts. Instead, markets and security take top priority. The Office of the Quartet, for example, proposes that Palestinian private sector should be the main driver of economic development:

> Though the Palestinian private sector has the potential to be a powerful engine, today the Palestinian economy suffers from underinvestment in Palestinian industry. Investment in plant and machinery in the West Bank and Gaza as a proportion of GDP has fallen from 12.9% in 2000 to 4.8% in 2014. The current annual level of underinvestment in plant and machinery amounts to about $1.4 billion a year.[59]

Leaving aside distributive justice concerns, the report ignores the complications, to put it mildly, of investing in an environment where goods must pass Israeli checkpoints or otherwise be subjected to Israel regulations. The insecurities and contingencies have proven too much for even the most resourced and dedicated investors. Market strategies in this context do not produce national growth for Palestinians but a substratum of cheap labour for foreign enterprises and Palestinian economic elites.

The USSC, for its part, is even more removed from Palestinian priorities. It is not that Palestinians do not value security. They do. However, "security" in the Palestinian context has meant extended state power, including the power of the Israeli state, over Palestinian lives, with the result that Israeli security matters

57 *Ibid.* at 3–6, 13–14, 17.

58 Office of the Quartet, "Report for the Meeting of the Ad-Hoc Liaison Committee on Action in Support of Palestinian State Building" (2016) *Office of the Quartet* online: <https://unispal.un.org/DPA/DPR/UNISPAL.NSF/47d4e277b48d9d3685256ddc00612265/552a9aad68473fa88525803000680492?OpenDocument> [Office of the Quartet].

59 *Ibid.* at 4.

while Palestinian security does not. It has become axiomatic that security coordination does not entail equal security. The Palestinian security forces do not have jurisdiction over Israelis, regardless of where they are, while the Israeli army continues to have jurisdiction over Palestinians, either directly or by proxy, regardless of where they are.[60] Efforts purportedly aimed at appeasing Israeli anxiety or building trust between Israeli and Palestinian forces has translated into Palestinian forces policing their own people and putting down popular protests, or coordinating with Israel against political opponents. A resident of the Jenin refugee camp expressed a popular Palestinian sentiment in response to the situation where Palestinians are subject to both forces while Israelis are subject to none:

> I don't have a problem with the security collaboration if it is reciprocal. However, there is domination only. When the PA can ask Israel to arrest a settler to protect the Palestinian people's security, that will be a different story.[61]

Ultimately, donor coordination through the Ad Hoc Liaison Committee and the USSC have produced spending priorities within Palestine that benefit the Israeli economy, donors, and the colonial condition. Israel no longer has to spend from its own coffers on matters such as security or re-building Palestinian infrastructure, including infrastructure destroyed by Israeli military offences.[62] Moreover, one economist has calculated that "at least 72% of international aid ends up in the Israeli economy".[63] By these figures, aid has become yet another site for the colonial plunder of Palestinian resources.[64] Focusing on Canada, Jeffrey Monaghan has demonstrated that donors are the main beneficiaries of security aid that is purportedly given to benefit Palestinians. In the case of Canada, Monaghan details that enhancing Canada's international reputation and relationship with other donors, particularly the United States, proved a significant motivator for giving

60 Alaa Tartir, "The Evolution and Reform of Palestinian Security Forces 1993–2013" (2015) *Stability: Intl J Security & Dev* 1, DOI: <10.5334/sta.gi> [Tartir 2015].

61 Alaa Tartir, "How US Security Aid to PA Sustains Israel's Occupation" (2 December 2016) *Al-Jazeera*, online: <www.aljazeera.com/indepth/features/2016/11/security-aid-pa-sustains-israel-occupation-161103120213593.html> [Tartir 2016].

62 Lee Berthiaume, "Israel Urged Canadian Government Not to Cut Aid to Palestinians Over UN Vote: Documents" (2013) *National Post*, online: <http://news.nationalpost.com/news/canada/canadian-politics/israel-urged-canadian-government-not-to-cut-aid-to-palestinians-over-un-vote-documents> [Berthiaume].

63 Shir Hever, "How Much International Aid to Palestinians Ends Up in the Israeli Economy" (2015) *Aid Watch* 15, online: <www.aidwatch.ps/sites/default/files/resource-field_media/InternationalAidToPalestiniansFeedsTheIsraeliEconomy.pdf> [Hever 2015]. See also Shir Hever, "The Political Economy of Israel's Occupation: Repression Beyond Exploitation" (2010) *Holy Land Stud* at 131–133 [Hever 2010].

64 Peter Baker & Julie Hirschfeld Davis, "US Finalize Deal to Give Israel $38 Billion in Military Aid" Press Report (2016) *New York Times*, online: <www.nytimes.com/2016/09/14/world/middleeast/israel-benjamin-netanyahu-military-aid.html?_r=0> [Baker & Davis].

aid to Palestinians and that the proponents of security aid considered themselves directly accountable to other donors, not Palestinians.[65]

Mastery in project implementation

Once approved through donor coordination mechanisms, development priorities have to be turned into projects which require implementation. Donor agencies generally contract out specific implementation projects, often but not always to corporations from their own jurisdiction. We entered the Palestinian development fray in 2005, as two universities – Windsor and Birzeit – having received a financial contribution from CIDA, as it was then, to develop a judicial education program with human dignity as its focus. Our initiative was called Karamah. At that time, donors gravitated towards judicial education in part because, consistent with liberal and neoliberal aspirations, they imagined the judiciary as an institution that can protect investors, check executive excesses, dispense justice to disputing parties, and transform conflict into peaceful dispute resolution.

At this point in our analysis, we directly draw on our experiences with Karamah to explain how control of Palestinian decision-making, coupled with the benevolence narrative, also shape Palestinian-donor relations at the point of project implementation through aid delivery contracts. We turn an analytical lens on the management tools used by foreign development agencies to manage and evaluate development projects. The aid agency and the policies that guide the implementation of the aid agenda merit greater scrutiny. The agency's very raison d'être requires the imagination of Palestine as a nation asking for technical assistance rather than liberation, thus replicating and concretizing the benevolence narrative. Agency management tools, particularly the *logic model* and *risk matrix*, serve the interests of agency control, feed a variant of the benevolence narrative, and ultimately render working towards justice through international development a risky endeavour. In the aid bureaucracy's "meticulous, often minute techniques" and the "multiplicity of often minor processes", we find "the blueprint for a more general method".[66]

Agencies use logic models to define desired results and help ensure that their interventions lead to sustainable change. Accordingly, agencies determine which projects get funded on the basis of the efficacy of the logic model proposed and funded projects are evaluated against the logic model in the short, medium, and long terms.[67] Logic models purport to create transparency by helping agencies

65 Jeffrey Monaghan, "Security Development and the Palestinian's Authority: An Examination of the 'Canadian Factor'" (2016) 16:2 *Conflict Security Dev* 125.

66 Michel Foucault, *Discipline and Punish: The Birth of the Prison* (London: Penguin, 1975) at 138–139 [Foucault].

67 Global Affairs Canada, "Results-Based Management Tools at Global Affairs Canada: A How-to Guide" Press Report (2017) *Global Affairs Canada*, online: <www.international.gc.ca/development-developpement/partners-partenaires/bt-oa/rbm_tools-gar_outils.aspx?lang=eng> [Global Affairs Canada 2017]. Global Affairs Canada explains the central role that logic models play in the agency's commitment to results based management

structure communication about investments and their intended and actual results. If the results identified at the end of the logic chain are not achieved, the donor investment is considered a poor one. If the results are achieved but not according to the plan set out in the logic model, the change is considered "unexpected" or, alternatively, inconsequential to the donor investment. Again, the donor investment might be considered a poor one because the results could have been achieved without it. Adherence to the logic model is thus the *sine qua non* of international development project management.

While different donors adopt slightly different schemas to represent their logic models, all share a common framework that moves proponents from activities to an increasingly higher order of sought-after results: effort is expended at the activity level, activities have to be defined in advance and often repeated to get results, the arrows (or some other metaphor) represent a causal force, and the higher-level boxes are effects that are the product of effort expended plus causal forces. CIDA, the United States Agency for International Development (USAID), and the World Bank agree that properly conceptualized and implemented activities should, by some causal force, produce the effects defined in higher-level boxes.[68]

The causal force that purportedly propels a project from one level of result to another is actually a theory of change. Some donors, like USAID, explicitly recognize that a theory of change is acting behind the scenes while others do not. Global Affairs Canada – previously CIDA – remains committed to the notion that activities produce results in a clear, concise, and predictable manner through causal connection between the various levels of the logic model chain: "A result is a describable or measurable change that is derived from a cause-and-effect relationship".[69]

When read from bottom to top, the logic model purports to explain *how* work should be structured to produce results. In the judicial education context, activities such as preparing educational materials are defined and expected to produce short-term results, such as improved understanding of human rights principles on the part of judicial participants. The short-term results are to be repeated so that eventually, compounded over time, they produce longer-term results such as better judicial decision-making in light of human rights principles; and, those results themselves propel change at the ultimate level such as improved rule of law, access to justice or justice (depending on the prevailing terminology). When read from top to bottom, the model purports to explain *why* activities are undertaken: a desired goal such as supporting justice, access to justice or the rule of

(RBM): "RBM has a long history at DFATD: it has been used, in one form or another, for more than thirty years. DFATD's first official RBM policy was released in 1996, and a revised and updated policy was approved in June 2008."

68 L. G. Morra & R. C. Rist, "The Road to Results: Designing and Conducting Effective Development Evaluations" (2008) *The World Bank* [Morra & Rist]. USAID and the World Bank, for example, also have adopted a logic model framework.

69 Global Affairs Canada 2017, *supra* note 68. Global Affairs Canada has instructions for the use of their three main results-based management working tools: the logic model, performance measurement framework, and risk register.

law is defined; this goal in turn relies on improved decision-making, which in turn relies on enhanced knowledge, which in turn requires the development of educational materials.

Beyond the activity level, each box represents a desired result. The budget must correspond to the logic model with a set percentage of the total budget allocated to each box. Regardless of the content of each box, the relationship between the boxes must be defined in terms of cause and effect. The plan had to be clear, largely knowable in advance, and sequential. Most importantly, it has to make sense to the desk officer who might have little to no knowledge of law, legal education, or social change but who approves narrative and financial reports before disbursing funds.

Driven by the need for clarity, the logic model distils complex issues into simple statements and transforms wicked questions into tame ones.[70] Judicial education is imagined as a set of pre-planned activities rather than a dynamic process of engagement between actors across jurisdictions and sectors. In Karamah's case, the demand for simplistic cause-and-effect planning moulded into the logic model structure imported invalid assumptions into the change process no matter how many times we tried to revise or perfect our version of the logic model.

For example, our logic model presumed that change arises out of activities that transfer knowledge from expert knower to judicial target. On this view, the more information or knowledge transferred, the better. Consistent with colonial projects that presume a need for change only in the colonial subject and harness education towards such benevolent results, the logic model does not admit or value the possibility that all actors in the relationship may benefit and change. Moreover, enhanced capacity in and of itself does not in itself change individuals. People do not examine or alter their behaviour because they have picked up a new fact or theory. Individuals change their behaviour because they have built relationships and professional identities that explain their relationship with their larger world differently.[71]

70 H.W.J. Rittel & M. M. Webber, "Dilemmas in a General Theory of Planning" (1973) *Pol'y Sciences*, online: 4. <www.cc.gatech.edu/fac/ellendo/rittel/rittel-dilemma.pdf> [Rittel & Webber].

71 Joy Amulya, Christie O'Campbell & Ceasar McDowell, "Transformative Learning in Social Justice Organization through Reflective Practice" (delivered at the Fifth International Conference on Transformative Learning, New York City, 2003), online: <www.racialequitytools.org/resourcefiles/crcp1.pdf> [Amulya et al.]. See also Jack Mezirow, "Transformative Learning as Discourse" (2003) *J Transformative Educ* 58, DOI: <10.1177/1541344603252172> [Mezirow]; Kathleen M. Brown, "Leadership for Social Justice: Weaving A Transformative Framework and Pedagogy" (2004) 40:1 *Educ'l Admin Q* 77 [Brown 2004]; Kathleen M. Brown, "Leadership for Social Justice and Equity: Evaluating a Transformative Framework and Andragogy" (2006) *Educ'l Admin Q*, online: <http://journals.sagepub.com/doi/abs/10.1177/0013161X06290650> [Brown 2006]; R. Land, J.H.F. Meyer & C. Baillie, "Editors' Preface: Threshold Concepts and Transformational Learning" in R. Land, J.H.F. Meyer and C. Baillie, eds., *Threshold Concepts and Transformational Learning* (Rotterdam: Sense, 2009) [Land et al.] and Ray Land, "Threshold Concepts and Troublesome Knowledge (3): Implications for Course Design

Second, the logic model imposed the assumption that changed decision-making by judges would produce larger changes in society, even though we knew that there is no direct line or simple causal relation between judicial decision-making and social change, and that law on the books often diverges from law in action. Judicial impact studies have demonstrated this to be the case across jurisdictions.[72] It is not that judges do not matter. They do. However, legal reforms, including judicial decision-making, must work in concert with social, economic, or political forces to affect behaviour. The activities that must be undertaken, the changing context, the interaction between actors, the nature of changes required, and the types of relationships that must be fostered cannot adequately be captured through logic models which emphasize streamlined and focused decision-making by individual elites that transit change through repetition of activities rather than strategic relations. Logic models cannot capture the complexity of activity, relationships, or decision-making that is required to produce promised results.

Of course, change processes can be understood differently. Tactical mapping, for example, eschews properly sequenced activities in favour of fostering productive networks and relationships.[73] Tactical mapping strategies contemplate that law has an important but not exclusive role to play in social change, including social change that defines itself as building the rule of law. Legal, social, economic, and political abuses

> are sustained by a complex system of relationships that mutually reinforce the role of abuse and violations of power. Some of these relationships are hierarchical or otherwise structural; others are informal. Each of these relationships is a potential site of intervention and might respond to a different tactic.[74]

Tactical maps also recognize that "the status quo generally does not yield to a single tactic. Multiple strategies are needed".[75] Viewed through a logic model lens, implementation resources are best spent on logistics, preparing and planning for events. Viewed through a tactical planning model, implementation resources are best spent on relationship-building that leads to the events and activities that in turn produce results.

Karamah promised to deliver a new model of judicial education, one that supported the independence of the judiciary itself while also creating a platform for

---

and Evaluation" (2005) *Improving Student Learning – Diversity and Inclusivity* (Oxford Centre for Staff and Learning Development) 53 [Land].

72 Gerald N. Rosenberg, *The Hollow Hope* (Chicago: University of Chicago Press, 1991) [Rosenberg].

73 Reem Bahdi, "Women's Access to Justice: Texts and Contexts" (2010) *SSRN* 26, online: <http://papers.ssrn.com/sol3/papers.cfm?abstract_id=1716883> at 21–22 [Bahdi 2010].

74 *Ibid.* See also the materials at New Tactics in Human Rights, online: <www.newtactics.org/en/tactical-mapping> [New Tactics].

75 Reem Bahdi, *Women's Access to Justice: Texts and Contexts* (UK and Canada: Department for International Development & International Development Research Centre, 2010) at 21.

members of the judiciary to reflect upon the meaning and significance of human dignity in judicial decision-making. We achieved this by thinking of our work more through a tactical mapping than a logic model frame. The key is that relationships drive strategies or tactics and events rather than the other way around. Ironically, although the necessity of a new model of judicial education was recognized and funded by CIDA, CIDA officers insisted on reading our work and its results through the logic model. There was no option. Not surprisingly, they found it extremely difficult to understand our methods or the successes that our approach engendered.[76]

If logic models and risk registers force false cause-and-effect relationships, why do aid agencies remain committed to these management tools? Why, in other words, remain faithful to a model that time and time again has stacked the deck against the possibility of success? It is not because agencies do not, or at least cannot, know better. Aid agencies have policy branches that are mandated to examine the efficacy of tools and processes adopted by the agency. And as we have already noted, a plethora of easily available literature questions the assumptions inherent within the logic model, raises questions about the risk register, and can point to alternatives.

Nonetheless, the logic model remains the bureaucratic instrument of choice because it packs a powerful bureaucratic and political punch. It creates spaces of bureaucratic discretion by placing implementers in an impossible predicament, always vulnerable to bureaucratic criticisms of insufficiency and failure: follow the logic model and diminish the possibility of results, or deviate from the model and risk charges of contract breach.

Logic models and risk registers permit desk officers to equate accountability with inflexibility and control with understanding. In their insightful paper, "The Colonial Foundations of the State of Exception: Juxtaposing the Israeli Occupation of the Palestinian Territories with Colonial Bureaucratic History", Shenhav and Berda identify intentional and systemic unpredictability as the basis of colonial bureaucratic rule. Weber's classic account of rule-based bureaucracy does not account for the ways in which the exception is built into colonial systems of control. Systematized unpredictability makes a moving target of accountability.[77]

The targets, modes, consequences, and context of colonial bureaucratic rule differ drastically from the modern development bureaucracy. But embedded uncertainty plays the same role. Žižek's[78] master who, imbued with discretion,

76 Bahdi & Kassis: Decolonization, *supra* note 1.

77 Yehouda Shenhav & Yael Berda, "The Colonial Foundations of the State of Exception: Juxtaposing the Israeli Occupation of the Palestinian Territories with Colonial Bureaucratic History" in Adi Ophir, Michal Givoni & Sārī Ḥanafī, eds., *The Power of Inclusive Exclusion: Anatomy of Israeli Rule in the Occupied Palestinian Territories* (New York: Zone Books, 2009), online: <www.faculty.umb.edu/heike.schotten/readings/Shenhav%20and%20Berda,%20Colonial%20Foundations.pdf>.

78 Žižek, *supra* note 2 at 34.

transforms complexity "into a simple, decisive Yes or No" appears again. The logic model permits development officers the illusion of mastery, but mastery of what? Mastery of boxes and arrows that purport to capture the aspirations of people and nations through a series of three or four layers of discrete columns of boxes and arrows. Certainly not mastery of the complicated, conflicting, and changing decision-making terrain. The rationale for "Yes or No" can thus be made knowable to the bureaucrat sitting thousands of miles away. If a "No" is given, funding stops and activities cease. The "No" is always available because the logic model lays down an unachievable path even if the ultimate results are achievable by other routes.

Of course, as we detailed in the first section of this chapter, governments can say either "Yes" or "No" as purely political acts.[79] Such responses, however, risk public scrutiny and discussion.[80] The "Yes" given in the shadow of the always present, structurally sustained possible "No" gives the agency control over rule of law programming, whatever their rhetoric about "aid effectiveness", valuing "the local" or participatory decision-making. It is precisely the arbitrariness of the logic model which breeds uncertainty and instability for initiatives by holding them to illogical methodologies and modalities that enables agency control; the possibility of demonstrating merit or results is rendered subjective and placed in agency hands. The logic model reproduces power relations by charting a path to failure while funnelling discussions about results through a prism that deflects, marginalizes, and warps the considerations that need to be highlighted and the discussions that need to be exchanged for change to take root.

Just as it is erased at the point of donor coordination, occupation barely matters at the bureaucratic project implementation level. It factors in project management through the risk register merely as a logistical concern. Companion to the logic model, the risk register requires regular updating by project managers whose job it is to identify, grade, and minimize risks. Examples of occupation related risks include restrictions on travel because of checkpoints. Occupation barely matters beyond the risk register. For example, the evaluation of CIDA programming in the West Bank and Gaza finalized in July 2015 reviews 25 CIDA projects but does not mention the word "occupation" once, preferring instead the terms "history of conflict" and "ongoing political instability".[81]

79 The Canadian government, for example, said "no" to funding in Palestine after the election of Hamas to the Palestinian Legislative Council in 2006. All CIDA programming was "suspended" until the politicians worked out arrangements that proved politically acceptable.

80 Jamey Essex, "The Politics of Effectiveness in Canada's International Development Assistance" (2012) 33:3 *Can J Dev Stud* 338 online: <www.tandfonline.com/doi/abs/10.1080/02255189.2012.713856> [Essex].

81 Global Affairs Canada, "Evaluation of Canada's Development and Humanitarian Assistance Programming in West Bank and Gaza" Press Report (2015) *Global Affairs Canada*, online: <http://international.gc.ca/department-ministere/evaluation/2015/eval_cdhapwbg-eval_pdahccbg.aspx?lang=eng> [Global Affairs Canada 2015].

As Jeremy Wildeman's review of donor aid effectiveness to Palestinians demonstrates, context denial and historic amnesia are typical of most donors:

> Strong analysis of the context of an intervention is crucial to a donor not doing harm in a fragile and conflicted state. This analysis does not seem always to be present with donors active in the OPT, especially the powerful North American based ones. This can be observed in how they perceive and account for the fundamental factors driving conflict between Israel and the Palestinians, such as occupation, settlements, settlers and colonisation. Here some donors rarely, if ever, identify those factors, even though they are the main causes for Palestinian poverty, the failure of the Oslo Process, continuous violence and instability.[82]

Wildeman concludes that Canada stands out among donor countries as one of the worst deniers. Eliminating occupation as a factor that drives Palestinian poverty and institutional weaknesses reinforces the illusion at all bureaucratic levels that Palestinians are a people who need technical training rather than liberation. This inversion turns the agency into a benefactor, renders gratitude a decisive factor in development programming, and reinforces the narrative of debt as the narrative for North-South engagements.

We close this chapter by relaying a personal encounter with aid bureaucracies that was reflective of several others. We do so mindful of Obiora Okafor's reflections on practicing Third World Approaches to International Law (TWAIL) through close engagement with institutions and the importance of institutional insider perspectives to "enact our dramas of close engagement".[83] Throughout our seven years of engagement with CIDA and its bureaucracy, we encountered kind and caring individuals who worked hard to understand our work and its context. Too often, however, officials acted as though they are not subject to laws, including the overriding judicial review principles that circumscribe their decision-making.[84] Rather, they imagine themselves as unfettered decision makers who confer a unilateral benefit onto others and who had granted us a personal favour by contributing to our project through a contribution agreement. As one senior bureaucrat put it to us in asserting his power over our knowledge, "I am in the Queen". Alluding to our contract with the Queen in Right of Canada, he was insisting that his interpretation of our contract would prevail without having to provide reasons. With these words, he highlighted, perhaps unwittingly, his expectation of mastery over subjects who are expected to know their place and show appropriate gratitude for the generosity that has been bestowed upon them.

82 Wildeman, *supra* note 50.

83 Obiora Okafor, "Praxis And The International (Human Rights) Law Scholar: Toward The Intensification Of Twailian Dramaturgy" (2016) 33:3 WYAJ 1 at 30.

84 The principles of judicial review were recently explained in *Kattenburg v. Canada*, 2019 FC 1003, online: <https://decisions.fct-cf.gc.ca/fc-cf/decisions/en/item/419068/index.do> [*Kattenburg*].

Conclusion

Aid has reframed the space in which Palestine engages with the "international community". Led by the United States, northern countries have worked to deflect decision-making away from international bodies that have conventionally been involved in the human rights of the Palestinian people. To that end, United Nations decisions and reports that highlight violations of Palestinian human rights including, inter alia, Special Rapporteurs whose mandates include the human rights of the Palestinian people, and two United Nations investigations into violations of international law in Gaza in 2009 and 2014 have been the subject of campaigns to discredit them. Palestinian appeals to the General Assembly, the Security Council, the International Court of Justice, and the International Criminal Court have similarly faced resistance from the United States and its allies that have sought to work against declarations of Palestinian rights by these bodies and thwart any possibility of remedies for rights violations by them.

Engagement between the Global North and Palestine is increasingly directed away from law towards aid and aid agencies whose work results in the erasure, denial, or minimization of the occupation as the primary mischief to be remedied in the pursuit of peace and justice in Palestine-Israel. Aid and international law need not be alternative frameworks, but they have been posited and treated as such by the Global North with reference to Palestine, advancing the narrative that Palestinians are a people in need of technical assistance, not liberation.

5 Rethinking international legal education in Latin America*

Exploring some obstacles of a hegemonic colonial academic model in Chile and Colombia

Paola Andrea Acosta-Alvarado, Amaya Álvez Marín, Laura Betancur-Restrepo, Enrique Prieto-Ríos, Daniel Rivas-Ramírez and Fabia Fernandes Carvalho Veçoso

Introduction

During the international academic conference Decolonizing Law? Methods, Tactics and Strategies, held in Windsor University in April 2018,[1] we discussed how colonialism and imperialism continue to have a direct impact on the existing economic, legal and intellectual relationships between the Global North and the Global South – specifically, how the law has served as an instrument to reinforce colonial and imperial practices, but also how to think on alternative methods, tactics, and strategies to decolonize law. In this chapter, we bring this discussion in the context of education[2] and we focus on international law, analyzing the cases of Chile and Colombia.

Education is a powerful tool that can reinforce a certain collective conscience under the veil of neutrality,[3] but it can also be used to question models and paradigms and propose alternative ways to explore various conceptions of decolonization. Following Antonio Gramsci´s approach, we consider important to question whether legal education in the domain of international law in Latin

* REDIAL, by its acronym in Spanish, stands for Rethinking International Legal Education in Latin America.

1 Organized by Windsor School of Law, Osgoode Hall Law School, Ontario, Canada, and Water Research Center for Agriculture and Mining CRHIAM at the University of Concepción, Chile, held in Canada on 2–3 April 2018. University of Windsor, "Decolonizing Law? Methods, Tactics & Strategies", online: *University of Windsor* <www.uwindsor.ca/law/1102/decolonizing-law-methods-tactics-strategies>.

2 In the term "education" we include aspects related to teaching and learning, academic research, and leadership and service.

3 Paul Ransome, *Antonio Gramsci: A New Introduction* (London: Harvester Wheatsheaf, 1992) at 193. Eagleton has similarly concluded that education takes to hegemony as long as it manages to lead to general consensus thanks to the transmission of moral, social and intellectual patterns. Terry Eagleton, *Ideología. Una Nueva Introducción* (Barcelona: Paidós, 1997) at 153.

America follows (or not) a colonialist hegemonic model based on epistemological domination.[4]

This discussion is part of an ongoing research project called REDIAL (Rethinking International Legal Education in Latin America).[5] REDIAL is a collaborative academic research project that brings together Latin American researchers interested in exploring the current stakes of international legal education in the region.[6]

Despite the great tradition of Latin American scholars present in international law, featuring well-known names such as Andrés Bello, Carlos Calvo or Alejandro

4 Gramsci's theory advocates for the linkage between education systems and politics by understanding that education is one of the most important means in order to establish and sustain any ideology in power and in consequence, to strengthen ruling classes' hegemonies. Thus, education (and the functional intellectuals) aims to develop and settle a certain collective conscience under the veil of neutrality.

5 In Spanish: Repensar la Educación del Derecho Internacional en América Latina. In Portuguese: Repensar a educação em Direito Internacional na América Latina.

6 This project emerged in 2014 in the context of the workshop held by the Institute for Global Law and Policy at Harvard Law School. As workshop participants from Latin America, we shared common concerns about teaching and research in international law in the region. These concerns were further explored and became our guiding questions in the project: How and what is taught in international law in Latin America today? Are there common Latin American elements? What aspects can we rethink to modify the way in which international law is taught in this region? Despite the fact that our intellectual networks and trajectories relate to our educational paths in Latin America, but also the North and West, REDIAL does not intend to reproduce a critical legal studies movement in Latin America. With REDIAL we seek to raise awareness of these biases in our own work, understand the influences that shape our approaches, but not to simply reproduce a pre-existing model in Latin America. Prior REDIAL publications include Paola Andrea Acosta-Alvarado, "REDIAL e Imperialismo y Derecho Internacional. Oportunidad para la reflexión" (2017) 39 *Derecho del Estado* 3; Amaya Álvez Marín & Armulf Becker Lorca, "Los Pueblos Originarios Y La Práctica Del Derecho Internacional En Chile: Nuevos Horizontes Ante El Debilitamiento De Los Legados Del Autoritarismo" (2017) 39 *Derecho del Estado* 21; Laura Betancur-Restrepo & Enrique Prieto-Ríos, "Educación Del Derecho Internacional En Bogotá: Un Primer Diagnóstico A Partir Del Análisis De Los Programas De Clase Y Su Relación Con Las Epistemologías Del No Conocimiento" (2017) 39 *Revista Derecho del Estado* 53; Adriane Sanctis de Brito & Salem Hikmat Nasser, "Ensinar Direito Internacional No Brasil: Panorama De Una Práctica E Seus Desafios" (2017) 39 *Derecho del Estado* 119; Fabia Fernandes Carvalho Veçoso, "História E Crítica Em Direito Internacional Na América Latina: Revisitando Discussões Pretéritas Sobre Ensino Jurídico Na Região" (2017) 39 *Derecho del Estado* 91; Jimena Sierra-Camargo, "La Importancia De Decolonizar La Enseñanza Del Derecho Internacional De Los Derechos Humanos: El Caso De La Consulta Previa En Colombia" (2017) 39 *Derecho del Estado* 137; Paola Andrea Acosta-Alvarado, Amaya Álvez Marin et al. "Rethinking International Legal Education in Latin America: Reflections toward a Global Dialogue" (August 30, 2019) 1 *Twailr Reflections, https://twailr.com/rethinking-international-legal-education-in-latin-america-reflections-toward-a-global-dialogue/;* and Paola Andrea Acosta-Alvarado, Amaya Álvez Marin et al. "La construcción de un diálogo sobre cómo repensar la educación en derecho internacional en América Latina" in Enrique Prieto-Ríos, Paola Andrea Acosta-Alvarado & Daniel Rivas-Ramírez, eds., *Repensar la Educación en Derecho Internacional en América Latina: Avances y discusiones en 2019* (Bogotá: Universidad del Rosario, 2020).

Álvarez,[7] the domestic education on international law in Latin America has been characterized for being dogmatic based on a reproduction of a Western approach.[8] In this regard it has been adopted in an uncritical way, almost as something natural or as a given, following a Eurocentric and formalistic approach. REDIAL intends to create awareness about the advantages and disadvantages of an orthodox and "Western-centric" approach to international law, which includes re-examining the colonial past embedded in the field but also interrogating ways and possibilities of transforming it in the present.

Our interest in international law is twofold. On the one hand, it is explained by the fact that all the members of the project are dedicated to international law; we teach and investigate this area of law. On the other hand, international law is of great importance in our region. Unlike what happens in other areas, in Latin America international law has direct effects, so that in recent decades it has determined the contours of the most basic aspects of the state and the daily life of individuals. This is why it is important for us to recognize the international legal reality as an intersubjective construction that implies the recognition of international law as a political space. Thus, the traditional approach in international law that distinguishes between a strictly legal area and the political context constitutes an analytical option that reduces the political space and depoliticizes the discipline. The idea of "neutrality" provides disciplinary sensitivities to the depoliticization of practice in international law, strengthening the idea of the "inevitability" of an international system defined according to liberal ideologies.

The mainstream view is a formalist-positivist cut centered on formal rules, claiming objectivity in the formation of a legal space with a disciplinarily approach that aims to be only technical. The main criticism is the parochial and pragmatic character of the way of understanding and studying international law in the region, with an emphasis on its operation, that has a limited reflection and no interdisciplinary. However, there is also a particular critical development that attempts to challenge granted approaches to international law.[9]

7 See Liliana Obregón Tarazona, "Latin American International Law" in David Armstrong ed., *Routledge Handbook of International Law* (New York: Routledge, 2009) 154; Arnulf Becker Lorca, "International Law in Latin America or Latin American International Law? Rise, Fall, and Retrieval of a Tradition of Legal Thinking and Political Imagination" (2006) 47:1 *Harv Intl LJ* 283, and Jorge Esquirol, "Alejandro Álvarez's Latin American Law: A Question of Identity" (2006) 19:4 *Leiden J Intl L* 931.

8 It is important to note that this is common not only with the teaching of international law but also in other areas of law, as highlighted in an article titled "The Current State of Legal Education Reform in Latin America: A Critical Appraisal" written by Juny Montoya, (2010) 59:4 *J Leg Educ* 545. In the same vein Professor Jorge Esquirol points out that legal education in the region has also been influenced by the Western developmental agendas of the 1960s and '70s.

9 For an example of how other perspectives are silenced and how international law manages to keep being imperialist, see Luis Eslava, Liliana Obregón & René Urueña, "Estudio Preliminar" in Antony Anghie, Martti Koskenniemi & Anne Orford, eds., *Imperialismo Y Derecho Internacional: Historia Y Legado* (Bogota: Siglo del Hombre Editores, 2016). On the ways in which the Latin-American contributions to International Law have been "erased", see

This contribution aims at creating awareness and at opening spaces to rethink the practices of teaching and researching in international law in Latin America beyond the mainstream view in the field. With special attention to the current contexts of Chile and Colombia, the main objective is to interrogate the ways in which we can think on alternative methods, tactics and strategies to decolonize international legal education in the region.

The argument unfolds as follows. The next section will explore in more detail our ideas on what does it mean to put forward a critical Latin American thinking in international law. We then present the details of the current context of how international law is currently taught and researched in Chile and Colombia. To do this, we provide data on graduate legal education on international law in Chile and Colombia at the LLM level.[10] The chapter follows with a critical discussion on how to deal with a global system of publications from a Latin American perspective. For this, we reflect on the publication system required in global academia today and the burden we all face by the imposition of certain indexing system where Latin American academia is openly marginal. Based on the concrete Chilean and Colombian experiences, this contribution ends presenting ways forward to rethink international legal education in the region.

A paradigm shift towards critical and Latin American thinking

In order to be able to identify which are the main traits of the Latin American education model in international law, it is necessary to assess the state of the art of what the national markets have to offer. Thus, by studying and analyzing the different elements that determine education in international law in our countries, we will be able to show in more detail the formalist-positivist nature of our education in international law, and which ingredients we need to unlearn in order to be able to relearn those that will allow us to decolonize the discourses and histories taught in our region.

Interrogating, comparing and depicting legal education in Latin America does not constitute a new trend. In a study published in 1950 by the *Journal of Legal Education*, H. Claude Horack assessed 37 law schools from 16 Latin American countries.[11] This study was undertaken for the specific reason of supporting the Inter-American Bar Association's views related to the positive aspects of

---

Juan Pablo Scarfi, *The Hidden History of International Law in the Americas: Empire and Legal Networks* (Oxford: Oxford University Press, 2017).

10 In this piece we explore LLM programs in Chile and Colombia as previous REDIAL studies have focused on undergraduate programs in law, and these type of diagnoses and comparisons of programs and syllabuses are a path that interest us. For a study on the syllabus of international law courses at the undergraduate level, see Betancur-Restrepo & Prieto-Ríos, *supra* note 7 at 69.

11 H. Claude Horack, "Legal Education in the Latin-American Republics" (1950) 2 *J Leg Educ* 287.

the interchange of law students and law professors amongst the American countries.[12] Even considering the US-centric perspective of this study, Horack was able to notice long-lasting aspects of Latin American legal education:

> Teaching is largely by the lecture method except in seminars and practice court work. . . . All the schools have been influenced by the formal lecture methods of the continental law schools, particularly those of Spain, France, and Italy where until recent years many students and professors went for special or post-graduate study. Thus it is not unusual to find a lecturer who asks no questions of the students and permits no questions by them, but delivers a formal lecture that is mimeographed or printed and given out to the students. When this is not done a few students take shorthand notes of the lecture, which are then transcribed and given out to their fellows. In many schools this practice is encouraged.[13]

In Latin America, efforts directed at mapping and understanding legal education in our region are not a novelty either. Between 1959 and 1974, five international conferences put together representatives of Latin American law schools to exchange experiences regarding teaching law, a context described by one commentator as a process of modernization of law schools in Latin America.[14] The first of these Conferencias de Facultades y Escuelas Latinoamericanas de Derecho was held in Mexico City, in 1959. They were then convened in Lima (1961), Santiago de Chile (1963), Montevideo (1965) and Cordoba (1974). These meetings covered a broad range of topics. Among other issues, country reports depicting the status of legal education in various Latin American countries, teaching methods (with a strong critical view on the lecture method described by Horack above), and a call for a multidisciplinary approach to the study of law, including history, sociology, philosophy and politics, were all debated in these conferences.[15]

These examples illustrate the enduring character of the discussions on legal education in our region. However, endurance of these discussions does not mean that the Latin American context has been the same since the 1950s. According to recent publications, we keep on repeating past analysis on Latin American law, as "many of the old assumptions about Latin American legal institutions and culture continue to creep into contemporary scholarship and reform projects".[16] This is

12 American Bar Association, "1949 Proceedings of Section of International Law and Comparative Law. Part V, General Committee Reports" (1949) 5 *Horack Survey of Latin American Law Schools* 183 at 186–187.

13 Horack, *supra* note 12 at 288.

14 Héctor Fix-Zamudio, "Algunas Reflexiones Sobre La Enseñanza Del Derecho En México Y Latinoamérica" in Jorge Witker, ed., *Antología De Estudios Sobre Enseñanza Del Derecho* (Mexico City: UNAM, 1995) at 72.

15 For a more detailed analysis of the five Conferences of Latin American Law Schools held between 1959 and 1974, see Veçoso, *supra* note 7.

16 César Rodríguez-Garavito, "Remapping Law and Society in Latin America: Visions and Topics for a New Legal Cartography" in César Rodríguez-Garavito, ed., *Law and Society in Latin America: A New Map* (New York: Routledge, 2015) at 1.

due to the persistent influence of the law-and-development paradigm, especially the first wave of this scholarship and practice from the 1960s. In this setting, "such assumptions tend to depict Latin American legal fields as marked by large gaps between norms and practice, exacerbated legal pluralism, clientelistic legal cultures, and authoritarianism".[17]

This traditional critique of Latin American law has problems.[18] This view is problematic because the context that we experience today in our region is completely different from the one experienced in the 1960s in geopolitical, social and legal terms.[19] More important, beyond the fact that the context is changing, this traditional critique of Latin American law is based on an imprecise comparison made against the Global North, a comparison that presupposes certain characteristics of the legal institutions of the North that do not exist today.[20]

This asymmetrical comparison between the North and the South is still influential in our context, as Latin American scholars keep articulating legal materials produced in the North without challenging the traditional critique of Latin American law mentioned above.[21] In this setting, what we have is "a perspective of analysis that reconstructs and reinforces Latin America's place as a 'reception context' – of norms, theories and doctrines from 'production contexts' of the global North".[22]

Furthermore, it is necessary to remember that the return of international law in the second half of the 20th century refers simultaneously to the recognition of its relevance and the opening of intense debates about the uses and meanings of the discipline.[23] Some consider that the renewal is rather a continuity in what constitutes a broader trajectory of the discipline.[24] In general terms, we can see the emergence of deep splits within the thinking of contemporary international law between three great visions: the legalist-pragmatic, the liberal-cosmopolitan and the critical approaches to international law – the first constituting the traditional core of the discipline, the second ascribing to the disciplinary renewal

17 *Ibid.* at 2.
18 *Ibid.*
19 *Ibid.*
20 "In the meantime, in the midst of the economic crisis in Europe and the United States, unleashed by deregulation and austerity policies since 2008, the legal institutions of the Global North show many features that, according to law and development, characterize Latin America. The growing socioeconomic inequality in the North has led to small elites having a disproportionate and excessive amount of influence regarding the substance of laws; the precarious economy has created a steep rise in the informal sector and in legal pluralism; and the xenophobic reactions against immigration and the war against terrorism have given way to criminal laws and legal decisions typical of authoritarian regimes." *Ibid.*
21 *Ibid.* at 3–4.
22 *Ibid.* at 4.
23 Álvez Marín & Becker Lorca, *supra* note 7.
24 David Kennedy, "My Talk at the ASIL: What Is New Thinking in International Law? In Proceedings of the Annual Meeting (American Society of International Law)" (2000) 94 *Soc'y Int'l L* 104.

and the third opposing both currents in general.[25] Our project is ascribed to the critical side of international law.

This calls for new maps and critical approaches to rethink legal studies and practices in Latin America today to fully resonate with REDIAL's main objectives related to opening spaces to decolonize international legal education in the region. Without merely reproducing past critiques to legal education in the region, we aim at producing a new engaged map of international legal education in Latin America. Studies on legal education in the region rarely choose international law as an important focus of analysis, even considering that international law plays an influential role in Latin America today, as illustrated by the role of the Inter-American System of Human Rights. Just to mention one example, the Inter-American Court of Human Rights developed international standards on transitional justice in its case law on domestic amnesties, asserting an indisputable duty to punish serious human rights violations related to contexts of regime change.[26] These standards have been playing a decisive role in the Colombian peace process, which showed the limits of the nation-state as the only source of human rights in Latin America today.[27] Other examples would include global economic regulations, transnational claims of migrants, transnational spaces of deliberation and transnational mobilization of indigenous groups.[28]

Arnulf Becker underlines how a regional project called "American International Law" in the first half of the 20th century allowed human rights to embody structural transformation based on a political ideology of regional solidarity rejecting a moral conception of human rights. For Becker, in Latin America human rights empowered states to adopt social and economic policies.[29] In the 1970s this was replaced by a new development paradigm centered on a market structure. This also affected the human rights movement. This is a call to reclaim particularities of the human rights movement in Latin America.

Furthermore, there is also an extensive literature on subaltern studies and decolonial approaches towards epistemologies and power. Some of the literature has

25 Gerry Simpson, "The Situation on The International Legal Theory Front: The Power of Rules And The Rule Of Power" (2000) 11:2 *Eur J Intl L* 439.

26 For more on the "Inter-American view on amnesty", see Fabia Fernandes Carvalho Veçoso, "The Inter-American View on Amnesties: Human Rights Absolutism?" (2015) 35 *Revista Derecho Del Estado* 3; Fabia Fernandes Carvalho Veçoso. "Whose Exceptionalism? Debating the Inter-American View on Amnesty and the Brazilian Case" in Karen Engle Zinaida Miller & Dennis Davis, eds., *Anti-Impunity and the Human Rights Agenda* (Cambridge: Cambridge University Press, 2016) at 185.

27 On different relations between international law and the Colombian Peace Process, see Laura Betancur-Restrepo, "The Legal Status of the Colombian Peace Agreement" (2016) 110 *AJIL Unbound* 188; Juana Acosta-López, "The Inter-American Human Rights System and the Colombian Peace: Redefining the Fight Against Impunity" (2016) 110 *AJIL Unbound* 178; Nelson Camilo Sanchez, "Could the Colombian Peace Accord Trigger an ICC Investigation on Colombia?" (2016) 110 *AJIL Unbound* 172, among others.

28 Rodríguez-Garavito, *supra* note 17 at 16–17.

29 Arnulf Becker Lorca, "Human Rights in International Law? The Forgotten Origins of Human Rights in Latin America" (2017) 67:4 *UTLJ* 465.

focused on the relationship between settler state and indigenous peoples in many parts of the world.[30] From a Latin American perspective, the terms "coloniality" and "decolonial turn" have been used as theoretical tools to create awareness about the current political, institutional, socio-economic and cultural arrangements as direct consequence of past colonial arrangements.[31] This position argues that the world has not been fully decolonized, and as such the decolonial turn aims at re-signifying the importance of recognizing multiple epistemological, racial, economic and gender perspectives, among others, that challenge an Euro- and US-centric approach. Accordingly, "the history of modernity itself began with the violent encounter between Europe and America at the end of the fifteenth century", and Latin America's colonial relationship to Europe has had a prolonged duration, which has not completely ended.[32]

In this context, in the REDIAL project we have decided to advance a detailed assessment of the current status of international legal education in the region. In 2017, the *Revista Derecho del Estado* published a special issue on this topic that included different articles from REDIAL members.[33] The published papers included an exploration on the relationship between imperialism and international law, an analysis of the practice of international law in Chile in light of indigenous peoples, an assessment of international legal education in Bogotá and a history of past discussions on legal education in the region in Latin America. In this chapter, we would like to build up from those reflections and deepen this path of analysis by assessing the main features of graduate programs on international law in Chile and Colombia. We also explore the publishing system established

30 Eve Tuck & K. Wayne Yang. "Decolonization Is Not a Metaphor" (2012) 1:1 *Decolonization: Indigeneity, Education & Society* 1; Tshepo Madlingozi, "On Settler Colonialism and Post-Conquest Constitutions: The Decolonising Constitutional Vision of African Nationalists of Azania/South Africa" (2019) [Draft], <www.academia.edu/33747352/On_Settler_Colonialism_and_Post_Conquest_Constitutionness_The_Decolonising_Constitutional_Vision_of_African_Nationalists_of_Azania_South_Africa>.

31 See, among others, Aníbal Quijano, "Modernity, Identity, and Utopia in Latin America" (1993) 20:3 *Boundary* 2 140; Santiago Castro-Gómez & Ramón Grosfoguel, *El Giro Decolonial Reflexiones Para Una Diversidad Epistémica Más Allá Del Capitalismo Global* (Bogota: Siglo del Hombre Editores, 2007); Ada María Isasi-Díaz & Eduardo Mendieta, *Decolonizing Epistemologies: Latina/o Theology and Philosophy* (New York: Fordham University Press, 2012); Enrique Dussel, *1492 El Encubrimiento del Otro: Hacia el Origen del Mito de la Modernidad* (La Paz: Plural Editores – Facultad de Humanidades y Ciencias de la Educación – UMSA, 1994) at 19 and 74; Enrique Prieto-Rios & Kojo Koram, "Decolonising Epistemologies, Politicising Rights: An Interview with Eduardo Mendiet" (2015) 3:1 *Birkbeck Law Review* 13; Nelson Maldonado-Torres, "Thinking through the Decolonial Turn: Post-Continental Interventions in Theory, Philosophy, and Critique: An Introduction" (2011) *Transmodernity* 1.

32 Aníbal Quijano, "Modernity, Identity, and Utopia in Latin America" (1993) 20:3 *Boundary* 2 at 140.

33 The special issue is fully available as "Educación y derecho internacional: Reflexiones a propósito de la publicación de *Imperialismo y derecho internacional*" (2017) *Revista Derecho del Estado* 39, 3–186, online: <https://revistas.uexternado.edu.co/index.php/derest/issue/view/479>.

in these two countries in order to question whether there are tools to help us to decolonize international law in our contexts, or whether the practice that we analyze in this contribution is a reproduction of a colonialist and hegemonic model of education in international law. The next two sections of this contribution present the results of our research on graduate programs in international law and the publishing system in both Chile and Colombia.

Local postgraduate limited offer in international law

Amaral Palevi Gómez Arévalo stated that a colonial legacy might be identified in the Latin-American history of education. There are at least five main characteristics of this legacy: (1) the scholastic and the castellanization,[34] (2) the illustration influence, (3) the conception of education as a progress indicator, (4) the liberal myth about education as a solution for everything and (5) the irruption of neoliberalism as educative philosophy.[35] All of these factors are a consequence of a psychosocial and cultural dependence between our countries and the Global North as an inexplicable necessity to resemble them.

According to Enrique Dussel, the myth of modernity began in 1492 with the colonization of the Americas.[36] It was the beginning of the construction of a European imaginary of racial and intellectual superiority and the construction of the Other as intellectually and racially inferior. This imaginary construction materialized in the imposition of legal, social and economic structures as well as in the monopolization of knowledge and disciplines, creating situations of epistemic superiority in different disciplines, including international law.

Historically, the first universities in Colombia and Chile were founded during colonial periods and by an initiative of the Dominican and Jesuit religious orders. The scenario of epistemic superiority created an aspirational academic framework in the periphery to become a copy of the civilized academy in the metropolis. As stated by Frantz Fanon: "The native intellectual accepted the cogency of these ideas, and deep down in his brain you could always find a vigilant sentinel ready to defend the Greco-Latin pedestal".[37] One of the research questions we dealt with is if an aspirational academic framework in Colombia and Chile translated

34 By *castellanization* we refer to the process that took place during the colonization of Latin America in which the Spanish cultural, social and economic standards were imposed to the indigenous communities. These transformations gravely affected the original and ancestral traditions and manners that the original and indigenous peoples had. According to Gómez Arévalo, in terms of education, castellanization refers to the treatment given to the indigenous peoples, the *mestizos* and the afro descendants by forbidding and preventing them from any understanding further than a rudimentary reading and the imposed catechism in Spanish [Our own translation].

35 Amaral Palevi Gómez Arévalo, "Ideas Y Pensamientos Educativos En América Latina: De La Escolástica Colonial Al Posneoliberalismo Educativo" (2010) 11:2 *Revista Latinoamericana de Estudios Educativos* 115 at 117.

36 Dussel, *supra* note 32 at 19 and 74 [our own translation].

37 Frantz Fanon, *Black Skin, White Masks* (New York: Grove Press, 1967) at 37–38.

into a cult towards the academy and the intellectuals of the Global North. In the case of Colombia and Chile, this has led to the construction of an ideal of getting academic training in institutions of the Global North. There is a tradition of privileging studies abroad, mainly in universities in the United States or Europe.

And yet, legal education offered in these countries is not small. Colombia has more than 400,000 active lawyers, and there are 195 law schools and 147 master's degree programs (MDPs) related to law.[38] Chile has a much smaller legal community, with 60,000 active lawyers and 141 law schools (which is the result of an aggressive privatization and commodification of legal education in Chile since the 1980s), with 75 MDPs related to law.[39] But if legal *training* has a strong tradition and roots, it is possible to say that legal *academia* is quite young. Traditionally law schools have been run by practitioners and not by full-time scholars, but this has begun to change incrementally with the hiring of more professors with doctoral training dedicated exclusively to teaching and research and with the creation and strengthening of graduate programs. In Chile this change happened in the last decade, and there is no official record of it.

Most of the scholars who started this academic wave were trained abroad. The youth of the legal academia in these countries and the short (or non-existent) offer of doctoral programs in law partly explain the need that existed for a long time to study abroad. This has also meant an important impetus for the internationalization of the Colombian and Chilean academia and has enriched the legal and cultural exchange. However, it may also have led to increase the cult towards foreign academia and the intellectual production of the Global North.[40]

Studying abroad is enriching and positive on many levels, but it is as important to have a strong and attractive offer of national graduate programs (and to assess them as equivalent to foreign programs). On the one hand, strong national graduate programs can be a tool to decolonize the law and to emphasize and deepen on issues and needs specific to local and regional contexts, as well as to account for gaps, blind spots and epistemologies of ignorance that have traditionally been imported from other areas without major criticisms and that have ended up reproducing uncritical standards. On the other hand, in one of the

38 According to the Ministry of National Education, in Colombia there are 4,349,823 people eligible to enroll in higher education programs, out of a total of 48,203,405 inhabitants. Of these, 550,462 are enrolled in undergraduate courses (54,203 in law programs) in the country and 21,214 in master's degrees. Ministerio de Educación Nacional, "Compendio Estadístico de Educación Superior" (2016), online: *Ministerio de Educación Nacional* <www.mineducacion.gov.co/1759/articles-360739_recurso.pdf>.

39 Data information obtained from crossing the Supreme Court database and the Chilean National Ministry of Education. Chilean National Ministry of Education, "Higher Education Institutions' Directory" (April 2018) *Chilean National Ministry of Education*, online: <https://divesup.mineduc.cl>.

40 For instance, see the influence in the diagnose of the bibliography proposed in international law syllabi in Bogota (at undergraduate level), in Betancur-Restrepo & Prieto-Ríos, *supra* note 7 at 69–72.

Table 5.1 Available information on MDP offered in Colombia and Chile (prepared by authors)

Universities That Offer MDPs in International Law in Colombia and Chile			
	Name of University	*Type of Institution*	*Master's Degrees*
Colombia	Escuela Superior de Guerra	Public	1
	Universidad Católica de Colombia	Private	1
	Universidad de La Sabana	Private	1
	Universidad de los Andes	Private	1
	Universidad de Medellín	Private	1
	Universidad del Rosario	Private	1[1]
	Universidad Externado de Colombia	Private	2[2]
	Universidad Santo Tomás	Private	1
Chile	Universidad de Chile	Public	2
	Universidad Diego Portales	Private	1
	Universidad San Sebastián	Private	1[3]

1 The MDP in international law at Universidad del Rosario has three emphases the student can choose: international criminal law and IHL, international economic law and critical studies.

2 According to the National Ministry of Education, Universidad Externado de Colombia has only two MDP in international law, one in international law and another one in international taxation; nevertheless, the MDP in international law (in general) has two different emphases that the student might choose: international public law and international business law.

3 Universidad San Sebastián, "Máster de doble titulación en Derechos Humanos, Estado de Derecho y Democracia en Iberoamérica" *Universidad San Sebastián*, online: <www.uss.cl/centros-uss/idej/magister/>.

most inequitable regions of the world, a vigorous national offer of graduate programs is, for many people, indispensable and the only option available.

In this sense we want to examine the offer of MDPs related to international law in Colombia and Chile to determine the most important trends in specialized education in international law. In concrete, we pretend to identify some patterns regarding the geographical location of the programs, the main emphases that they have and the type of methodologies and teaching strategies they use. With these elements we will be able to start showing how a Western-centric perspective is favored and how the center-periphery logic is replicated in the Global South.

Among 147 MDPs in Colombia, only nine are in international law, with most of them offered by private institutions.[41] In Chile, amongst 75 MDPs, there are four in international law offered by public and private universities of Chile (Table 5.1).[42] In both countries, most of the MDPs are concentrated in the major cities of each country. In the Colombian case, the offer of MDPs is concentrated in Bogotá (the capital of the country) and Medellín (the country's second most important city) (Figure 5.1). In Chile, they are all based in Santiago (the capital city) (Figure 5.2). There is one (online) program that establishes a dual degree

41 Colombian National Ministry of Education, "National System of Information of Higher Education (SNIES)" (July 2018) *Colombian National Ministry of Education*, online: <https://snies.mineducacion.gov.co/consultasnies/programa>.

42 Chilean National Ministry of Education, "Higher Education Institutions' Directory" (April 2018) *Chilean National Ministry of Education*, online: <https://divesup.mineduc.cl>.

Figure 5.1 Geographical distribution of MDPs in international law in Colombia

Source: The authors, based on the ScimagoJR Ranking 2017, Scielo, Redalyc, DOAJ, Dialnet and LatinIndex databases.

with a Spanish law school, whose main topics are human rights, the rule of law and democracy in Iberoamerica.

In Chile, the ways of practicing the discipline of international law, for example through the offer of graduate studies, are functional to the characteristics of a Chilean political model that is understood mainly in terms of economic international insertion responding to power relations of the international system, and specifically to the hegemony of a neoliberal discourse. Therefore, many programs are focused on international law, commerce and investments.[43] There is also a relevant recent development of programs with main focus on human rights. The MDP in international economic law is offered in conjunction with a German university. Hence, most of its content focuses on European and German experiences.[44] Part of this international neoliberal model applies also for the offer

43 MDP in conjunction with Heidelberg University and another with a focus on arbitration. Information available at Comisión Nacional de Acreditación website. Comisión Nacional de Acreditación, "Búsqueda Avanzada de Acreditaciones" *Comisión Nacional de Acreditación*, online: <www.cnachile.cl/Paginas/buscador-avanzado.aspx>.

44 It is the case of the courses about Chilean cases before the WTO, economic integration in Latin America and international arbitration in Chile.

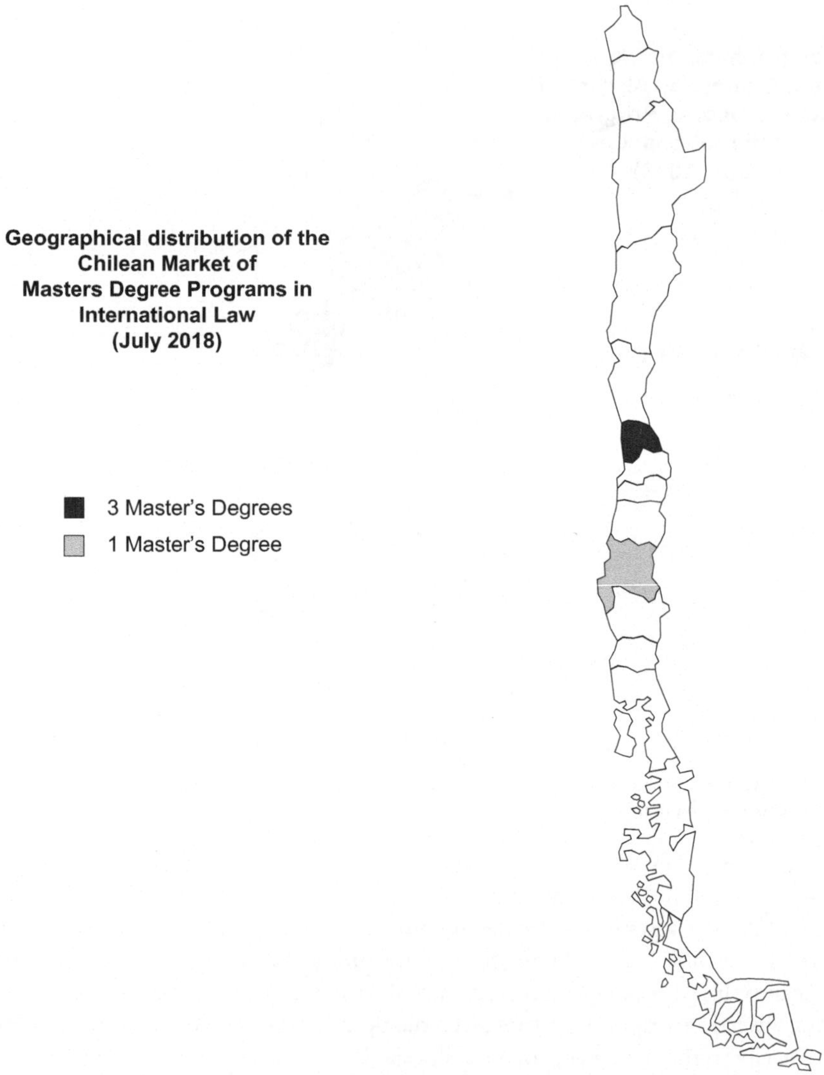

Figure 5.2 Geographical distribution of MDPs in international law in Chile

Source: The authors, based on the Chilean National Ministry of Education database.

of graduate programs. In Chile, universities of the Global North offer graduate programs mainly in international law in different modalities: online, partially online or even through institutional offices in the country. Information about this graduate program is presented as any other commodity.[45]

45 One example is Educaedu Chile, "19 Masters y Cursos de Derecho Internacional en Chile" *Educaedu Chile*, online: <www.educaedu-chile.com/derecho-internacional>.

In Colombia, 50% of the MDPs propose a comprehensive study of international law, while most of the remaining programs focus on international human rights law and international humanitarian law (IHL). The emergence of MDPs focused on international human rights Law and IHL occurred after the enactment of domestic normative instruments that recognized the existence of the armed conflict and established different mechanisms for the victims' reparation.[46] Interestingly, this could show a correspondence between programs offered and local needs, but it also suggests a limitation in the topics addressed in the international legal programs. This is probably because in Colombia, for a long time, the interest in international legal issues was limited to aspects related to the armed conflict (including the international obligations of Colombia that regulated the conflict, the struggle of the victims and the intervention of international institutions in this regard). There is a long Colombian tradition to equate studies in international law with human rights and IHL. In this sense, the first generalist master's program on international law began to work only in 2010, since all the other previous postgraduate programs (different to MDPs) were limited to aspects of human rights and IHL.[47]

We must recognize that the international legal academia in Chile and Colombia is experiencing a growing process that has allowed the consolidation of MDPs specializing in international law. Naturally, in the first stages of this process scholars have been keen with introducing some basic notions of international law and entailing them with the local context and necessities. In that sense, we see how Colombia has historically privileged education in international human rights law and IHL, while Chile has favored international economic law and recently international human rights law (Figure 5.3).

This correspondence between education and local context might be positive but might also be problematic. Confining specialized education with certain topics restricts both scholars' and practitioners' perspectives, preventing them to perceive and study some other issues that are also important for the country. A good example of this is how in Colombia the issues related to international economic law and international investment law were rarely studied until a couple of years ago, even when they had serious and important effects not only to the national economy but also in human rights and environmental law.

Furthermore, from the contents studied in the existing MDP, there might also arise some problematic issues related to the understanding of international law. For instance, in the case of Chile MDPs, it is feasible to see how international

46 The first MDP on international human rights law and international humanitarian law was offered in 2013. For 2017 the offer increased to four MDP focused on these topics.

47 In Colombia there is an important tradition of offering graduate programs called "specializations" (which are a degree superior to the undergraduate but lower than the master's degree). With the tendency to professionalize the legal academia and to unify criteria between international and national diplomas, MDPs on offer have increased (and many former specializations have become MDP). In this sense, the offer of specializations in international law for a long time was dominated to programs on human rights and IHL. The first specialization in human rights and IHL was offered in 1999. Nowadays, there is still an offer of more than 16 specializations limited to these topics.

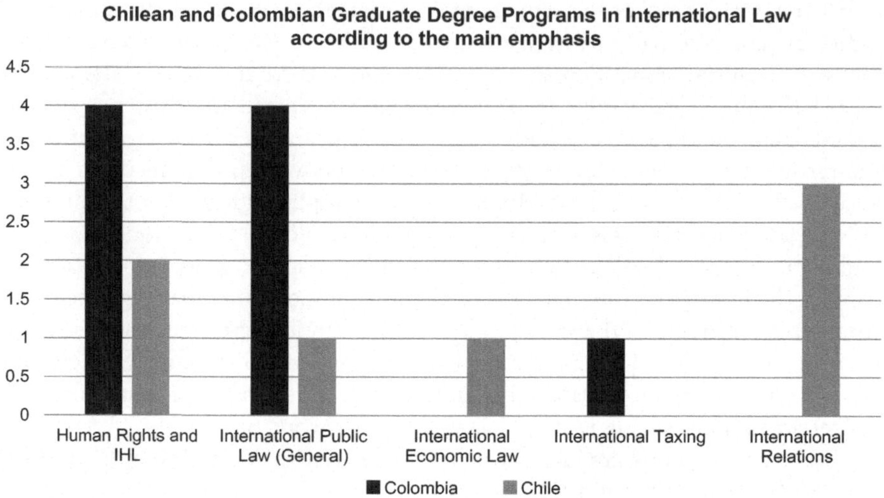

Figure 5.3 Chilean and Colombian MDPs in international law, according to their main emphasis

Source: The authors, based on the National System of Information of Higher Education of the Colombian National Ministry of Education database and Chilean National Ministry of Education.

economic law is taught from an orthodox perspective where it is understood as positive and necessary for development.

It is also important to recognize that MDPs in these countries incorporate a fragmented conception of international law due to the specialized lenses they have. In that sense, the study of topics as international human rights law and IHL is usually done without acknowledging other branches of international law that might be relevant for the local context, even within the frame of the Colombian armed conflict. In the Chilean case, the perspective is mainly focused on economic perspectives, equally fragmented. Regardless of whether this is conscious or unconscious, it contributes to reinforcing epistemologies of ignorance and promotes a limited conception of international law.

There is also a relevant common note between Chile's and Colombia's MDPs. In both cases, the specialized education in international law offered by the MDPs is limited to very few cities, normally located in the most important regions of each country. In part this implies that this type of education is concentrated in some "centers", leaving the less important (in the national economy) areas in the "periphery", replicating the colonialist formula of "inclusion-exclusion". In addition, as a consequence of the highly inequitable social and economic conditions of the population in both countries, this type of geographical limitation strengthens a knowledge gap and promotes the lack of interest and perceived relevance of international law in the regions.

In our opinion, the current state of the MDPs in international law in Chile and Colombia reproduces and maintains some characteristics of a hegemonic model of education in international law. The offered programs promote limited and biased conceptions of international law but also replicate a model of exclusion, which holds international law as an area for privileged minorities that have some resources that allow them to get to the MDPs. Nevertheless, we gladly recognize that there are some recent developments and some new proposals that intend to broaden the study in international law in order to present and teach a wider range of international law theories and perspectives. But on the concentrated offer in the main cities, there is still much to be done.

Continuing with those efforts, we firmly believe that education and the MDPs constitute an important tool to decolonization in our countries. The MDPs are the perfect scenario to promote and strengthen the ability to discern as well as to develop critical thinking in Chilean and Colombian scholars and practitioners of international law. It is only by promoting and developing strategies towards a wider and diverse education in international law that acknowledges the peripheral position that we occupied that we recover our historical particularities in the Latin American International Law Project.

Dealing with an imposed "global" system of publications

After reflecting on the dynamics of the MDPs on offer in international law, in this section we will reflect on the existing epistemological limitations derived from rankings and academic databases. Publications are means by which academics share questions, interests and research results. They should reflect the diversity within academia, be able to discuss global, regional and local needs, enrich and open new dialogues with peers, and serve as essential materials for the classroom.

Nowadays, publications are also an important mean to evaluate the performance of academics by institutions. This last aspect seeks in principle to guarantee the quality of the research and strengthen internationalization. To do this, universities and national institutes have tended to adopt standardized international rankings established by international index platforms such as ScimagoJR Ranking 2017 (Scopus), Web of Science (WOS) or Open Researcher and Contributor ID (ORCID). These indexing systems use different indicators in order to determine the quality of the journal, the book series or the publishing house that is being evaluated. Other indicators used are the H Index, the level of international collaboration, the citation and the circulation of the publication.[48]

These international ranking systems have been broadly criticized, among other reasons, because they fail to take into consideration some factors as the asymmetries among the publications and the geopolitical influence that some countries might have.[49] Nonetheless, in Colombia and in Chile, the National Ministries of

48 "Help" *Scimago Journal & Country Rank*, online: <www.scimagojr.com/help.php>.

49 For some critics on rankings see Alma Maldonado, "¿Qué Dicen Y Qué Omiten Los Rankings De Universidades En América Latina?" (13 July 2016) *Nexos*, online: <https://educacion.

Education and the institutions in charge of the research policies – Departamento Administrativo de Ciencia Tecnología e Innovación (Colciencias) and Comisión Nacional de Investigación Científica y Tecnológica (Conicyt), respectively – have replicated the same logic promoted by international databases such as Scopus, WOS or ORCID. In the case of Colombia, the platform used by Colciencias classifies scholars' publications in five categories, based exclusively on the indexing system of the journal in which the article was published, which copies the Scopus classification.[50] In Chile, Conicyt has adopted an analogous logic by coupling with the WOS, Scopus and Scielo indexing databases.[51]

The public institution in charge of the certification process called Comisión Nacional de Acreditación (CNA) through a group of experts established a chart of academic scientific productivity in law in 2015. This group of experts established a minimum of 80 points to be a professor in a doctoral graduate program, 40 points for an research master's degree and 20 points for a professional master's degree. The list of activities to gain points rewards the highest to publish in a WOS journal (12 points) or with a prestigious international publisher (36 points) from a strict and selected list. In both cases, the scholar needs to publish in a foreign imperial language (English) and for a small elite audience.[52]

However, one of the problems of replicating these indexes without alteration lies in the small number of local journals that are indexed in those foreign databases. For instance, in Scopus there are 602 law journals worldwide and 25 in Latin America, but there only seven Colombian law journals[53] (all of them in the two lowest quartiles) and seven Chilean law journals (one of them in the first quartile, four in the second, one in the last, and one without classification).[54] Nevertheless, according to the collected information from several minor and Latin American databases (LatinIndex, Scielo and Redalyc, among others), we find that there are at least 50 law journals in Colombia and 78 in Chile. It means

nexos.com.mx/?p=279>; Felipe Martínez Rizo, "Los Rankings De Universidades: Una Visión Crítica, Revista De La Educación Superior" (2011) 40:157 *Rev. Educ. Sup* 77; PTM Marope, Peter J Wells & Ellen Hazelkorn, *Rankings and Accountability in Higher Education Uses and Misuses* (Paris: UNESCO, 2013).

50 Colciencias, "Manual del Aplicativo CvLAC: Curriculum Vitae para Latinoamérica y el Caribe" (2016) *Colciencias*, online (pdf): <http://colciencias.gov.co/sites/default/files/ckeditor_files/manual-de-usuario-cvlac.pdf>.

51 Conicyt, "Scielo Chile Incorpora Cinco Nuevas Revistas A Su Colección" (6 June 2016) *Conicyt*, online: <www.conicyt.cl/informacioncientifica/2016/06/06/scielo-chile-incorpora-cinco-nuevas-revistas-a-su-coleccion/>.

52 Comisión Nacional de Acreditación de Postgrado, "Orientaciones Sobre Productividad Por Comités De Área" *Comisión Nacional de Acreditación de Postgrado*, online (pdf): <www.cnachile.cl/Documentos%20de%20Paginas/ORIENTACIONES%20DE%20PRODUCTIVIDAD%20POR%20COMIT%C3%89S%20DE%20AREA%2018-06-2015.pdf>.

53 Anuario Colombiano de Derecho Internacional, Universitas, Jurídicas, Revista de Derecho Privado, Revista Derecho del Estado, Revista Criminalidad and Revista Republicana.

54 Revista Chilena de Derecho, Política Criminal, Revista de Derecho, Estudios Constitucionales, Ius et Praxis, Revista de Estudios Histórico-Jurídicos and Revista Chilena de Derecho y Tecnología.

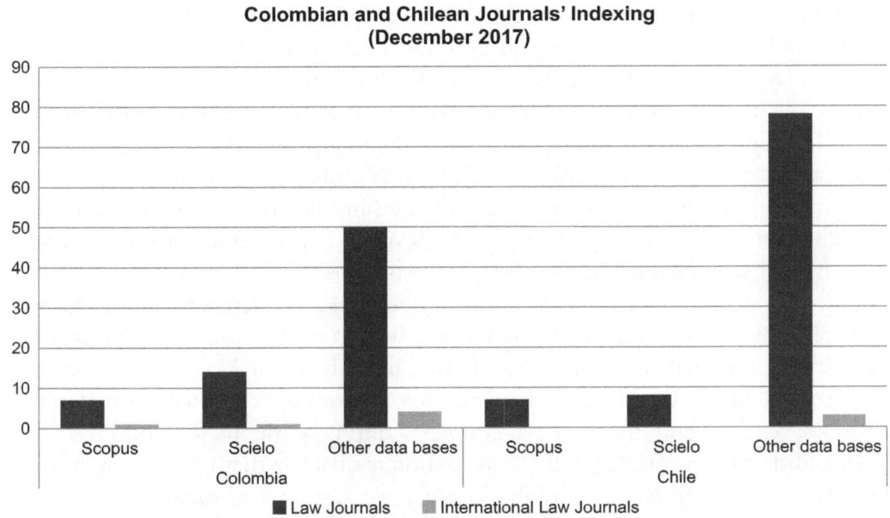

Figure 5.4 Index of legal journals in Chile and Colombia

that more than 86% of Colombian specialized journals and more than 91% of Chilean law journals are not considered quality publications. Furthermore, there are only three specialized journals in international law (in each country),[55] but only one (the *Anuario Colombiano de Derecho Internacional*) is indexed in the Scopus database and one in Scielo (*Revista de Relaciones Internacionales, Estrategia y Seguridad*) (Figure 5.4).

As a result, Colombian and Chilean scholars need to target mainly foreign journals to publish their articles if they want to comply with the requirements of their institutions and national research agencies that, in the end, define their position and salary. Publishing abroad has without any doubt many advantages, as it allows broader academic dialogues and, in many cases, implies an effort for improving the quality of the publication. But besides the problems that any indexing system has, it is particularly problematic that the only indexes accepted are those in which Latin American academia is openly marginal.

It is important to consider that countries such as the United States, the United Kingdom, Germany, Japan, France and Canada have the highest numbers of journals indexed in the most important databases accepted by Chilean and Colombian

55 In Colombia, Anuario Colombiano de Derecho Internacional, Revista de Relaciones Internacionales, Estrategia y Seguridad and Perspectivas Internacionales. A few years ago there was also the "International Law-Revista Colombiana de Derecho Internacional" that recently disappeared. In Chile they are Boletín Nexos, Revista de Estudios de la justicia and Tratados de Chile.

research guidelines but also for the global academic market.[56] With this limited origin and scope of publications, Colombian and Chilean scholars are forced not only to publish in an alien language but also to address some specific audiences and discuss topics and debates that interest those contexts. This and leaves aside and makes invisible concrete political projects, including the aim to decolonize law. The imposition of English as the main language to publish in high-ranked publications makes it impossible to engage with traditionally excluded communities that do not read foreign languages (something not unimportant in contexts of high inequality such as Latin America). Inevitably, those publications (and rankings) have their own agendas that hinder the possibility to address topics only relevant to local and regional contexts but probably not attractive to those journals and epistemic centers. This situation must lead us to ask whether these barriers are silencing Colombian and Chilean (and more broadly, Latin American) voices and whether academics are entering into a race for citations in order to be valued in the national, regional and international contexts limiting academic freedom.

In addition to the above, there is an economic obstacle that is worth highlighting. Many of the indexed journals do not have any type of open access to the publications, and subscriptions tend to be too expensive for the local context, hampering the circulation of knowledge in these countries.[57] For example, the subscription to the *European Journal of International Law* (published by Oxford and which includes online access to only four issues) costs US$430,[58] almost 1.7 times the minimum wage in Colombia and almost equal to the Chilean one. This is relevant because publishing in journals and databases is so expensive and in languages that are not accessible to a big part of the population, limiting more equitable dialogues that involve a larger scope of scholars and students in the region.

If part of our project includes strengthening local and regional academia, including epistemic issues left aside by mainstream scholarship and proposing an alternative and decolonial vision of international law, we have to find a way to engage in conversations with local and regional peers traditionally disregarded and make an effort to help circulate knowledge among countries within the South.[59]

Conclusion

The growing but still limited offer of MDPs in Chile and Colombia has the potential to be a tool of decoloniality, of inclusion and of expanding the visions

56 ScimagoJR, "Ranking 2017, Country Rankings" *ScimagoJR*, online: <www.scimagojr.com/countryrank.php>.

57 Open access has also been criticized for its dangerous effects in poor countries. Brenda Wingfield & Bob Millar, "How the Open Access Model Hurts Academics in Poorer Countries" (17 April 2019) *University Affairs*, online: <www.universityaffairs.ca/opinion/in-my-opinion/how-the-open-access-model-hurts-academics-in-poorer-countries/>.

58 Prices and fees according to the *European Journal of International Law* web page. European Journal of International Law, "Purchase" *Oxford Academic*, online: <https://academic.oup.com/ejil/subscribe>.

59 There are some interesting efforts in this regard, such as the creation of the *Third World Approaches to International Law Review (TWAILR)*.

of international law in accordance with national and regional contexts. It may also be the opposite: a tool for reproducing traditional standards and epistemic blind spots and strengthening hierarchies. We have seen that the topics of most MDPs are limited but also that there are some recent examples in Colombia and Chile that begin to change and expand the traditional view of international law. We have also seen that there is still much to be done in terms of centralizing knowledge and including regions in the national academic offer.

On the other hand, the literature published and used is another crucial issue. It is important to strengthen the publication processes in a rigorous way but without having to ignore most publications in the region and be forced to publish only in English. Reproducing foreign indexes and rankings in an uncritical manner as if they were objective and consistent with all the contexts is problematic and can have very negative consequences: instead of strengthening regional academia, it can weaken local production and limit the selection of topics and alternative publications relevant for local needs.

Finally, we must account for the voices and the problems of the region. Knowing ourselves, reading us, studying us and criticizing us are the main tasks in this decolonial effort. In this sense, our project advocates the need to be aware of what we do and from there to assume the role of an academic activist under which we seek to account for what should be the law, not only in terms of its validity but also of its correction in light of the standards of justice.

Part 2
Sites of engagement

6 Indigenous peoples and Belo Monte Hydroelectric Plant

The mobilization of displaced Indigenous peoples in the urban area of Altamira

Estella Libardi de Souza and Assis da Costa Oliveira

Introduction

The Belo Monte Hydroelectric Power Plant (HPP) on the Xingu River, constructed in the municipalities of Altamira, Vitória do Xingu and Brasil Novo in the state of Pará, has been a site of conflict between the Brazilian State and Indigenous peoples for more than 30 years. In the late 1980s, Eletronorte (Centrais Elétricas do Norte do Brasil S.A.) announced its plans to deploy, in the Volta Grande do Xingu (VGX),[1] the Kararaô HPP. This was to be the first step in a project that included the construction of six plants on the Xingu River and one on its main tributaries, the Iriri River, forming the "Hydroelectric Complex Xingu," which would flood parts of 12 Indigenous territories.[2]

The construction of hydroelectric dams on the Xingu River was studied and planned by the federal government since the mid-1970s, during the period of the military dictatorship in Brazil (1964–1985) when large "development" projects were implemented in the Amazon, with devastating effects for Indigenous peoples. In 1977, Shelton H. Davis argued that Indigenous peoples were the "victims of the miracle," that is, the economic development policy, responsible for high growth rates of the Brazilian gross domestic product (GDP) in the period known as "economic miracle," was the direct cause of deaths, diseases, cultural destruction and suffering that spread among Indigenous peoples, especially from the beginning of the 1970s.[3]

The hydroelectric plant planned by the military dictatorship for the Xingu River would have added to the list of major projects in the Amazon that caused genocide and ethnocide; however, it was avoided by the tenacious confrontation

1 The Volta Grande do Xingu is a stretch of about 180 km with rich biodiversity, consisting of islands, channels and rapids, where the Xingu River makes a huge curve after passing through the town of Altamira, in Pará State.

2 Fany Ricardo, "As usinas hidrelétricas e os índios" (1991) Centro Ecumênico de Documentação e Informação [CEDI 1991].

3 Shelton H. Davis, *Victims of the Miracle: Development and the Indians of Brazil* (Cambridge: Cambridge University Press, 1977).

by the people that would be affected. Indigenous peoples living in the Xingu basin, especially the Kayapó, strongly resisted this project and they mobilized, denouncing the damage to their territories and the lack of dialogue with the Brazilian government. The Xingu Indigenous Peoples Meeting (promoted by the Kayapó in Altamira in February 1989) against the construction of the Kararaô HPP brought together approximately 600 Indigenous peoples; this included 24 peoples from Brazil and abroad as well as environmentalists, anthropologists and journalists, among others.[4] This event had an enormous impact in Brazil and abroad, forcing the federal government to delay and reshape the hydroelectric project. The government renamed the project Belo Monte and, in the years that followed, there were many battles fought between the successive governments trying to establish the plant and the population struggling to stop it.[5]

The long and strong resistance undertaken by Indigenous peoples resulted in the project being postponed for decades. In the period in which the project was suspended, there were significant constitutional and international law changes, in Brazil and abroad, which ensured important achievements in the field of Indigenous rights. It is noteworthy that Brazil ratified the International Labour Organization Convention (No. 169) concerning Indigenous and Tribal Peoples in Independent Countries and supported adoption of the United Nations Declaration on the Rights of Indigenous Peoples. Therefore, Brazil has a commitment to advance the rights of Indigenous peoples, among which is the right to consultation and free, prior and informed consent (FPIC) in the decisions that affect them within the states in which they live.

Consultation is a duty of the states and is an instrument for the effective participation of Indigenous peoples on measures that may directly affect them. The aim of any consultation process is to reach agreement or obtain consent, which means that Indigenous peoples must be able to exercise significant influence in the decision-making process. The perspectives and concerns of Indigenous peoples must be accommodated, which implies demonstrable and verifiable changes in the project's objectives, parameters or design. On the other hand, in large-scale projects (such as the Belo Monte HPP), there is not only the duty of

4 Amazonia Hoje, "Kararaô, as águas vão rolar?" (1989) 1:3, 28, CEDI 1991, *supra* note 2; Arsênio Oswaldo & Seva Filho, "Tenotã-Mõ: alerta sobre as consequências dos projetos hidrelétricos no rio Xingu" (2005) São Paulo: IRN, 2005.

5 Alexandra Martins Silva, "Megaprojetos, conflitos e processo decisório – a análise de uma controvérsia intemporal chamada Belo Monte" (2015) *Universidade de Coimbra, Faculdade de Economia, Programa de Doutoramento em Governação, Conhecimento e Inovação, Coimbra*, online (pdf): <https://estudogeral.sib.uc.pt/bitstream/10316/29442/1/Megaprojetos%2C%20conflitos%20e%20processo%20decis%C3%B3rio.pdf>.

Silva, who analyzes the decision-making process that led to the construction of the Belo Monte SA, states that it cannot be considered only as a water project, since it represents "a symbol of resistance and also persistence marked on the one hand by the struggle of indigenous peoples and on the other hand by the desire of successive Brazilian rulers to build it" (p. 2). In addition, other segments of social movements such as those related to women, people affected by dams, children, the elderly, blacks and riverside communities, among others, had a relevant role leading the resistance against hydroelectric projects. However, they did not have the same visibility and efficiency obtained by indigenous people.

accommodation but the obligation of the State to obtain the consent of Indigenous peoples, as understood by the Inter-American Commission on Human Rights.[6]

The new constitutional and international standards, especially the rights of participation, consultation and free, prior and informed consent of Indigenous peoples in relation to the state measures that affect them, are central to the proposal to establish non-colonial relations. Before this new framework of rights, states considered that the territories where Indigenous peoples lived, and the peoples themselves, were under their control and tutelage and, therefore, under their sole decision. However, the right to consultation and FPIC reaffirms the principle that Indigenous peoples have equal dignity to all peoples and cultures and have the same capacity to control their institutions and freely determine their ways of life and development model.[7]

Nevertheless, this new legal framework for the rights of Indigenous peoples did not alter the governmental plans for the construction of the Belo Monte HPP nor the authoritarian practices of the Brazilian State in the implementation of major projects in the Amazon, as we will discuss below. After more than two decades of conflicts,[8] the construction of the Belo Monte HPP started in 2011 and was concluded in November 2019. No consultation process, according to the international standards, has been carried out.

With an installed capacity of up to 11,233.1 megawatts (MW) and costs currently estimated at over US$7 billion, Belo Monte is the largest public works project in Brazil. The federal government presents the plant as "clean energy, renewable and sustainable"[9] and advertises that it does not adversely affect

6 CIDH, "Pueblos indígenas, comunidades afrodescendientes y recursos naturales: Protección de derechos humanos en el contexto de actividades de extracción, explotación y desarrollo" (2015) *Organización de los Estados Americanos*, online (pdf): <www.oas.org/es/cidh/informes/pdfs/IndustriasExtractivas2016.pdf>.

7 Raquel Yrigoyen Fajardo, "De la tutela a los derechos de libre determinación del desarollo, participación, consulta e consentimiento: fundamentos, balance y retos para su implementación" (2009) 1:2 *Amazônica – Revista de Antropologia*.

8 Beto Ricardo & Fany Ricardo, "Povos Indígenas no Brasil: 2006/2010" (2011) *São Paulo: Instituto Socioambiental.*

Despite the defeat suffered by Eletronorte in 1989, the company continued working to implement the hydroelectric project on the Xingu River. The Belo Monte project was re-presented at the late 1990s, with several changes, but was still contested by social movements and indigenous peoples; the environmental licensing was judicially invalidated by the court in 2003. In 2005, the third attempt to implement the project began. Indigenous peoples and social movements mobilized intensely against the project; the mobilization included meetings and other events in various cities of the country and abroad. An emblematic moment of the mobilization against Belo Monte was the Xingu Vivo Para Sempre Meeting, held in Altamira in May 2008, with participation of indigenous peoples, social movements, civil society organizations, researchers, and environmentalists, among others. The meeting was attended by about 3,000 people, including about 800 indigenous people, from more than 20 indigneous communities.

9 Daniele Bragança, "Dilma inaugura usina hidrelétrica de Belo Monte" (5 May 2016) *OECO*, online: <www.oeco.org.br/noticias/dilma-inaugura-belo-monte-maior-obra-do-seu-governo/>; CEDI 1991, *supra* note 2.

Indigenous peoples because it does not flood Indigenous lands.[10] The problems encountered by Indigenous peoples are nonetheless serious.

In addition to reducing the flow of the Xingu and jeopardizing the maintenance of the ecosystem and the livelihoods of Indigenous peoples in Volta Grande do Xingu, the Belo Monte HPP displaced hundreds of Indigenous families. The Xipaya and Kuruaya peoples residing in the city of Altamira, which had part of its territory affected by the plant's reservoir, were especially affected. The enormous population influx that the construction of the project brought to the region also a had major impact on the Indigenous peoples and their territories.

Throughout the construction and the operation of the Belo Monte HPP, the Indigenous peoples affected by Belo Monte engaged in several political actions to denounce the effects of the project and to demand that the Brazilian State and the consortium responsible for the implementation of the plant, Norte Energia, comply with their demands. In addition, the struggle of Indigenous peoples is also a part of the decision-making processes of the Belo Monte HPP, so that they can be heard and have their positions considered with regard to the compensation and mitigation actions that affect them.

In this chapter, we discuss the political mobilization of Indigenous people, specifically the Xipaya and Kuruaya residing in the urban municipality of Altamira who were compulsorily displaced from the area that was destined to be the reservoirs of the Belo Monte HPP. We discuss their political mobilization using field research developed between 2015 and 2017 through interviews[11] with Indigenous leaders, direct action monitoring and documentary research. In the first part of the chapter, we outline the presence of Indigenous peoples in the city of Altamira and the social and political processes the Xipaya and Kuruaya have articulated since the 1990s, as well as their demands for ethnic recognition and territory. These demands run parallel to the attempts of the Brazilian State to implement the hydroelectric plant at Volta Grande do Xingu. Then we examine the implementation of Belo Monte HPP from the latter part of 2000s, when Indigenous peoples in Altamira demand the recognition of their ethnic identities, consideration of the specificity of their livelihoods and participation in the process of registration, negotiation and resettlement of the affected Indigenous families.

The case of HPP Belo Monte reveals the profound implications of the colonial history in the treatment of Indigenous people: their territories, identities and voices. It shows that relations between the Brazilian State and Indigenous peoples remain based on colonial and tutelary bases, resulting in the limitation and

10 BRASIL, "Belo Monte transforma a vida de 11 cidades do Pará" (25 May 2015) *ZE DUDU*, online: <www.zedudu.com.br/belo-monte-transforma-a-vida-de-11-cidades-do-par/>.

11 Indigenous persons interviewed in this research were previously informed of the objective of the research and the questions they would answer, and the publicization of their names and information. The people interviewed previously agreed with these ethical procedures orally, and it was recorded as a register for them and the researchers.

violation of the exercise of citizenship by Indigenous peoples, their autonomy and free determination.

The perpetuation of colonial relations, expressed in the tutelary practices related to Indigenous peoples and in disrespect for Indigenous rights, can be understood in the context of Aníbal Quijano called coloniality of power. Coloniality was developed in the context of colonialism, however it is more lasting and profound than this, having become the "foundational stone of the capitalist world power, colonial/modern and Eurocentric."[12] In this sense, coloniality originates from European colonialism but differs from it insofar as it refers to a pattern of power that structures social relations in Latin America.

The case also reveals the way Indigenous peoples face contemporary colonial dilemmas, including their strategies of "cultural rescue" and indigenization of the city, in which they produce a political use of collective memories.

Indigenous peoples and the history of Altamira

The presence of Indigenous people in the urban area of Altamira is tied to the origins of the city.[13] The first non-Indigenous occupation referred to is the Tavaquara Mission, founded by Jesuit priests in 1750 near the Igarapé Panelas, which brought together the Juruna, Xipaya, Kuruaya and Arara peoples. However, the presence of Indigenous peoples in the city is not the result of the old Tavaquara Mission alone. Simoni and Dagnino point out that the Indigenous presence in Altamira follows the occupation cycles of the Middle Xingu region and the establishment of the city, highlighting three important periods in the process of establishing the city: missionary settlements (1750–1880); two moments during the rubber cycle (1879–1945); and developmentalist expansion (from 1970 until today).[14]

According to Simoni and Dagnino, despite the importance of the mission as a reference point for Indigenous populations, as it is still part of their social memory, missionary occupation was not permanent. The village was definitively established only during the rubber cycle, as of 1879. According to these authors, the Xipaya, Kuruaya and Juruna peoples played an important role in this economic cycle either because of their knowledge of the region or because they worked in the rubber plantations. Many Indigenous people were enslaved and had been forced to travel to work in those plantations. The Xipaya and the Kuruaya were

12 Aníbal Quijano, "¡Qué tal raza!" (2000) 6:1 *Rev. Venez. de Economía y Ciencias Sociales* at 37, translated by the authors.

13 The town Altamira had, in the 2010 census, 99,075 habitants (for 2018, it is estimated 113,195 people) in an area of 159,533.328 square kilometer (IBGE, 2017), land area which makes it the largest Brazilian municipality and one of the largest in the world. Much of the territory of the municipality covers indigenous lands and conservation units. The urban area of the municipality, the city of Altamira, is situated on the banks of the Xingu River and is cut by the Transamazônica highway; it concentrates much of the population.

14 Alessandra T. Simoni & Ricardo S. Dagnino, "Dinâmica demográfica da população indígena em áreas urbanas: o caso da cidade de Altamira, Pará" (2016) 33:2 *R. bras. Est. Pop* 303.

also forced to move because of conflicts with the Kayapó people. In this context, there was a wide circulation between rubber extraction and production sites along the Xingu and Iriri Rivers and the city of Altamira. In this process, relations between Indigenous and non-Indigenous peoples intensified and many marriages took place between Indigenous peoples and the "rubber soldiers."[15] At the end of the rubber cycle in 1945, "the populations involved in rubber production began to find better living conditions in the city of Altamira and settled there."[16] From the 1970s onwards, with the construction of the Trans-Amazonian Highway, the Indigenous people living in Altamira suffered real-estate cost increases that forced them to live in more distant neighborhoods. They moved closer to the border of the Altamira and Ambé Igarapés as well as the Panelas.

Parente suggests that the movement of the Xipaya and the Kuruaya (the two most populous groups) towards Altamira stems from social and historical reasons.[17] For example, they moved because of the territorial conflicts with the Kayapó and with non-Indigenous peoples. According to Parente, in addition to the context of violence and expropriations to which the Xipaya and Kuruaya peoples were subjected, the city was seen as a space where they could have their demands for health and education met.[18] It was seen as a space for reconstruction of the territory and ethnic identity with the relatives who lived in the city.

"Mixed" in with the non-Indigenous society and therefore considered as "extinct," the "dispersion" towards the city did not result in the disappearance of the Xipaya and Kuruaya peoples. They engendered strategies to (re)construct their ethnic identities in the city, branding identities that distinguish them from each other and non-Indigenous peoples. According to Parente,[19] the "blood" is a metaphor that evokes (and "proves") the Xipaya and Kuruaya's ancestry based on the memory of the elders. They tell the stories of their peoples and maintain the

15 Isabel Cristina Martins Guilhen, "A batalha da borracha: propaganda política e migração nordestina para a Amazônia durante o Estado Novo" (1997) 9 *Revista de Sociologia e Política* 95. "Soldiers of Rubber" was the expression used to categorize the migration of the northeastern workers to the Amazon during period of the Estado Novo (1937–1945), when it promoted the national campaign "Battle of Rubber ", a result of agreements between Brazil and United States (the Washington Agreements) that had a focus on the increasing of production strategic raw material (especially rubber and minerals) for the equipment used in World War II, which lasted from 1939 to 1945, in exchange for technical and financial support from the Americans. According to Guillen (1997), the ideas of "soldiers of rubber" and "battle of rubber" were used to promote the involvement of Brazilian society in the effort of cooperation for the war. The migration to the Amazon had government incentives, and, "as a result of drought in 1942, about 50,000 Northeastern workers destinations volunteered (or were willing) to face the battle of production" (p. 95).

16 Simoni & Dagnino, *supra* note 14 at 309 (translated by the authors).

17 Francilene de Aguiar Parente, "Eles são indígenas e nós também: pertenças e identidades étnicas entre xipaya e kuruaya em Altamira/Pará. Tese (Doutorado)" (2016) Universidade Federal do Pará, Instituto de Filosofia e Ciências Humanas, Programa de Pós-Graduação em Antropologia, Belém.

18 *Ibid.*

19 *Ibid.*

consciousness of belonging to their respective group. Therefore, the blood and the memory of the elders are the central elements to assert themselves as Xipaya people and Kuruaya people.

Parente argues that despite the apparent dispersion and mixture in the process of production of difference and belonging in Altamira, the Xipaya and Kuruaya, grouped in neighborhoods or associations, recreated their world in the city, reconstructed their life and its territory and marked these areas of the city as Indigenous peoples' places. Yet the territory is recreated in a discontinuous way, sometimes in the plots of land, farms, sites and villages where they transit, sometimes in the city, which is a place of reproduction of life: "meetings, socialization of stories, revitalization of language, strengthening of culture, discussion of demands and strategies of struggle."[20] In this sense, Parente notes that the city is not thought of as the place of the Other but the Indigenous as well, although it was appropriated by non-Indigenous peoples.

The strategies of the Xipaya and Kuruaya peoples to re-elaborate their ways of life and to reconstruct their ethnic identities in the city are part of the processes of resistance of these peoples to the violence of contact with non-Indigenous society, which almost resulted in the end of their existence.

They are also form the "re-existence" of the Xipaya and Kuruaya peoples, a category adopted by Adolfo Albán-Achinte to analyze the process of emancipation and struggle of Afro peoples in the Americas, which considers the development of ways of existing, that is, to be in the world in the condition of subjects, and not only to resist the condition of subjugation. Re-existence refers to the process of "re-elaborating life in adverse conditions, in an attempt to overcome these conditions to occupy a dignified place in society"[21] and which remains present in our racialized and discriminatory societies.

In this way, the Xipaya and Kuruaya peoples resist and "re-exist" in the city of Altamira, facing violence and genocidal and ethnocidal actions practiced by non-Indigenous society.

Struggle and political organization by ethnic recognition in the context of the Belo Monte HPP

When, at the end of the 1980s, Eletronorte attempted to build the Kararaô HPP, it knew of the presence of Indigenous peoples who lived in the city of Altamira and understood that they would be affected by construction. In the Report on Indigenous Populations in the Area of Influence of the Kararaô HPP to CNEC S.A. (1988), the anthropologist Regina Müller confirmed that the Indigenous population in the area around the Kararaô HPP consisted of 3,600 people and 11 officially recognized territories with enormous sociocultural, demographic diversity and history of contact and relation with the territory. According to Müller,

20 *Ibid.* at 243.

21 Adolfo Albán Achinte, "Epistemes 'otras': ¿epistemes disruptivas?" (2012) 6 *KULA Antropólogos del Atlántico Sur* at 30, translated by the authors.

this diversity ranged from those that were more recently encountered Indigenous peoples (whose contact occurred in the 1980s) to those that had centuries of coexistence with non-Indigenous peoples. Many of these communities include those that inhabit places in the Amazon rainforest inaccessible to those who lived in the city. Of the 15 peoples identified by Müller (1988) as affected by the Kararaô HPP, four are considered directly impacted. They are the Juruna, the Xikrin, the Xipaya and the Kuruaya. The Xipaya and the Kuruaya lived around the borders of the Xingu, Iriri and Curuá Rivers and also live in the urban area of Altamira.

The feasibility studies of the Kararaô HPP included a survey of Indigenous peoples in the city, conducted in 1988 by CNEC, Eletronorte and Fundação Nacional do Índio (Funai), with the objective of identifying the population that would be in the area directly affected by the plant. In the survey, it was found that "the majority of the [i]ndigenous people of the domiciles interviewed had settled in Altamira in the 1940s, most of them being Xipaya and Kuruaya, born in the Iriri and Curuá areas."[22]

In the 1989 document prepared by Eletronorte titled "Information to Indigenous Communities on Hydroelectric Facilities on the Xingu River," the company states that "in the city of Altamira, 42 indigenous families live today. There are 213 indigenous people and 30 non-indigenous people married to indigenous people. They belong to the groups Curuaya, Xipaya, Arara of Xingú, Karajá, and Kayabi."[23] Eletronorte presents a map of the places where the Indigenous population lived in Altamira, distributed in several neighborhoods. According to the company, the houses of the Indigenous people of Altamira would not be affected by the reservoir. It did, however, note that

> with the construction of the Kararaô plant and the growth of the city, the problems of these indigenous people will increase. Eletronorte with Funai can develop actions to improve the standard of living, in the same way it will be done with the Indigenous peoples of the area of impact.[24]

After the defeat suffered in 1989, Eletronorte resumed the attempt to establish the hydroelectric plant in the late 1990s under the name Belo Monte Hydropower Complex (CHBM). In the reformed project, the reservoir of the plant would not flood Indigenous lands in the VGX, but it would nonetheless reach the city of Altamira, causing the compulsory displacement of part of the population. Those affected by this displacement would include hundreds of Indigenous families, especially those living on the edge of the Xingu River and other small rivers in the city.

At that moment, the Indigenous peoples of Altamira had gained some visibility. In the mid-1990s, they mobilized to recognize the presence of Indigenous

22 Simoni & Dagnino, *supra* note 14 at 321.
23 Eletronorte, Informações às comunidades indígenas sobre os aproveitamentos hidrelétricos no rio Xingu (1989) at 8.
24 *Ibid.*

families in the city and demand assistance from the Indigenous government body, Funai. Elza Xipaya,[25] a leader of Indigenous families in Altamira, reports that when she returned to Altamira in 1994, she saw the situation of the Indigenous people in the city. According to Elza, the community was "mistreated" without care by Funai. Moreover Funai affirmed that it had no responsibility for the Indigenous peoples of the city. At the same time, she participated in a meeting at the invitation of the Indigenous Missionary Council, which discussed the articulation of a movement to recognize Indigenous people living in the city. Elza proposed to carry out a survey of the Indigenous peoples in Altamira, which began in 1995, elaborating a registry of Indigenous families with the aim of being recognized as Indigenous people living in the city. Thus, in 1999, when a team approached Elza to carry out the environmental impact assessment of the CHBM project,[26] more than a thousand Indigenous people had already been registered.[27]

The environmental licensing of CHBM was invalidated by the court in 2003, setting the second defeat of the Belo Monte project.[28] The threat of being forcibly displaced by the project, while still struggling for recognition as Indigenous peoples along with the differentiated public policies, boosted and strengthened the mobilization of Indigenous peoples in Altamira. Supported by social movements and by Indigenous Missionary Council in 2000, the movement of Indigenous women extended to the Movement of the Indigenous Families Residents of the city of Altamira and formed an association. Created in 2001, the Association of Indigenous Residents in Altamira initially added 380 Indigenous people, according to an interview with Elza Xipaya.

In addition to the importance of the associations for the social and political organization of Indigenous people in Altamira,[29] Parente also emphasizes its significance as spaces of congregation and coexistence of the Indigenous peoples in

25 Interview of Elza Xipaya, aged 49, by Estella Libardi de Souza (February 2017) at her home, located in collective urban resettlement (RUC) São Joaquim.

Elza Xipaya was the main articulator of the movement of indigenous families in the city of Altamira, and president of the Association of Indigenous Residents of Altamira (Aima) from its creation until 2010, when she was appointed to a post in Funai to work with the indigenous population in Altamira, where she still works today. Estella Libardi de Souza interviewed her on two occasions in February 2017.

26 The environmental impact assessment (EIA) of the CMBM was carried out by the Amparo Foundation and Research Development (FADESP), linked to the Federal University of Pará (UFPA). However, the EIA was invalidated by a decision handed down by the Federal Public Prosecution Service filed by the Federal Public Ministry (MPF), which required the nullity of the agreement between Eletronorte and FADESP.

27 Simoni & Dagnino, *supra* note 14. It is interesting to note the discrepancy in the numbers referring to the indigenous population in the city of Altamira, obtained in several local surveys, carried out either by the indigenous people, or by researchers, or by the EIA of the Belo Monte project, in relation to censuses demographics 2000 and 2010, being the census are always lower than those of local surveys, as highlighted by Simoni and Dagnino.

28 Oswaldo & Filho, *supra* note 4.

29 In 2003, another indigenous association, Akarirá, was created and later renamed Kirinapan. Since 2012, other associations have been formed.

the city. These were understood as collective spaces: "associations appeared as the place of congregation of the struggle and community in urban contexts, where culture transcends domestic spaces for the collectivization of ethnicity."[30]

In 2000, the Xipaya, Kuruaya, Juruna and Arara peoples demanded that Funai recognize and demarcate the territory where the Tavaquara Mission was located. In response to the letter sent to Funai by the Movement of the Indigenous Families Residents of the city of Altamira in September of the same year, the claim was included in the "Basic Survey of Indigenous Land Information to be Defined, Identified and Reviewed in the Ethnographic Area VII – Xingu," coordinated by the anthropologist Maria Elisa Guedes Vieira in 2001. In the report, Vieira[31] informs that the Xipaya and Kuruaya who lived in the city totaled approximately 800 people, as well as another 400 Juruna, Arara and Kayapó people, a Xucuru family and a Guarani family.

The survey work consisted of "recognition of places that are still in memories of the Kuruaya and Xipaya townspeople,"[32] with the participation of a group of Indigenous Xipaya and Kuruaya, including Elza, which crossed the borders of the Xingu River on the city's pier, passing through the region of the former Tavaquara Mission. Two possible areas claimed for the delimitation of an Indigenous land or reserve were discussed with the Indigenous peoples: the first, in the São Sebastião and Independente II and III districts, which included the Panelas Creek; the second, alternatively, in the Transamazonica, in the area of the Altamira Creek. However, there were problems in both areas, such as their intense occupation and proximity to the airport in the first case and proximity to a landfill in the alternative area. Vieira suggests that the Xipaya and Kuruaya wanted to be close to the city, in an area that did not flood and where the land is flat and not far from the center of Altamira, where they could continue their economic and educational activities developed through the association. This would include making handicrafts and meetings for cultural and linguistic activities that were important to each ethnic group. We include transcripts of Elza Xipaya's speech in July of 2001, which explains this particular claim:

> I always thought that if we had a land, we would be able to take at least half the indigenous people of the city and ask them to work the land, to cultivate, to work with crops like beans, rice, corn, coffee, black pepper, cocoa. Because today the majority of indigenous people pay rent, so they live a sad life. So, when we sat down, we drafted a document and sent it to Brasilia. Because we were very worried about those indigenous people who are suffering from their needs. And if we gained this land, they will live on this land. . . . We want to form a village and start to return to culture, to dance, to paint, to make the indigenous rhythm to all, what they did. I take advantage

30 Parente, *supra* note 17 at 229.

31 Maria Elisa Guedes Vieira, "Relatório do Levantamento Básico de Informações das Terras Indígenas a Definir, a Identificar e a Revisar na Área Etnográfica VII-Xingu" (2002).

32 *Ibid.* at 9.

of these eight old elders to teach the younger ones. So our concern is that. So we drafted this document.[33]

(Elza Xipaya, July 2001, cited by Vieira)

The Vieira report indicates the Belo Monte HPP, scheduled for 2002, as a "threat to the territorial integrity" of the Indigenous peoples and suggests the creation of a technical group by Funai for the identification of an area where an Indigenous reserve for the Indigenous peoples of the city of Altamira would be formed.[34] In 2003, a new survey was conducted by the anthropologist Louis Carlos Forline about the possibility of demarcating a land for the "urban Indians" in the city of Altamira. Forline suggests that the "urban Indians" claimed an Indigenous Reserve within Altamira since the 1980s. He points out that

> it is considered essential to establish an Indigenous Area in Altamira for reasons of security and self-esteem, and thus contribute to a redirection of the indigenous trajectory in that city. . . . Moreover, the establishment of the Indigenous Area would not be the only and definitive solution, but it is assumed that this space, coupled with the dynamics of the indigenous movement witnessed in the last 15 years in Altamira, would consolidate the effort of agglutinating an expressive part of the Indian actors in this city.[35]

There were no further references regarding the claim of the Indigenous area in the city of Altamira because a technical group for studies on the identification of the Tavaquara Indigenous land or for the constitution of an Indigenous reserve was never formed.

Although it is not possible to affirm that the Belo Monte HPP was the reason for not meeting the demand for an Indigenous territory in the city of Altamira, it is evident that the formal recognition by the Brazilian State of this Indigenous

33 *Ibid.* at 10.

34 The demarcation of indigenous lands is an administrative procedure, regulated by law, by which the Brazilian government represents and recognizes the original right of indigenous peoples to territories traditionally occupied by them, identifying them and delimiting them. The Indigenous reservation is a different form of recognition of the territorial rights of indigenous peoples as provided in article 26 of Law No. 6001/1973, known as the Indigenous Statute, through which the Union purchase, evict or receive in donation property for the establishment of the indigenous reservation. According to Fundação Nacional Do Índio – Funai, "Entenda o processo de demarcação" (2017), online: <www.funai.gov.br/ index.php/2014-02-07-13-24-53>[Funai (2016)], the reserves are constituted "in extraordinary cases, such as irreversible internal conflict, impacts of large enterprises or technical impossibility of recognition of land of traditional occupation," and although they are lands that also belong to the patrimony of the Union and are destined to the permanent possession of the indigenous peoples, they are not confused with the lands of traditional occupation, which article 231 of the Brazilian Federal Constitution deals with. However, there are indigenous lands constituted by means of reserves that are recognized as of traditional occupation.

35 Louis Carlos Forline, "Estudo e Levantamento Prévio de Identificação e Delimitação da Terra Indígena Tavaquara – Relatório final" (2004) at 26.

territory could hinder government plans to construct the hydroelectric plant, as it would flood part of the city (possibly the Indigenous territory itself) and would compulsorily displace thousands of people, including hundreds of Indigenous families.

It is noteworthy that the Brazilian Constitution prohibits the compulsory removal of Indigenous peoples. In addition, International Labour Organization (ILO) Convention 169 has been in force in Brazil since July 25, 2003, making it mandatory for the Brazilian government to promote a process of consultation with Indigenous peoples on the construction of the Belo Monte HPP. The Indigenous territory in the city of Altamira would reinforce the mandatory consultation, which was not carried out at any time by the Brazilian State, neither before nor during the construction of the hydroelectric plant.

The compulsory displacement of Indigenous peoples affected by Belo Monte

In 2005, the third attempt to create the Belo Monte HPP on the Xingu River began with the publication by the National Congress of the Legislative Decree No. 788, which authorized the Executive Branch to implement the project. After several court decisions that paralyzed the licensing process, the Environmental Impact Assessment related to Indigenous peoples (called the "Indigenous component")[36] began in 2008. The assessment covered 10 Indigenous lands as well as the Indigenous families living in the urban area of Altamira and along the VGX.[37]

The assessment indicated the presence of 340 Indigenous families in the city of Altamira – a total of 1,622 people – who identified themselves as Xipaya, Kuruaya and Juruna.[38] Among the possible impacts on the Indigenous inhabitants of Altamira, the assessment pointed to the de-structuring of existing social networks and land removal, although there was a possibility of creating a "visibility and political empowerment" group.[39] The assessment noted:

> The filling of the reservoir of the Belo Monte Dam, if the dam is built, will drastically interfere with the living conditions of the indigenous population living in Altamira, leaving it permanently in flood conditions and the indigenous population of Volta Grande, leaving it permanently in a drought

36 Funai calls *indigenous component* the assessment, within the process of environmental license, about the impacts about indigenous peoples and lands, as well as compensation actions and mitigation later proposed and implemented as a result of such assessment.

37 The indigenous lands were Paquiçamba; Arara Volta Grande do Xingu; Juruna of km 17; Arara; Cachoeira Seca; Araweté do Igarapé Ipixuna; Koatinemo; Kararaô; Apyterewa; and Trincheira Bacajá. Subsequently, the Xipaya and Kuruaya indigenous lands were included.

38 Eletrobrás, "Aproveitamento Hidrelétrico Belo Monte: Estudo de Impacto Ambiental/ Relatório de Impacto Ambiental (EIA/RIMA)" (2009) 35 *Rio de Janeiro*.

39 Fundação Nacional Do Índio – Funai. *Parecer Técnico Nº. 21* CMAM/CGPIMA. 30 set. 2009 [Funai (2009)].

> situation. This situation will be aggravated, especially in the city of Altamira, by the expected flow of almost 100,000 people attracted by the works. Today, the living conditions of these populations, as well as a large part of the Xingu River's riverside peoples, are already very precarious. . . . Therefore, due to its vulnerability and the cultural restoration moment that is going through, for this population, the impact of the possible construction of the Belo Monte Dam will be even greater.[40]

Elza Xipaya relates the concern with the area to which they would be displaced at the time. When she participated in a meeting with Funai in Brasília in 2009, she was informed about the specific registration of the Indigenous people who lived in Altamira and who would be displaced by the plant, but the removal of Indigenous people would occur along with the general affected population, without differentiation as part of the Basic Environmental Plan (PBA) of the project.[41] Elza states:

> We just knew we were going out, but I did not know what location they were going to put us. We spent some time worrying because we thought, we live inside the city center, and today they want to put us near from Vitória, or towards Medicilândia. . . . we stayed like this, with so much things said, we did not know what the locality was. We only knew about this in 2009. . . . was in 2009 when I went there in Brasilia for a meeting at the Funai. . . . Several leaders from here too, for this meeting, that we put as it was going to be the situation of the indigenous people that live in the city and the ones who live in riverside. . . . And it was I who sat down with Janete and Fabio, and she said: "Look, Elza, the team is gone, we are going to send the team back to work with you, but it will be a differentiated work, Funai will follow the registration, the PBA." [. . .] So it was that she went to talk about the PBA, that it was going to be all together, it was not going to be differentiated. I said, "No, Janete, we want a PBA for indigenous people." When I saw a team coming to work in a different PBA for the indigenous people in the villages, I said, "No, I want a team that works with the indigenous people in the city also differentiated, that we will also have opinions, and we will choose what we want. Because if we are to stay together with the population, they will put us where they want, when we are going to ask Funai for help." Funai says "No, it's ready, you cannot go back.". . . So that was the difference, the reallocation, for Funai to go along, to see the structure of the houses, the opinions, and the indigenous people who had to decide which neighborhood he was going to go to, it was not Norte Energia to do as they

40 *Ibid.* at 212.

41 The PBA is provided by the Resolution No. 006 of 16 September 1987 from the National Council for the Environment (CONAMA), and presents a breakdown of all environmental programs and projects to be implemented by the entrepreneur foreseen in the EIA or requested by the licensing agency. It is a prerequisite for obtaining the installation license (LI).

> want. . . . We even put Funai from Brasília, an indigenous neighborhood. As it is different, we wanted a different neighborhood, a neighborhood only for the indigenous people.[42]

As the construction of Belo Monte HPP provided the possibility for the resettlement of affected families in new neighborhoods constructed for reallocations, the Indigenous peoples required a district where they would be resettled. According to Elza Xipaya's report, the demand for the "indigenous people neighborhood" was connected to the former claim of the Xipaya and Kuruaya for the Indigenous Tavaquara territory in Altamira. Funai never responded to their initial claim. For this reason, according to Elza's account, "Indigenous neighborhood" and "Indigenous land" are terms that appear to have the same meaning:

> Because in 1994, I had already discussed an indigenous neighborhood, I think you should have already seen the history of this neighborhood, which was in the Independente. . . . [*But how did this story of the indigenous neighborhood come about?*] From Tavaquara, have you heard of Tavaquara? It came out like this. Because that's where Independent I is, when I started working, they said, "Look, Elza, this place was a place that when we came, we stayed here." There it was called "The Oca," at that time. Then the indigenous peoples who came from the Xingu and the Iriri, the Xipaya, Kuruaya, and Juruna, all their locality and was there, in that place. There it was called "The Oca." . . . And we put the name "Tavaquara." . . . Independent II, it is not Independente I. This area was very large. . . . And then the indigenous people wanted it to be a village, an indigenous neighborhood.[43]

Elza Xipaya states that she was giving up the Tavaquara land because she was afraid for her life. The area where Tavaquara land was supposed to be, near the Independente II neighborhood, was intensely occupied by non-Indigenous. The Indigenous peoples had not accepted the proposal of an alternative place, as Elza suggested, in an area on the banks of the Xingu known as Pedral, because the Indigenous peoples claimed the Independente II neighborhood as their territory. Thus, according to Elza's account, the claim for the Indigenous territory in the city remained "quiet" until the studies related to the Belo Monte HPP began, when the demand resumed in the form of a resettlement only for the Indigenous people, an Indigenous neighborhood, which would take the form of an Indigenous land:

> Then it got quiet. When this team already came to us to see, then I said: "Let's work on an indigenous neighborhood." Because there was in the questionnaire, an indigenous neighborhood. . . . We had a lot of discussion

42 Interview of Elza Xipaya (February 2017).
43 *Ibid.*

with indigenous people about the indigenous neighborhood. And we also talked: "Look, if an indigenous neighborhood will be formed, it will be only for indigenous people live there, in that neighborhood we will not allow parties, we will not allow alcohol, it will be a village, we're going to work to build a heritage of the association, a good thing that comes to the benefit of everyone."[44]

The Belo Monte Hydroelectric Environmental Impact Assessment highlights that in the meetings with Indigenous leaders and families living in Altamira, the group's decision was about the structuring of an Indigenous neighborhood for the resettlement of Indigenous families affected by the reservoir plant. This was not the same as the claim for the demarcation of the Indigenous land Tavaquara to be held by Funai:

> During the interviews, besides the ratification of the continuity of the process of identification of urban indigenous land (Funai attribution), it was demanded an indigenous neighborhood in an area to be identified in Altamira, to house the indigenous families affected directly by the Xingu reservoir (about 200 families) or even all those living in the city (estimated at 340, plus about 50 still unregistered).[45]

In the report that evaluated the environmental impact assessment, Funai considered that the claims about Tavaquara land and noted that "the question of the identification of an Indigenous Land in the city of Altamira, whose suit was referred to Funai at the beginning of 2000, still needs to be better evaluated by the official indigenous body."[46] As well, in relation to the claim of the Indigenous neighborhood:

> The structuring of a neighborhood for the indigenous families that will eventually be relocated from the Altamira creeks presents itself in a very timely manner. It will be necessary to discuss and plan with the families all the configuration of this new neighborhood, its location, spatial organization and internal regiment. If, on the one hand, the new indigenous neighborhood was intended only for those families impacted by the construction of the reservoir, we agree with the perspective pointed out in the studies that the programs of differentiated care should extend to all indigenous families of Altamira, independent of whether or not they are directly impacted by the work. In this way, problems of discrimination and favoritism would be avoided, also avoiding divisions and intensification of internal disputes between the indigenous families living in Altamira. In addition, it

44 *Ibid.*
45 Forline, *supra* note 35 at 448.
46 Funai (2009), *supra* note 39 at 84.

is recalled that they may also receive basic health care and education in a differentiated way.[47]

On February 1, 2010, the Brazilian Institute for the Environment and Renewable Natural Resources (Ibama) issued the prior license to Belo Monte HPP; and on April 20, 2010, the auction of the plant was held, with the Norte Energia consortium as the successful contender. In that year, Norte Energia began the elaboration of the Indigenous Component Basic Environmental Guide (PBA-CI), which consolidated the programs and actions under the responsibility of the consortium, to mitigate and compensate the impacts of the plant on Indigenous peoples. While the PBA-CI was prepared, in January 2011, Ibama issued a permit authorizing the installation of construction sites of Belo Monte Hydroelectric Plant and, in June of the same year, issued an installation license to start the plant.

The PBA-CI, directed by Norte Energia and approved by Funai, reiterates the demand for an Indigenous neighborhood, pointing out that it would be the project to "adapt the time and the pace of settlement processes of agreement about resettlement, taking into account the needs of resettled indigenous families,"[48] and that "sufficient time should be allowed for them [Indigenous peoples], in accordance with their habits, cultural and political practices, to discuss and make all decisions collectively."[49]

The PBA-CI stresses that in the collective urban resettlement option, the demands and specificities of Indigenous families for collective urban resettlement should be negotiated with the entrepreneur. Also, to ensure access to information and to "permit the participation of the population throughout the process, from the choice of areas for resettlement, housing typology, eligibility criteria and others,"[50] the PBA-CI envisaged participatory workshops with Indigenous peoples affected, in order to reach agreements with Indigenous families regarding their collective urban resettlement proposals.

In early 2013, Norte Energia initiated meetings with the affected population, Indigenous and non-Indigenous, about the resettlement process. The Indigenous people participated in the meetings, but there were no specific meetings with the Indigenous families affected to discuss and agree on the resettlement process, as it was foreseen in the PBA-CI. Elza Xipaya, displaced by the Belo Monte project, attended the meetings and noted that those affected – Indigenous and non-Indigenous – had no information about where the collective urban resettlement would be deployed.[51] Subsequently, Norte Energia stated that the houses to be

47 *Ibid.*

48 Norte Energia, "PBA do Componente Indígena da Usina Hidrelétrica Belo Monte" (2011) *Programa Médio Xingu* at 1098.

49 *Ibid.*

50 *Ibid.* at 1101.

51 Elza Xipaya's report is ratified by Ibama, in the analysis of the report presented by Norte Energia in May 2013: "This situation [non-construction of model houses, that is, demonstration houses of the material and the construction patterns which will be used in the housing units to be offered to the resettled], added to the lack of definition of areas for

built for resettlement would be made in concrete, with an area of 63 metres, in five areas where the collective urban resettlement would be implemented, called "new neighborhoods."

All areas defined by the Norte Energia for resettlement are far from the Xingu River border, and only one – the collective urban resettlement (RUC) Larangeiras – has access to the river through the Panelas Creek. In view of this, the Indigenous associations of Altamira (Aima, Kirinapan and Inkuri) questioned the proposed housing model and the locations defined for the collective urban resettlement. They convened a meeting in Altamira in July 2013 with Ibama, Funai, the Federal Public Ministry (MPF) and Norte Energia, and they began to demand the acquisition of a new area near the Xingu for the resettlement of Indigenous families. The first area claimed by Indigenous people in Panelas Creek, near the Xingu, was requested in a list signed by more than 300 Indigenous people.

However, the reply from Norte Energia was that "the recommendation of the licensor was to avoid construction in Altamira neighborhoods that could lead to segregation."[52] Thus, Norte Energia ignored what was foreseen in the environmental impact assessment and the PBA-CI, proposed by the company itself. Using the "promise" to avoid any *segregationist* differentiation in the treatment of Indigenous and non-Indigenous families, the company violated the right of Indigenous peoples to participate in the decision-making process and did not take into account their demands regarding the relocation process.

At that time, although Indigenous families were no longer concentrated in one place, as in the past, when the place occupied by the Xipaya and Kuruaya in the city was known as "village" or "mission" there were still groups of families in some regions of the city. Under the argument of avoiding the segregation of Indigenous families, Norte Energia intended to provoke, or accentuate, the "dispersion" of Indigenous peoples living in the city and, with this, the disintegration and breaking of the bonds of solidarity that united Indigenous families. As we can see, Norte Energia used a reference of equal treatment between Indigenous and non-Indigenous peoples to re-force the violation of Indigenous autonomy and the disqualification of Indigenous voices.

It should be noted that to deny the possibility of collective urban resettlement deployment in the area indicated by the Indigenous people, the company said that although it was possible, its acquisition "would require a process of negotiation with the owners with deadlines incompatible with the Belo Monte environmental licensing schedule."[53] Thus, instead of the environmental licensing

resettlement, to the non-disclosure of the price book, to the standardization of the size of the houses in 63sqm (unlike the three different sizes announced in the entrepreneur's newsletter), the lack of information on how the resettlement process will be conducted and, above all, a process of social illumination for the population, has generated dissatisfaction and instability among the affected residents" (Ibama, 2013).

52 Norte Energia. CE 075/2013 – DS, de 21 ago. 2013.

53 *Ibid.*

process of Belo Monte HPP respecting the time needed for Indigenous people to discuss and make their decisions, the Indigenous people had to adapt to the time of the environmental licensing of Belo Monte and the deployment schedule of the plant.

The process of reallocation proceeded at an accelerated pace, as Norte Energia still intended to obtain the operating license for Belo Monte HPP in 2014. In order to do so, it would have to conclude the "negotiation" to reallocate the 7,790 registered families[54] in the urban area, including 776 Indigenous families located next to the Creeks Ambé, Altamira, Panelas and the borders of the Xingu. When the "negotiations" were initiated, the affected people denounced the denial of the option for a house in one of the collective urban resettlement and the pressure to accept the low value of the indemnities, among other violations discussed in a public hearing promoted by MPF in November 2014 in Altamira.

Although the removal of those affected people was ongoing, the Indigenous associations resisted and insisted on guaranteeing the Indigenous people affected the possibility of resettlement in a close area to the Xingu. In early 2014, as part of the demand for associations and as a determination of Funai, there were "participatory workshops" with Indigenous families to discuss the relocation process and agreement concerning the resettlement areas. Of the 654 families registered so far, only 181 participated in the workshops. The participating families (almost 70%) expressed a desire to be resettled in an area on the borders of the Xingu, known as Pedral.

Despite the fact that Norte Energia denied the possibility of deploying a collective urban resettlement in the area of Pedral (which also was hampered by Ibama for not fitting the criteria in the PBA), the Indigenous claim was added to the fishermen's demand, represented by the Z-57 Fishing Colony through the Pedral area, for resettlement on the banks of the Xingu River. Both Indigenous peoples and fishermen (a category that included many Indigenous fishermen) claimed the Pedral area as the most adequate to maintain their ways of life, in close relation to the Xingu River. Ibama (in the case of fishermen) and Funai (in the case of the Indigenous people) stated that the areas envisaged by Norte Energia thus far did

54 Assis da Costa Oliveira, "Atingidos pela Usina Hidrelétrica Belo Monte: mobilização político-organizacional da luta por direitos humanos" in Arruda, *Conflitos jurídico-políticos na Amazônia e processos de enfrentamento* (São Paulo: Ícone Editora, 2018) at 52. In fact, the identification and quantification of families registered as affected were in dispute over the period of implementation of the Belo Monte HPP. According to Oliveira (2018), despite having been registered 7,790 families, the unique design of the urban resettlement only 3,980 families, and disregarded the registration of hundreds of families. As a result of this, the Movement of Dam Affected people (MAB) began to organize, from 2014, a process of preparation of statistical and nominal surveys, through personal data population and signatures collected fortnightly meetings monitoring of the affected families in neighborhoods of Altamira, to provide visibility to the exclusion of thousands of registration conducted by NESA [Norte Energia]" (p 60). From this popular census, MAB came to the quantity of about 50,000 non-indigenous people who would be affected in the urban area of Altamira, has already recognized an additional 1,300 families, representing about 4,888 people.

not stratify the expectations of the affected population. Finally, in 2014, Norte Energia announced that it would implement a collective urban resettlement in the Pedral area for the resettlement of Indigenous people and fishermen.

The negotiation process with the affected people, including the 776 Indigenous families, was completed by the end of 2015, and families were removed. Those who opted for RUC Pedral were provisionally resettled in other collective urban resettlements, maintaining the possibility of being resettled in Pedral when it is completed. On November 24 of that year, Belo Monte HPP obtained the Operation License (LO), which determined that RUC Pedral should be concluded by November 2016.

The RUC Pedral was concluded in 2019, almost three years after the deadline foreseen in LO. One hundred and fifty houses have been built, in addition to a school, a daycare center, a health center and other basic services. There are, however, pending adjustments in the houses, such as adding balconies and walls. The process of "re-offering" the houses available in RUC Pedral to Indigenous families and fishermen provisionally settled in other collective urban resettlements is also undefined.

For Claudio Curuaia,[55] an Indigenous leader, president of the Inkuri Indigenous association and secretary of the Working Group to follow up on the implementation of RUC Pedral, the delay in implementing it was a strategy of Norte Energia for families to give up on the area. Today, there would be only about 30 families to be transferred to RUC Pedral. Curuaia, however, believes that many other families would opt for the transfer to RUC Pedral after the "re-offer," which Norte Energia would be resisting, although it is an obligation of the company. For this reason, Indigenous associations and their representatives continue to be mobilized for the transfer of Indigenous families.

During the process of implementing RUC Pedral, the Indigenous associations of Altamira expanded their initiatives to make it a "differentiated neighborhood" in order to give visibility to the Indigenous presence in the city and to strengthen the process of "cultural rescue" of Indigenous peoples who live in Altamira. In addition to building Indigenous associations' offices and cultural spaces within RUC Pedral, the associations demand that the streets of the neighborhood be named after the Kuruaya, Xipaya and Juruna peoples and their leaders[56] in order

55 Interview of Claudio Curuaia Cambuí, president of the Inkuri association, by Estella Libardi de Souza (July 2015 and February 2017 in Altamira). The references to his speech are also part of the recent conversations they had, between April and June of 2019, in the city of Altamira.

Claudio Curuaia Cambuí has been the main articulator of the indigenous struggle in Altamira for RUC Pedral.

56 In Canada, the Ogimaa Mikana Project has developed a similar initiative to restore Anishinaabe means in the place-names of the streets, avenues, roads, paths, and trails of Toronto, or the nomination in Anishunaabe language of this territory: *Gichi Kiiwenging*. More information at Lacey Mcrae Williams, "Reclaiming Spaces/Places: Restoring Indigenous Street Names in Toronto" (4 November 2014) *Spacing National*, online: <http://spacing.ca/national/2014/11/04/reclaiming-spacingplaces-restoring-indiginous-street-names-toronto/>.

to register Indigenous protagonism in the constitution of the "neighborhood" and honor their ancestors. They also require that the public facilities (school, daycare and health centers) be painted with graphic design motifs of the Xipaya, Kuruaya and Juruna peoples.

In this way, the demands of the Indigenous peoples for RUC Pedral are connected with the longing of these populations for a territory in which it is possible to reproduce and reconstruct their ways of life, continuing the process of "cultural rescue" started in the 1990s, where they can "return to culture, to dance, to paint, to make the indigenous rhythm to all," as Elza Xipaya explained in 2001.

In addition, the Indigenous associations managed to change the name of the "neighborhood" from RUC Pedral to RUC Tavaquara. At the same time, the claim of the Indigenous area in the city of Altamira, called Tavaquara Reserve, was resumed, proposing to Funai the creation of an Indigenous reserve in the area surrounding the collective urban resettlement. In evoking the name of the old mission/village, the Indigenous peoples living in the city want to "mark" the Indigenous presence in Altamira and also emphasize the history of Indigenous peoples in the territory that is now part of the city. As Claudio Curuaia says, the Kuruaya, Xipaya and Juruna are not newcomers to the city but they are "native" peoples, originally from Tavaquara territory.

Conclusion

In this chapter, we have discussed the political mobilization of the Xipaya and Kuruaya peoples, who were displaced by the Belo Monte HPP project in Brazil. These Indigenous peoples mobilized in the form of various Indigenous movements and associations; the main demand of these communities was for an Indigenous resettlement solely for Indigenous peoples – an Indigenous neighbourhood in Pedral, which was later called Tavaquara.

As we have seen, there was no consultation process with Indigenous peoples who were compulsorily displaced by the Belo Monte HPP and no mechanism for effective participation of Indigenous peoples in the process of relocation and resettlement of those affected by the hydroelectric plant, through which Indigenous demands were accommodated. The case of HPP Belo Monte points, therefore, to the persistence of colonial practices that disregard Indigenous peoples as political subjects, resulting in the violation of the citizenship of Indigenous peoples, their autonomy and free determination. "Development" policies and projects, such as the Belo Monte HPP, are ways of updating the coloniality relations that shape the formation of the Brazilian State; for this reason, there is so little difference in the practices adopted when implementing "development" projects in Brazil, either during the military dictatorship or during democracy.

Nevertheless, in the case of the Belo Monte HPP, Indigenous peoples mobilized and sought ways to claim rights and make themselves heard, devising strategies to influence the decision-making process on the relocation and resettlement of the affected population. Despite the authoritarianism and the speed of implementation of the project, Indigenous peoples resisted and produced political responses capable of influencing the course of events, which is important to emphasize when analyzing the social effects of large-scale projects.[57]

The mobilization of Indigenous peoples in the city of Altamira and the conquest of RUC Pedral/Tavaquara demonstrate the tenacity of Indigenous resistance. Indigenous peoples did not passively accept Norte Energia's plans. They sought a territory that could maintain and strengthen the bonds of solidarity between Indigenous families and that would be suitable for its political and historical projects of "cultural rescue" and reconstruction of their ethnic identities, based on a territory that demarcates the Indigenous presence in the city – and this way, "indianizes" the city. RUC Tavaquara points out that the city of Altamira has a history, that the history of the city is also the history of Indigenous peoples, and that the presence of Indigenous peoples in the city is part of the process of "re-existence" of the Xipaya and Kuruaya peoples.

57 Lygia Sigaud discusses the construction of the Sobradinho dam, in Brazil, in the 1970s. The author highlights that the literature drew attention to the fragility of the population and the lack of reaction to state authoritarianism, as it was concerned with emphasizing the negative social effects of the project and thus ignored the population's political responses. On the other hand, the author emphasizes the political responses of the population that suffered the social effects of the project and points out that, although limited by the dimensions of what was imposed on it, and unable to prevent the destruction of its social organization, the population was not entirely passive to the events, and reacted to the point of influencing the direction of the solutions that were being given by the State. Lygia Sigaud, *Efeitos sociais de grandes projetos hidrelétricos: as barragens de Sobradinho e Machadinho* (Rio de Janeiro: Programa de Pós-Graduação em Antropologia Social, Museu Nacional – UFRJ, 1986) or online: <www.ppgasmn-ufrj.com/uploads/2/7/2/8/27281669/c9.pdf>.

7 Unearthing (de)colonial legal relations

Mining law in Aotearoa New Zealand

Estair Van Wagner and Maria Bargh

The structure of relations produced through environmental law affects not only the relationships between different levels of decision makers and between decision makers and constituents but also critically shapes "the subjective relationships of people with each other and with the environment."[1] In particular, control over people-place relations is a foundational element of colonial power.[2] Therefore, unsettling dominant people-place relations is central to the work of decolonization.[3] Here we examine how the work of shaping people-place relations occurs through law in the context of mineral prospecting, exploration, and extraction in Aotearoa New Zealand.

Minerals in Aotearoa New Zealand are regulated by the *Crown Minerals Act, 1991* (the CMA). Like other statutes in New Zealand, the CMA recognizes Te Tiriti o Waitangi (the Treaty of Waitangi), signed by the British and Māori in 1840, and therefore the relationship between Māori and the lands and resources governed by the Act. The Treaty relationship continues to play a crucial role in conflicts about land and resources and is central to the practice of decolonization for Māori. However, as we argue, the governance of relationships between people and minerals, as foundational elements of material systems, extend much further to the Māori legal orders developed throughout Aotearoa. The Treaty brought these systems of law and governance into a relationship with British colonial law. However, the CMA fails to recognize and accommodate Māori jurisdiction over territory, including the mineral resources in a particular *rohe* (traditional territory). While Māori must be consulted when the state considers whether to open up lands to mineral exploration, prospecting, or mining, the CMA consultation regime is used to reinscribe the colonial order of people-place relations on the

1 Maria Carmen Lemos & Arun Agarwal, "Environmental Governance" (2006) 31 *Annual Rev of Environment & Resources* 297 at 297–325, 304.

2 Shiri Pasternak, *Grounded Authority: The Algonquins of Barriere Lake against the State* (Minneapolis: University of Minnesota Press, 2017) at 10; see also Glen Sean Coulthard, *Red Skin, White Masks* (Minneapolis: University of Minnesota Press, 2014).

3 Margaret Mutu, "Maori Issues" (2015) 27:1 *Contemporary Pacific* 273 at 273, 274; Moana Jackson, "Colonization as Myth-Making: A Case Study in Aotearoa" in Stephen Greymorning, ed., *A Will to Survive: Indigenous Essays on the Politics of Culture, Language, and Identity* (New York: McGraw Hill, 2004) at 5, 95–108.

area of a proposed permit. Crown relations to mineral resources are placed at the peak of a hierarchy of interests. Despite the explicit recognition of the Treaty and provision for engagement with *iwi* (tribe) and *hapū* (sub-tribe), the CMA consultation process undermines the *tino rangatiratanga* (self-determination/chiefly authority) protected by the Treaty and the jurisdictional authority over lands and resources flowing from it. We examine the ways in which Māori participation in the CMA process disrupts and contests these relations, and yet why Māori submissions are rarely able to influence the outcome of the block offer process.

Below, we explore Māori contestation of colonial people-place relations through a case study of a block offer – the national minerals exploration tendering process – for epithermal gold in the Central North Island of Aotearoa New Zealand. We examine the process through iwi and hapū submissions as well as data from key informant interviews in local and national government. Our case study draws attention to mining not only because it is often a highly impactful, transformative, and often destructive land use, but also because it is raises complex issues about the relationship between law and place. Open pit mining, such as epithermal gold mining, is transformative – a particular place simply no longer exists once the minerals and the land, waters, plants, and animals surrounding and connected to them are removed. For Māori, this does not only have material impacts; Māori legal orders and authority are rooted firmly in particular places and intergenerational and metaphysical relationships of kinship and responsibility with that place.[4] We argue decolonial relations with minerals require the transformation of Crown-Māori relations to meaningfully recognize *mana* as place-based authority, practiced and upheld by maintenance and care for the complex Māori kinship relations with the physical and metaphysical world. In this way, people-place relations and the place-based laws flowing from these enduring kinship relations will not only be considered by Crown decision makers, they will be a source of jurisdiction for iwi and hapū to fulfil their obligations and responsibilities.

Methodology

Our approach to this research is informed by Kaupapa Māori methodologies.[5] According to authors such as Linda Smith, Fiona Cram, and Graham Smith, who have written extensively about Kaupapa Māori methodologies, the core principles include the following: (a) establishing relationships with Māori as part of the research; (b) maintaining respectful and culturally appropriate behaviours towards participants; and (c) reflecting on the political role that research plays in either protecting the political, economic, and legal status quo or changing

4 Carwyn Jones, *New Treaty, New Tradition: Reconciling New Zealand and Maori Law* (Vancouver: UBC Press, 2016); Nin Thomas, "Maori Concepts of Rangatiratanga, Kaitiakitanga, the Environment, and Property Rights" in David Grinlinton & Prue Taylor, eds., *Property Rights and Sustainability*, Vol. 11 (Leiden: Martinus Nijhoff, 2011) at 219–248.

5 Linda Smith, *Decolonizing Methodologies: Research and Indigenous Peoples* (Otago: Otago University Press, 1999).

it.[6] These principles guided the ways that information was collected and prioritized. While our focus in this research is examining and exposing the structure of state mining law and not a detailed examination of *tikanga* (Māori system of law) in relation to minerals and land use, our research intentionally foregrounds Māori views. We do so in order to emphasize the need for Indigenous knowledge to be a central consideration in land use and natural resource decision-making. Further, we aim to use our scholarly research to disrupt the status quo and support Māori aspirations and assertions of jurisdiction and tino rangatiratanga with respect to their lands, resources, and legal orders.

Core concepts in the Māori worldview

The Māori perspectives examined below are based on a particular worldview and system of law (tikanga), which flows from several core concepts: relationships (*whanaungatanga*), guardianship (*manaakitanga/kaitiakitanga*), authority (mana), spiritual quality (*tapu*), and balance (*utu*). These core concepts assist in understanding the centrality of people-place relations and the genealogical connections between people and the environment. Positive relationships amongst people and between people and landscape features and flora and fauna play a crucial role in maintaining peace and balance.[7] Through caring relations and guardianship, particular kinds of behaviours to promote sustainability within human and environmental relations are encouraged and reinforced. Authority, or mana, relates not only to the individual authority of people and leaders but also to the authority that particular groups have over specific resources and areas, and therefore the responsibilities they hold. Behaviours in Māori society are also regulated through the concept of tapu or the spiritual element of all things. The concept of utu, or balance, is a key mechanism to ensure the maintenance of relationships. When rules are breached, or a loss or change occurs, there must be an action (utu) to restore the balance.[8] These concepts inform all areas of Māori law, including the use and management of natural resources such as minerals.

Ownership and jurisdiction in relation to mineral resources

In Western colonial thought, minerals are understood primarily through their ability to be extracted from their surroundings and made useful for humans,

6 *Ibid.* See also Linda Smith, "On Tricky Ground: Researching the Native in the Age of Uncertainty" in Norman K. Denzin & Yvonna S. Lincoln, eds., *The Sage Handbook of Qualitative Research* (Thousand Oaks, CA: Sage, 2005) at 1–12; Graham Smith, "Mai I te maramatanga ki te putanga mai o te tahuritanga" (2004) 37:1 *Education Perspectives: Indigenous Education* 46 at 46–52; Fiona Cram, "Developing Partnerships in Research" (1997) 35 *Sites* 44 at 44–63.

7 Hirini Moko Mead, *Tikanga Māori*, Revised ed. (Wellington: Huia, 2016) at 32–33. See also Jones, *supra* note 4 at 65–86.

8 *Ibid.*

without agency or relations to humans or the more-than-human world.[9] However, this view of minerals as primarily "resources" has not always been the dominant understanding of these foundational inorganic elements of the environment. Māori have long-standing relations with minerals, including a history of their use in various areas of Aotearoa.[10] These relations are not preservationist, as minerals have long played key roles in Māori society. However, Māori environmental relations, including those with mineral resources, are embedded in *te ao Māori* (the Māori worldview), in which the use of and benefit from natural resources results in a "reciprocal obligation to care for those resources, their environment, and even enhance their 'energy' (*mauri*)."[11] Therefore, natural features can be *tupuna* (ancestors), with mauri of their own that must be respected. The land itself is Papatuānuku, the earth mother, with Ruaumoko, god of earthquakes inside. As Justice Joe Williams of the New Zealand Court of Appeal notes, "the fundamental law of the maintenance of properly tended relationships" serves as the guiding principle of Māori resource management: "No right in resources can be sustained without the right holder maintaining an ongoing relationship with the resource. No relationship; no right."[12]

Māori continue to assert ownership rights and contest the foundations of colonial claims to mineral ownership, including in the case study we discuss below.[13] As Ruckstuhl et al. conclude, the contemporary Māori response to mining is embedded in "a long legacy of 'constitutional' struggles and a sustained adherence to traditional values and practices."[14] In submissions relating to the block offer case study discussed below, several iwi asserted their ownership of minerals. The Tūwharetoa Māori Trust Board asserted their "customary rights and interests to Ngā Ōpapa [minerals]" in their tribal area.[15] Ngāti Rangitihi argued that "the reservation of minerals to the Crown is contrary to the Treaty of Waitangi"

9 "Minerals" are defined by s 2 of the *Crown Minerals Act* as "generally as a naturally occurring inorganic substance beneath or at the surface of the earth, whether or not under water, and includes all metallic minerals, non-metallic minerals, fuel minerals, precious stones, industrial rocks and building stones, and prescribed substances within the meaning of the Atomic Energy Act 1945."

10 Katharina Ruckstuhl et al., *Maori and Mining* (Otago: Te Poutama Maori, University of Otago, Maori and Mining Research Team, 2013), online: <hdl.handle.net/10523/4362> at 3.

11 *Ibid.* at 310.

12 Joseph Williams, "Lex Aotearoa: An Heroic Attempt to Map the Maori Dimension in Modern New Zealand Law" (2013) 21 *Waikato L Rev* 1 at 1, 5.

13 Waitangi Tribunal, *Petroleum Report* (Wellington: Waitangi Tribunal, 2003), online: <forms.justice.govt.nz/search/Documents/WT/wt_DOC_68187177/Petroleum%20Report.pdf> [*Petroleum 1*]; *Greenpeace of New Zealand v the Minister of Energy and Resources*, [2012] NZHC 1422, online: <www2.ecolex.org/server2.php/libcat/docs/COU/Full/En/COU-159586.pdf>; Andrew Erueti & Joshua Pietras, "Extractive Industry, Human Rights and Indigenous Rights in New Zealand's Exclusive Economic Zone" (2013) 11 *NZYB Intl L* 37.

14 Ruckstuhl et al., *supra* note 10 at 311.

15 Tūwharetoa Māori Trust Board, *Submission on Proposed Tender, Epithermal Gold 2013* (19 July 2013) at 3.

and that they believed they have "equal status with the Crown in decision making for mineral allocation and exploitation in their rohe [traditional area]."[16] Indeed, while asserting and acting upon ownership claimed through statutory vesting under the CMA and its predecessors, the Crown acknowledged these questions as unresolved in the required report to the minister, noting this legal uncertainty as one of the primary "risks" of going ahead with the tender process.[17] The Crown has recognized the rights of some Māori groups to specific minerals, such as *pounamu* (greenstone or jade).[18] However, it is Crown policy not to consider minerals-based remedies for Treaty settlements, and they have also ignored successful claims before the Waitangi Tribunal, such as the claim by Ngā Hapu o Ngā Ruahine and Ngāti Kahungnunu and other interested parties asserting a proprietary right in petroleum resources, and a subsequent inquiry into the management of petroleum under the CMA.[19] Outside of these Tribunal claims, there has been very limited judicial consideration of the CMA framework, likely due to the limited ability to challenge a minerals decision.[20]

Māori perspectives on minerals

While iwi and hapū have a range of perspectives on mining, there is broad agreement that mineral extraction should be sustainable, maintain the stability of the environment, avoid or mitigate negative impacts, and provide benefits for iwi

16 Te Mana o Ngāti Rangitihi, *Submission to the New Zealand Epithermal Gold 2013: Proposed Competitive Tender Allocation of Exploration Permits in the Central North Island* (May 2013) at 2–3.

17 S. Darby, *New Zealand Epithermal Gold 2013 Minerals Competitive Tender: Results of Consultation* (19 August 2013), released under the *Official Information Act* at 4 [*Darby Report*].

18 An iwi in the South Island, Ngāi Tahu, took a case to the Waitangi Tribunal and alleged the Crown breached its Treaty of Waitangi obligations when it failed to ensure Ngāi Tahu retained ownership of pounamu (greenstone or jade) in rivers and adjacent land when they sold land to the Crown. See Waitangi Tribunal, *Ngai Tahu Land Report* (1991); *Ngai Tahu (Pounamu Vesting) Act 1997* (NZ), 1997/91.

19 *Petroleum 1*, *supra* note 12. See also Waitangi Tribunal, *Report on the Management of the Petroleum Resource* (2011) [*Petroleum 2*]. The resulting 2003 Stage 1 Petroleum Report concluded that prior to the nationalization of petroleum in 1937, Māori had legal title to the resource as an incident to land ownership. Therefore, the loss of legal title by pre-1937 Treaty breaching alienations *and* expropriation of those resources without compensation or royalties breached the Treaty. They also concluded that the Crown's refusal to consider petroleum-based remedies was in breach of the Treaty. The Crown refused to recognize the Tribunal findings and no other mineral ownership claims have been pursued in the Courts to challenge the original vesting of mineral resources in the Crown. The Stage 2 report examined both the CMA and the *Resource Management Act 1991* under which environmental impacts of mining activity are regulated. The Tribunal concluded that the CMA was in breach of the Treaty because of the failure to ensure Māori interests are adequately protected and Māori perspectives are adequately considered. They also found a failure to ensure Māori had the capacity and resources to effectively engage with the processes under the CMA.

20 *Petroleum 2*, *supra* note 19.

and hapū.[21] Mineral resources are not easily extricated from the environment in which they are embedded in te ao Māori.[22] This is in recognition of the complex and necessary geological and hydrogeological functions they serve, but also because the natural environments in which minerals are embedded, such as mountains, are tapu (sacred) and deserving of care and respect. For example, Māori legal scholar Jacinta Ruru explains, "Māori interact and care for mountains and resources found on mountain slopes as *taonga* (treasures). It is an ethic that embodies the historical, spiritual and cultural association with land."[23] Indeed, Māori environmental management focuses on these broader ecological systems as central to sustaining not only human life, but all parts of the natural and spiritual worlds and future generations. Dame Nganeko Minhinnick notes, "in environmental terms the kaitiaki [guardianship] approach is holistic," and it provides for "restoration of damaged ecological systems, restoration of ecological harmony, increased usefulness of resources, and reduced risk to present and future generations."[24] Humans have direct responsibility as *kaitiaki* of particular places to ensure the mauri (life force) of the land is respected through only sustainable use of resources. Indeed, mana is directly related to the ability of an individual or community to maintain and enhance mauri of taonga (treasured resources).[25] Therefore, while Māori environmental management does not necessarily result in a prohibition on mining and the use of minerals for human benefit, it does import a different set of values and relationships than the Anglo-colonial worldview in which current mining law is embedded.[26] As the Waitangi Tribunal has noted, "nothing about tino rangatiratanga [self-determination], nor anything in Maori customary law, confers on Maori the right to destroy natural resources."[27]

Framing the relations of mining law

We also rely on both relational legal theory and legal geography to understand the structure of people-place relations under the CMA. Relational theory scholar Jennifer Nedelsky argues the structuring of relationships is a key, but underexamined, function of law.[28] Extending this analysis to people-place relations exposes the structural work effected through property relations and land

21 Ruckstuhl et al., *supra* note 10 at 15.

22 *Ibid.* at 16.

23 Jacinta Ruru, "Indigenous Peoples' Ownership and Management of Mountains: The Aotearoa/New Zealand Experience" (2004) 3 *Indigenous LJ* 111 at 116.

24 N. Minhinnick, *Establishing Kaitiaki* (Auckland: The Print Centre, 1989), cited in Hirini P. Matunga, *The Resource Management Act 1991 and Maori Perspectives* (Canterbury: Centre for Maori and Indigenous Planning and Development, Lincoln University, 1995) at 23, online: <http://researcharchive.lincoln.ac.nz/handle/10182/5119>.

25 *Petroleum 2*, *supra* note 19 at 30.

26 Ruckstuhl et al., *supra* note 10 at 26.

27 Waitangi Tribunal, *Central North Island Report* at 1246.

28 Jennifer Nedelsky, *Law's Relations: A Relational Theory of Self, Autonomy, and Law* (New York: Oxford University Press, 2011).

use laws.[29] As legal geographer Nick Blomley notes, through law "a set of relations specified as legally consequential are bracketed and detached from entanglements (ethical, practical, ecological, ontological) that are now placed outside the frame."[30] The use of law to structure and bracket relations is, as Blomley notes, always limited and partial. However, it is also always political because not all parties have equal ability to shape the frame and determine what is in and what is out.[31] Indeed, as Canadian geographer Shiri Pasternak points out, the concept of jurisdiction becomes a critical tool in unpacking the claims at the heart of land and resource disputes in settler colonial contexts. While Indigenous parties bring forward assertions of ownership and governmental authority, the presumption of the Crown's ownership and jurisdiction over land use and resource development is used to transform their claims to "reflect state frames of recognition."[32]

Further, in the context of land use and natural resource planning, the rationality of technical expertise is often mobilized to justify and enforce prior political decisions about spatial order.[33] The resulting "narratives of necessity" place conceptual limits on the terms of debate about specific land use decisions with important implications for attempts to assert alternative or non-extractive relations with place.[34] In the context of settler colonial nations, this closure has important consequences for Indigenous Peoples whose legal orders are embedded in worldviews with profoundly different values and principles than settler colonial state law.[35] As legal geographers Carolyn Harrison and Tracey Bedford argue, reliance on technical experts and the resulting instrumental rationality can result in "institutional closure" to the range of value orientations engaged by environmental decisions.[36]

29 Estair Van Wagner, "Putting Property in Its Place: Relational Theory, Environmental Rights and Land Use Planning" (2013) 43 *RGD* 275. See also Estair Van Wagner, "Law's Ecological Relations: The Legal Structure of People-Place Relations in Ontario's Aggregate Extraction Conflicts" (2016) *MIT J of Planning* 35.

30 Nicholas Blomley, "Disentangling Law: The Practice of Bracketing" (2014) 10 *Annual Rev of L & Social Science* 133 at 133–148, 136.

31 *Ibid.* at 139.

32 Pasternak, *supra* note 2 at 17. See also Shaunnagh Dorsett & Shaun McVeigh, "Questions of Jurisdiction" in Shaunnagh Dorsett & Shaun McVeigh, eds., *Jurisdiction* (London: Routledge, 2012).

33 Bent Flyvbjerg, *Rationality and Power: Democracy in Practice* (Chicago: University of Chicago Press, 1998) at 27. See also Jon Murdoch, *Post-Structuralist Geography: A Guide to Relational Space* (London: SAGE, 2005) at 147.

34 Susan Owens & Richard Cowell, *Land and Limits: Interpreting Sustainability in the Planning Process*, 2nd ed. (London: Taylor & Francis, 2010).

35 Emma Battell Lowman & Adam J Barker, *Settler Identity and Colonialism in 21st Century Canada* (Hatfield: University of Hertfordshire, 2016) at 49.

36 C. M. Harrison & T. Bedford, "Environmental Gains? Collaborative Planning, Planning Obligations and Issues of Closure in Local Land-Use Planning in the UK" in J. Holder & C. M. Harrison, eds., *Law and Geography: Current Legal Studies* (Oxford: Oxford University Press, 2003) at 343.

Mining and the Treaty relationship

Our analysis is also embedded in broader debates about the Treaty partnership between the Crown and Māori. As Māori scholar Margaret Mutu notes, "decolonization in Aotearoa/New Zealand has focused on honouring, upholding, and implementing the treaty."[37] Notably there are differing interpretations of the Treaty, in part because there are two versions: one in English and one in the Māori language. Most of the Māori signatories signed the Māori language version.[38] Major differences in interpretation arise in part because in the English version, Māori cede sovereignty to the British whereas in the Māori language version, Māori allow the British to set up a government but retain tino rangatiratanga over their lands, villages, resources, and taonga. Both Māori and the Crown recognize the Treaty as a foundational part of the constitutional framework of Aotearoa New Zealand.[39] However, debates about the meanings and status of the Treaty are ongoing,[40] and the differing interpretations and broad wording of the provisions have led to the development of an evolving set of principles by the Crown, the courts, and the Waitangi Tribunal.[41]

In their Report on the Management of the Petroleum Resource, the Tribunal found the following principles to be particularly relevant: partnership, the principle of active protection, and redress.[42] The principle of partnership refers to the nature of the relationship between the Crown and Māori as being one of equal partners who act in good faith. The Tribunal has stated this can be achieved in the most straightforward way by having each partner on the decision-making body.[43] The courts have been less definitive about the relative status of the partners but have nonetheless noted the honour of the Crown requires it act with "the utmost good faith" towards its Treaty partner and to make informed decisions.[44] The principle of active protection indicates that the Crown has a duty to actively protect Māori rights and interests, which

37 Mutu, *supra* note 3 at 274.

38 Mason Durie, *Ngā Tai Matatū: Tides of Māori Endurance* (Auckland: Oxford University Press, 2005).

39 *New Zealand Maori Council v Attorney General*, [1987] 1 NZLR 641 (CA) at 656.

40 See Malcolm Mulholland & Veronica Tawhai, *Weeping Waters: The Treaty of Waitangi and Constitutional Change* (Wellington: Huia, 2010). See also Jones, *supra* note 4 and Moana Jackson, "The Treaty and the Word: The Colonisation of Māori Philosophy" in G. Oddie & R. Perett, eds., *Justice, Ethics and New Zealand Society* (Auckland: Oxford University Press, 1992).

41 Waitangi Tribunal, *The Principles of the Treaty of Waitangi as Expressed by the Courts and the Waitangi Tribunal* (Wellington: Waitangi Tribunal, 2002), online: <www.waitangitribunal.govt.nz/assets/Documents/Publications/WT-Principles-of-the-Treaty-of-Waitangi-as-expressed-by-the-Courts-and-the-Waitangi-Tribunal.pdf>.

42 *Petroleum 2*, *supra* note 19 at 148.

43 *Ibid.* at 150–151.

44 *New Zealand Maori Council v Attorney General*, [1994] 1 NZLR 513 (PC); *New Zealand Maori Council v Attorney General*, [1987] 1 NZLR 641.

the courts and the Tribunal have found cannot necessarily be satisfied by consultation alone.[45] Indeed, with respect to petroleum, the Tribunal concluded Treaty-compliant outcomes can only be ensured where all key decision-making processes involve Māori participation of a kind that is appropriate to the decision being made.[46] Further, consultation must be meaningful and the decision maker must have an open mind rather than presenting a *fait accompli*.[47] The principle of redress suggests "past wrongs give rise to the right of redress" and imposes a positive obligation on the Crown to take steps to remedy breaches. Further, contemporary minerals and resource management should not compound past injustices or breaches.[48]

We examine Māori participation under the CMA in the context of these principles. At the same time, we recognize a wider range of sources of law and jurisdiction in relation to the ownership and governance of mineral resources. We view the existing statutory and policy framework as contingent and therefore as having the potential to be disrupted and transformed through the ongoing negotiation of a meaningful partnership and by Māori contestation of dominant people-place relations. As Mason Durie has noted, "at the heart of the Treaty is the promise of a mutually beneficial relationship between Māori and the Crown, a partnership."[49] At the same time, we follow Māori scholars such as Mutu and Moana Jackson in arguing that decolonization requires remedying Treaty breaches and "restoring the balance" between Māori as owners and decision makers, and settlers as guests invited to share in accordance with tikanga, the law of the land.[50]

Case study: the 2013 Epithermal Gold Block Offer

As noted in the Tribunal's 2008 Report on Central North Island Claims (CNI):

> From the evidence before us it is obvious that, to Central North Island Maori, land and resources had (and have) a spiritual and metaphysical significance that often go to the essence of tribal and personal identity. They are also a link with the past that roots people in their environment.[51]

45 *Ngai Tahu Maori Trust Board v Director General of Conservation*, [1995] 3 NZLR 553 at 560; *New Zealand Maori Council v Attorney General*, [1987] 1 NZLR 641.

46 *Petroleum 2*, *supra* note 19 at 150.

47 *Wellington International Airport Ltd v Air NZ*, [1991] 1 NZLR 671 [*Wellington Airport*]; *Petroleum 2*, *supra* note 19 at 150.

48 Waitangi Tribunal, *The Principles of the Treaty of Waitangi as Expressed by the Courts and the Waitangi Tribunal* (publisher unknown, 2002) at 100, online: <www.waitangitribunal.govt.nz/assets/Documents/Publications/WT-Principles-of-the-Treaty-of-Waitangi-as-expressed-by-the-Courts-and-the-Waitangi-Tribunal.pdf>.

49 Mason Durie, "Universal Provision, Indigeneity and the Treaty of Waitangi" (2002) 33 *VUWLR* 167 at 175.

50 Mutu, *supra* note 3 at 274. See also Jackson, *supra* note 3 at 101.

51 Waitangi Tribunal, *He Maunga Rongo: Report on Central North Island Claims* (2008) at 92 [*CNI Report*].

The 2013 Epithermal Gold Block Offer was proposed over a large area in the Central North Island of Aotearoa New Zealand, primarily in the Bay of Plenty area.[52] The original proposed area encompassed the rohe of several iwi (Te Arawa, Ngāti Awa, Ngāti Rangi, Ngāti Ranginui, Tuhoe, Ngāti Tuwharetoa, Ngāti Maniapoto, Tainui) and cut across areas governed by several local authorities, including the Bay of Plenty Regional Council. Approximately 31.5% of the Bay of Plenty area is land owned by Māori entities and held in Māori land title and general title.[53] The area has been the subject of 16 Waitangi Tribunal historical inquiries into breaches of the Treaty, including the Central North Island Report,[54] and eight major Treaty Settlements, with approximately another 10 being negotiated.[55] These include the major forestry settlement, the Central North Island Iwi Collective Crown Forest Settlement in 2008, and the Te Arawa Lakes Settlement in 2006, which established the first iwi-Council co-governance model for a natural resource in New Zealand.[56] As one local council noted, "the Treaty settlement landscape is a significant feature of our region."[57] According to the Crown, the Block Offer area was selected "to take account of geology and prospectivity" in a "prime region for epithermal gold and silver deposits."[58]

In 2008, the Tribunal released their findings in their inquiry into breaches in the Central North Island. They concluded the Crown had failed to protect the tino rangatiratanga of Central North Island iwi and hapū, actively undermining Māori legal and governance systems.[59] The Tribunal also made important findings in relation to the loss of control over resources, particularly geothermal resources. This is notable in the context of the 2013 Block Offer because the gold deposits located in the area are produced by heat at shallow depths in relationship to hot springs and volcanic features.[60] These types of gold deposit are referred to in the mining industry as "bonanza" deposits because they can be very

52 While New Zealand Petroleum and Minerals does post information about block offers online, information about the 2013 Epithermal Gold Minerals Block Offer is no longer available on their website. Indeed much of the information collated for this chapter required numerous Official Information Act 1982 requests between 2016 and 2017 to obtain.

53 Māori Land is a specific title of land governed under the Māori Land Act/Te Ture Whenua Māori 1993. Te Puni Kōkiri, *Report on the Māori Asset Base in the Waiariki Economy* (2010) at 4, online: <www.tpk.govt.nz/en/a-matou-mohiotanga/business-and-economics/te-ripoata-ohanga-maori-mo-te-waiariki>.

54 All five volumes of the report are available online: <www.waitangitribunal.govt.nz/publications-and-resources/waitangi-tribunal-reports/>.

55 Bay of Plenty Regional Council, *Treaty of Waitangi Toolkit* (2015), online: <www.boprc.govt.nz/about-council/kaupapa-maori/treaty-of-waitangi-toolbox/>.

56 *Central North Island Forests Land Collective Settlement Act 2008* (NZ), 2008/99; *Te Arawa Lakes Settlement Act 2006* (NZ), 2006/43.

57 Bay of Plenty Regional Council, *Submission to Proposed Competitive Tender–Epithermal Gold 2013* (28 May 2013).

58 *Darby Report*, *supra* note 17 at 6.

59 *CNI Report*, *supra* note 51 at 1674.

60 *Darby Report*, *supra* note 17; see also Chris Ralph, "Epithermal Gold and Silver Deposits" (2017) *ICMJ's Prospecting and Mining Journal*, online: <www.icmj.com/magazine/article/epithermal-gold-and-silver-deposits-3618/>.

rich and easy to extract.[61] As noted by the Tribunal, these geothermal features are taonga, including the subsurface elements of the Taupo Volcanic Zone.[62] They were "struck" by "the exercise of authority over geothermal resources that has remained unbroken for hundreds of years." Therefore, the gold being offered up for exploration is in direct relationship with, and even constituted by, the geothermal systems at the heart of Māori kinship relations in the CNI, and therefore tino rangatiratanga and "onerous" kaitiaki responsibilities and obligations. As the tribunal noted, the legal relationships with geothermal resources are

> based on intense associations with the resources, an extensive accumulated knowledge of its behaviour, and the varying characteristics of different surface and subsurface manifestations – as with every other aspect of Māori knowledge of the natural world with which they claimed a close relationship.[63]

The 2013 Block Offer process

Affected iwi and hapū were notified of the proposed offer area in March 2013 with approximately two months of consultation following the initial notifications. There were 15 iwi and hapū submissions, as well as seven from councils. Māori submitters overwhelmingly rejected the proposed offer area, with all submitters noting significant concerns about the proposals.

The Te Arawa Coalition[64] held several meetings with New Zealand Petroleum and Minerals officials and the Minister of Energy and Resources and Minister of Māori Development. Te Arawa hapū also held separate hui (gathering) in and around Rotorua, including a Hui on Mining at Kearoa *marae*, Horohoro in June and a *hui-a-iwi*. The Te Arawa hui-a-iwi passed a resolution stating that they "do not support epithermal gold mining in the Te Arawa rohe."[65] Most of the iwi and hapū submissions requested their entire rohe or significant areas be excluded from the Block Offer.[66] If all of these exclusions had been granted, there would have been no Block Offer area at all. In addition, several iwi and councils requested specific sites be excluded.[67] Opposition to the offer area was

61 Priscila Barrera, "An Overview of Epithermal Gold Deposits" (24 May 2017) *Investing News*, online: <investingnews.com/daily/resource-investing/precious-metals-investing/gold-investing/an-overview-of-epithermal-gold-deposits/>.

62 *CNI Report*, *supra* note 51 at 1543.

63 *Ibid.* at 1543.

64 The Coalition is comprised of representatives from Te Arawa Federation of Māori Authorities, Te Arawa Lakes Trust, Te Pūmautanga o Te Arawa, Te Arawa Primary Sector Inc, Te Arawa River Iwi Trust and Tapuika Iwi Authority.

65 Te Arawa Hui-a Iwi, "NZ Epithermal Gold Hui-a-Iwi o Te Arawa Resolution" (13 July 2013).

66 The following iwi groups requested their entire tribal areas be excluded: Te Arawa, Raukawa Charitable Trust, Tapuika Iwi Authority, Te Maru o Rereahu, Maniapoto M ori Trust Board, Ngāti Koroki Kahukura, and Ngāti Tūwharetoa.

67 Ngāti Rangiwewehi, Te Maru o Rereahu, Te Arawa River Iwi Trust, Tūwharetoa Māori Trust Board, Bay of Plenty Regional Council, Matamata-Piako District Council, Waipa District Council and the Waikato Regional Council.

firmly rooted in an understanding of Māori holding a level of jurisdiction over land and over the specific resource. This was expressed both in written submissions and at face-to-face meetings.[68]

Following from the recommendations of the Results of Consultation Report to the Minister, the tender proceeded.[69] In May 2014, a five-year permit was granted to Silver City Ltd.[70] for a 33 km^2 area in the Central North Island. By 2016, Silver City had quietly relinquished their permit.[71]

The structure of mineral relations in Aotearoa New Zealand

Sources of law

Iwi and hapū rely on a range of sources of law and jurisdiction beyond the CMA. These include tikanga and inherent jurisdictions such as *mana whenua* and kaitiakitanga; Treaty settlements and statutory acknowledgements; Agreements with the Crown about particular places; Accords with the Crown; Waitangi Tribunal reports; and instruments under the CMA and the *Resource Management Act 1991*, such as iwi management plans or official plans.[72] The primary source for the majority of iwi and hapū submitters was tikanga and the assertion of their

68 *Darby Report*, *supra* note 17 at 2.

69 *Ibid.*

70 New Zealand, Minister of Energy and Resources Hon Simon Bridges, "Epithermal Gold Exploration Permit Awarded" (9 May 2014) *Media Statement*, online: <www.scoop.co.nz/stories/PA1405/S00173/epithermal-gold-exploration-permit-awarded.htm>.

71 "Going for Kawerau Gold" *Rotorua Daily Post* (5 May 2015), online: <www.nzherald.co.nz/rotorua-daily-post/news/article.cfm?c_id=1503438&objectid=11443969>.

72 The majority of submissions pointed to existing recognitions by the Crown of their mana, through Deeds of Settlement or protocols or statutory acknowledgements. Of the 15 submissions, eight have Deeds of Settlement or Protocols or Statutory Acknowledgements or Iwi Management Plans that set out protections or acknowledgements of the mana of those groups over their particular areas. Included amongst these are: Ngāti Rangiwewehi Te Tāhuhu o Tawakeheimoa Trust – Crown Minerals Protocol and Conservation Protocol, Ngāti Rangiwewehi Deed of Settlement; Ngāti Tūwharetoa Statutory acknowledgements for Tarawera and Rangitaiki Rivers and Kawerau Geothermal System. Deed of Settlement 2005; Ngāti Tuwharetoa Hapū Forum Terms of Negotiation 2013; Raukawa Deed of Settlement 2012 (includes statutory acknowledgement areas formally registering Raukawa's connection to these places), Raukawa Energy Accord with Minister of Energy and Resources and Ministry of Business, Innovation and Employment; Tapuika Iwi Authority Trust, Deed of Settlement (before Parliament 2013 and includes Crown Minerals Protocol); Te Arawa Lakes Settlement 2006; Ngāti Tuwharetoa, Raukawa, Te Arawa River Iwi Waikato River Act 2010; Te Arawa River Iwi Energy and Resources Accord – with Minister of Energy and Resources and MBIE 2012; Te Mana o Ngāti Rangitihi Trust, Iwi Environmental Management Plan (lodged with Whakatane District Council and Bay of Plenty Regional Council 2012); Tūwharetoa Environmental Iwi Management Plan. Many of these high-level agreements or Settlements have taken years to negotiate and some involve legislative backing (e.g. *Waikato-Tainui Raupatu Claims (Waikato River) Settlement Act 2010*). Several of these Accords commit the Crown and iwi to "giving effect to the principles of Te Tiriti o Waitangi/Treaty of Waitangi."

mana, including as recognized in these various instruments. Their inherent jurisdiction over the lands and resources was linked to assertions of their ownership of mineral resources in some cases.[73] However, even where ownership was not referenced, submitters made broad claims to jurisdiction over resource management decision-making in their rohe.[74] The Tapuika Iwi Authority noted the role of customary traditions and tikanga in regulating the use of resources: "Tapuika tikanga was that in order to ensure the wellbeing of the people, it was necessary to maintain the balance between the physical realm, the natural realm and the realm of mankind hence the enforcement of conservation through tapu."[75]

In the CNI report, the Tribunal concluded the Crown must "actively protect the exercise of rangatiratanga (including customary law and values) in environmental and resource management, not reduce the duty of active protection merely to taking these relationships and values into account."[76] However, in the 2013 Block Offer process, the Crown relied solely on the CMA and its instruments as the source of legal authority. No reference was made to tikanga or to relevant Tribunal reports as guiding the process or as relevant in the analysis post-consultation. State mining law in New Zealand is divided between allocative functions under the CMA and the governance of environmental and social effects under the *Resource Management Act 1991*. These functions were intentionally severed when sweeping law reform brought the majority of environmental and planning law under the RMA in 1991. Notably, minerals are the only resource singled out in this way from the integrated approach under the broad environmental planning RMA.

As the first step, the allocation permitting process provides the Crown critical chronological power to determine when the process begins and when and how other parties must engage and respond. For Māori, this chronological power indicates the hierarchy of relations. The Crown's relations are positioned as primary. State law is the relevant legal framework, and iwi and hapū are submitters who must fit into its frame to make claims cognizable. Māori relations with place and the mineral resource at stake are subordinated to the primary statutory purpose and "balanced" against a variety of other Crown-determined factors in

73 Ngāti Tuwharetoa Settlement Trust, *Response to Crown Consultation on the 'Proposed Competitive Tender Offer for Metallic Minerals Exploration Permits: Part of Bay of Plenty and Waikato'* (19 July 2013); see also Tūwharetoa Māori Trust Board, *Submission on Proposed Tender, Epithermal Gold 2013* (19 July 2013).

74 Ngāti Kea Ngati Tuara, *Submission on Sichuan Tianbao Minerals Exploration Permit Application* (20 April 2015). See also Te Arawa River Iwi Trust, *Submission to the Ministry of Economic Development Regarding the Epithermal Gold 2013 Proposed Tender* (2013) and Te Mana o Ngāti Rangitihi Trust, *Submission to the New Zealand Epithermal Gold 2013: Proposed Competitive Tender Allocation of Exploration Permits in the Central North Island* (May 2013).

75 Tapuika Iwi Authority Trust, *Submission from Tapuika Iwi Authority on the Proposed Competitive Tender Offer for Metallic Minerals Exploration Permits: Epithermal Gold 2013 Proposed Tender* (14 July 2013).

76 *CNI Report*, *supra* note 51 at 1245.

determining when exploration and extraction will take place.[77] This balancing act is also expressly structured by the CMA to prioritize the extraction of minerals. As Ministry officials told us, "We've got our hands tied because of our legislation."[78] The Tribunal, including in both the Central North Island Report and the Report on the Management of Petroleum, has noted the potential for Māori to be prejudiced by such balancing exercises.[79] Indeed, former National Manager Sefton Darby, who led the 2013 Block Offer process, characterized the role of the Ministry as "cheerleading instead of regulating" the mining industry.[80]

The purpose of the CMA

When the Crown Minerals Bill was before Parliament in 1991, the Minister of Energy dismissed opposition to mining.[81] The government's position was that sustainable management of mineral resources was "more likely to be achieved through ensuring there are as few barriers as possible to invest in exploration" and "with as few Government interventions as possible."[82] Opposition members opposed the Bill, characterizing it as prioritizing development.[83] A purpose clause was inserted by the 2013 reforms, which defines the purpose as the promotion of "prospecting for, exploration for, and mining of Crown owned minerals for the benefit of New Zealand."[84]

The scheme presumes extraction to be in the public benefit rather than initiating an inquiry into whether or how it will, or will not, be of benefit in the particular circumstances. A proposed development therefore goes forward from an initial stage with "rights" to engage in this presumptively beneficial activity regardless of the impact it may have, which are to be dealt with at a later stage under the RMA consent process. Despite evidence to the contrary, particularly in relation to gold and silver mining, there is no opportunity to contest the presumption of investment and employment benefits in the CMA process.[85] The presumptive benefit clearly outweighs even the Treaty relationship at the core of New Zealand law, despite strong criticism of the Ministry's failure to undertake a cost benefit analysis of mining activity and the "absolutely fantastical" numbers

77 *Petroleum 2*, *supra* note 19 at 163, 171.

78 Interview of Ministry of Business, Innovation and Employment officials (23 May 2017) [*Interview*].

79 *CNI Report*, *supra* note 51 at 1248. See also *Petroleum 2*, *supra* note 19 at 163, 171.

80 Sefton Darby, *The Ground Between: Navigating the Oil and Mining Debate in New Zealand* (Wellington: Bridget Williams Books, 2017) at 23 [*The Ground Between*].

81 New Zealand, House of Representatives, *Parliamentary Debates (Hansard)*, 43rd Parl, 2nd Session, No 516 (4 July 1991) (Hon John Luxton) [*Hansard 43*].

82 *Ibid.*

83 *Ibid.* at 695 (Pete Hodgson).

84 *Crown Minerals Act 1991* (NZ), 1991/70 at s 1A [*Crown Minerals Act*].

85 Geoff Bertram, "Mining in the New Zealand Economy" (2011) 7 *Policy Q* 13; Gundars Rudzitis & Kenton Bird, "The Myth and Reality of Sustainable New Zealand: Mining in a Pristine Land" (2011) 53:6 *Environment: Science and Policy for Sustainable Development* 16.

to describe the contribution of the mining sector to the economy.[86] While iwi submitters called for the inclusion of Māori interests directly in the purpose clause during the most recent CMA reform processes in 2013, the government rejected these calls.[87]

Understanding Treaty relations: the section 4 Treaty clause

The Treaty relationship was a central element of iwi and hapū submissions, particularly the concept of partnership. Ngāti Tuwharetoa noted Treaty partnership "would require Crown and Ngāti Tuwharetoa to make decisions together in respect of whether licences ought to be granted within our area of interest and on what conditions."[88] Ngāti Rangitihi asserted "equal status with the Crown in decision making for mineral allocation and exploitation in their rohe."[89] This conception of the partnership is consistent with the findings of the Central North Island Report.[90]

The Crown's view of the Treaty relationship under the CMA is set out in the stand-alone Treaty clause in section 4. It requires anyone exercising functions under the *Crown Minerals Act, 1991* to "have regard" to the principles of the Treaty of Waitangi. Given that there are no general requirements for public consultation in the Act, this suggests Māori views will be of particular significance in minerals decisions. However, not only is the CMA clause a weak Treaty clause, but it clearly positions Treaty relations as peripheral to the promotional purposes of the Act.

Māori members and others noted the weakness of the Treaty clause during debate when the Act was first introduced, noting that the minerals bill was not consistent with the Māori engagement and sustainability objectives set out in the companion RMA bill and was weaker than other statutes.[91] The Tribunal recommended the Treaty clause be revised to be "at least" the level of the *Conservation Act 1987* and the *State-Owned Enterprises Act 1986*.[92] These statutes respectively require the Crown to administer and interpret the respective Acts so as to "give effect to the principles of the Treaty" or state the Act cannot be interpreted to "permit the Crown to act in a manner that is inconsistent with the principles of the Treaty."[93]

86 *The Ground Between*, *supra* note 80.
87 New Zealand, Ministry of Business, Innovation and Employment, *Departmental Report on the Crown Minerals (Permitting and Crown Land) Bill: Preliminary Report* (December 2012) [*Departmental Report*].
88 Tūwharetoa Māori Trust Board, *supra* note 73.
89 Te Mana o Ngāti Rangitihi Trust, *supra* note 74.
90 *CNI Report*, *supra* note 51 at 1673.
91 *Hansard 43*, *supra* note 81 (Tirikatene-Sullivan).
92 *Petroleum 2*, *supra* note 19.
93 *Conservation Act, 1987* (NZ), 1987/65 at s 4; *State-Owned Enterprises Act 1986* (NZ), 1986/124 at s 9.

The courts have interpreted the phrase "have regard to" conservatively in the context of other statutes, such as the RMA:

> The tribunal may not ignore the statement. It must be given genuine attention and thought, and such weight as the tribunal considers appropriate. But having done that the tribunal is *entitled to conclude it is not of sufficient significance either alone or together with other matters to outweigh other contrary considerations* which it must take into account in accordance with its statutory function.[94]

In this context, it is clear the wording of the CMA Treaty clause requires iwi or hapū views to be weighed against other matters rather than considered in their own right, and certainly not given effect to. The facilitative purpose clause works in tandem with the weak Treaty clause to uphold colonial people-place relations. As a result, the 2013 Block Offer Report on Consultation concluded the Te Arawa request for the exclusion of their rohe – about half the tender area – was not in the public interest as it "would substantively restrict the Crown's ability to manage its mineral assets in the region."[95] Instead of responding substantively to assertions of jurisdiction and equal partnership by multiple submitters, the Crown reiterated ownership, allocation decision-making, and royalties are not subject to negotiation.[96] Even a request for a permit condition requiring "proactive engagement" was denied as "unenforceable" because of "iwi and hapū who may choose not to engage."[97] This, the report concluded, unacceptably "takes decision making authority out of the hands of the Crown and places it in the hands of iwi." These examples demonstrate how through the consultation process, the Crown fixes the conception of the Treaty partnership in accordance with their presumptive jurisdiction rather than in relation to Māori perspectives and laws. These are structurally excluded from decision-making under the CMA by the consultation process itself.

The Minerals Programmes: the consultation policy

The content of the section 4 duty is contained in the mandatory policy instruments, the Minerals Programmes developed by the minister.[98] They are the central mandatory instruments created by the Act to provide the details of the management regime for allocation decisions and guide the significant discretionary power under the Act.[99] The Programmes emphasize two interrelated

94 *New Zealand Co-operative Dairy Co Ltd v Commerce Commission*, [1976] 1 NZLR 436.
95 *Darby Report*, *supra* note 17.
96 *Ibid.* at 21.
97 *Ibid.* at 20.
98 *Crown Minerals Act*, *supra* note 84 at s 14(1)(b), 15.
99 The Act requires two minerals programs, one for Petroleum and one for Minerals (Excluding Petroleum). While both engage similar issues and raise similar concerns, this research is

aspects of the Treaty clause: consultation and exclusion requests. Through the Programmes, the Treaty principles are effectively narrowed down to a duty to consult, an approach directly rejected by the Tribunal in the Central North Island Report and the Report on the Management of the Petroleum Resource.[100]

Consultation

The current Programme requires consultation where an iwi's or hapū's rohe includes some or all of the permit area or an iwi or hapū will be "directly affected."[101] Consultation principles include acting reasonably and in good faith, making informed decisions, including being informed of the Māori perspective and tikanga, and having regard to Treaty principles.[102] The Programme requires meaningful consultation, which includes a number of commitments: "early consultation" to inform of "any Treaty implications or any other matters about which iwi and hapū may wish to express their views"; ensuring sufficient information to make informed decisions and to participate; providing enough time; and ensuring that Crown decision makers will have "an open mind on the views received" and give these views "full and genuine consideration." This definition is consistent with the jurisprudence on consultation more broadly.[103]

The Programme maintains this form of consultation is flexible and mentions face-to-face meetings and *hui*. However, Ministry officials told us they were "simply unable" to undertake these types of consultation with all iwi and hapū despite acknowledging, "each group for the most part prefers to meet face to face, and us come up to the rohe, and that by far is probably our preference as well."[104] Therefore, staff must determine whom they are going to engage with most deeply, and consequently, with whom they will not. Consistent with the purpose of the Act, to promote and facilitate extraction, Ministry officials advised us, "we would probably be more likely to want to sit down with a group who is both willing to negotiate and there are parameters to reach some sort of outcome." Iwi and hapū submitters and councils both criticized the consultation process.[105] Ngati Rangiwewehi noted: "The receipt and acknowledgement of

---

focused on the later. The 2011 Tribunal report was focused on the former. New Zealand Petroleum and Minerals, Ministry of Business, Innovation and Employment, "Minerals Programme: Minerals Programme for Minerals (excluding Petroleum) 2013" (2013), online: <www.nzpam.govt.nz/assets/Uploads/our-industry/rules-regulations/minerals-programme-2013.pdf>.

100 *CNI Report*, *supra* note 51 at 1236, citing *New Zealand Maori Council v Attorney General*, [1996] 3 NZLR 140 (CA) at 169; *Petroleum 2*, *supra* note 19 at 150.

101 *Crown Minerals Act*, *supra* note 84 at s 2.2.

102 *Crown Minerals Act*, *supra* note 84 at s 2.3: "Where consultation with iwi and hapū is required by this Programme, it must be carried out in accordance with the consultation principles and procedures set out below or in accordance with any agreed protocol."

103 *Wellington Airport*, *supra* note 47.

104 *Interview*, *supra* note 78.

105 Email from Maniapoto Māori Trust Board, "Proposed Competitive Tender Offer" (23 May 2013) to Rob Robson; Ngāti Tuwharetoa Settlement Trust, *supra* note 73; Raukawa

advice letters from the Ministry must not in any way be regarded as an appropriate consultation process from our perspective."[106]

The consultation section of the Programme notes the Ministry has also entered into specific Accords or protocols with iwi or hapū and that these set out how the Crown will engage with them. These instruments are intended to guide how consultation and engagement will occur with the Ministry. The Accords were noted in submissions as recognizing the mana of the signatories. However, Ministry officials told us, "the reality is the accords aren't binding." In their view, the meaning of the Accords is explanatory: "Listen, the Crown Mineral Act is messy and it's hard to interpret so here's how it affects you directly. The main thing is, here is how we are going to communicate with you."[107] The Ministerial officials told us Statutory Acknowledgements and Deeds of Recognition did not affect their process because they deal with environmental matters, which they consider not to fall under the CMA. These are included in Treaty settlements to acknowledge areas or sites with which iwi have a special relationship and were cited by many submitters as recognizing their mana and kaitiaki responsibilities. This narrow interpretation of the importance of Crown Acknowledgements to the Treaty relationship compounds the effects of the weak Treaty and facilitative purpose clauses described above to further shift Māori relationships with land outside the minerals framework.

Exclusions and conditions

Part of the consultation regime under the Programmes is the opportunity for iwi or hapū to request the exclusion of "defined areas of land of particular importance to the mana of the iwi or hapū."[108] Schedule 3 of the Programme contains a list of "land that is significant to iwi" to be excluded from the operation of the Programme or not to be included in any permit at the request of an iwi or hapū. However, the Programme also provides for requests during the consultation relating to a block offer or permitting process.[109] The Tribunal found iwi and hapū continually engage in this process in good faith.[110]

In 2013, the Programmes were amended to provide for iwi and hapū to request conditions on the proposed activity in addition to requesting exclusion. While according to the Ministry report the amendment was made in response to

Charitable Trust, *Proposed Competitive Tender Offer for Metallic Minerals Exploration Permits: Part of Bay of Plenty and Waikato* (19 July 2013); Te Mana o Ngāti Rangitihi Trust, *supra* note 74, Tūwharetoa Māori Trust Board, *supra* note 73; Bay of Plenty Regional Council, *Submission to Proposed Competitive Tender: Epithermal Gold 2013* (28 May 2013); Waikato Regional Council, *Proposed Competitive Tender Offer for Metallic Minerals Exploration Permits: Part of Bay of Plenty and Waikato* (27 May 2013).

106 Ngāti Rangiwewehi, *Submission* (18 July 2013).

107 *Interview*, *supra* note 78.

108 *Crown Minerals Act*, *supra* note 84 at s 14.

109 *Ibid.* at s 2.7.

110 *Petroleum 2*, *supra* note 19 at 165.

iwi submissions during the reform process, it clearly shifts the emphasis from the ability of iwi and hapū to engage with underlying questions about *whether* mining activity should occur, to a managerial approach focused on *how* mining will occur in a particular place. Conditions are more consistent with the facilitative statutory purpose. Indeed, while we did not see the submission requesting the change, we might query whether the difficulty in having areas excluded in the past influenced the request for alternative measures.[111] The Ministry officials we spoke to confirmed the emphasis on conditions rather than exclusion when describing a typical follow up conversation with submitting iwi and hapū: "Help us out here. What would be acceptable to you? Are there specific conditions you are looking for? Or are there specific areas that are really, really important to you?"[112]

Requests for exclusion or conditions require reasons for the exclusion or conditions including why the area is important to the mana of iwi and hapū; whether it is a *known wāhi tapu* site; what makes the area unique; whether the area has been recognized as important through Treaty claims and settlements, and objections under other legislation; relevant Treaty claims and the potential to "impede the prospect of redress of grievances"; *Marine and Coastal Area (Takutai Moana) Act 2011* rights or interests; and exclusions specified in iwi management plans. However, as the Tribunal noted, the minister relies on the Ministry officials for expertise in making exclusion decisions, not on Māori elders or other experts on local tikanga.[113] The Programme does provide considerations in addition to the reasons of the iwi and hapū.[114] These include Māori interests in the foreshore and seabed,[115] existing legislative protections, viability concerns, and "the size of the area and the value of the potential resource affected if the area is excluded." The Act explicitly requires the minister to balance existing and recognized iwi and hapū Treaty interests against potential or theoretical benefits.

One Ministry official reflected on the need to balance iwi and hapū concerns with their mandate and the shift away from exclusion requests, particularly large-scale exclusion, towards very site specific restrictions and minor restrictions like iwi monitoring or notification:

> I think over the time I have been here I have seen the dialogue move from, "No, we hate mining, go away, and this is all really too culturally significant," and when we front up and say, "Look that is really hard for us to just categorically say no because there are other factors and our Act says we have to facilitate development, help us out here guys, we really want to understand this."[116]

111 In *Petroleum 2*, *supra* note 19, the Tribunal notes the sense that iwi and hap iwi and hap fail to have land excluded.
112 *Interview*, *supra* note 78.
113 *Petroleum 2*, *supra* note 19 at 170.
114 *Crown Minerals Act*, *supra* note 84 at s 2.8.
115 See the *Marine and Coastal (Takutai Moana) Act 2011* (NZ), 2011/3.
116 *Interview*, *supra* note 78.

In the view of one official, more positive outcomes have emerged from a dialogue about *how* rather than *if* exploration, prospecting, or extraction will occur. In their view, the "best case-scenario is when we get the iwi group speaking directly with the permit holder and they work through their concerns together."[117] However, in this way, the Crown's Treaty responsibilities are outsourced to private entities and are no longer governed by the formal legal relations guiding the Treaty partnership. Rather, they rely on the willingness and capacity of private actors going beyond the minimum requirements of exercising their statutory rights. As one Ministry official put it, "really good permit holders will say, 'Cool, come and help us monitor this', or 'Come out onsite with me and show me the areas that we need to avoid.'"[118] While some such arrangements could be conditions of the permit, the Ministry officials we spoke to implied that much of this relationship building would be voluntary on the part of industry and their role was as a "matchmaker" rather than an enforcement authority. Iwi and hapū submitters expressed strong concern about the iwi engagement reporting requirements for industry because there is no requirement for iwi input to the annual report and no means for iwi to verify or contest proponent data provided to the Ministry.[119]

Despite the guidance in the Programme, decisions on exclusion or conditions requests remain highly subjective. The Tribunal specifically noted the lack of transparency in the process in relation to petroleum.[120] The minister retains discretion to exclude lands or to reject such a request either at the Programme level or during a permit or block offer process. As one Ministry official told us:

> the struggle that we deal with every day is the fact that we have a sense in terms of when something is important, where it should be excluded, but there's no actual number of weighting that has been created through the legislation.[121]

In 2011, the Tribunal also noted the very limited success of exclusion requests.[122] In the 2013 Block Offer, the entire area of the tender was subject to requests for exclusion by iwi and hapū. However, the post-consultation report states just two exclusion requests were received from iwi and hapū. Submissions of outright opposition to the tender where not characterized or considered as requests to exclude as they "were not based on protecting sites of significance but broader issues around the Crown's management of the Crown minerals estate." Similarly submissions alleging the process was a breach of the Treaty were dismissed, as they did not request specific "parcels of land be excluded due to importance to mana." However, even requests with very specific details

117 *Ibid.*
118 *Ibid.*
119 *Departmental Report*, *supra* note 87 at 17.
120 *Petroleum 2*, *supra* note 19 at 171.
121 *Interview*, *supra* note 78.
122 *Petroleum 2*, *supra* note 19 at 65.

were denied on the grounds they "lacked due specificity." The requirement for specificity not only imposes spatial limits on exclusions; with respect to wāhi tapu sites, it requires iwi to share sensitive and undisclosed information. Ngāti Raukawa specifically noted that they found it offensive to be asked to disclose these sites.[123]

In the case study, the only requests for exclusion granted after the consultation process were two requests for small areas by local councils, both with low or no prospectivity.[124] Notably, unlike iwi and hapū, councils have no statutory right to consultation or to request exclusions and are only consulted as a matter of internal policy. Waikato and Bay of Plenty Regional Councils also unsuccessfully sought the removal of significant and geothermal resources protected under current planning instruments. As the report noted: "some of the most prospective areas are located over, in, and around geothermal systems."[125] When we spoke with local council officials, this disregard for the "robust" policies resulting from their lengthy public consultative process, including significant work developing relationships with iwi and hapū, was a clear source of frustration. One interviewee noted, New Zealand Petroleum and Minerals think "they have a preeminent right over any other legislation."[126] Our interviewees were not only concerned with poor planning outcomes that may result but also the potential for the minerals process to undermine the extensive relationship building work they had undertaken in response to both Treaty settlements and past conflicts and challenges.[127] Indeed, the Tribunal raised a cautionary note about this possibility in relation to petroleum.[128]

The limited success of exclusion requests is not surprising in the context of a facilitative regime aimed at promoting one particular activity, and one narrow view of relations with land. As one Ministry official noted, "unfortunately there is only so much we can do." In their view, the statutory scheme results in "a really strong development focus and really clear criteria."[129] It is, however, nonetheless concerning in the context of the Treaty relationship. It is particularly troubling amid moves towards partnership models in other natural resource contexts.[130] While there remains much work to be done to improve and enforce Māori engagement and jurisdiction under the RMA and *Conservation Act*, as Ruckstuhl et al. argue, "the Treaty-based *partnership* approach . . . has much to

123 Raukawa Charitable Trust, *supra* note 105.

124 *Darby Report*, *supra* note 17 at 19–20.

125 *Ibid.* at 18–19.

126 Interview of Bay of Plenty Local Officials 1 (28 March 2017) at 4 [*Interview 1*].

127 *Ibid.*; Interview of Bay of Plenty Local Officials 2 (28 March 2017) [*Interview 2*].

128 *Petroleum 2*, *supra* note 19 at 165.

129 *Interview*, *supra* note 78.

130 See *Resource Management Act 1991* (NZ), 1991/69 at s 58M (Mana Whakahono-a-Rohe: Iwi Participation Agreements); *Te Awa Tupua (Whanganui River Claims Settlement) Act 2017 (NZ)*, 2017/7; *Te Urewera Act 2014* (NZ), 2014/51. Note, however, the status of Crown-owned minerals is not affected by the vesting of *Te Urewera* in itself as a legal entity, as per s 93.

offer as a process for engaging in meaningful dialogue with Māori communities to assess the impacts of mining."[131]

In addition to exclusion requests, a number of submissions raised environmental concerns such as toxic damage, loss of habitat and resources, health impacts, and water contamination and usage.[132] Indeed, Ministry officials told us approximately 80% of the concerns raised in CMA consultations are environmental in nature. They told us while environmental effects "create context," they cannot actually weigh these issues in assessing exclusions or conditions.[133] However, the 2013 Block Offer submissions demonstrate this characterization relies on a fundamental mischaracterization of the role people-place relations in the Māori worldview and legal order. A majority referenced kaitiaki relationships and obligations, including duties to both ancestors and future generations. By narrowly construing these assertions of tikanga processes and relations as 'environmental issues', the Crown is able to make an important jurisdictional move. They can exclude not only Māori perspectives, but the very basis of Māori legal and political authority and identity: the relationships of Māori with their land and resources. As the Tribunal noted in the CNI Report:

> from the evidence before us it is obvious that, to Central North Island Maori, land and resources had (and have) a spiritual and metaphysical significance that often go to the essence of tribal and personal identity. They are also a link with the past that roots people in their environment.[134]

Conclusion

While creative and landmark settlements are being made in relation to freshwater and protected areas to recognize Māori relations with place, the mining regime continues to attempt to exclude the basis of such relations with minerals and mining sites. Despite close to three decades of Māori participation in the CMA process, clear findings that the processes breached the Treaty, and clear recommendations for improvement from the Tribunal, our case study demonstrates little has changed to ensure Māori jurisdiction in relation to onshore mineral resources in Aotearoa New Zealand. Through the jurisdictional division between the Crown's allocative functions and environmental decisions under the RMA, CMA decision makers lawfully exclude not only the majority of concerns expressed by iwi and hapū, but the very foundations of their interest in and responsibility to their territory.

131 Katherina Ruckstuhl, Michelle Thompson-Fawcett & Hauauru Rae, "Māori and Mining: Indigenous Perspectives on Reconceptualising and Contextualising the Social Licence to Operate" (2014) 32:4 *Impact Assessment and Project Appraisal* 305.

132 For example, Te Arawa Coalition, *supra* note 64; Tapiuka Iwi Authority Trust, *supra* note 72; Ngāti Tuwharetoa Settlement Trust, *supra* note 73; Tūwharetoa Māori Trust Board, *supra* note 73.

133 *Interview*, *supra* note 78.

134 *CNI Report*, *supra* note 51 at 92.

The Tribunal made concrete suggestions about realizing partnership between the Crown and Māori with respect to the petroleum resource, including co-management models, commissioning cultural impact reports, resourcing Māori bodies to engage in the process, and the creation of local Māori boards to evaluate permit applications and Ministerial decisions, as well as to provide advice.[135] None of these suggestions have been taken up with respect to minerals – petroleum or otherwise. Indeed, the failure of the minerals regime in this regard was a pressing concern for the interviewees we spoke to at the Council level, where much of the day-to-day work of building and realizing partnerships is undertaken.[136]

Implementing the Tribunal's suggestions would go a long way to address some of the most pressing concerns about the CMA Block Offer process. We would go further. We agree with Erueti and Pietras who note attention to kaitiakitanga and Treaty principles at the exclusion of tino rangatiratanga fails to address the concerns of iwi and hapū, as demonstrated in our case study. In the 2013 Block Offer, the Crown used kaitiakitanga as a shield, both by claiming its own kaitiaki responsibilities as a kind of public interest obligation and by transforming the laws of Māori people-place relations into "environmental concerns" rather than assertions of jurisdiction. As Tomas argues, full recognition of Treaty partnership requires changes to the "internal structure of the state to overtly recognize Māori as a political, Treaty-based, entity at both local and national levels."[137] According to Tomas, while the structures for Māori decision-making and autonomy emerging from Treaty settlements are important, they are not enough. "There must be corresponding acknowledgment from the government that their own actions are constrained and that they cannot unilaterally take away Māori rights without Māori consent."[138] Decolonizing mining law, and natural resource law more broadly, requires a restructuring of people-place relations, one which upholds Māori people-place relations as a source of legal relationships and obligations rather than simply one of many factors to be balanced in a broad and defined public interest.

135 *Petroleum 2*, *supra* note 19 at 184–185.
136 *Interview 1*, *supra* note 126. See also *Interview 2*, *supra* note 127.
137 Nin Tomas, "Indigenous Peoples and the Māori: The Right to Self Determination in International Law–From Woe to Go" (2008) 4 *NZLR* 639 at 682.
138 *Ibid.* at 682.

8 Comparative law and epistemologies of ignorance in Chilean constitutional adjudication

A case study

*Amaya Álvez Marín, Tatsuhiko Inatani and Marta Infantino**

The debate over a civilizing mission in comparative and constitutional law

The origin of comparative legal studies has many common elements with the colonial constitutional history in Latin America. Comparative studies began at the Congress of Paris in 1900 and aimed at a convergence among different legal regimes towards the discovery of universal law produced by civilized nations.[1] Colonialism is conceptualized as a practice of domination, which involves the subjugation of one people to another.[2] In Latin America, it was mainly the Spanish Empire that imposed its laws and institutions from 1492 onwards. One of the ways in which this was justified was through a "civilizing mission" towards "barbaric" societies through dependence until they were developed or capable of imitating European governmental institutions, thereby becoming "enlightened". In Latin America, the emancipation process of the 19th century that created independent countries did not allow Indigenous Peoples to be represented at the constitutional level. On the contrary, constitutions made Indigenous legal, social, and cultural institutions invisible and voiced the necessity of adopting the only acceptable worldview: leaving behind their "savage" status.

* The ideas discussed in this chapter are part of a Collaborative Research Network between Professors Infantino, Inatani and Alvez started in 2014 at the Institute for Global Law and Policy (IGLP) at Harvard Law School. Data reported in the chapter was supported by the Chilean Research Funding Council CONICYT through a Fondecyt 11121371 "The Use of Comparative Law by the Chilean Constitutional Court (2006–2012): Theory and Practice", in which Amaya Álvez Marín was the main researcher.

1 Bénédicte Fauvarque-Cosson, "Development of Comparative Law in France" in Mathias Reimann & Reinhard Zimmermann, eds., *The Oxford Handbook of Comparative Law*, 2nd ed. (Oxford: Oxford University Press, 2019) at 29.

2 Margaret Kohn & Kavita Reddy, "Colonialism" in Edward N. Zalta, ed., *The Stanford Encyclopedia of Philosophy* (Fall 2017 Edition), accessed 22 August 2019, online: <https://plato.stanford.edu/archives/fall2017/entries/colonialism/>.

Comparative law, as a legal discipline denomination, is not univocal or unambiguous.[3] According to the mainstream view, comparative law is the "comparison of the world's present legal systems or particular elements thereof in pursuit of a variety of academic and practical objectives"[4] – a definition apparently too broad. Many comparatists, however, would adopt a more specific approach. For some, comparative law is mainly the study of legal transplants – that is, of the borrowing of ideas between legal cultures over time.[5] For others, comparative law is primarily about exploring the relationship between law and society,[6] focusing on the mentalities and perceptions of law in a given space and time,[7] observing how official rules live side by side with other (supranational or domestic) unofficial sources of law.[8] By contrast, others would define comparative law more generally as an intellectual adventure: "an opportunity for learning, for organizing and allowing us intimacy with the world".[9] Some authors perceive that the precise territory and stakes of engagement between socio-legal studies and comparative law have often seemed somewhat unsettled,[10] maybe as the result of outsider perspectives on law developed by the law and society project, on one hand, and the comparison of norms backed up by the coercive force of the state only, on the other.

This chapter proposes a parallel between criticism about the constitutional invisibility of Indigenous Peoples in Latin America and the struggles of comparative law as a legal discipline. The aim of Professors Saileilles and Lambert, about the very possibility of finding a universal civilized law, was limited to a marginal status throughout the 20th century. Therefore, we can rightly ask, what

3 Mauro Bussani & Ugo Mattei, "Diapositives versus Movies: The Inner Dynamics of the Law and Its Comparative Account" in Mauro Bussani & Ugo Mattei, eds., *Cambridge Companion to Comparative Law* (Cambridge: Cambridge University Press, 2012) at 3.

4 Mathias Reimann, "Comparative Law and Neighbouring Disciplines" in Bussani & Mattei, eds., *supra* note 3 at 34.

5 Alan Watson, *Legal Transplants: An Approach to Comparative Law*, 2nd ed. (Athens, GA: University of Georgia Press, 1993) at 6.

6 On law see, David S. Clark, ed., *Comparative Law and Society* (Cheltenham: Edward Elgar, 2012) at 1; Roger Cotterell, "Comparative Law and Legal Culture" in Reimann and Zimmermann, eds., *supra* note 1, 710; on history, see James Gordley, "Comparative Law and Legal History" in Reimann & Zimmermann, eds., *supra* note 1, 754; Reinhard Zimmerman, *Roman Law, Contemporary Law, European Law: The Civilian Tradition Today* (New York: Oxford University Press, 2012); Harold J. Berman, *Law and Revolution: The Formation of the Western Legal Tradition* (Cambridge: Harvard University Press, 1983).

7 See for instance Jorge L. Esquirol, "The Impact of Transnational Comparativism on Law in Latin America" in Mauro Bussani & Lukas Heckendorn Urscheler, eds., *Comparisons in Legal Development: The Impact of Foreign and International Law on National Legal Systems* (Zurich: Schulthess, 2016) at 185–218.

8 H. Patrick Glenn, *Legal Traditions of the World: Sustainable Diversity in Law*, 4th ed. (Oxford: Oxford University Press, 2014).

9 Günter Frankenberg, "Critical Comparisons: Re-Thinking Comparative Law" (1985) 26 *Harvard International Law Journal* 411 at 412.

10 Annelise Riles, "Comparative Law and Socio-Legal Studies" in Reimann & Zimmermann, eds., *supra* note 1 at 772–804.

is comparative law ultimately about? Is comparative law a method or an academic discipline, or is it perhaps a field of knowledge in its own right?[11]

If we were to analyze internal colonialism understood as a legal framework to dominate Indigenous Peoples and their territories without their consent, even against centuries of resistance, comparative law might provide some tools. For example, for some authors, comparative law serves to advance knowledge of legal diversity or to construct and sustain domestic visions of others' "otherness". Maybe comparative law is aimed primarily to deliver arguments for legitimating policy decisions, legal harmonization, and import and export of the law.[12] Comparatists have debated these fundamentals for many decades within the boundaries of their own field without a satisfactory agreed-upon answer.

Since its birth and growth as a self-standing field, comparative law has been surrounded by a combination of enthusiasm and doubt. Critiques have been raised in many quarters against the very idea and practice of comparative law, or certain ways of idealizing and practicing it. Some have claimed that comparative law – whether made in a structuralist or in a functionalist fashion – is too legocentric, state-centric and Western-centric, and comparative lawyers are seldom willing to discuss the purity of their motives, the objectivity of their methods and the correctness of their results.[13] Others claim that too often comparative lawyers deal with "ideas and notions that cannot be put to practical use"[14] and devote too scant attention to the compelling questions underlying their own work (e.g. what is the "law" and the "legal system" we care about when we compare?).[15] Still others have criticized the alleged neutrality of comparative law vis-à-vis its object of study, noting that comparative lawyers tend to downplay the political aspects of law, have a project of comprehension rather than governance, and depict themselves as "the last honest m[e]n, whose goal is merely that of understanding or contributing to a broadly humanist understanding of a universal phenomenon called law".[16] Some have gone so far as to conclude that comparative law is a struggle with the impossibility of understanding others from the outside[17] or to

11 Mathias Reimann, "The Progress and Failure of Comparative Law in the Second Half of the Twentieth Century" (2002) 50 *American Journal of Comparative Law* 671 at 684–685.

12 For a summary of the possible purposes of comparative law, see Sebastian McEvoy, "Descriptive and Purposive Categories of Comparative Law" in Pier Giuseppe Monateri, ed., *Methods of Comparative Law* (Cheltenham: Edward Elgar, 2012) at 151–162; H. Patrick Glenn, "Comparative Legal Families and Comparative Legal Traditions" in Reimann & Zimmermann, eds., *supra* note 1 at 423–441.

13 See for instance Mauro Bussani, "Comparative Law Beyond the Trap of Western Positivism" in Tong-Io Cheng & Salvatore Mancuso, eds., *New Frontiers of Comparative Law* (Hong Kong: Lexis Nexis, 2013) at 1–9; Frankenberg, *supra* note 9 at 416–426.

14 Basil Markesinis, *Comparative Law in the Courtroom and Classroom* (Oxford: Hart, 2003) at 61.

15 Frankenberg, *supra* note 9 at 416–417.

16 Upendra Baxi, "The Colonialist Heritage" in Pierre Legrand & Roderick Munday, eds., *Comparative Legal Studies: Traditions and Transitions* (Cambridge: Cambridge University Press, 2003) at 59.

17 Pierre Legrand, "On the Singularity of Law" (2006) 47 *Harvard International Law Journal* 517.

proclaim that the 21st century is seeing the decline, or maybe even the end, of comparative legal studies.[18]

These debates could dialogue with the ways in which internal colonialism tried to extinguish Indigenous Peoples' rights over their territories limiting their self-government. The strategies have been explained by Tully as threefold: the doctrine of discovery, *terra nullius*, which in the Spanish case was accompanied by religious mandate to convert and conquer was made by the Pope Alexander VI through the *Inter Caetera* bulls (1493); the disappearance of Indigenous Peoples through unilateral measures like conquest or uniform laws and voluntarily through the signature of treaties; and the incorporation of Indigenous Peoples to the dominant society in order to force them to lose their identity through assimilation and light accommodation.[19] There is substantial agreement that comparative lawyers' considerations about the theories and methods underlying their studies have so far largely missed the point, but we would like to expand this claim to mainstream constitutional scholars in Latin America. One set of reviewers is focused on the widespread lack of self-reflection and self-criticism displayed by many comparative and constitutional lawyers. Critics also underline the naïveté with which they tend to conceive themselves as residents of a "non-ethnocentric neutral territory",[20] and their task as that of merely collecting items and telling the "true story of similarities and dissimilarities between legal cultures, traditions, systems, families, styles, origins, solutions and ideas".[21] In the constitutional realm, this has been noticeable through neutral analysis of the assimilation laws and the light accommodation of Indigenous Peoples by downplaying political aspects of constitutional laws that aimed to perpetuate their invisibility.

Boaventura de Sousa Santos proposes the idea of an "ecology of knowledge" affirming "there is no ignorance or knowledge in general; all ignorance is ignorant of a certain knowledge, and all knowledge is the triumph of a particular ignorance".[22] In this way, we try to expand the possibilities that follow of the coexistence of the different cultures that make up the world, in order to achieve a "more balanced distribution of scientific knowledge".[23] This idea recognizes the effect of what de Sousa Santos calls *abysmal thought*, which represents the indifference with which traditional Western thought has made the ancestral knowledge typical of Indigenous Peoples invisible.

The impact caused by colonialism, whether external through comparative law or internal through constitutional law, continues to this day in the form of

18 Mathias Siems, "The End of Comparative Law" (2007) 2 *Journal of Comparative Law* 133.

19 James Tully, "Las luchas de los pueblos indígenas por y de la libertad" in Roger Merino & Areli Valencia, eds., *Descolonizar el derecho. Pueblos indígenas, derechos humanos y Estado plurinacional* (Lima: Palestra Editores, 2018) at 49–96.

20 Frankenberg, *supra* note 9 at 425.

21 *Ibid.* at 426.

22 Boaventura de Sousa Santos, *Refundación del Estado en América Latina* (Lima: Instituto Internacional de Derecho y Sociedad, 2010) at 44.

23 *Ibid.* at 45.

coloniality, since traditional Western thought "has sought to universalize and naturalize the conception of the world from the cognitive, evaluative and normative framework of a particular cultural tradition".[24] Making people believe that there is only one possible way of knowing the world from a given rationality, language, and culture – this could be referred as epistemology of ignorance. For Santos, comparative studies require to work properly between Indigenous Peoples and the rest of the population of a certain country an intercultural translation. One intellectual exercise that questions the very pillars on which the modern liberal state was built, such as separation of powers, representativeness, or human rights, in light of the knowledge and practices of Indigenous Peoples. The main notion is to force a consideration of Indigenous knowledge as legitimate and equal, with respect to Western or "Eurocentric" dominant formulations. The purpose is to find a common ground through a "translation work" with respect to knowledge and practices (institutions), a process that assumes the form of a *diatopical hermeneutics*, that is, "a work of interpretation between two or more cultures with the aim of identifying isomorphic concerns between them, and the different responses they provide".[25]

There are concrete studies of epistemologies of ignorance in the legal education sphere in Latin America, particularly on public international law. Laura Betancur-Restrepo and Enrique Prieto-Ríos, as part of the REDIAL project,[26] conducted an empirical study analyzing 24 syllabi of public international law courses from 10 universities in Bogotá, Colombia. The paper argues that how international law is taught in Bogotá creates epistemological blind spots, which limits the perception and problematization of international lawyers, mainly with its relationship with colonial and imperial projects and its relationship with the local context.[27]

Much comparative analysis has been confined to loose references or to a simplistic cut-and-paste exercise lacking adequate theoretical grounding. The problem with the way in which actors are exercising the power of comparative inquiry is not that they choose to refer to a particular foreign law but rather the lack of explanations or reasoning behind the actor's choices.

The thin methodology upon which much comparative legal research is based, it has been claimed, partially accounts for the marginalization of comparative law from the curricula of Western legal education and the (self-)estrangement of the comparative lawyer amidst legal sciences in the Western legal academia. Whatever

24 Pedro Garzón, "Pueblos indígenas y decolonialidad, sobre la colonización epistemológica occidental" (2013) 10:22 *Andamios* at 307.

25 De Sousa Santos, *supra* note 22 at 46.

26 REDIAL stands for 'Repensar la Educación del Derecho Internacional en América Latina' (Rethinking International Legal Education in Latin America).

27 Laura Betancur-Restrepo & Enrique Prieto-Ríos, "Educación del derecho internacional en Bogotá: un primer diagnóstico a partir del análisis de los programas de clase y su relación con las epistemologías de no conocimiento" (2017) 39 (Julio–Diciembre) *Derecho del Estado Universidad Externado de Colombia* 53 at 54.

the reasons, what is undeniable is that comparative lawyers often fail to get their voices heard outside the inner circle of their fellow colleagues.

These failures – to draw thick foundations for comparative legal studies and to make them known and easy to grasp for inside and outside observers – have reinforced and widened the reach and gravity of the Cinderella syndrome. This metaphor, first used by Harold Gutteridge, considered comparative law as a sleeping Cinderella, waiting for a Blue Prince that would recognize her beauty and kiss her into life.[28] Günter Frankenberg adds a new twist to it, considering that comparatists could come across as the owners of truth and as the representatives of a higher professional ethic in a reverse version of the same syndrome.[29]

Chilean constitutional judges: the possibility of epistemologies of ignorance through an empirical study

The case study is part of a research project titled The Use of Comparative Law by the Chilean Constitutional Court (2006–2012): Theory and Practice from a Critical Perspective. The aim was to statistically examine all cases decided by the Constitutional Court in order to establish, with certainty, if comparative law was being used in court decisions. Once we knew the data, the next aim was to discover the ways in which comparative law has been used. This research is a response to the gap detected by Groppi and Ponthoreau. They stated: "few studies have tried to base their considerations upon effective empirical data, probably discouraged by the practical difficulty and width of this type of research".[30] The project sought to create a quantitative analysis of explicit references to the cases and the ways in which comparative law has been used so far. The project examined the period between 2006 (when the 2005 "democratic makeover" of the Constitutional Court was implemented) and 2012 (the year that the research fund was adjudicated).

Empirical constitutionalism is a new academic path still undeveloped in Chilean doctrine, with few exceptions. A scarce reference can be found in a book by a former judge of the Chilean Constitutional Court,[31] but only a few articles so far have been fully devoted to the topic. For example, Humberto Nogueira argues that there is a lack of method in which foreign materials are used, with little recognition of the relevance of the resources at hand, reliance upon the preference of the judge, and even the influence of the graduate studies pursued by the judge

28 Harold Gutteridge, *Comparative Law: An Introduction to the Comparative Method of Legal Study and Research*, 2nd ed. (Cambridge: Cambridge University Press, 1949) at 23.

29 Frankenberg, *supra* note 9 at 418–421.

30 Tania Groppi and Marie-Claire Ponthoreau, "Introduction: The Methodology of the Research: How to Assess the Reality of Transjudicial Communication?" in Tania Groppi & Marie-Claire Ponthoreau, eds., *The Use of Foreign Precedents by Constitutional Judges: Hart Studies in Comparative Public Law* (Oxford: Hart, 2013) 1 at 3.

31 Jorge Correa Sutil, *Inaplicabilidad por inconstitucionalidad en la jurisprudencia del Tribunal Constitucional* (Santiago: Abeledo Perrot–Legal, 2009) at 51.

defining the type and origin of the comparative sources.[32] Judith Schonsteiner offered an empirical study of the use of human rights treaties by the Constitutional Court and the different reflections to consider it a source of constitutional law. Her claims resonate with the ones developed throughout this study about a "cherry-picking" exercise and not the consideration of human rights law as a constitutional groundwork.[33] More recently, we proposed a study with categories of comparative references: references that aim to demarcate the legal resolution of the case, and other references that aim to confirm the decision already adopted or to show a different legal alternative. We answer the question regarding the relevant, strategic, or merely decorative role of comparative law in the jurisprudence of the Chilean Constitutional Court based on empirical legal data.[34]

Following Frankenberg's work, it is worthwhile to consider how ideas, ideals, and ideology travel from one jurisdiction to another.[35] Various new terms are being used for this process, including "legal transplants",[36] "the migration of constitutional ideas",[37] and the theory of "constitutional transfer",[38] with each term defining the openness of a court to engage with foreign materials, although with slightly different degrees and accents. The actual practice of courts in various countries has been inconsistent about the use of foreign law. On one end of the spectrum, the United States Supreme Court has rejected the use of foreign precedents and is, arguably, even unreceptive to foreign case law.[39] On the other end of the spectrum, the South African Constitutional Court, among others, is invited by its own constitutional text to interpret cases with assistance from foreign case law.[40]

Out of 721 final decisions adopted by the Chilean Constitutional Court, 246 judicial decisions contained some form of reference to foreign law, using comparative law as a legal discipline to solve the conflict brought before them (Figure 8.1). This represents approximately one-third of the cases decided before the Constitutional Court in Chile. Questions arise from this situation: How

32 Humberto Nogueira, "El Uso del Derecho Convencional Internacional de los Derechos Humanos en la Jurisprudencia del Tribunal Constitucional Chileno del Período 2006–2010" (2012) 39:1 *Revista Chilena de Derecho* 149.

33 Judith Schonsteiner, "El Derecho Internacional de los Derechos Humanos en el Tribunal Constitucional Chileno: el mínimo común denominador" (2016) 39:1 *Revista de Derecho Universidad Austral de Chile* 197.

34 Amaya Álvez Marín & Benjamín Vicente, "Estudio legal empírico sobre el uso del Derecho Comparado por parte del Tribunal Constitucional de Chile" (2018) 31:2 *Revista de derecho* (Valdivia) 155.

35 Günter Frankenberg, "Comparing Constitutions: Ideas, Ideals, and Ideology–toward a Layered Narrative" (2006) 4:3 *International Journal of Constitutional Law* 439 at 440.

36 Watson, *supra* note 5.

37 Sujit Choudhry, *The Migration of Constitutional Ideas* (Cambridge, UK: Cambridge University Press, 2006).

38 Günter Frankenberg, "Constitutional Transfer: The IKEA Theory Revisited" (2010) 8:3 *International Journal of Constitutional Law* 563.

39 *Lawrence v. Texas* (2003) 539 U.S. 588; *Roper v. Simmons* (2005) 543 U.S. 551.

40 South African Constitution (1986) s 39.

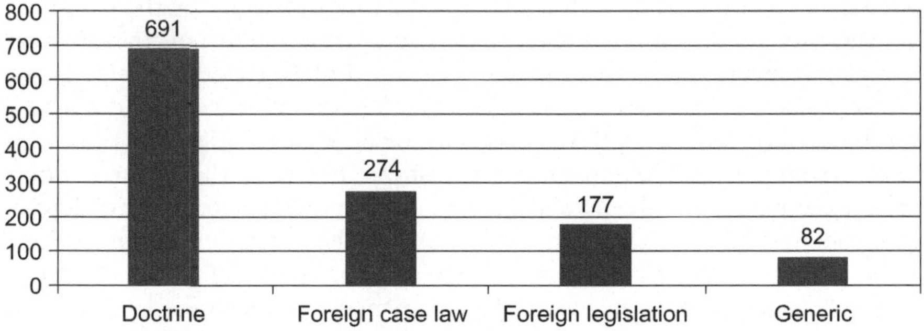

Figure 8.1 Categories of comparative law cited at the Constitutional Court in Chile (2006–2012)

Source: Own elaboration; *N* = 721 judicial decisions.

deep should our knowledge of legal systems go in order to allow us to draw sound comparative conclusions? Or to what extent should comparative law chip away at distinctions between the national and the international legal spheres, the private and the public legal domain, and substantive and procedural law?

The Chilean Constitutional Court, however, displays an uncomfortable double standard on the matter. The court does not explicitly accept the influence of foreign case law, nor has it established a method for its use (Figure 8.1). There is an implicit understanding that most of the arguments used in solving constitutional cases are based on, or have features in common with, foreign law. Chilean judges often refer to foreign law as part of a decision, particularly the jurisprudence of foreign tribunals; legislation of other national, international, or transnational entities; and doctrine of foreign authors. By far the most frequent reference is to Spanish doctrine and the judgments of its Constitutional Court as a natural parameter for Chile. We offer data obtained on the concrete use of comparative law, one scenario that gives meaning to the debate summarized in the first part over comparative law as a legal discipline.

We aim to reflect on a potential framework for the use of comparative law in Chile. One of the difficulties in this forum is the constant mixing of references to international law and foreign law, without a methodological approach of the legal discipline of comparative law. International law in Chile can be a mandatory reference due to the acceptance of international human rights treaties as part of the catalogue of fundamental rights. Doctrine and jurisprudence supports the recognition of major human rights treaties above legal rank but still considers them to be infra-constitutional as legal norms. A 1989 amendment of section 5 of the 1980 constitution incorporated international obligations on human rights at the domestic level. The text recognizes that human rights treaties ratified by Chile are a limitation on sovereignty, handing them a "constitutional status" and, therefore, adding new obligations to the state in the field of fundamental rights.[41] As a result, we tried to exclude international law from the research database, except when the judge's reference is voluntary with Chile not being a part of the particular treaty. An example of this would be references to European Union treaties or case law of the European Court of Human Rights.

These distinctions, although basic, proved to be sometimes difficult. For example, doctrine revealed to be a difficult source because it is difficult to know whether a particular piece of doctrine was written for a specific jurisdiction or was simply written as a highly theoretical enterprise with no specific audience. Therefore, we decided to use the geographical origin of the work as criteria for doctrine. In terms of foreign precedents, we were careful not to consider a comparative exercise when an international court has some jurisdiction over the country under examination. In the Chilean case, the jurisprudence of the Inter-American Court of Human Rights is binding through the American Convention on Human Rights and, therefore, it is international and not comparative law. However, reference to the European Court of Human Rights in several Chilean cases is comparative law. Foreign legislation was easier to isolate as a category of comparative law, although the amount of context necessary to understand the reference was challenging. In most cases, the information provided was insufficient to determine whether the foreign legislation being cited was positive or negative borrowing. Finally, it was necessary to create a category where we could incorporate references that were so general or imprecise that it was impossible to reconstruct the source of foreign law cited.

The argument made here is that constitutional judges, by referring to foreign law in concrete constitutional cases, would need to use discretion to determine whether there are any social or political conditions or historical developments that will differentiate the local and foreign system to a degree that would render impractical any comparative inquiry. Therefore, what is proposed is a cautious inquiry of the rationale of comparative constitutionalism in every case. Some of the research questions are: How can comparative law go beyond the comparison between national legal systems (a notion often equated to that of States) and official rules? What difference does it make to expand the comparative analysis to unofficial or customary layers within legal systems? In addition, if we support a contextual analysis for comparative law, which methodological tools can be offered to relate culture, society, and politics to law?

The study of the judicially driven transplants from Europe and the United States into Latin American courts may unveil how law in postcolonial settings may have perpetuated the historical balance of power between the West and its former colonies. Along the same lines, exploring the Latin American constitutional moment may provide a litmus test for Frankenberg's layered narrative on "constitutions as law, as culture and as imaginations of community".[42] Think,

41 Humberto Nogueira, "Los derechos esenciales o humanos contenidos en los tratados internacionales y su ubicación en el ordenamiento jurídico nacional: doctrina y jurisprudencia" (2003) 9:1 *Revista Ius et Praxis* 403.

42 Frankenberg, *supra* note 35 at 451.

for instance, of how Latin American constitutional comparative lawyers tend to take the Spanish or the US experiences as the parameter for comparison, thus reinforcing a trend which is tantamount to a form of cultural subordination. Our reflections on constitutional law adjudication in Chile aimed also to explain the strategies already tackled to render Indigenous Peoples and their legal claims invisible – for example, through uniform laws, the signature of treaties and the incorporation of Indigenous Peoples to the dominant society in order to force them to lose their identity through assimilation and light accommodation. There is also a particularity in the Latin American constitutional realm. Where many countries like Colombia (1991), Ecuador (2008), Perú (1993) and Bolivia (2009) have moved toward a recognition of Indigenous Peoples, Chile isolated and therefore rejected the use of comparative law from Latin America.

As previously asserted, Constitutional Court judges frequently reference foreign law using Eurocentric references, primarily Spanish doctrine and judgments of the Spanish Constitutional Court as a sort of "natural parameters" for Chile (Figure 8.2). A challenge is whether the constant tendency to use Spain as a parameter is tantamount to a form of subordination or not. It is also interesting to interrogate if the epistemology of ignorance could be a systemic one, according to which knowing(s) and unknowing(s) serve to differentiate the powerful from the powerless in relation to a specific area following Alcoff's work.[43]

So far, there is no other empirical or doctrinal study in Chile (that we are aware of) about the way in which comparative studies applied by constitutional judges

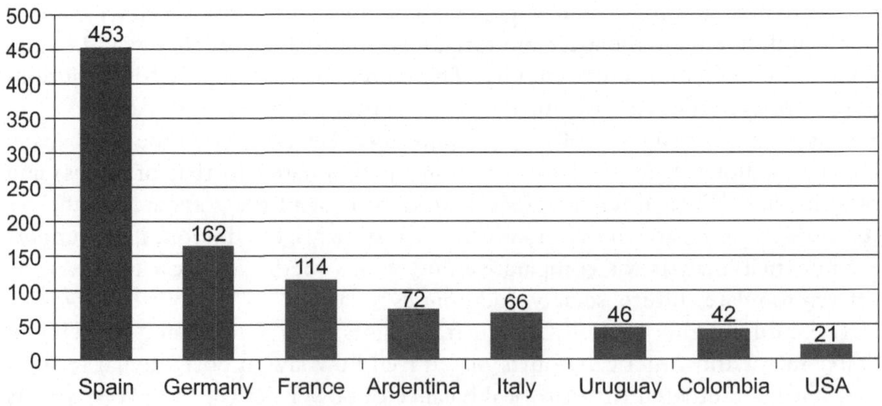

Figure 8.2 Origins of the principal foreign jurisdictions cited by the Chilean Constitutional Court (2006–2012)

Source: Own elaboration; $N = 976$ foreign references.

43 Linda Martin Alcoff, "Epistemologies of Ignorance: Three Types" in Shannon Sullivan & Nancy Tuana, eds., *Race and Epistemologies of Ignorance* (Albany: State University of New York Press, 2017) at 54.

ignore Indigenous Peoples' legal knowledge by deciding on foreign examples that reinforce the civilizing paradigm in place since the Spanish conquest five centuries ago. By describing the "cultural production of ignorance", Robert Proctor enumerates part of the reasons that could explain the phenomenon: "neglect, forgetfulness, myopia, extinction, secrecy, or suppression".[44] This reflective exercise is part of the task constitutional lawyers and judges could pursue in order to make the choice of remaining ignorant a conscious one.

The road forward: invitation to release comparative law's critical potential as a tool in constitutional adjudication

Praised at the beginning of the 20th century for its potential to explore the globe's legal diversity, comparative law is now struggling to maintain that role in a much more interconnected and globalized world where the need for, and the capacity of, comparative legal research to unravel legal phenomena seems to be waning. As David Kennedy once put it, "post-war comparatists seemed determined to establish a professional practice more earnest and boring that many of them could actually stand to pursue".[45]

In spite of the debates, doubts, and critiques just mentioned, there are reasons to think that comparative law still has an important role to play in dealing with legal rules, expectations, and practices at any level – be it national, international, transnational, or global. We are particularly interested in opening a space for constitutional judges to reflect on Indigenous legal cultures and comparative constitutional orders that consider them relevant in the Latin American space. This chapter would like to reflect a step further on the possibility that judges could be actively participating in the creation of a *lacuna* or silence. This has been named, by authors like Eduardo Mendieta, as epistemologies of ignorance.[46] This could also be a way in which the silence over the legal system of Indigenous Peoples in Chile could be unearthed, as well as the comparative studies used to adjudicate constitutional cases with examples of legal systems that already turned towards a plural legal system, or opened the sources of law, or worked towards ensuring cultural diversity in the legal system.

Many of these reasons relate to the critical potential of comparative law – that of probing legal cultures for sources of their change or resistance to change, for their implicit judgments and assumptions about the usual way of doing things, and for the ways in which people's identities and narratives are intertwined with their daily

44 Robert N. Proctor & Londa Schiebinger, eds., *Agnotology: The Making and Unmaking of Ignorance* (Palo Alto: Stanford University Press, 2008) at 312.

45 David Kennedy, "The Methods and the Politics" in Legrand & Munday, eds., *supra* note 16 at 351–352.

46 Eduardo Mendieta, "The Ethics of (not) Knowing: The Care of Ethics and Knowledge Will Come on Its Own Accord" in Adia Maria Isasi-Díaz & Eduardo Mendieta, eds., *Decolonizing Epistemologies: Latina/o Theology and Philosophy* (New York: Fordham University Press, 2011) at 252.

practices of law. In this respect, we rely on comparative law's potential to expand the horizons of legal research, a potential which is fully yet to be explored.

Comparative law has great potential to provide those who practice it with a mindset whose conditions are the same as those required for critical legal thinking. Moreover, the comparative critical lawyer does not expect law to be easy to grasp, displaying a relentless tendency to contest entrenched beliefs, established domains, self-fulfilling explanations, easy answers, and often the questions themselves. Like any critical thinker, the comparative lawyer has a sensitivity for the complexity and the ambiguity of the law and is aware of her relative ignorance about how law actually works and is dissatisfied with mainstream explanations about how and why law is the way it is.

From the data gathered, we know that Chilean Constitutional judges choose to use comparative law. We would like to offer at least five reasons why we believe that comparative law could potentially nurture critical (comparative) legal thinkers; this also includes the type of exercises that judges confront while comparing foreign doctrine, jurisprudence, legislation, and constitutions in order to decide a case before them. This is also a way in which the criticism against comparative studies as too logocentric, state-centric, and Western-centric could be answered, including the discussion about the purity of the judges' motives, the objectivity of their methods, and the correctness of their results.[47]

Getting beyond ourselves

It is generally held that comparative law is about knowing the Other. Yet, insofar as the Other is always defined in relation to the self, comparative law is mostly about knowing oneself. The lawyer or judge who moves only within the framework of her own discipline or formal legal system unconsciously tends to ask herself questions and look for answers which are consistent with the possible ways of viewing the world under that framework (only). But questions and answers that work in a given environment (besides origins coming from other frameworks) may have a different, or little, sense in other settings. By looking beyond the boundaries of her own frameworks, the comparative lawyer or judge tries to see herself through (what she thinks) are others, to resist the power of prejudice and ignorance, to appreciate the relativity of her own firmly held beliefs and well-settled knowledge, and to understand how her standpoint affects her own visions of life, perceptions of problems, and needs for solution.

Against overconfidence

As noted above, comparative law's focus is generally held to be that of knowing others – whatever the "others" may be. Yet knowing others is for the comparative

47 See for instance Bussani, *supra* note 13 at 1; Frankenberg, *supra* note 9 at 416–426.

lawyer more an aspiration than an achievement. Comparative law makes one aware of the many obstacles that, when dealing with a discipline, system, or culture new to, or different from, our own may hinder our capacity to understand what is different from us. We may, for instance, unknowingly embrace a given perspective or interpretation of what we are studying simply because that perspective or interpretation fits with our own mentality or pre-existing knowledge. This could be potentially the case of seeing Spain as the natural parameter. Hidden biases such as these may easily lead the researcher to project her own way of thinking onto the objects of her scholarly attention and to prioritize some questions, approaches, or solutions over other ones only because she knows and has internalized the former better than the latter. Comparative law is no cure for these problems. However, by developing and practicing a sharp sense for diversity and heterogeneity, comparative law warns the researcher against the risk of agnotology and about being overconfident in terms of our own knowledge on and ability of understanding others.

Emphasis on understanding

At whatever level it is exercised, no (serious) legal comparison is easy. It is (or should be) a tenet of comparative law that no legal system can be understood without considering the multiple layers that make up its structure,[48] the mixed origins of its components,[49] the gaps between law's narratives and practices,[50] and the

> set of deeply rooted, historically conditioned attitudes about the nature of law; about the role of law in the society and the polity; about the proper organization and operation of a legal system, and about the way law is or should be made, applied, studied, perfected, and taught.[51]

Comparative law's emphasis on the relevance (and the immensity) of investigating these aspects to study, criticize, or reform a legal system makes knowledge both an aim and a methodological guidance for the comparative lawyer, turning any comparative legal research into an endless quest for more and better understanding – of the self and of others.

48 Mauro Bussani, "A Pluralist Approach to Mixed Jurisdictions" (2011) 6:1 *Journal of Comparative Law* 161.

49 Esin Örücü, "Family Trees for Legal Systems: Towards a Contemporary Approach, Epistemology and Methodology of Comparative Law" in Mark van Hoecke, ed., *Epistemology and Methodology of Comparative Law* (Oxford: Hart, 2004) at 361.

50 Rodolfo Sacco, "Legal Formants: A Dynamic Approach to Comparative Law" (1991) 39 *American Journal of Comparative Law* 343.

51 John H. Merryman, *The Civil Law Tradition: An Introduction to the Legal Systems of Western Europe and Latin America*, 3rd ed. (Palo Alto: Stanford University Press, 2007) at 2.

Engaging with complexity

As stated above, comparative law is not afraid of the complexities of laws. The comparative lawyer or judge knows that law is not always what it claims to be. She is committed to staying close to how law lives in different settings. Although historically, comparative law has developed as a method to compare legal rules from different states (or, at best, legal systems), today's comparative lawyer takes for granted that states (and legal systems) are only one of the many sites where law lives. Rather, she acknowledges that law is produced by (and contributes to produce) many different actors and institutions playing different roles as rule-makers and rule-takers, and produced by many different identities, narratives, and interpretive patterns which shape people's ways of organizing social experience, giving it meaning and qualifying it as normal and just.[52] Under comparative law's perspective, law becomes a ubiquitous, pluralistic, and ambiguous phenomenon that can be traced everywhere: in texts, institutions, actions, ideas, expectations, and fantasies. This is the rather disquieting but also fascinating prospect for the comparative law scholar.[53]

A quest for interdisciplinarity

Despite its limited capacity for dialogue with lawyers who are not comparatists, comparative law has always been a field open to interactions and exchanges with other disciplines. This is partly because comparative law, like many non-legal disciplines, offers a chance to look beyond law's institutional and positivistic framework, to delve into those hidden and much more pervasive legal rules that frame minds, kindle fantasies, structure social visions, and influence actions.[54]

Much of the comparative law's toolbox is indeed borrowed or developed in close consonance with that of other disciplines, such as history, sociology, anthropology, and linguistics. Some exchanges with other disciplines have given rise to new methodological approaches, such as the case of "comparative law and economics".[55]

Many other potentially fruitful directions are to be further explored: comparative international law;[56] comparative human rights law (which in a paradoxical way, despite the subject being taught in many universities, very few studies have

52 George P. Fletcher, "Comparative Law as a Subversive Discipline" (1998) 46 *American Journal of Comparative Law* 683.

53 Frankenberg, *supra* note 9 at 454.

54 *Ibid.* at 447.

55 Nuno Garoupa & Tom Ginsburg, "Economic Analysis and Comparative Law" in Bussani & Mattei, eds., *supra* note 3 at 57.

56 On the possible relationships between comparative law and public international law, compare Anthea Roberts, *Is International Law International?* (Oxford: Oxford University Press, 2017); Boris Mamlyuk and Ugo Mattei, "Comparative International Law" (2011) 36:2 *Brooklyn Journal of International Law* 385; Martti Koskenniemi, "The Case for Comparative International Law" (2011) 20 *Finnish Yearbook of International Law* 1 at 1–8.

attempted to investigate how human rights law could be examined in comparative legal terms); comparative law and development;[57] and critical comparative law.[58]

Conclusions

At the origin, comparative legal studies aimed at a convergence among different legal regimes of civilized nations. It was praised at the beginning of the 20th century for its potential to explore the globe's legal diversity; nonetheless, right now comparative law is struggling to maintain that role. Since 1900, there have been many questions surrounding what comparative law's aims are and the ways in which constructions of "others" are presented. This chapter focused on the potential of comparative law as a legal discipline; therefore, we criticized the lack of self-reflection and self-criticism displayed by many comparative lawyers.

This is also the case of Chile, a country situated at the periphery of the so-called civilized nations. For a long period of time, the comparative exercise has been limited to legal transplants from a Western perspective mainly anchored in European examples. The empirical research shows how central Europe is a parameter, a sort of mandatory role model. Constitutional judges refer very often to foreign doctrine, legislation, and judicial cases, but in most cases they downplay the political aspects of those laws. We particularly focused on the epistemology of ignorance created through the silence over the legal framework of Indigenous Peoples in constitutional adjudication by the Chilean Constitutional Court. As showed empirically, much comparative analysis has been confined to loose references or to a simplistic cut-and-paste exercise lacking adequate theoretical grounding and perpetuating the civilizing paradigm of comparative law.

We think that part of the marginalization of comparative law is due to the thin methodology upon which much comparative legal research is based. Nevertheless, we reflect that there are reasons to think that comparative law still has an important role to play in dealing with legal rules, expectations, and practices at any level – be it national, international, transnational, or global.

Comparative law has much to learn and might have something to give – from its great sensibility for the "self" and the "other" to its challenge to cultural prejudice, its tolerance for ambiguity, its refusal to oversimplify (or deny) complexity, its openness to "other" approaches to law, and its potential for empowering and liberating our taken-for-granted perspectives on what the law is and how we would like it to be.

57 Jedidiah Kroncke, "Law and Development as Anti-Comparative Law" (2012) 45 *Vanderbilt Journal of Transnational Law* 477.
58 Frankenberg, *supra* note 9 at 411.

9 Not empty of laws

Indigenous legal orders and the Canadian state

Mary Eberts

Indigenous law is one of the three pillars of Canadian law[1] yet has no place in the Canadian constitutional order.[2] By Indigenous[3] law-making, I mean the creation and maintenance of laws, and an order of laws, by an Indigenous collectivity pursuant to power that is not delegated to it by the Canadian state, but rather is its own inherent power. Indigenous law-making predates contact and the assertion of sovereignty by Europeans.

Although Indigenous nations were never conquered,[4] they were colonized: their homeland was included in a larger state against their will.[5] The goal of the settler state was to consolidate its hold on the land by making the original inhabitants disappear, through a long and brutal attempt at assimilating them, and sometimes literally by death.[6]

Indigenous Peoples had no part in the drafting of the *Constitution Act, 1867*,[7] which allocated jurisdiction between Canada and the provinces[8] and gave Canada

1 *Edwards v. Attorney General of Canada*, [1930] AC 124 at 136 [*Edwards*].

2 Philip Girard, Jim Phillips & R. Blake Brown, *A History of Law in Canada, Vol. 1: Beginnings to 1866* (Toronto: University of Toronto Press, 2018) at 9 [Girard et al.].

3 In this chapter, I use *Indigenous* by preference whenever I can, as it includes but is not limited to First Nations, Métis and Inuit peoples. I use aboriginal with a lowercase "a" when it is an integral part of terminology in common usage, like "aboriginal rights", when it used in a court judgment and cannot be paraphrased away, and when it is used in an enactment. Where it does not seem possible to avoid the term "aboriginal" but it can be spelled with an uppercase "A", I do that.

4 Peter H. Russell, *Canada's Odyssey: A Country Based on Incomplete Conquests* (Toronto: University of Toronto Press, 2017) [Russell].

5 Michael Asch, *On Being Here to Stay: Treaties and Aboriginal Rights in Canada* (Toronto: University of Toronto Press, 2014) at 61, quoting Will Kymlicka, *Politics in the Vernacular: Nationalism, Multiculturalism and Citizenship* (New York: Oxford University Press, 2001) at 148 [Asch].

6 James Tully, "The Struggles of Indigenous Peoples for and of Freedom" in Duncan Ivison, Paul Patton & Will Saunders, eds., *Political Theory and the Rights of Indigenous Peoples* (Cambridge: Cambridge University Press, 2000) at 39–40 [Tully].

7 *Constitution Act, 1867*, (UK), 30 & 31 Vict, c 3, s 91(24) [*Constitution Act, 1867*].

8 House of Commons, *Minutes of Proceedings of the Special Committee on Indian Self-Government* Issue No. 40 (12 and 20 October 1983) (Chair, Keith Penner), *Second Report* at 39–40 [*Penner Report*].

jurisdiction over "Indians and lands reserved for Indians". There was no place in this constitution for Indigenous law-making or legal orders.

In this chapter, I examine the treatment of Indigenous law and law-making in the context of Canada's recognition of self-government as an inherent right under section 35 of the *Constitution Act, 1982*,[9] particularly the extent to which the inherent right policy permits the recuperation of Indigenous legal orders and recognition of their place within federalism. The Penner Report speculated that if the right to self-government is an "aboriginal right" under section 35 of the *Constitution Act, 1982*, "there could be a substantial re-ordering of powers" with Indigenous governments having "explicit legislative powers that are now unrecognized".[10]

A review of section 35 jurisprudence on self-government, and of Canada's "self-government" policies shows that they have produced no new constitutional room for Indigenous law-making. In fact, we have seen a vigorous new round of colonization. The court refuses to acknowledge any general power of self-government protected by section 35. The state regulates, not recognizes, aspects of Indigenous law-making. The state delegates law-making authority, instead of recognizing that it already exists. The state enters into arrangements and agreements that are not recognized and protected as treaties under section 35. None of these agreements meets the strict test for extinguishing Indigenous law-making power. Any of them will make it all the more difficult for Indigenous law-making to assert a place in any renewed federalism. These initiatives tear at the fabric of Indigenous legal orders, cherry-picking certain topics for attention in the colonizer's regime, and leaving the rest shrouded in obscurity.

The first section of the chapter sets out the subject of my inquiry, namely Indigenous legal orders, not just singular instances of Indigenous law-making. I then examine the doctrine of continuity, pursuant to which Indigenous law-making power has survived into the 21st century. I next set out the self-government policy of Canada and examples of "self-government", which are really just exercises in delegating legislative power for administrative purposes. There follows a discussion of the interpretation of section 35 of the *Constitution Act, 1982*, and the compromised Indigenous jurisdiction over land under both the self-government policy and section 35 jurisprudence.

Finally, I offer suggestions for matters to address as a priority so that Indigenous law-making will be able to flourish as part of the "living tree"[11] that is the Canadian Constitution.

9 Canada, Indigenous and Northern Affairs Canada, *The Government of Canada's Approach to Implementation of the Inherent Right and the Negotiation of Aboriginal Self-Government* (15 September 2010), online: <www.rcaanc-cirnac.gc.ca/eng/1100100031843/1539869205136#inhrsg> [Inherent Right Policy].

10 *Penner Report*, *supra* note 8 at 43.

11 *Edwards v. Attorney General of Canada*, [1930] AC 124 at 136 [*Edwards*].

Indigenous legal orders

In the *Manitoba Language Reference*,[12] the Supreme Court stresses that the rule of law requires "the creation and maintenance of an actual order of positive laws which preserves and embodies the more general principles of normative order".[13] John Borrows drives home the connection between survival of Indigenous legal orders and the maintenance of an orderly society: "Failure to recognize and affirm the positive customary laws of Aboriginal peoples, which preserve and embody the general principles of their ancient normative orders, has sustained near-anarchy and constant strife within Aboriginal communities".[14]

Recognizing another order of law-making in Canada involves more than just accepting the results of its operation on a case-by-case basis. At a deeper level, it must involve an acceptance of the values and perspectives of that order of laws.

We are now likely to meet Indigenous law and law-making when an Indigenous person turns to a Canadian court to reconcile his or her circumstances under Indigenous law with Canadian law (as in the case of adoption or marriage), or when there is an overt conflict between the requirements of Indigenous law and the law of the modern state (as in conflicts over resource exploration and extraction). Cases involving individual circumstances rarely place in conflict the legal systems of Canada and the Indigenous nation. Clashes between Indigenous opponents of development and developers acting under authorization of provincial law are more likely to raise systemic issues.

Systemic issues in the domain of the criminal law have been resolved in favour of the primacy of Canadian law, with small embellishments at its margins which purport to be elements of Indigenous law. These go by the name of "restorative justice", a concept that makes its appearance in the Canadian legal system only at the point where an Indigenous person has been accused, tried, and convicted under Canadian law.

Frank Iacobucci has observed that "First Nations observe the Canadian justice system as devoid of any reflection of their core principles or values, and view it as a foreign system that has been imposed upon them without their consent".[15] Three decisions of the Supreme Court of Canada have acknowledged the systemic discrimination against Indigenous peoples in the Canadian criminal law.[16] The Supreme Court noted in *Ipelee* in 2012 that the over-representation of

12 *Reference re Manitoba Language Rights*, [1985] 1 SCR 721 [Manitoba Language Reference].

13 *Ibid.* at 750.

14 John Borrows, *Recovering Canada: The Reemergence of Indigenous Law* (Toronto: University of Toronto Press, 2002) at 118 [Borrows: *Recovering Canada*].

15 Ministry of the Attorney General, *First Nations Representation on Ontario Juries: Report of the Independent Review Conducted by the Honourable Frank Iacobucci* (February 2013) at para 211 [Iacobucci].

16 *R. v. Williams*, [1998] 1 SCR 1125 [*Williams*]; *R. v. Gladue*, [1999] 1 SCR 688 [*Gladue*]; and *R. v. Ipelee*, 2012 SCC 12 [*Ipelee*]. *R. v. Hamilton (and Mason)*, [2004] OJ No. 3252 (Ont CA) [*Hamilton and Mason*].

Indigenous persons in the criminal justice system has increased since 1999, to the point where it is worse than ever.[17]

Canada has taken no steps to change the content of the criminal law in order to respond to its devastating effect on Indigenous Peoples. Canada's policy on the inherent right of self-government specifically states that Canadian criminal law will continue to apply to Indigenous entities with self-government agreements.[18] Nor, unfortunately, have there been any marked changes in discretionary law enforcement practices pursuant to which disproportionate numbers of Indigenous persons are arrested and charged. In the case of Indigenous Peoples and the criminal law, the state is not just the "singular antagonist of the individual", as stated in *Irwin Toy*,[19] but of whole peoples. This characterization fits with Canada's historic reality, where police authorities have played a pivotal role in enforcing compulsory attendance at residential schools and many other oppressive measures.

The doctrine of continuity

Chief Justice McLachlin in *Mitchell*[20] states that English law accepted that Indigenous peoples possessed pre-existing laws and interests and recognized their continuance in the absence of extinguishment, by cession, conquest, or legislation.[21] Such interests and laws

> were presumed to survive the assertion of sovereignty, unless (1) they were incompatible with the Crown's assertion of sovereignty, (2) they were surrendered voluntarily via the treaty process, or (3) the government extinguished them. . . . Barring one of these exceptions, the practices, customs and traditions that defined the various aboriginal societies as distinctive cultures continued as part of the law of Canada.[22]

The intention to extinguish by legislation must be clear and plain and must meet a strict test. Regulation does not amount to extinguishment, nor does legislation that is necessarily inconsistent with the continuation of the Indigenous interests or laws. The onus of proving extinguishment is on the Crown.[23]

17 *Ipelee*, *supra* note 16, quoted in *Iacobucci*, *supra* note 15 at 56, para 222.

18 Inherent Right Policy, *supra* note 9 at 5 of 17 preserves for the exclusive jurisdiction of Canada "maintenance of national law and order and substantive criminal law, including offences and penalties under the Criminal Code and other criminal laws."

19 *Irwin Toy Ltd. v. Quebec (AG),* [1989] 1 SCR 927 at 994 [*Irwin Toy*].

20 *Mitchell v. MNR*, 2001 SCC 33 [*Mitchell*].

21 *Ibid.* at para 9.

22 *Ibid.* at para 10. The CJC relies in this passage on Brian Slattery, "Understanding Aboriginal Rights" (1987) 66 *Can Bar Rev* 727 [Slattery, *Understanding*] and see Binnie J. in *Mitchell, supra* note 20 at paras 141–142 quoting Slattery, Understanding at 738 and Brian Slattery, "Making Sense of Aboriginal and Treaty Rights" (2000) 79 *Can Bar Rev* 196 at 201 [Slattery, *Making Sense*].

23 R. v. *Van der Peet*, [1996] 2 SCR 507, per CJC Lamer, at para 133 [*Van der Peet*].

In her dissent in *Van der Peet*, Justice McLachlin quotes Justice Brennan's observation in *Mabo* that "an inhabited territory which became a settled colony was no more a legal desert that it was a 'desert uninhabited'".[24] McLachlin J. specifically agrees with this dismissal of the doctrine of *terra nullius*, citing the *Royal Proclamation of 1763*.[25] The doctrine of terra nullius posited that newly encountered lands were empty of people who owned them, thereby legitimating their "settlement" by incomers. Ovide Mercredi argues that the presumption that Indigenous Peoples and Nations are "empty of laws"[26] is still in existence. This certainly accords with Canada's policy of relying on delegation to "give" First Nations law making powers, discussed below.

After recognition: regulation by the state?

As Borrows points out, the integrity of a legal system depends on a system's recognition, which "secures a jurisdictional space for its operation that encourages the respect of the public and facilitates access to resources".[27] Experience with the doctrine of continuity shows that after court recognizes a product of Indigenous law-making, there is a risk that the state will move in to regulate the area, superseding the Indigenous legal order. The case of custom adoption shows both this danger and also that it can be avoided.

Recognition of custom adoption as valid under the common law came about, in part, as a way of dealing with pressure from the bureaucratic state on those who had been adopted according to custom. In *Re Adoption of Katie E7–1807*, Sissons J. of the Northwest Territories Territorial Court states that "there are some hundreds of adoptions in accordance with Eskimo [*sic*] custom going back many years in which there has been no application to the Court for an adoption order pursuant to provincial legislation".[28] He continues:

> These applications to the Court are made because the white man says there should be an adoption order, and because it is well to have something of Court record establishing the adoption and proving it for purposes of Family Allowances, School Registration, Succession, and to avoid dispute or question.[29]

24 *Ibid.* at para 265, citing Brennan J. in *Mabo v. Queensland* [*No. 2*] (1992) 175 *CLR* 1 at 58 [*Mabo*].

25 *Royal Proclamation, 1763*, RSC 1985, App. II, No. 1, referred to in *Van der Peet*, *supra* note 23 at para 270 [*Royal Proclamation of 1763*].

26 Ontario, Law Society of Ontario, *Review Panel on Regulatory and Hearing Processes Affecting Indigenous Peoples*, *Report to Convocation*, 24 May 2018, which includes *Supplementary Report* and *Report of the Independent Reviewer Ovide Mercredi, Additional Recommendations* [Mercredi]. The expression "empty of laws" is found at page 3 of Mercredi.

27 John Borrows, *Canada's Indigenous Constitution* (Toronto: University of Toronto Press, 2010) at 116 [Borrows: *Constitution*].

28 *Re Adoption of Katie E7–1807*, (1961) 32 DLR (2d) 686 at 688 [*Re Katie*].

29 *Ibid.* at 688.

Sissons J. held that custom adoption was an adoption "made according to the laws of the territories" as required by the *Child Welfare Ordinance*.[30] In *Casimel v. Insurance Corporation of British Columbia*,[31] the BC Court of Appeal held that custom adoption is a right under section 35 of the *Constitution Act, 1982*.[32]

After *Casimel*, BC and the Northwest Territories passed legislation providing for the recognition of custom adoptions.[33] In Nunavut, which inherited the NWT statute, a Law Review Commission study[34] presented substantive concerns about unregulated custom adoption[35] and the need to be responsive to changes in custom adoption brought about by changing demographics and lifestyles. The Law Review Commission observed that "there is a strong consensus that something does have to be done before custom adoption is continued in the current haphazard way".[36] Concluding that custom adoption is "a strong and a unique characteristic of Nunavut and will continue to be for years to come", it recommends that there be legislation which preserves the original concepts of custom adoption while recognizing the adaptation of today's Inuit society.[37]

Regulation by those other than Indigenous law-making authorities in fact negates recognition, the whole point of which is to honour Indigenous law-making, not supplant it. Nunavut is itself an Indigenous government, created by the Nunavut Land Claims Agreement, *Land Claims Agreement Act*,[38] and *Nunavut Act*.[39] One might say that its involvement in reforming the law is the Indigenous law-maker changing its own law. In actuality, it is at this stage

30 *Ibid.* at 690.

31 *Casimel v. Insurance Corporation of British Columbia*, (1993) 30 B.C.A.C. 279 (C.A.). The grandparents of the deceased had adopted him under customary law after he had been abandoned by his mother, their daughter. They treated him, in all respects, as if he were their son, until his death at the age of 28. The Court held that they would qualify as dependent parents under the *Insurance Act* of BC and could claim his no-fault death benefit.

32 *The Constitution Act, 1982*, s 25, being Schedule B to the *Canada Act 1982* (UK), 1982, c 11 [*Constitution Act, 1982*].

33 *Adoption Act*, RSBC, c 5, s 46 [*Adoption Act*]. See also *Aboriginal Custom Adoption Recognition Act*, SNWT 1994, c 26, as amended [*Aboriginal Custom Adoption Recognition Act*].

34 Maligarnit Qimirrujht & Nunavut Law Review Commission, *Issue: Aboriginal Custom Adoption*, n.d. at 1–2 [Nunavut Law Review Commission]. The Report notes that custom adoption is more prevalent today than it was in historic times.

35 Such concerns are also coming to the fore in judicial decisions: Steve Ducharme, "Nunavut Judge Says Inuit Custom Adoption Law Needs a Makeover" (21 March 2017) *Nunatsiaq News*; and Canadian Press, "Judge Questions Nunavut Custom Adoption Procedures after Quashing Certificate" (20 March 2017). See also Richard Gleeson, "NWT Judge Overturns Custom Adoption after Father Files Lawsuit" (18 July 2017) *CBC News*.

36 Nunavut Law Review Commission, *supra* note 34 at 25.

37 *Ibid.* at 30.

38 *Nunavut Land Claims Agreement Act*, S.C. 1993, c 29, which provides in s.23(1)(l) that the legislature has power legislate with respect to property and civil rights in Nunavut.

39 *Nunavut Act*, S.C. 1993, c. 28.

difficult to identify a particular Indigenous law-maker which originated the rules about custom adoption. The origins of these laws seem diffuse, varying from region to region, with adoption practices responding to individual and community needs.[40]

Amendment of the Quebec *Civil Code* has been accomplished in a way that recognizes customary adoption without regulating it in a way that negates traditional Indigenous law-making authority.[41] It was done after a thorough study of the issue by a Working Group composed of Quebec government authorities, representatives of self-governing nations, and Indigenous "civil society" organizations.[42] The Report of the Working Group aims at finding "a simple and effective solution that would create a bridge between statutory law and Aboriginal custom and expressly recognize its effects without undermining its nature, purpose, conditions or effects",[43] specifically adopting the approach of recognition not regulation.[44] A brief to the Quebec National Assembly pointed out that since customary adoption is a matter of Aboriginal rights recognized under section 35, "customary adoption is already part of the law applicable in Quebec".[45] This language is crucial: the brief does not say that customary adoption is part of the law *of* Quebec but of the law applicable *in* Quebec. The brief makes absolutely clear that "custom adoption continues under the laws of First Nations".[46]

The new provisions of the *Civil Code* provide for the recognition of any custom adoptions that are in harmony with the principles of the interest of the child, respect for the child's rights, and the consent of the persons concerned. They establish a system whereby adoptions will be vetted by the authority that is competent for the Aboriginal community or nation of either the child or the adopter and a certificate issued if the adoption is consistent with the legislative criteria.

40 Nunavut Law Review Commission, *supra* note 34 at 4–6.

41 Bill 113, *An Act to Amend the Civil Code and Other Legislative Provisions as Regards Adoption and the Disclosure of Information*, 1st Sess, 41st Leg, Quebec, (assented to 16 June 2018), SQ 2017, c 12.

42 Quebec, Government of Quebec, *Working Group on Customary Adoption in Aboriginal Communities*, Report (Quebec: Government of Quebec, 16 April 2012 [Report of the Working Group]).

43 *Ibid.* at 137.

44 *Ibid.* at 138.

45 Assembly of First Nations Quebec-Labrador and First Nations of Quebec and Labrador Health and Social Services Commission, Brief on *Recognition of Effects of First Nations Customary Adoption in and for the Purposes of* Quebec *Legislation*, to the Committee on Institutions, National Assembly of Quebec, 23 November 2016 (studying Bill 113) at 22 [Brief].

46 *Ibid.* at 8; see also First Nations of Quebec & Labrador Health and Social Services Commission, *Reference Guide: Appointing a Competent Authority for Customary Adoption and Tutorship in First Nations Communities/Nations* (2018) at 4.

Canada's self-government policy: delegated authority since 1982

Canada has been negotiating arrangements with Indigenous Peoples since 1973.[47] Following the Supreme Court decision in *Calder*,[48] the government developed the Comprehensive Land Claims Policy in 1973.[49]

In its 1982 submissions to the Penner Committee, Canada proposed The Alternative of Optional Indian Band Government Legislation, which involved passage of legislation giving Indian Bands powers to tax, pass authoritative by-laws, enter into agreements with other bands or government authorities or agencies to provide services on reserve, control reserve lands, and determine membership.[50] The legislation would vary from band to band, as no single approach was regarded as universally appropriate, and a band would have to formulate a charter describing its relations with its members and government in order to enter into Indian Band Government legislation.[51] The Penner Committee unanimously rejected this proposal because it represented a delegation of power rather than a recognition of sovereignty.[52]

The Penner Committee urged passage of a constitutional amendment to bring self-governing First Nations into the constitutional order of Canada,[53] with a legislative backup plan to accomplish as much as possible pending achievement of that amendment.[54] It recommended passage of legislation under s. 91(24) which would recognize all areas of law-making competence necessary

47 Canada, Crown-Indigenous Relations and Northern Affairs Canada, *Treaties Agreements and Negotiations*, online: <www.rcaanc-cirnac.gc.ca/eng11001000-28574/1529354437>, at 4 of 7 (in second paragraph of section on Modern Treaties).

48 *Calder v. Attorney General of British Columbia*, [1973] SCR 313 [*Calder*].

49 Minister of Indian Affairs and Northern Development, *Comprehensive Land Claims Policy* (Ottawa: Minister of Supply & Services Canada, 1986) at 5–6.

50 The power to determine Band membership was delegated to Band Councils in 1985 by *Bill C-31*, as part of a purported reform of long-standing sex discrimination in the *Indian Act: An Act to Amend the Indian* Act, S.C. 1985, c 27, s 4. This power, however, still operates within the confines of the *Indian Act's* registration system, and federal funding to First Nations is determined on the basis of the number of status Indians they include, not the number of members they recognize. Funding on the basis of the number with Indian status, as opposed to the number of members recognized by a self-governing Nation, was found to be unacceptable in *Teslin Tlingit Council v. Canada*, 2019 YKSC 3 [*Teslin*]. However, in a useful move, the power to make membership rules is subject to the requirement that a membership code passed under section 10 may not exclude from membership a woman who was restored to status pursuant to Bill C-31, after being deprived of her status on marriage to a non-status male.

51 *Penner Report*, *supra* note 8 at 22.

52 *Ibid.* at 24. See also *An Act to Amend the Indian Act*, RSC 1985, c 27, s 4. *Penner Report*, *supra* note 8 at 22.

53 *Ibid.* at 44, 50. The Penner Committee mandate included only consideration of band councils under the *Indian Act:* House of Commons, Orders of Reference, Special Committee on Indian Self-Government (Task Force), 22 December 1982 [*Penner Report*, *supra* note 8 at v]. Thus, its recommendations did not deal with Métis or Inuit, only with what it called Indian First Nations [*Penner Report*, *supra* note 7 at 59].

54 The legislative backup plan is described in *Penner Report*, *supra* note 8 at 59.

to permit "Indian First Nations" to govern themselves and ensure that provincial laws would not apply on First Nations land except by agreement with the First Nations government. The Report says: "Self-government would mean that virtually the entire range of law-making, policy, program delivery, law enforcement and adjudication powers would be available to a First Nations government within its territory",[55] although it also considered health, education and child welfare to be three of the most important powers. Recommendation 21 lists the law-making (governance) jurisdiction of the First Nation government as "social and cultural developments, including education and family relations, land and resource use, revenue-raising, economic and commercial development, and justice and law enforcement".[56]

In a move it says was partly in response to the Penner Report, Canada announced the Community-Based Self-Government Policy in 1985.[57] Under this policy, Canada would delegate a range of "jurisdictions" (i.e. powers to legislate) to individual First Nations on reserve. One such arrangement was reached with the Sechelt Indian Band of British Columbia; it was not included in an agreement, but there is legislation bringing it into being.[58] This Act did not create a modern treaty protected under section 35 of the *Constitution Act, 1982*.[59] Few agreements were reached under this policy; Canada says that one of the key reasons for this was the delegated nature of law-making powers.[60]

In 1995, consistent with the recommendations of the Royal Commission on Aboriginal Peoples, Canada recognized the inherent right of self-government as an existing right within section 35 of the *Constitution Act, 1982*.[61] Canada stated that recognition of the inherent right is based on the view that

> the Aboriginal peoples of Canada have the right to govern themselves in relation to matters that are internal to their communities, integral to their unique cultures, identities, traditions, languages and institutions, and with respect to their special relationship to their land and their resources.[62]

55 *Penner Report*, *supra* note 8 at 63.

56 *Ibid.* at 64.

57 Canada, Crown-Indigenous Relations and Northern Affairs Canada, *General Briefing Note on Canada's Self-Government and Comprehensive Land Claims Policies and the Status of Negotiations*, online: <www.rcaanc-cirnac.gc.ca/eng/1373385502190/1542727338550> at 2 of 62 [General Briefing Note].

58 *Ibid.* at 12 of 62. See also *Sechelt Indian Band Self-Government Act*, SC 1986, c 27 [*Sechelt*] and *Sechelt Indian Government District Enabling Act*, RSBC 1996, c. 416 [*Sechelt Enabling Act*].

59 General Briefing Note, *supra* note 57 at 12.

60 *Ibid.* at 2.

61 Canada, Minister of Public Works and Government Services Canada, *Gathering Strength: Canada's Aboriginal Action Plan* (Ottawa: Minister of Indian Affairs and Northern Development, 1997) at 8 [Gathering Strength].

62 Inherent Right Policy, *supra* note 9 at 2.

The intent of the inherent right policy was to set aside legal debates in favour of practical arrangements that operate within the framework of the Canadian Constitution, that is, without interfering with the existing division of powers between Canada and the provinces.[63]

The 1995 policy document states that the government views the scope of Aboriginal jurisdiction or authority as likely extending to matters that are internal to the group, integral to its distinct Aboriginal culture, and essential to its operation as a government or institution, and proposes that negotiated agreements can set out law-making authority in many areas, including governance, social and economic development, education, health, and lands.[64] The list reflects an understanding of what an Indigenous legal order would have been preoccupied with historically. This sensitivity is blunted, however, by the requirement in the inherent right policy that Indigenous laws made pursuant to a self-government agreement should harmonize with the laws of other jurisdictions. Only Indigenous laws protecting culture and language generally take priority if there is a conflict.[65]

Despite its rejection by the Penner Committee and the later rejection of the Community-Based Self-Government policy, Canada has continued to delegate power to make laws. It delegated to bands the power to make membership rules in the 1985 amendments to the *Indian Act* status provisions,[66] and then in 1999 it used delegated power in the area of management of reserve lands. The *First Nations Land Management Act* (*FNLMA*)[67] brings into effect the 1996 Framework Agreement on First Nations Land Management negotiated between a group of First Nations and the federal government. Subsection 20 of the *FNLMA* provides that the council of a First Nation has the power to enact laws respecting interests or rights, and licences, in relation to First Nation land. The development, conservation, protection, management, use and possession of First Nation land, and any matter arising out of or ancillary to the exercise of that power and subsection 2(1) defines such a law as "First Nation law". The *FNLMA* also specifically grants a First Nation power to manage First Nation land and the legal capacity necessary to exercise its powers and perform its duties and functions.[68]

Defining "First Nation laws" as laws made pursuant to legislative power delegated by Canada is also found in the *Family Homes on Reserves and Matrimonial Interests or Rights Act*,[69] passed because the Supreme Court of Canada

63 General Briefing Note, *supra* note 57 at 3.

64 Canada, Crown-Indigenous Relations and Northern Affairs Canada, "Self-Government", online: <www.rcaanc-cirnac.gc.ca/eng/1100100032275/15293545447314, at 3 of 5 at 2 of 5 ["*Self-Government*"].

65 *Ibid.* at 5.

66 See *supra* note 50.

67 *First Nations Land Management Act*, SC 1999, c. 24 as amended [*FNLMA*].

68 *Ibid.* at s. 18(1)(2).

69 *Family Homes on Reserves and Matrimonial Interests or Rights Act*, SC 2013, c. 20 [*Family Homes Act*].

held that provincial matrimonial property law is inapplicable to reserve lands.[70] Section 7(1) of the *Act* provides that

> A First Nation has the power to enact First Nation laws . . . respecting the use, occupation and possession of family homes on its reserves and the division of the value of any interests or rights held by spouses or common-law partners in or to structures and lands on its reserves.[71]

In December 2018, Canada began co-developing legislation with the three national Indigenous groups to deal with family and child welfare issues.[72] The first reading of *An Act Respecting First Nations, Inuit and Metis Children, Youth and Families*[73] took place in February 2019.

Its stated purposes include the affirmation of the rights and jurisdiction of Indigenous Peoples in relation to child and family services.[74] Section 18(1) of the Act states that the inherent right of self-government recognized and affirmed by section 35 of the *Constitution Act, 1982*, includes jurisdiction in relation to child and family services, including legislative authority in relation to those services and authority to administer and enforce laws made under that legislative authority. These are all welcome features. However, the federal government retains the controlling hand by subjecting Indigenous child welfare laws and activities under them to the criteria set out in the legislation,[75] which also applies to provincial authorities who continue to participate in the child welfare area.

The Act provides that if an Indigenous group wishes to exercise its legislative authority in the child welfare area, it should give notice to the governments of each province in which it intends to exercise that authority and request that they enter into a coordination agreement with the Indigenous group and the federal minister.[76]

Canada negotiates several different types of self-government agreements. Claims-related self-government is negotiated in concert with comprehensive land claims agreements. Stand-alone self-government arrangements are usually negotiated with *Indian Act* First Nations and cover the First Nations reserve. Stand-alone agreements can be comprehensive and cover a range of subject areas, or sectoral, covering governance arrangements and one or two additional subjects like education or child welfare. Public government arrangements deal with

70 *Derrickson v. Derrickson*, [1986] 1 SCR 285 [*Derrickson*]; *Paul v. Paul*, [1986] 1 SCR 306 [*Paul*].

71 *Family Homes Act*, s 7(1).

72 See Government of Canada, Indigenous Services Canada, Backgrounder November 30, 2018: Federal legislation as an important step toward reducing the number of Indigenous children in foster care.

73 Bill C-92, *An Act Respecting First Nations, Inuit and Metis Children, Youth and Families*, 1st Sess, 42nd Parl., 2019 (first reading 28 February 2019) [Bill C-92].

74 *Ibid.*, s 8(a).

75 *Ibid.*, s 23 and criteria in ss 9, 10.

76 *Ibid.*, ss 20–24.

Aboriginal self-government negotiated within the context of broader, public government, as is the case in Nunavut.[77]

The 1995 Inherent Right Policy states that Canada is prepared to protect some of the elements of negotiated self-government agreements as modern treaties, where the other parties agree.[78] However, not all of the self-government agreements have that protection. For example, the Final Agreement between Canada and the Tesla Tlingit Council is a section 35 treaty, but its Self-Government Agreement is not.[79]

More recently, Canada has been at discussion tables "to explore new ways of working together to advance the recognition of Indigenous rights and self-determination".[80] These tables are open to all Indigenous groups with section 35 rights to address long-standing issues that may fall outside the scope of other federal policies and processes like treaty and self-government negotiations.[81] At these tables, Canada and Indigenous groups "can explore new ideas and ways to reach agreements that will recognize the rights of Indigenous groups and advance their vision of self-determination".[82] These largely sectoral agreements will not have the protection of section 35 of the *Constitution Act, 1982.*

Given the clarity of intention needed to establish extinguishment, it is unlikely that the exercise of delegated power would result in extinguishment of Indigenous law-making power. However, Canada's policy gives resources and recognition to the exercise of delegated power in certain areas, tearing them away from the overall fabric of the Indigenous legal orders continued under the common law doctrine of continuity. These orders were left to continue, if they could, in circumstances of dire poverty, dislocation, and oppression. Knowledge about law-making, and the language in which it was conducted, are rare because of residential schools and other forms of cultural oppression. The heightened attention to delegated power is yet another burden hindering the recuperation of these venerable orders of law.

Canada's policies on self-government are designed to function with the existing division of powers in the constitution. In formulating and applying them, Canada has paid no attention to the 2000 decision of Williamson J. of the Supreme Court of British Columbia that the *Constitution Act, 1867*, did not distribute all legislative power to Parliament and the provincial legislatures.[83] What was distributed in sections 91 and 92 was all of, but no more than, the powers which until June 30, 1867, had belonged to the colonies. Anything outside of

77 General Briefing Note, *supra* note 57 at 3.

78 Inherent Right Policy, *supra* note 9 at 6.

79 *Teslin*, *supra* note 50.

80 Canada, Crown-Indigenous Relations and Northern Affairs Canada, "Exploring New Ways of Working Together", online: <www.rcaanc-cirnac.gc.ca/eng/1511969222951/1529103469169> at 1 [Exploring New Ways].

81 *Ibid.* at 2.

82 *Ibid.*

83 *Campbell v. British Columbia (Attorney General)*, 2000 BCSC 1123 at para 180, [2000 BCJ No. 1524 Williamson J. [*Campbell*].

the powers enjoyed by the colonies at that time remained outside of the powers of Parliament and the legislatures under the 1867 legislation.[84] Aboriginal rights survived, particularly what Williamson J. calls "a right of self-government akin to a legislative power to make laws".[85] This decision, given in an unsuccessful challenge to the *Nisga'a Final Agreement*,[86] was never appealed and is not contradicted by any subsequent decision of any court of equivalent or superior rank. When the Supreme Court decided in *Tsilhqot'in*[87] that "aboriginal rights" under section 35 are a limit on both federal and provincial jurisdiction,[88] it did not refer to the *Campbell* decision.

Section 35 jurisprudence

Section 35 of the *Constitution Act, 1982*, provides: "The existing aboriginal and treaty rights of the aboriginal peoples of Canada are hereby recognized and affirmed"[89] Subsection (3) of section 35 states that "'treaty rights' includes rights that now exist by way of land claims agreements or may be so acquired".

Lamer CJC states in *Van der Peet:* "In order to be an aboriginal right an activity must be an element of a practice, custom or tradition integral to the distinctive culture of the aboriginal group claiming the right".[90] The chief justice does not focus on the continuity of law from past to present, but rather on the continuity between the past activities of the Indigenous claimant and those of the present day. He does so within the narrow compass of the "integral to a distinctive culture test". The historical action must have been "integral" rather than incidental or so modest or routine it was not worthy of particular notice; and the activity must have been distinctive in the sense "that this tradition or custom makes the culture what it is".[91]

Walters states that there is no case under the doctrine of continuity that protected only distinctive cultures. To have been so restrictive

> would have violated the rule of law by undermining civil order, stability, and legal certainty in the territory by introducing confusing and (from the local perspective) arbitrary rule that deprived culturally non-integral parts of the legal system of any force. Even if culturally unimportant laws could be identified by judges swiftly, rationally, and comprehensively so as to avoid

84 *Ibid.* at para 76.
85 *Ibid.* at paras 81–96.
86 Put in place by *Nisga'a Final Agreement Act*, SBC 1999, c 2 [*Nisga'a* BC] and *Nisga'a Final Agreement Act*, SC 2000, c 7 [*Nisga'a*].
87 *Tsilhqot'in Nation v. British Columbia*, 2014 SCC 44, [2014] 2 SCR 256 [*Tsilhqot'in*].
88 *Ibid.* at para 118.
89 *Constitution Act, 1982*, ss 35(1) and (3), *supra* note 31.
90 *Van der Peet*, *supra* note 22 at para 46.
91 *Ibid.* at para 71.

> chaos . . . the sudden invalidity of these laws might have deprived the legal order of rules that, in practical terms, were indispensable to its continued functioning.[92]

The exceedingly narrow range of the *Van der Peet* test has had a devastating effect on claims that self-government is a right protected by section 35. In *Pamajewon*,[93] the appellants claimed that certain gambling activities in which they took part, and their Nations' regulation of those activities, came within section 35. Chief Justice Lamer holds that this claim must be assessed according to the test in *Van der Peet*: "claims to self-government are no different from other claims to the enjoyment of aboriginal rights and must, as such, be measured against the same standard".[94]

The first step in such analysis is to define the activity in respect of which the right is claimed. In *Pamajewon*, the court characterizes the claim as "to participate in, and to regulate, gambling activities on their respective reserve lands".[95] The appellants characterize the claim as "the broad right to manage the use of their reserve lands", which Lamer CJC dismisses as "a level of excessive generality".[96] It is clear from his reasons that the self-government issue is to be considered activity by activity.[97] He concludes that while the evidence does demonstrate that the Ojibwa gambled, "it does not demonstrate that gambling was of central significance" and in no way addresses the extent to which it was subject to regulation by the community.[98]

The activity-by-activity approach to self-government embraced in *Pamajewon* allows for the deconstruction of the orders of Indigenous law which the doctrine of continuity recognized as existing when British sovereignty was asserted. From those deconstructed orders will be cherry-picked powers of self-government over only certain topics, which are considered to have been important enough to the traditional society to meet the *Van der Peet* test. Doing that cherry-picking will be judges who are, for the most part, non-Indigenous. Under Canada's self-government policies, the cherry-picking will be done at negotiation tables. However, unlike the results of judicial cherry-picking, the results of negotiations will not necessarily be protected by section 35. They must be modern treaties to secure such protection. When all the cherries have been picked, there may well be something left of the old orders of Indigenous law-making, under the doctrine of continuity, but the practical and legal position of these remnants is not immediately apparent.

92 Mark D. Walters, "The 'Golden Thread' of Continuity: Aboriginal Customs at Common Law and Under the Constitution Act, 1982" (1999) *McGill L.J.* 711 at 741–742 [Walters].
93 *R. v. Pamajewon*, [1996] 2 SCR 821 [*Pamajewon*].
94 *Ibid.* at paras 23–34.
95 *Ibid.* at para 26.
96 *Ibid.* at para 27.
97 *Ibid.*
98 *Ibid.* at para 28.

The land question

Philip Girard et al. identify as one of the three major characteristics of Indigenous legal traditions that "they assumed and sought to perpetuate a sustainable relationship between human beings and the natural world".[99] Marianne Ignace and Ron Ignace say that at its core the multi-dimensional system of resource access, use and management practiced by the Secwpemc "has always been sustained by a system of spiritual beliefs and sanctions that underlie the laws of good conduct, access to resources and trespass of land manifested in . . . our laws".[100] In Anishinabe belief, the Earth is seen is a living entity with thoughts and feelings; it can exercise agency by making choices and is related to human beings at the deepest generative level of existence. What Borrows calls the land's "sentience" is a fundamental principle of Anishinabe law, informing its legal personality.[101]

In order to ensure that this ethos of respect for the land and its inhabitants is preserved, it would be necessary for Canadian governments to recognize orders of Indigenous laws predicated on these beliefs. In virtually every aspect of its dealing with Indigenous lands, Canada has failed to do this.

Canada undertakes that modern treaties will provide Aboriginal parties with secure title to treaty settlement lands.[102] Subsurface rights to resources are in federal or provincial jurisdiction, and the Interim Policy on comprehensive claims provides that "holders of subsurface rights must have fair access to settlement lands, where necessary, for exploration, development and production of resources".[103] The exercise of such rights is to be subject to fair compensation as determined through timely negotiations or by arbitration. The policy contains no explicit reference to the need to respect or preserve the land while exercising such "fair access" rights.[104] Only where the subsurface rights are on federal Crown land is there a possibility that the Aboriginal party might have access to such rights and thus the ability to control the manner and consequences of their access.[105]

Under *Haida Nation*,[106] where a First Nation has asserted but not yet established Aboriginal title, the Crown has a duty to consult about proposed development on the land, and if necessary and appropriate, accommodate the concerns expressed.

99 *Supra* note 1 at 2.

100 Marianne Ignace & Ronald E. Ignace, *Secwepemc People, Land and Laws* (Montreal: McGill-Queens University Press, 2017) at 209–210 [Ignace & Ignace].

101 Borrows: *Constitution*, *supra* note 27 at 242–243.

102 Indigenous and Northern Affairs Canada, *Renewing the Federal Comprehensive Land Claims Policy: Towards a Framework for Addressing Section 35*, online: <www.rcaanc-cirnac.gc.ca/eng/1408631807053/1544123449934#sube> at s 2, item e [Renewing].

103 *Ibid*., s 2, item j.

104 *Ibid.*

105 *Ibid*., s 2, item j.

106 *Haida Nation v. British Columbia (Minister of Forests)*, 2004 SCC 73, [2004] 3 SCR 511 [*Haida Nation*].

Cases arising from conflicts between developers and protesters trying to assert Indigenous law show that the duty to consult arises in circumstances where Canadian law has already authorized development activity or exploration. The duty to consult does not entail an obligation to stop a proposed development project if Indigenous consent is withheld. Rather, the project will continue, with whatever adjustments to its features are necessary to reach a deal. The resource development orientation of Canadian law and society will, inevitably, prevail to some degree over the orientation of Indigenous law to safeguard the land. If the victory of the resource exploitation perspective is complete enough, the land may no longer be able to be used in a way consistent with the Indigenous interest, and the development might thus defeat the title claim.[107]

The conflict between the approaches of the two legal systems, if it reaches court, will be adjudicated upon by a Canadian court applying Canadian law.

In *Frontenac Ventures Corporation v. Ardoch Algonquin First Nation*,[108] the trial judge summarizes the evidence of someone protesting uranium exploration as "while he respects the rule of law, he cannot comply because his Algonquin law is supreme. He says he finds himself in a dilemma".[109] Then he continues: "It is a dilemma of his own making. His apparent frustration with the Ontario government is no excuse for breaking the law. There can only be one law, and that is the law of Canada, expressed through this court".[110]

The Court of Appeal states that injunctions sought by private parties to protect their interests should only be granted where every effort has been made by the court to encourage consultation, negotiation, accommodation and reconciliation among competing rights and interests.[111] This fails to acknowledge that the position of Algonquin law, forbidding the mining exploration, could never be vindicated in a process of consultation and accommodation. While acknowledging that the shortcomings of the consultation and accommodation process could produce "unsatisfactory, indeed tragic" results, the Supreme Court in *Ktunaxa* says that "in the difficult period between claim assertion and claim resolution, consultation and accommodation, imperfect as they may be, are the best available legal tools in the reconciliation basket".[112]

Where a court has found that Aboriginal title exists in land, the First Nation may, in theory, have greater ability to prevent or curtail resource development.

Chief Justice McLachlin in *Tsilhqot'in* says: "The right to control the land conferred by Aboriginal title means that governments and others seeking to use the land must obtain the consent of the Aboriginal title holders".[113] Without

107 *Delgamuukw v. British Columbia*, [1997] 3 SCR 1010 at para 117 [*Delgamuukw*].

108 *Frontenac Ventures Corporation v. Ardoch Algonquin First Nation*, 2008 ONCA 534 [*Frontenac*].

109 *Ibid.* at para 40.

110 *Ibid.*

111 *Frontenac*, *supra* note 107 at para 46.

112 *Ktunaxa Nation v. British Columbia (Forest, Lands and Natural Resource Operations)*, 2017 SCC 54, [2017] 2 SCR 386 at para 86 [*Ktunaxa*].

113 *Tsilhqot'in*, *supra* note 87 at para 77.

such consent, the government's only recourse is to establish that the proposed incursion on the land is justified under section 35. To do that, it must show that it has discharged its procedural duty to consult and accommodate, that its actions are backed by a compelling and substantial objective, and that the governmental action is consistent with the Crown's fiduciary obligation to the group.[114] The compelling and substantial objective must be considered from the Indigenous perspective and from the perspective of the broader public.[115] To constitute a compelling and substantial objective, the broader public goal asserted by the government must further the goal of reconciliation, having regard to both the Indigenous interest and the broader public objective.[116]

This consent requirement accords with article 19 of the UN *Declaration on the Rights of Indigenous Peoples*,[117] which provides that states shall consult and cooperate in good faith with the Indigenous Peoples concerned, through their own representative institutions, in order to obtain their free, prior and informed consent before adopting and implementing legislative or administrative measures that may affect them. Significant also is that the test the government must meet to justify its actions when there is no consent requires that the Indigenous perspective be considered at each of its stages. Through this test, the requirements of Indigenous land law will be brought to bear on a conflict about land use, something that does not occur in the ordinary consultation and accommodation case.

Chief Justice McLachlin adds to her reasons in *Tsilhqot'in*: "Governments and individuals proposing to use or exploit land, whether before or after a declaration of Aboriginal title, can avoid a charge of infringement or failure to adequately consult by obtaining the consent of the interested Aboriginal group".[118]

I would add to this excellent advice that such consent should not be sought with the modern-day equivalent of trinkets, that is a few jobs that will disappear when the construction phase of a big project is over, or some relatively modest investment in community development or training. Rather, consent should be sought by adopting and acting in accordance with the ethos of Indigenous law, that is based in respect for the land and harmony between it and all its inhabitants, including people.

Indigenous legal orders in a "self-governing" world

"Self-government" agreements are required to operate within the existing distribution of powers under the constitution. The exercise of powers delegated from

114 *Ibid.* at para 77.
115 *Ibid.* at para 81.
116 *Ibid.* at para 80.
117 *United Nations Declaration on the Rights of Indigenous Peoples*, GA Res 61/295, UNGAOR, 61st Sess., Supp No 49, Vol III, UN Doc A/61/49 (2007) [*Declaration*]. Canada signified its unconditional acceptance of the *Declaration* in May 2016: Tim Fontaine, "Canada Officially Adopts UN Declaration on Rights of Indigenous Peoples" (10 May 2016) *CBC News*, online: <www.cbc.ca/news/indigenous/canada-adopting-implementi>.
118 *Tsilhqot'in*, *supra* note 87 at para 97.

Canada is required to be done in harmony with other jurisdictions and in a spirit of cooperation. Those operating under these agreements, are more like municipal governments. They do not constitute a third order of government in Canada.

The sectoral agreements now being negotiated by Canada do not implicate the whole of an Indigenous legal order. They thus contribute to the fracturing of the legal orders that have been recognized, but not actively protected or promoted, by the doctrine of continuity. They mirror the approach of the Supreme Court to self-government claims under section 35 of the *Constitution Act, 1982.* The difference between the two approaches is that a segment of the legal order recognized under section 35 is protected, whereas a sectoral agreement offers no section 35 protection and can be withdrawn or altered. Both shatter the coherence of the Indigenous legal order.

The Indigenous legal orders which predate contact and the assertion of sovereignty have not been extinguished by any act of government that meets the strict test for extinguishment. It would be appropriate under section 35 to hold that there is an aboriginal right at common law to the continuity of the legal order and the law-making historically undertaken by the plaintiff nation. This would not be a one-size-fits-all right; its assertion would require that proof be adduced of the historical situation. Accepting that there is a section 35 right to the continuance of one's legal order would have a powerful beneficial influence on Canada's approach to self-government: an Indigenous polity could resist the imposition of delegated power and insist on the deployment of its own inherent law-making jurisdiction.[119]

Ending the assault on Indigenous legal orders through section 35 is a necessary element of reconciliation.[120] It is also necessary under article 5 of the UN *Declaration on the Rights of Indigenous Peoples*, which provides that Indigenous Peoples have the right to maintain and strengthen their distinct political, legal, economic, social, and cultural institutions while retaining their right to participate fully, if they so choose, in the political, economic, social, and cultural life of the state. Article 34 provides that Indigenous Peoples have the right to promote, develop, and maintain their institutional structures and their distinctive customs, spirituality, traditions, procedures, and practices; and, in the cases where they exist, juridical systems or customs, in accordance with international human rights standards.

Even before any case changing the Supreme Court jurisprudence on section 35, Canada can specify that its interpretation of section 35 includes protection

119 We already see assertions of inherent law-making jurisdiction in these stand-alone agreements. The Preamble to the Anishinabek Nation Education Agreement states "Whereas the Participating First Nations assert that they have law-making power and other authority with respect to education which they have never relinquished." Enacted by *Anishinabek Nation Education Agreement Act*, SC 2017, c. 32 [*Anishinabek Education Act*].

120 Mary Eberts, "Reconciliation and the Rule of Law" in Janine L'Espérance et al., eds., *Canada and the Rule of Law: 150 Years after Confederation* (Ottawa: International Commission of Jurists Canada, 2018) at 241–246 [Eberts].

of Indigenous legal orders, thereby moving beyond the *Van der Peet* test. This is not such a big step: Canada already acknowledges in its policy that section 35 protects a right of self-government. While noting that Canada and Indigenous nations may have different views about the scope and content of the inherent right, it acknowledges that the courts have not yet authoritatively defined the right.[121]

Canada missed a significant opportunity to acknowledge that section 35 protects Indigenous legal orders in 2018, when it issued its *Recognition and Implementation of Indigenous Rights Framework*,[122] intended to replace the Comprehensive Claims and Inherent Rights Policies with a more up-to-date approach. Nowhere in this Framework does Canada recognize Indigenous legal orders surviving since before contact, even though contributing to meaningful reconciliation with Indigenous Peoples is one of the Framework's purposes.[123]

One of the most effective strategies for the advancement of Indigenous law-making and legal orders is for Indigenous Peoples simply to exercise their historical law-making jurisdiction, continuing all the while their advocacy for recognition of that inherent jurisdiction. The case of adoption, in particular, has shown that strong capacity in Indigenous nations, and strong advocacy, can contribute to appropriate state legislation recognizing, rather than regulating, the exercise of Indigenous jurisdiction. Building and re-building capacity will be enhanced by fulfilment of Call to Action 50 of the Truth and Reconciliation Commission, which calls upon Canada, in collaboration with Indigenous organizations, to fund the establishment of Indigenous law institutions for the development, use, and understanding of Indigenous laws and access to justice in accordance with the unique cultures of Aboriginal peoples in Canada.[124]

A place for Indigenous law-making in the legal and constitutional arrangements of Canada will benefit not only Indigenous polities emerging from the horrors of colonization. It will benefit the Canadian legal order as a whole to embrace principles of Indigenous law throughout the criminal law, in resource and environmental law, and in the treatment of children and families, to mention three key areas.

121 *Westbank First Nation Self-Government Agreement between Her Majesty the Queen in Right of Canada and Westbank First Nation* at Preamble and Article 1(b) [*Westbank Self-Government Agreement*]. Enacted by *Westbank First Nation Self-Government Act*, SC 2004, c 17 [*Westbank Self-Government Act*].

122 Canada, Crown-Indigenous Relations and Northern Affairs Canada, *Overview of a Recognition and Implementation of Indigenous Rights Framework*, online: <www.rcaanc-cirnac.gc.ca/eng/1536350959665/1539959903708> at 12 [Framework].

123 *Ibid.* at 5.

124 *Final Report of the Truth and Reconciliation Commission of Canada, Volume One: Summary, Honouring the Truth, Reconciling for the Future* (Toronto: James Lorimer, 2015) at 327 [TRC Final Report].

10 The right to free, prior, and informed consent (FPIC)

Reflections on experiences of two Indigenous communities in northern regions of Canada and Chile

Terry Mitchell, Courtney Arseneau, José Aylwin, and Darren Thomas

We wish to acknowledge the leadership role played in the development of this chapter by the chiefs of the Matawa First Nations with the support of their tribal council support staff. We also wish to thank Dr. Peggy Smith, Professor Emerita of Lakehead University, for her community engagement and intellectual leadership, and the Diaguita leaders from Chile who engaged in the research partnership in Chile and the FPIC workshop in Matawa. The authors have sole responsibility for the final content. We also wish to thank the Social Sciences and Humanities Research Council for their generous support.

The emergence of an international Indigenous rights regime, most strongly signaled by the United Nations Declaration on the Rights of Indigenous Peoples,[1] is slowly changing the playing field for resource development around the globe.[2] Advancing Indigenous rights, particularly the right to free, prior, and informed consent (FPIC) regarding development on Indigenous territories, will be essential for reconciling economic development agendas with the inequalities and injustices endured by Indigenous Peoples. This is especially true for Canada, given the country's economic dependence on resource extraction both domestically and internationally. In this chapter, we focus on the ongoing pressures faced by Indigenous communities in responding to growing global investments in extractive activities such as mining. In highlighting the obligations of states and businesses to adhere to consultation processes and practices of the right to FPIC, we will provide a comparative analysis of the barriers faced by Indigenous Peoples

1 UN General Assembly, United Nations Declaration on the Rights of Indigenous Peoples: resolution adopted by the General Assembly (2 October 2007), A/RES/61/295, online: <www.refworld.org/docid/471355a82.html> [UNDRIP].

2 James Anaya, *International Human Rights and Indigenous Peoples* (New York: Aspen, 2009) [Anaya 2009]; José Aylwin, Matias Meza- Lopehandia & Nancy Yanez, *Los pueblos indigenas y el derecho* (Indigenous Peoples and the Law) (Santiago: LOM Ediciones, 2013); Claire Charters & Rodolfo Stavenhagen, *Making the Declaration Work: The United Nations Declaration on the Rights of Indigenous Peoples*, IWGIA Document no. 127 (Denmark: International Work Group for Indigenous Affairs, 2010).

in mining-affected communities in northern Ontario (Canada) and in northern Chile. We also call attention to the extraterritorial responsibilities of Canada's mining investments in Chile presenting the situation of global extractive practices as a new wave of colonialism known as extractive imperialism.

As members of the Pan-American Indigenous Rights and Resource Governance Network and a team of Indigenous and non-Indigenous scholars and community leaders from across the Americas, we have worked together over several years with the aim of advancing the understanding of Indigenous Peoples' right to FPIC from an interdisciplinary and intercultural perspective. This research was funded by the Social Sciences and Humanities Research Council of Canada (SSHRC) Grn-435–2015–1302-Mitchell. The research program received ethics review and approval from Laurier University's Research Ethics Board. Three of the authors are community psychologists who have been working in partnership with the Matawa tribal council and their nine-member First Nations communities in the context of the "Ring of Fire" in northern Ontario. The fourth author is a human rights lawyer who has been working with the Observatorio Ciudadano (Citizen's Watch) in conducting a human rights impact assessment of Canadian mining activities in the Atacama Desert of northern Chile with the Diaguita people of Huasco Alto.[3] Together, we adopt a critical lens to analyze the impact of the ongoing colonial forces involved in extractive industries across our case study sites. We draw from our comparative analysis to report on the challenges of asserting Indigenous rights to self-determined development and exercising the right to FPIC. We will discuss the key Pan-American findings of (1) a lack of consultation and information; (2) inducement and division; and (3) environmental impacts, as parallel experiences across both regions. We conclude with reflections on decolonial approaches to consultation and policy recommendations for the implementation of FPIC and the monitoring of Indigenous rights in Canadian mining activities across the Americas.

Background

The United Nations Declaration on the Rights of Indigenous Peoples (UNDRIP), approved in 2007 with Chile's support and with a delayed signing by Canada in 2010, is an important international consensus document, setting "the minimum standards for the survival, dignity and well-being of the Indigenous peoples of the world".[4] Building on previous international norms, such as those enshrined in the International Labour Organization (ILO) Convention 169 on Indigenous and Tribal Peoples,[5] the Convention on Biological Diversity (1993),

3 El Observatorio Ciudadano and Oxfam, "Canadian Mining Projects in the Territory of the Diaguitas Huasco Altinos agricultural community in Chile: Human Rights Impact Assessment" (2016), online (pdf): Oxfam <https://policy-practice.oxfamamerica.org/static/media/files/Chile_HRIA_English.pdf> [Observatorio, 2016].

4 UNDRIP, *supra* note 1 art 43.

5 *Indigenous and Tribal Peoples Convention, 1989* (27 June 1989), 1650 UNTS, 5 September 1991 [ILO #169, 1989].

and the International Convention on the Elimination of All Forms of Racial Discrimination (1969), the UNDRIP reinforces the global movement toward a human rights framework expressed and defined through international law. Central to UNDRIP is the right to consultation, and in certain circumstances, the right to FPIC as an expression of the right to self-determination.

Canada has a contradictory relationship with Indigenous rights and UNDRIP. Despite Canada's significant role in advancing the internationalization of Indigenous rights, the government of Canada is not a signatory to ILO Convention 169 and refused to sign UNDRIP at its adoption in 2007. The Canadian government eventually became a signatory to UNDRIP in 2010, with qualifications referring to the Declaration as an "aspirational document". In 2014, the Canadian government under Prime Minister Harper was the only UN member to refuse to adopt the outcome document of the Indigenous World Conference, citing objections to article 20 of the document due to its explicit commitment to the implementation of FPIC.

Unfortunately, it is evident that the principles set out in the UNDRIP are often neglected in practice. As such, international scrutiny of states that have significant Indigenous populations, such as Canada and Chile, has put increasing pressure on policy makers to reform legal norms and administrative structures at the national level. For instance, in reporting on his visit to Canada in October 2013, James Anaya, former UN Special Rapporteur on the Rights of Indigenous Peoples, articulated that despite a strong legal framework, Indigenous rights in Canada are in crisis. He highlighted the multiple social problems faced by Indigenous peoples across the nation, stating that "it simply cannot be acceptable that these conditions persist in the midst of a country with such great wealth".[6]

Nowhere is this contradiction between legal order and policy practice more apparent than in the multiple cases of social conflict around resource development on Indigenous traditional territories. In the absence of an intercultural, rights-based framework, Indigenous Peoples have been positioned as "standing in the way of progress",[7] while being disproportionately and negatively affected by industrial processes.[8] This situation creates economic and cultural contexts for

6 James Anaya, "Statement upon Conclusion of the Visit to Canada: United Nations Special Rapporteur on the Rights of Indigenous Peoples" (15 October 2013), online: *James Anaya Former United Nations Special Rapporteur on the Rights of Indigenous Peoples* <www.unsr.jamesanaya.org/statements/statement-upon-conclusion-of-the-visit-to-canada> at para 12; James Anaya, "Report of the Special Rapporteur on the Rights of Indigenous Peoples, James Anaya, on the Situation of Indigenous Peoples in Canada" (7 May 2014), online: *James Anaya Former United Nations Special Rapporteur on the Rights of Indigenous Peoples* <http://unsr.jamesanaya.org/country-reports/the-situation-of-indigenous-peoples-in-canada>.

7 Ken Coates, *A Global History of Indigenous Peoples: Struggle and Survival* (London: Palgrave Macmillan, 2004) at 262; Thierry Rodon, Francis Levesque & J. Blais, "De Rankin Inlet a Raglan, le developpement minier et les communautés inuit" (2014) 37 *Etudes/Inuit Studies* 103; Thierry Rodon & Stephan Schott, "Towards a Sustainable Future for Nunavik" (2013) 50 *Polar Record* 1.

8 Terry Mitchell, "CIGI Special Report: The Internationalization of Indigenous Rights: UNDRIP and the Canadian Context" (2014) *Centre for International Governance Innovation*.

enduring social and economic disparities and escalating social conflict between states and Indigenous populations nationally and globally, increasingly characterized by violence, particularly in Latin America. As Anaya noted in his report, there is an atmosphere of increasing distrust between Indigenous Peoples and Canadian governments, especially in light of the lack of appropriate consultation with Indigenous communities in advance of resource development in their territories. The disjuncture between emerging international rights standards and Canadian policy is of grave concern, especially given the push to amplify Canada's position as a powerhouse in resource exports by expanding mineral and energy extraction in regions like northern Ontario's Ring of Fire and northern areas of Chile.

Canada is not alone in such contradictions. Chile has also repeatedly come under international scrutiny for the fraught relationship between the government and Indigenous peoples. The Chilean Constitution does not recognize Indigenous Peoples or their rights. Although ILO Convention 169 on Indigenous and Tribal Peoples of 1989 was ratified by the Chilean state in 2008, Indigenous Peoples' rights are regulated by Law No. 19,253 of 1993 on the Promotion, Protection and Development of the Indigenous, a law that does not meet the standards of international law on the rights of Indigenous Peoples. This persists particularly in relation to rights to lands, territories, and natural resources traditionally occupied or used, self- determination, autonomy, and the right to FPIC. Public policies implemented by the Chilean state in the last decades have been aimed at promoting foreign investment, largely on natural resource extraction. Indeed, the Chilean government has signed free trade agreements with all large economies, including Canada. Such agreements have had a direct effect on the increase of investment in the extraction of natural resources and in infrastructure – mining in the north of the country; forestry and fish farming in the south; and energy and infrastructure projects throughout the country, in land and territories legally belonging to, or traditionally occupied by Indigenous Peoples.[9] The installation of mines, hydroelectric dams, and other infrastructure projects have generated social conflict as Indigenous communities demand meaningful participation in decisions around resource development.[10] As in Canada, the Chilean government has consistently resisted fulsome interpretation of its duties under the emerging

9 José Aylwin, Emanuel Gomez & Luis Vittor, *El TPP y los derechos de pueblos indígenas en América Latina* (Copenhagen: IWGIA – Observatorio Ciudadano, 2016).

10 *Supra* note 3; Charters & Stavenhagen, *supra* note 2; Chilean Cooper Commission Research Department, *Investment in the Chilean Mining Industry, Project Portfolio: 2013–2021* (Santiago: Chilean Copper Commission, 2013) [COCHILCO 2013]; Diane Haughney, "Neoliberal Policies, Logging Companies, and Mapuche Struggle for Autonomy in Chile" (2007) 2 *Latin American and Caribbean Ethnic Studies* 141; Diane Haughney, "Defending Territory, Demanding Participation: Mapuche Struggles in Chile" (2010) 39 *Latin American Perspectives* 201; Francisco Molina Camacho, "Competing Rationalities in Water Conflict: Mining and the Indigenous Community in Chiu Chiu et Loa Province, Northern Chile" (2012) 33 *Singapore Journal of Tropical Geography* 93; Patricia Richards, "Of Indians and Terrorists: How the State and Local Elites Construct the Mapuche in Neoliberal Multicultural Chile" (2010) 42 *Journal of Latin American Studies* 59.

international Indigenous rights regime. If such shortcomings in Chilean policy echo challenges faced in Canada, they also present a direct concern as Canadian companies represent the most significant source of foreign investment in Chile's mining sector.[11]

Colonialism and extractivist imperialism

Canada, with its resource-based economy, is emerging as a global mining superpower with considerable mining interests within Canada and abroad.[12] Much of Canada's global dominance in mining is exerted in Latin America, predominantly on Indigenous territories.[13] This new era of resource extraction, funded by global capital and dominated by Canadian mining companies, has been termed extractivist imperialism.[14] Extractive imperialism is defined as a global political economy of natural resource extraction. Extractive industries engage in colonial forms of territorial displacement characterized by environmental degradation, denuding and polluting of Indigenous territories, and dispossessing Indigenous Peoples from their territories and natural resources.[15]

Extractivist imperialism commits the violence of gross interference of Indigenous territories and Indigenous lifeways by viewing water, minerals, land, and trees through the lens of market value rather than through the lens of relationship. As stated by Indigenous scholar and activist Leanne Simpson:

> Extraction and assimilation go together. Colonialism and capitalism are based on extracting and assimilating . . . The act of extraction removes all

11 *Supra* note 3; Anaya 2009, *supra* note 2; COCHILCO 2013, *supra* note 10; Coates, *supra* note 7; Ronald Niezen, "Recognizing Indigenism: Canadian Unity and the International Movement of Indigenous Peoples" (2000) 42 *Comparative Studies in Society and History* 119.

12 Government of Canada, "Exploration and Mining in Canada: An Investor's Guide" (February 2016), online (pdf): *Ministry of Natural Resources, Canada* <www.nrcan.gc.ca/sites/www.nrcan.gc.ca/files/mineralsmetals/pdf/mms-smm/poli-poli/pdf/Investment_Brief_e.pdf>; Mining Association of Canada, "Facts and Figures 2017" (5 March 2018), online: *The Mining Association of Canada* <http://mining.ca/print/69>.

13 International Council on Mining & Metals, "Indigenous Peoples and Mining: Position Statement" (2013), online: *International Council on Mining & Metals* <www.icmm.com/document/5433>; Mining Watch, "Report to the U.N. Committee on the Elimination of Racial Discrimination 93rd session, July–August 2017 for Its Review of Canada's 21st–23rd Periodic Reports UN" (2017), online (pdf): <https://tbinternet.ohchr.org/Treaties/CERD/Shared%20Documents/CAN/INT_CERD_ICO_CAN_27943_E.pdf>; Working Group on Mining and Human Rights in Latin America/Grupo de Trabajo sobre Minería y Derechos Humanos en América Latina, "El impacto de la minería canadiense en América latina y la responsabilidad de Canadá" (2013), online: <www.dplf.org/sites/default/files/informe_canada_resumen_ejecutivo.pdf>.

14 Henry Veltmeyer, "The Natural Resource Dynamics of Postneoliberalism in Latin America: New Developmentalism or Extractivist Imperialism?" (2012) 90 *Studies in Political Economy* 57 [Veltmeyer, 2012].

15 Henry Veltmeyer & James Petras, *The New Extractivism: A Post-Neoliberal Development Model or Imperialism of the Twenty-First Century?* (United Kingdom: Zed Books, 2014).

> of the relationships that give whatever is being extracted meaning. Extracting is taking. Actually, extracting is stealing – it is taking without consent, without thought, care or even knowledge of the impacts that extraction has on the other living things in that environment. That's always been a part of colonialism and conquest.[16]

Due to the high demand of resources on Indigenous territories and a conflict in worldviews, Indigenous Peoples in Canada and elsewhere have been positioned as standing in the way of progress.[17] Increasing conflict has, therefore, arisen between the rights of Indigenous Peoples and the far reach of global capital in the form of extractivist imperialism both in Canada and Chile. Canadian mining investments in Canada and Chile have not only failed to provide social and economic benefits to Indigenous communities, but they have had major negative socioeconomic and environmental costs causing cultural disruption and political conflict.[18]

Extractivist imperialism undermines the very existence and reality of Indigenous law through the dominating forces of colonial state law and business practices. Indigenous self-determination is further undermined as national governments sign new global economic treaties such as the Trans-Pacific Partnership (TPP), signed by Canada, Chile, and nine other countries in March 2018[19] central to an international expression of extractivist imperialism.

Description of case study sites

Within the context of this new wave of colonialism, we will report on Canadian mining activities in two case study sites: in northern Ontario and in northern Chile. We will begin by providing a description of both cases and will subsequently discuss the key themes that have emerged as common experiences faced by Indigenous Peoples across these two regions. We compare these case sites for two key reasons. First, colonialism has seriously impacted Indigenous Peoples globally. Despite differences in political and economic contexts, and diverse histories and cultures, Indigenous Peoples in both North and South America are impacted by extractive imperialism. Canada, one of the biggest mining stakeholders in the world, has led extractive projects that grossly impact Indigenous Peoples' social,

16 Leanne Simpson, quoted in Naomi Klein, "Dancing the World into Being: A Conversation with Idle No More's Leanne Simpson" (3 March 2013) *Yes! Magazine*, online: <www.yesmagazine.org/peace-justice/dancing-the-world-into-being-a-conversation-with-idle-no-more-leanne-simpson>.

17 Mario Blaser, Harvey A. Fleit & Glenn McRae, *In the Way of Development: Indigenous Peoples, Life Projects, and Development* (London: Zed Books in collaboration with IDRC, 2004).

18 Veltmeyer & Petras, *supra* note 15.

19 Government of Canada, "Comprehensive and Progressive Agreement for Trans-Pacific Partnership" (2018), online: *Government of Canada* <https://international.gc.ca/trade-commerce/trade-agreements-accords-commerciaux/agr-acc/cptpp-ptpgp/index.aspx?lang=eng> [Govt. of Canada, 2018a].

cultural, environmental, and political livelihoods across the Americas. Second, the emerging international Indigenous rights standards should hold the same weight and substantive nature in both North and South America, given that all Indigenous Peoples should be able to enjoy the rights set out by the UNDRIP. Our goal as a research team is to invite the voices and to understand the experiences of Indigenous Peoples in the North and South to engage in the interpretation and meaning of FPIC. In doing so, we offer a comparative perspective on the similarities and differences in the Pan-American implementation and uptake of FPIC.

Case study site 1: the "Ring of Fire" and the Matawa First Nations communities, Canada

Nine Ojibway and Cree communities in northern Ontario, Canada, form the Matawa First Nations tribal council (pop. 10,000). Following the discovery of a large chromite deposit in 2008, with an estimated value of over $60 billion,[20] the Matawa First Nations communities have been actively involved in deliberations, negotiations, and capacity building in response to the proposed mine and associated development coined the "Ring of Fire". The mining and processing of chromite, used primarily in stainless steel processing, is of notable environmental concern given the vast muskeg, intricate watersheds, and pristine boreal forests of the north. The mineral-rich Matawa region also holds deposits of nickel, copper, zinc, and other metals and has since attracted hundreds of mining claims by numerous proponents, with Noront Resources acquiring the majority of active claims in the immediate Ring of Fire area (ROF).

The ROF is located approximately 540 kilometers northeast of Thunder Bay, Ontario.[21] This area is within the Treaty 9 (1905–1906, adhesions 1929–1930) area and is the ancestral home of Anishinaabe (Ojibway), Mushkegowuk (Cree), and Oji-Cree Nations. Matawa First Nations Management is a tribal council formed in 1988 to support nine First Nation member communities in the region: Aroland, Constance Lake, Eabametoong, Ginoogaming, Long Lake #58, Nibinamik, Marten Falls, Neskantaga, and Webequie. With a total membership population of 9,500, the Matawa First Nations have unique sets of needs and priorities, with some communities accessible by road (Aroland, Constance Lake, Ginoogaming, and Long Lake #58) and others accessible by air or winter roads (Eabametoong, Nibinamik, Marten Falls, Neskantaga, and Webequie).

Several Matawa First Nations are familiar with forestry and some may have benefited from employment opportunities in the forest sector. With the

20 Jed Chong, "Resource Development in Canada: A Case Study of the Ring of Fire" (2014) Economics, Resources, and International Affairs Division, Parliamentary Information and Research Service: Library of Parliament Background Paper No. 2014-17-E.

21 Ontario Chamber of Commerce, "Beneath the Surface: Uncovering the Economic Potential of Ontario's Ring of Fire" (2014), online (pdf): *Ontario Chamber of Commerce* <www.occ.ca/wp-content/uploads/Beneath_the_Surface_web-1.pdf>.

modernization of the *Mining Act* (1990) in 2009 and the introduction of the *Far North Act* (2010),[22] the Province of Ontario is developing protocols for actively engaging Indigenous communities to consider resource extraction, with a focus on mining, as an economic strategy to enhance their infrastructure development. The Matawa First Nations are engaged in a process of discussing scientific reports, full of complex technical language, in their efforts to develop a common understanding and collective decision-making process on whether or not to proceed with the proposed development in their territories.

Although the nine communities have a shared Unity Declaration (Mamow-Wecheekapawetahteewiin), the communities have distinct histories, experiences, and priorities. Overall, the communities report that they are supportive of development but only if the benefits of the proposed development are maximized and environmental damage is limited. Matawa First Nations are considering the options and opportunities of industrial development in large part because many communities lack basic infrastructure such as adequate housing. Several communities have been on a water boil advisory for over 25 years. In some of these communities, people continue to live off of the land as part of the ecosystem. In facing this proposed mining activity and associated development (e.g. road development/infrastructure), member communities in the Matawa region have reported experiences of coercion and lack of adequate consultation. Despite ongoing pressures from both industry and the provincial government, community leadership within the nine communities and representatives of their various local and regional working groups continue to assert that development will not proceed without their FPIC.

The case study research in the Matawa region officially began in 2015 with the establishment of a research protocol in partnership with the Matawa First Nations Management and with the support of the Matawa Chiefs Council. Over the past three years, we have been visiting with leadership, management, and members from the Matawa First Nations communities to learn about their experiences of consultation and consent and their efforts at asserting their rights to self-determined development. In addition to individual interviews, focus groups, and community visits, we also organized a workshop on FPIC with Matawa, where members discussed and defined the principles of FPIC in the context of proposed development on their lands and territories. Notably, Matawa hosted two leaders at this workshop from the Indigenous Diaguita community from the northern Atacama Desert in Chile. This coming together of Indigenous communities facilitated the sharing of experiences, strategies of resistance, and Indigenous perspectives of consultation and FPIC from across the Americas. In the spring of 2018, there was a change in the political leadership of the province of Ontario, and the Matawa chiefs received no communications from the new premier's office and no responses to their inquiries for a year. It was unclear if, in the absence of any formal provincial consultation processes, whether the

22 *Far North Act, 2010*, SO 2010, c 18.

province was no longer pursuing access to the ROF or if the premier did not see the necessity of maintaining relationships to advance meaningful consultation. In the meantime, Matawa First Nations, with the support of the federal government, continued to meet to discuss their regional priorities with a renewed focus on their unity agreement.

Case study site 2: Canadian mining on the territories of the Diaguita people, Chile

Our research in Latin America has centered around two large mining projects in Chile, Pascua Lama and El Morro, owned by Canadian transnational corporations. Both projects are located in the traditional territory of the Diaguita people, with a population of 50,000, in northern Chile along the border of Argentina, in the dry desert of Atacama. Pascua Lama is a mining project of the Nevada Mining Company (Compañía Minera Nevada SpA), a subsidiary of Barrick Gold in Chile, incorporated in Canada. Pascua Lama is an open-pit gold and silver mine, located at more than 4,000 meters of elevation on the border of Chile and Argentina. In Chile, Pascua is in Huasco Province, in the Atacama region; Lama is situated in Argentina's San Juan Province.

The project in Chile is located at the headwaters of the El Estrecho and El Toro Rivers, and it involves the exploitation of a mineral deposit existing under the glaciers that sustain the Huasco Valley hydrological system. These glaciers irrigate ancestral territory of the Diaguita people (Diaguitas Huasco Altinos Agricultural Community), a territory usurped through legal loopholes in the early 20th century and purchased by the Compañía Minera Nevada for the implementation of the Pascua Lama project. Despite this fact, the community was not consulted before operations began. This led the Diaguita people to file a complaint to the Inter-American Commission on Human Rights that was declared admissible in 2009. In addition to the Pascua Lama mining project's violation of the fundamental right of consultation and the other human rights violations noted and FPIC, it has failed to fulfill the environmental requirements of Chile's Environmental Qualification Resolution. As a result of this non fulfillment, the project was halted on the basis of lack of compliance to the environmental impact assessment. Moreover, in 2018, the Chilean environmental authority fined the company for its harms to the environment; however, it is currently in the process of being re-evaluated with Chinese investors with the intention to re-establish the project as an underground mine.

The second project under study is the El Morro mining project, originally owned by Goldcorp Inc., also headquartered in Canada. The project involves the exploitation of an open-pit gold and silver mine. El Morro's worksites, located in Huasco and Copiapó Provinces, cover an area of approximately 2,460 hectares, out of which 1,420 hectares correspond to legally registered territory of the Diaguita people. In 2008, the Sociedad Contractual Minera El Morro submitted an environmental impact assessment (EIA) to the Regional Environmental Committee of the Atacama region, thereby presenting the El Morro project to the

Environmental Impact Assessment System. After a series of addenda, the project was approved by the environmental authority. Soon thereafter, judicial actions were filed against the El Morro project for violation of constitutional guarantees, in particular because the Indigenous consultation was not performed as established in the ILO Convention 169 on Indigenous and Tribal Peoples in Independent Countries.[23] These actions found acceptance in the courts, which ordered the annulment of the authorization issued by the Chilean government. Owing to this judicial decision, the company decided to temporarily withdraw the project from the Environmental Impact Assessment System and to indefinitely suspend its execution. Nevertheless, in 2015 Goldcorp, with Teck Resources, a company also based in Canada, announced their intention to amend the original project to give rise to the Corredor project that combines the El Morro mining project with another adjacent project called Relincho. The combined project was later named New Union, or Nueva Unión, in reference to this merger. As in the case of Pascua Lama, the Nueva Unión project has not publicly stated whether this modification substantially affects the impacts of the project and/or allows compliance with the requirements imposed by the Diaguita people and citizens. In addition, the Indigenous consultation is still pending. In response to the threats posed by mining, the Diaguita peoples are seeking to protect their land as an Indigenous Conservation Territory under guidelines set out by the International Union for Conservation of Nature.

The human rights impacts of these two large mining projects were recently assessed by the Observatorio Ciudadano.[24] Among other rights that according to this assessment have been violated are the right to equality and non-discrimination; the right to self-determination, autonomy, and self-government; the right to maintain and strengthen their own political, legal, economic, social, and cultural institutions; the right to decide their own priorities for the process of development; the Indigenous Peoples' right to ownership of their lands, territories, and natural resources, including the right to own, use, develop, and control the lands and territories they possess by reason of traditional ownership or other traditional occupation or use; and the right to consultation and to FPIC. The assessment also found that those responsible for these human rights violations included both Chile, for the authorization of these projects without consultation and FPIC of the Diaguita people, and Canada, as a result of the refusal of its government to accept the recommendations of international human rights organizations. Said organizations have urged it to adopt legislative and policy measures to meet its extraterritorial obligations for the violation of human rights by companies domiciled in Canada acting outside the country to prevent, remedy, and sanction such violations. We also found that the companies behind the project described here were also responsible for the collective rights violations of the Diaguita people, in particular due to the lack of due diligence in securing these rights.

23 ILO #169, 1989, *supra* note 5.
24 *Supra* note 3.

Evidence of common experiences, when Indigenous Peoples are engaged with proposed development and resource extraction on their traditional territories, were identified. In the following section, we will highlight key themes that we have observed across the Canadian and Chilean cases study sites in order to compare the experiences of the Diaguita people in the Atacama region of Chile (as reflected in the human rights impact assessment) with the experiences of Matawa First Nations in northern Ontario, Canada. In order to understand the experiences of the latter, we conducted interviews, focus groups, and workshops about FPIC in a research partnership with the Matawa First Nations communities.

Comparative analysis: common experiences of Indigenous peoples in asserting FPIC

While the history and stages of development are different across the two cases, and each case exists within a distinct political and cultural context with different legal frameworks, nevertheless very similar strategies were reported being used by governments and mining corporations in both cases. Communities across both regions shared similar experiences of inadequate consultation and information sharing, experiences of inducement and community division, as well as reports of significant environmental impacts.

Lack of consultation and information

Across both cases, Indigenous communities have reported that they were not meaningfully consulted prior to the beginning of proposed development activities, such as before exploration permits have been issued. In Chile, in the Atacama region, one community member said that "we found out about the mining project when they began working and four-wheel drive vehicles and helicopters came".[25] Similar experiences were reported in northern Ontario, where companies have illegitimately viewed hosting a meeting in the community as fulfilling their consultation obligations. Indigenous communities in both the Canadian and Chilean cases were clear that this is not acceptable:

> A company can come in and engage community Elders. That's not a consultation, that's just an open house or a meeting . . . but then they use that later, they check it off as we consulted with the Elders . . . but it wasn't. No. Nobody conceded to it.
>
> (Matawa region)

Communities need to be adequately informed about the economic, environmental, social, financial, and legal aspects of proposed development. It takes time to do that. However, it has been reported and confirmed that First Nations in

25 Focus Group conducted by Mitchell et al. during the FPIC Conference held at the Matawa First Nations Management Office in Thunder Bay, Ontario, Canada, on 27 October 2016.

Ontario are expected to respond and provide input on proposed plans and government permits without having adequate resources, staff, and time to do so under very tight timelines (e.g. 30 days for reviewing and responding to proposed plans).[26] In Matawa, community members reported that they always feel like they have to catch up to the timelines and regulations set by others, the government, and the industry's agenda. Adding to this pressure is the need for communities to quickly learn specialized technical knowledge about development and the mining cycle:

> [The mining companies] use technical words; we are farmers and don't understand.
>
> (Atacama region)

> You're looking for community input but it seems to be unfair to the community members because if they don't know anything about the mining perspectives, the business side, or how they will be socially impacted, then they don't completely understand.
>
> (Matawa region)

Across both regions, there is a need to make all of this highly technical information more accessible, not just in plain language but also in the preferred language of the communities.

Inducement and division

The processes for consultation, the consideration of proposed development, and decision- making should be determined by Indigenous communities. Instead, we consistently hear community members expressing a feeling of having to work on other people's terms and that Indigenous communities continually have to "prove" their inherent rights. As one Matawa member said, "we're always proving to the government that we have a footprint on the land. It should be changed around. It should be the government proving it".[27]

Community members across both cases have also reflected on some of the industry and government strategies used. For example, some people discussed the fear of indirect forms of intimidation, such as their communities feeling pressured to make a decision. They also discuss the community division that can occur when communities are not given adequate time to reach consensus using their own traditional decision-making processes:

> The miners came to change our lives; they came to impose another way of life on us, so there is a lot of division.
>
> (Atacama region)

26 *Mining Amendment Act, 2009*, SO 2009, c 21 – Bill 173.

27 Focus Group conducted by Mitchell et al. during the FPIC Conference held at the Matawa First Nations Management Office in Thunder Bay, Ontario, Canada, on 27 October 2016.

> Divide and conquer tactics . . . so they are trying to diffuse our unity and strength, but I think that we maintain the original principles . . . but that is why the laws are different. Their ideology is different, our ideology is sharing.
>
> (Matawa region)

Environmental impacts

Indigenous Peoples have an inherent right and responsibility to make decisions about their lands and to make decisions that will protect their territories to sustain them for future generations. Communities have an intimate knowledge of their territories and despite companies coming in and saying that "environmental impacts will be mitigated", community members have already observed the harmful impacts of development, even at early stages of exploration. In both regions, communities have observed changes to the water and fish as a result of past development:

> [The mining company] tell us a beautiful story; they tell us that the water will not be dirty, but the valley is already dry. The little water that exists is for the vineyards and for the miners. The vineyards poison the water.
>
> (Atacama region)

> It's all going to change from the way we live now. You won't be able to eat the fish in about five, six years. Right now, it's starting. They don't even have sturgeon running in the rivers anymore because of the dams that are blocking the rivers.
>
> (Matawa region)

The economic model of development that is framed by Western governments and industries does not adequately consider the inherent relationship and duty to protect the environment that is so fundamental to the social, cultural, physical, and spiritual wellbeing of Indigenous communities:

> To be Huasco Altino means to defend the earth.
>
> (Atacama region)

> We told the industry and the government that they have to come to the table because our land, resources, water and trees are sacred and clean. It seems like they never wanted to learn to understand that . . . that is our livelihood, where we came from.
>
> (Matawa region)

The cultural responsibility to take care of the territory and to honour the sacredness of the living world is a critical point central to Indigenous law. This is not an echoing of a simple cultural anecdote; this philosophy is part of Indigenous Peoples' way of being. These ways of knowing and understanding the world and Indigenous Peoples' relationship to their environment is how Indigenous Peoples have lived since time immemorial. Indigenous laws are what have guided and constructed Indigenous societies, ceremonies, and civilizations and which are related to specific roles, duties, and obligations for members of an Indigenous society. Honouring, respecting, and protecting the land for future generations to enjoy is one of those laws. Indigenous people will never look at their resource-rich lands and think about its economic value alone.

Responsibilities of states and industries

The analysis of community data was based on the United Nations Guiding Principles on Business and Human Rights,[28] which acknowledges that both states and businesses have a responsibility regarding human rights. We reflect on the interpretation of UN treaty bodies that say states have human rights obligations to pursue not only within their borders but also outside their borders (i.e. extra-territorial obligations of the state). Both the Chilean and the Canadian states have fostered investment in mining through trade agreements. This emerging issue is a new expression of colonialism. Chile was the first country in Latin America to sign a free trade agreement with Canada after the North American Free Trade Agreement (NAFTA, originally signed in 1996 and recently renewed in 2017). Now, they are both signatories of the new TPP-11. Both states are responsible for the huge influx of investment in Chile of Canadian mining corporations. These trade agreements were never assessed from a human rights perspective, despite the United Nations recommendation that states implement human rights assessments of the implications of trade agreements. Although Chile ratified Convention 169, the country has been reluctant to comply to this international standard, particularly the principles of FPIC. The state of Chile never demarcated and has not respected rights of property based on registered lands or on rights of traditional occupancy of the lands (which in the Canadian context is known as Aboriginal title). The Canadian government has said it is responsible for fostering these investments; however, Canada has been reluctant to follow reparations as outlined by the UN treaty bodies to make Canadian businesses operating abroad responsible for human rights grievances and violations. Businesses are responsible when they have not done their due diligence to operate on Indigenous lands. Industrial proponents are responsible for not acknowledging and for not respecting the representative Indigenous organizations – by manipulating and generating new municipalities in order to bypass the Indigenous groups that have opposed them or seeking contracts with individual communities that are otherwise part of a regional group with a unity agreement.

28 Office of the High Commissioner for Human Rights, "Guiding Principles on Business and Human Rights: Implementing the United Nations 'Protect, Respect, and Remedy' Framework" (2011), online (pdf): *United Nations Global Compact* <www.unglobalcompact.org/library/2>.

Decolonial approaches to consultation and FPIC: an intercultural perspective

Decolonialism is about relationship. For Indigenous Peoples, it has been about remembering and reclaiming Indigeneity while actively resisting colonial relations. We have witnessed this in our work with Indigenous Peoples across our case study sites. Indigenous Peoples are seeking the freedom and support to be Indigenous – to reclaim and celebrate their Indigeneity; to relearn their languages; to engage more in fishing, hunting, sewing traditional garments; to engage in more out-on-the-land programs; and to seek ways to bring youth and Elders together again. Indigenous Peoples are in a time of reclaiming and restoring culture and well-being. Some communities talk about this time of reclaiming and restoration as healing.

Colonial trauma has disrupted Indigenous families for generations.[29] It will take time to restore, rebuild, and strengthen communities. When we speak about decolonizing, it includes Indigenous processes of reclaiming and restoring Indigenous Peoples' well-being. This involves returning to traditional ways of knowing and recognizing that traditional knowledge and ways of knowing are just as relevant today, if not more, as Indigenous Peoples' work to strengthen and rebuild the well-being of their communities and families. An Indigenous cosmology is what many Indigenous Nations refer to as their "original instructions", part of Indigenous legal traditions.[30]

As elsewhere, however, Indigenous Peoples in Canada have been positioned as "standing in the way of progress", while being disproportionately and negatively affected by industrial processes.[31] Increasing conflict has arisen due to a second wave of colonialism in the form of extractivist imperialism, in which governments and industries seek gold, silver, uranium, iron ore, copper, chromite, and other resources from Indigenous territories domestically and abroad.[32]

Contemporary colonial expressions emerge as extractivist imperialist business ventures which are tremendously persistent, pernicious, and threatening to Indigenous communities globally. Extractivist imperialism is generated and sustained by global capital, where basic rights are now traded for land and resources. The current era of extractive imperialism undermines the very existence and reality of Indigenous law and is currently upheld by Canadian state law and business practices. Canadian industries are affecting Indigenous territories across Canada and around the globe. Indigenous self-determination is further undermined as

29 Terry Mitchell & Dawn Maracle, "Healing the Generations: Post-Traumatic Stress and the Health Status of the Canadian Aboriginal Population" (2005) 1:2 *Journal of Aboriginal Health* 14.

30 John Borrows, "Indigenous Legal Traditions" (2005) *Journal of Law and Policy* 19.; Michael Coyle, "Indigenous Legal Orders in Canada: A Literature Review" (2017) 92 *Law Publications* 1.

31 Blaser, Fleit & McRae, *supra* note 17.

32 Veltmeyer, 2012 *supra* note 14.

national governments sign new global economic treaties such as the TPP, which Canada recently signed.

Extractivist imperialism is a contemporary form of settler colonialism that further displaces Indigenous Peoples from their lands and territories and traditional lifeways. Extractive industries engage in colonial forms of dispossession and displacement. For example, significant to this new era of extractive imperialism is the environmental degradation, denuding, and polluting of Indigenous territories. This displacement and dispossession of land and culture is grossly expressed by extractive industries within both Canada and Latin America. Current practices of mineral exploration and extractivism are premised upon a profound disregard of Indigenous values, views, and laws as confirmed by our community observations and interviews in Chile and Canada. In both cases, we observed that there is persistence of colonialism in the imposition of Western law and Western models of development and, as a result, expectations for consultation and FPIC are not being realized from either the perspective of Indigenous communities or the standard of the Canadian Supreme Court.

In our work, we have observed that many Indigenous leadership and community members are often unaware of international and domestic rights standards that could be applied in asserting their existing inherent and treaty rights and those rights protected under domestic and international rights frameworks. For many Indigenous People, a significant amount of their time, energy, and resources is spent responding to immediate issues and community concerns such as attending to housing crises, substandard healthcare, and education. The privilege of examining, learning, and exploring how to use domestic and international law in asserting their Indigenous rights is not always feasible.

The Diaguita peoples have, however, engaged in various strategies of resistance. They have reported that they need to challenge global investments and that it is difficult to do this at a local level. They took their case, therefore, to the Inter-American human rights system as well as the UN human rights system. They established partnerships with the Canadian Network of Corporate Accountability to bring their claims to the attention of Canada's Global Affairs and to build alliances with civil society organizations. The Matawa First Nations communities have also resisted ongoing pressures and have successfully asserted their rights to self-determined development. One example of this is Neskantaga First Nation's refusal to adhere to the controversial *Far North Act*[33] – provincial legislation that regulates land-use planning and protected areas – choosing to establish their own community protocols. Another example is Eabametoong First Nation successfully halting an exploration permit issued to Landore Resources that would allow drilling on their traditional territory. The decision of the Ontario Superior Court of Justice Divisional Court determined that the Ministry of Northern Development and Mines did not meet their constitutional duty to consult when issuing a permit to the mining company, citing the community's unfulfilled expectations

33 *Far North Act*, *supra* note 22.

of further engagement and desire to develop a memorandum of understanding in advance of exploration.[34]

Implementing UNDRIP, and FPIC in particular, means going beyond the predominant understanding of consultation and participation in resource management, requiring policy frameworks that emerge from intercultural engagement with Indigenous worldviews and ancestral connections to the land from which these rights emerge.[35] In the case of Canada, such engagement must also be closely linked to interpretation of Indigenous and treaty rights protected by section 35 of the Canadian Constitution.[36] These conversations reach beyond simply FPIC; they are discussions of true self-determination and, in the context of extraction, it is a matter of self-determined development.

Canada's extraterritorial obligations on human rights

In recent years, international human rights law has affirmed that states have extraterritorial obligations[37] and that states should take all possible measures to support human rights. In the context of globalization, this means that states have to prevent and redress human rights violations committed outside their borders by private domestic actors, such as mining corporations. This is a very sensitive issue for Canada, a country that plays a significant role in extractive investments internationally, and particularly in Latin America. According to the Working Group on Mining and Human Rights in Latin America[38] on the impact of Canadian mining in Latin America, 57% of mining companies at a global level were listed on the Toronto Stock Exchange by 2012. Out of the 4,322 projects carried out by these companies outside Canadian borders, 1,526 were in Latin America. By 2013, the Latin American countries where Canadian companies were the most active were Mexico ($20 billion) and Chile ($19 billion). The Canada Brand Report identified incidents involving 28 Canadian companies during the years 2000–2015, which resulted in 44 deaths, 403 injuries, and 709 cases of "criminalization" (e.g. legal complaints, arrests, detentions, and charges) in Latin America.[39]

34 Thomas Isaac & Arend JA Hoekstra, "Proponents and Government Compromise Consultation under Ontario's Mining Act in Eabametoong First Nation v Minister of Northern Development and Mines" (25 July 2018), online: *Cassels Brock Lawyers* <https://cassels.com/insights/proponents-and-government-compromise-consultation-under-ontarioa%C2%A2a%C2%ACa%C2%A2s-mining-act-in-eabametoong-first-nation-v-minister-of-northern-development-and-mines/>.

35 Marie Battise, *Reclaiming Indigenous Voice and Vision* (Vancouver: UBC Press, 2011); B. Fry & Terry Mitchell, "Towards Coexistence: Exploring the Differences between Indigenous and Non-Indigenous Perspectives on Land" (2016) 23 *Native Studies Review* 35.

36 James Youngblood Henderson, *Indigenous Diplomacy and the Rights of Indigenous Peoples: Achieving UN Recognition* (Vancouver: Purich, 2008).

37 Meghna Abraham et al., "Maastricht Principles on Extraterritorial Obligations of States in the Area of Economic, Social and Cultural Rights" (2011) 29:4 *Nethl QHR* 578.

38 *Supra* note 13.

39 Shin Imai, Leah Gardner & Sarah Weinberger, "The 'Canada Brand': Violence and Canadian Mining Companies in Latin America" (2016) *Osgoode Hall Law School Working Paper Justice and Corporate Accountability Project*.

Various United Nations human rights treaty bodies have observed the failure of Canada to prevent and redress these human rights violations.[40] Canada has failed to accept the recommendations that these treaty bodies have made in urging the government to adopt administrative legislative measures and policies to meet its extraterritorial obligations regarding the violation of human rights by companies domiciled in Canada acting outside that country, and to prevent, redress, and penalize such violations. The Inter-American Commission on Human Rights has had three hearings on the accountability of Canadian mining companies and has called on Canada to adopt measures to prevent multiple human rights violations.[41]

Until recently, Canada did not address the complaints of the affected communities and civil society organizations and their concerns about the detrimental impact of these mining projects on human rights. Canada has in fact continued to foster these investments through the functions of Export Development Canada, trade agreements, and diplomacy. Two initiatives currently promoted in Canada provide some hope that there could be a change in this state pattern of violating the rights of Indigenous Peoples nationally and internationally. One initiative is the Trudeau government's creation of the Canadian Ombudsperson for Responsible Enterprise (CORE),[42] whose mandate is to address complaints related to allegations of human rights abuses arising from a Canadian company's activity abroad. The CORE will undertake collaborative and independent fact-finding, make recommendations, monitor implementation of those recommendations, and report publicly throughout the process.[43] The other initiative is the preliminary approval in June 2018 of Bill C-262, *An Act to Ensure That the Laws of Canada Are in Harmony with the United Nations Declaration on the Rights of Indigenous Peoples*, promoted by the Cree MP Romeo Saganash.[44] The Bill acknowledged the need for full application of the UNDRIP in Canada without qualification. The approval and implementation of these initiatives would contribute substantially to the implementation of UNDRIP, including the principles of FPIC, both in Canada and abroad, in regions such as Latin America where Indigenous Peoples are significantly impacted by Canadian extractive enterprises.

40 UN Committee on the Elimination of Racism, *Concluding Observations on the 21st to 23rd Periodic Reports of Canada: Committee on the Elimination of Racial Discrimination: Draft / Prepared by the Country Rapporteur*, CERDOR, 2017, C/CAN/CO/21–23.

41 Imai, Gardner & Weinberger, *supra* note 39; Inter-American Court Human Rights, "Human Rights, Indigenous Rights and Canada's Extraterritorial Obligations: Thematic Hearing for the 153rd Session of the Inter-American Commission on Human Rights" (2014), online: <https://justice-project.org/wp-content/uploads/2017/07/canada-mining-cidh-oct-28-2014-final-2.pdf>.

42 Global Affairs Canada, "The Government of Canada Brings Leadership to Responsible Business Conduct Abroad" (17 January 2017), online: *Government of Canada* <www.canada.ca/en/global-affairs/news/2018/01/the_government_ofcanadabringsleadershiptoresponsible businesscond.html>.

43 *Ibid.*

44 Bill C-262, *An Act to Ensure That the Laws of Canada Are in Harmony with the United Nations Declaration on the Rights of Indigenous Peoples*, 1st Sess, 42th Parl, 2018 (third reading 30 May 2018) [Govt. of Canada, 2018b].

Policy recommendations

To conclude this chapter, we would like to offer our policy-related reflections for the advancement of FPIC and the monitoring of Indigenous rights in Canadian mining activities across the Americas, with attention to host countries of mining investments, such as Chile. Despite a succession of Supreme Court of Canada rulings in favour of Indigenous Peoples and their land rights, Indigenous Peoples are still unable to enjoy their rights to self-determination and self-determined development. We continue to observe that Indigenous Peoples in Canada have to enter into the Canadian legal system, often with protracted efforts of 10 years or more,[45] to assert their basic rights and to defend their Indigenous laws and jurisdiction over their traditional territories. Indigenous Peoples' inherent rights continue to be violated and Indigenous Peoples are forced to spend their time in state courts defending the inherent and treaty rights and those rights now outlined in the UNDRIP, such as FPIC.

We are, however, at a juncture with the growing internationalization of Indigenous rights and domestically, within Canada, the Truth and Reconciliation Calls to Action[46] and the federal government's current rhetoric of the full implementation of UNDRIP without qualification. Romeo Saganash's Private Member Bill C-262 to harmonize UNDRIP with Canadian law was a promising step forward; however, the ultimate failure of the bill is indicative of the significant work that will be required to redress and align Canadian laws and policies across diverse contexts. Importantly, this political opportunity is premised upon the acknowledgement that reconciliation is contingent upon the full recognition and respect of Indigenous ontologies and Indigenous laws. Challenges faced by Chile regarding mineral activity on Indigenous lands and territories have also been highlighted. The right to FPIC, including consultation and the full recognition of Indigenous rights to define priorities in their own development, must be acknowledged in extraterritorial relations. Human rights impact assessment of mining projects, both in the context of free trade agreements that facilitate Canadian mining investments in Chile, as well as of specific mining projects, are needed.

The demand for lands and resources on Indigenous territories is not going to go away. Indigenous Peoples occupy 24% of the world's land mass and territories that hold 80% of the world's biodiversity.[47] A strategy is needed to ensure stronger rights recognition to support Indigenous communities that are faced

45 *Attorney General of Quebec v Moses*, 2010 SCC 17; *Tsilhqot'in Nation v British Columbia*, 2014 SCC 44.

46 Truth and Reconciliation Commission of Canada, "Truth and Reconciliation Commission of Canada: Calls to Action" (2015), online (pdf): <www.trc.ca/websites/trcinstitution/File/2015/Findings/Calls_to_Action_English2.pdf>.

47 World Bank, "The Role of Indigenous Peoples in Biodiversity Conservation: The Natural but often Forgotten Partners, Written by Claudia Sobrevila" (2008), online: *World Bank* <https://siteresources.worldbank.org/INTBIODIVERSITY/Resources/RoleofIndigenousPeoplesinBiodiversityConservation.pdf>.

with this ongoing demand. If the traditional territories of Indigenous Peoples are destroyed, their rights to land and livelihood and their right to practice and preserve their cultures for future generations are violated. Proponents of extractivism, governments, and industry fail to adequately consider these rights from an Indigenous perspective, in particular through the lens of Indigenous legal systems and traditions. Extractivism is founded on capitalist logic with attention to Western views of economics. For the right to FPIC to be fulfilled, an Indigenous lens must be included in current processes. The realization of the potential of the UNDRIP, and the fulfillment of the principles of FPIC, will require a deep and respectful understanding of Indigenous laws and their meaning and practice in the intersection of proposed development and community consultation and decision-making.

The UN Declaration is the minimum standard for the recognition of Indigenous Peoples' inherent right to self-determination. For Indigenous Peoples' full human rights to be recognized, Indigenous Peoples must be at the table. Indigenous Peoples must be consulted early and often, at every stage of proposed development. FPIC must be considered as the norm. Indigenous Peoples must not just be invited to meetings or consultations; Indigenous Peoples and Indigenous voices must have legitimate power in decision-making processes. This will require innovative intercultural approaches that challenge the capitalist logic of extractivist imperialism in recognizing and applying Indigenous law and rights frameworks to self-determined development.

Summary

Over the last decade there has been a growing internationalization of Indigenous rights emerging in tandem with growing global pressure of extractivism on Indigenous lands. Canada, as one of the largest players in global mining and forestry, is called upon to examine its performance in implementing UNDRIP and observing Indigenous rights to FPIC in communities affected by Canadian extractivism. In this chapter, we provided a brief commentary on two case studies, which highlighted the Pan-American comparatives of industry processes and impacts. Based on our case study observations, we have identified strong parallels of rights violations and the challenges to the enjoyment of the rights to FPIC and self-determined development. Despite the variance in political structures, economic and social realities, and the cultural and geographic distinctions between the Indigenous communities in a region of northern Chile and a region of the far north of Ontario, Canada, we observed parallel issues of (1) a lack of consultation and information; (2) inducement and division; and (3) environmental impacts.

Indigenous law and respect for, and protection of, cultural lifeways are violated both in Canada and Chile through consistent failure of states and industry to appropriately consult with Indigenous leadership; through their failure to respect Indigenous community norms and Indigenous visions of self-determined development; and their consistent failure to implement, in good faith, international Indigenous rights standards such as UNDRIP and ILO Convention 169.

As Canada comes under increasing international scrutiny from the United Nations and human rights organizations, further research needs to be conducted to monitor the potentially promising impact of the Calls to Action of the Canadian Truth and Reconciliation Commission, the fledgling efforts to harmonize Canadian law with UNDRIP, and the formation of CORE. During this period of reconciliation, there is a strong need for a broader and deeper intercultural understanding of Indigenous rights from the perspective of Indigenous Peoples and Indigenous law to advance self-determined development and the regulation of extractivism within an Indigenous rights framework.

Decolonizing through Indigenous worldviews

11 Decolonizing corrections

Beverley Jacobs, Yvonne Johnson and Joey Twins

Introduction

Decolonizing corrections means that there is a complete transformative change of the criminal legal system called corrections – a foreign colonial prison system forced upon Indigenous peoples.[1] Indigenous peoples, and specifically Indigenous women, have borne the brunt of this system where we now see the highest statistics of Indigenous women in this system which "exemplifies Canada's racist legacy of colonization."[2]

The female Indigenous population is only 5% in Canada, but 38% of Indigenous women make up the female federal prison population, and Indigenous women make up more than 50% of the federal prison population in the Pacific and Prairie Regions.[3] Indigenous girls represent 6% of the Canadian girls' population, but 44% were Indigenous girls in custody in 2008–2009.[4] Indigenous girls are the fastest growing population in youth custody.[5] As noted by Patricia Monture-Angus:

> In 2000, Aboriginal women comprised 23% of the federal prison population when Aboriginal peoples made up only 2.8% of the general Canadian

1 As noted by Patricia Monture, "Our Peoples, as Nations, Have Never Consented to the Application of Euro-Canadian Legal Systems and the Corresponding Values" Patricia A. Monture, "Chapter II: The Voices of Aboriginal People" in *Creating Choices: Task Force on Federally Sentenced Women* (Canada: Task Force on Federally Sentenced Women, 1990) at 20. Also found online: <www.csc-scc.gc.ca/women/choice3e-eng.shtml>.

2 Native Women's Association of Canada, *Indigenous Women in Solitary Confinement: Policy Backgrounder* (Ottawa, ON: Native Women's Association of Canada, 2017), online: <www.nwac.ca/wp-content/uploads/2017/07/NWAC-Indigenous-Women-in-Solitary-Confinement-Aug-22.pdf>.

3 Canada. House of Commons. "A Call to Action: Reconciliation with Indigenous Women in the Federal Justice and Correctional Systems. Report of the Standing Committee on the Status of Women", online: <http://publications.gc.ca/collections/collection_2018/parl/xc71-1/XC71-1-1-421-13-eng.pdf>.

4 Statistics Canada. *Youth Custody and Community Services in Canada, 2008/2009*. Donna Calverley, Adam Cotter & Ed Halla (eds.), Statistics Canada catalogue no. 85–002-X. (Ottawa, ON: Government of Canada, 2010) at p. 14.

5 Native Women's Association of Canada, *Arresting the Legacy*, booklet, 11.

> population. . . . This over-representation has been steadily rising since the Task Force on Federally Sentenced Women reported in 1990. Then, Aboriginal women comprised 15% of the federal prisoners.[6]

The steady increase has not stopped. In only 10 years, the number of incarcerated Indigenous women in federal custody increased by 76.4%. In 2005–2006, there were 140 incarcerated Indigenous women compared to 247 in 2015–2016.[7] The United Nations Special Rapporteur on Violence against women, its causes and consequences provided a more grotesque statistic in a 10-year span: "Between 2001–2002 and 2011–2012, the incarcerated Indigenous population has increased by 37.3%, while incarcerated Indigenous women have increased by 109%."[8] This is disgusting.

Of Indigenous women who do end up inside, 42% of them end up being classified as maximum security.[9] As a result, they are not able to access programs and services to assist in their rehabilitation. Fifty percent of those inside are Indigenous women serving time in segregation/solitary confinement.[10] Solitary confinement and segregation are documented as human rights violations,[11] and yet it is Indigenous women who continue to suffer this inhumane treatment inside prison walls.

These statistics demonstrate that the system is in further decline. In 1990, almost 30 years ago, two Indigenous women, Lana Fox and Fran Sugar, addressed their experiences in prison during the Task Force on Federally Sentenced Women as follows:

> We have often said that the women inside have the understanding to help themselves, that all that is required is the right kind of resources, support and help. The money spent on studies would be much better spent on family visits, on culturally appropriate help, on reducing our powerlessness to heal ourselves. But the reality is that prison conditions grow worse. We cry out for a meaningful healing process that will have real impact on our lives, but the objectives and implementation of this healing process must be premised on our need to heal and walk in balance.[12]

6 Patricia Monture-Angus, *The Lived Experience of Discrimination: Aboriginal Women Who Are Federally Sentenced* (Ottawa, ON: Canadian Association of Elizabeth Fry Societies, 2002) at 1.

7 Canada. Department of Justice, "Just Facts: Trends in Adult Federal Custody Populations" online: <www.justice.gc.ca/eng/rp-pr/jr/jf-pf/2018/march01.html>.

8 Dubravka Simonovic, United Nations Special Rapporteur on Violence against Women, Its Causes and Consequences, "End of Mission Statement – Official Visit to Canada" (23 April 2018), online: <www.ohchr.org/EN/NewsEvents/Pages/DisplayNews.aspx?NewsID=22981&LangID=E>.

9 Howard Sapers, "Annual Report of the Office of the Correctional Investigator 2015–2016."

10 *Ibid.*

11 Debra Parkes, "Solitary Confinement, Prisoner Litigation, and the Possibility of a Prison Abolitionist Lawyering Ethic" (2017) 32:2 *CJLS* 165.

12 Fran Sugar and Lana Fox, *Survey of Federally Sentenced Women in the Community* (Ottawa, ON: Task Force on Federally Sentenced Women, 1990).

In 1999, Patricia Monture-Angus noted that since 1990, the year the Task Force on Federally Sentenced Women (TFFSW) reported, "further evidence was accumulated, such as the Arbour Inquiry, which demonstrates . . . that things have gotten worse for all federally sentenced women including Aboriginal women."[13] Things are beyond worse today, almost 30 years since TFFSW and 23 years since the Arbour Inquiry.

This chapter focuses on the experiences of two Indigenous women who were incarcerated at the same time as Lana Fox and Fran Sugar. Yvonne Johnson and Joey Twins share their experiences of how prison conditions continue to grow beyond worse. They have survived in a very dehumanized system that in many instances results in brutal human rights violations wherein the public is completely unaware of what happens inside jails.

Prior to colonization, Indigenous peoples did not have a prison system. Without consent or conquest, Indigenous peoples have been forced into a Eurocentric criminal legal system with foreign principles of conflict and punishment. I am not saying that Indigenous peoples did not have conflict. Humanness and conflict are inevitable, but Indigenous peoples had ways and means of addressing conflict according to their sources of Indigenous laws. Indigenous laws are about balance in all of creation and amongst human beings. Indigenous peoples, through the practice of Indigenous laws, had a way of understanding someone who may have missed something, a teaching or a purpose that had been missed in their teachings which may have caused harm to someone else for some reason. To utilize an Indigenous conflict system goes directly to the core of that and to understand why a person would want to cause harm to someone else. Starting with that, it was about an imbalance if something was out of place or if something was done wrong. There was always ceremony, for example, that brought Indigenous peoples back to their original life path.

The stories of experiential Indigenous women

During my previous life as president of the Native Women's Association of Canada, I met many powerful Indigenous women who ended up in confined cages and spaces. I saw their power and their resilience from experiences of being traumatized on the outside before they ended up in prison but even more so when they end up inside. In knowing about Yvonne and Joey's stories of their lives in jail, I have always been angry about the internal processes and human rights violations that occur on the inside. It is unbelievable what Corrections Canada gets away with inside.

Yvonne Johnson and Joey Twins are two *nehiyaw* (Cree) women whom I met along my path when they were serving life sentences in federal prisons and now

13 Patricia Monture-Angus, "Aboriginal Women and Correctional Practice: Reflections on the Task Force on Federally Sentenced Women" in Kelly Hannah-Moffatt and Margaret Shaw, eds., *An Ideal Prison? Critical Essays on Women's Imprisonment in Canada* (Halifax: Fernwood, 2000) at 58.

they are both on parole and leading healthy lives. I call Yvonne and Joey survivors of the colonial prison system because they both have been able to get out of the system: Yvonne was sentenced to life in prison with 25 years to apply for parole and Joey was sentenced to life with 10 years to apply for parole. Yvonne came out to look after her grandchildren. They both impressed me at how brilliant they are. I call them my friends today. I invited them to participate in the Decolonizing Law conference,[14] of which this publication is a result. Their powerful words need to be reiterated here because they experienced firsthand the colonial prison system and offered the best solutions to decolonizing corrections. The following sets out their experiences, which are edited transcriptions of their presentations at the conference.

Yvonne Johnson

I was born and raised in Montana until I was 16 years old. My father was an American of Norwegian descent and an ex-Marine. My mother was Cree from Red Pheasant Reserve in Saskatchewan. Sadly, she passed away on March 24th of 2018. I am of the Red Race, of the Cree Nation, of the human being. I like to acknowledge all the ancestors, the spirits, and the helpers. I would like to acknowledge my friends Bev, Joey, and all others that are present that I may know or not know.

When I was in the United States, the first time I ever hit jail I was six years old. In the jails down there, the toilet was a hole in the floor and a trough with running water through it, and the bed was steel frame with chain link to lay on. If they wanted to be extra mean, they took the mattress out. It was a real old city jail.

In 1971, my brother was killed in Butte County Jail when he was 19 years old. They claimed my brother was stoned out of his mind and admitted to being high, when he was to have committed an act that ended his life. My mother and father fought for a coroner's inquest. Their finding showed no drugs in his system. Self-inflicted death still stood as cause of death. Mom was not going to let them get away with killing her son and passing it off as suicide in the jail. Apparently, my brother was not the only one the police were to have killed. Mother wrote letters all the way up the line, with no support or acknowledgement of brother's death. Then they closed Butte jail.

My mother became the first woman truck driver in an open pit mine in Butte, Montana so that she could feed her kids. She said she was going to get trained for a man's job with a man's pay. She was to become the first woman in the Teamsters' Union, one of the toughest unions there was in 1972.

Mother bought a car and headed out to Wounded Knee, answering the call from the American Indian Movement (AIM). She went on and traveled with Dennis

14 Beverly Jacobs, Yvonne Johnson and Joey Twins, "Indigenous Women and Incarceration" (Decolonizing Law? Methods, Tactics, Strategies delivered at the Art Gallery of Windsor, 3 April 2018) [unpublished].

Banks and Russell Means. She was part of the caravan of broken treaties. She was almost shot in the standoff at the church in Wounded Knee. She was a cook, and the man that walked in front of her when she was cooking got shot in the chest and was killed instantly. She ended up in Washington, DC, when President Nixon got voted in. AIM at that time dissipated.

My mom came back to Montana, and she advised my father she wanted to move back to her peoples. Mom said she could not handle living in Butte anymore. Dad refused to come into Canada, so they divorced. She loaded us kids up and we went with her back to her reserve, to Red Pheasant Reserve, Saskatchewan. My mom married a white man, so they alienated us on the reserve and did not give us any support of any kind. We did not get Christmas gifts at Christmas time. We had to pay for all our firewood, haul our own water. Good thing Grampa was a good hunter.

My grandmother gave us use of her home and we lived on Red Pheasant for quite a few years. There was no running water. We would get itchy and sore between the legs from having to drink still water (sough water). All of us kids got severe diarrhea. We had no car, so we used an old car hood as a sled and pulled it by horse. We opened up an old oil drum with an ax and made sure any sharp pieces were curved back so as not to get stabbed or sliced on the metal. We walked the horse into the water and used a cloth to strain the buckets of water we took from what they say was a lake but it was a sough. We got sick but mom said we would get used to it and we did. At least in 1972 Gramma's house had electricity. We had a wood cookstove and heated and cooked by firewood. My grandparents lived next to us in an old school bus they used to live in with a wood cookstove inside.

I'm told my great-grandmother lived to be 116. She passed in 1976, the same year the United States celebrated being two hundred years old. She was free before they created reserves in Canada and then she was put on reserve. The government and churches moved in and started controlling and dominating everything. Prisons of grass, imprisoned by invisible walls, where the warden was the Indian Agent, the guards were NWMP, then RCMP, then city police. Reserves ran like prisons. They stole the children and would not allow persons off reserve without written consent by the Indian Agent. No native was allowed off reserve to seek education. They had to be granted work release passes for seasonal jobs, usually called Indian jobs like cleaning farms lands called rock pickers, fence builders, bailing hay, sugar beating, etc. Once all the wild game on reserve was gone, Grampa would sit for days and wait for the game to cross the line to feed his family. If the police were informed that we had wild meat, they would confiscate it. We would have to hide it in the bush when we knew they were coming. Persons were rewarded for ratting on others to gain favours or more funding from the Indian Agent. Grampa would leave the reserve if he found work, but the Indian Agent demanded his slice of his pay.

My great-grandfather was Chief Big Bear. He was hung in North Battleford in the so-called retribution of the Frog Lake Massacre. They took all the native peoples from reserves around the area and kids out of the local residential schools and they made them go into town and watch as they hung my relations out there. Big Bear's descendants. Big Bear's people. The kids cried and suffered and they told them over and over "this is what is going to happen to you." They went back into residential school and many were killed there too. Many of them didn't come out.

They started the "Wheat Trade" in Saskatchewan where they wouldn't allow native people to have anything but basic farm implements so they wouldn't be able to self-sustain themselves. My grandfather used to sneak off reserve to go hunting. There was nothing on reserve for them to be able to hunt to eat so they starved them. Work them one day then they starve them three days. Same thing inside the federal prisons.

Mother was born in a tent on the reserve. They didn't report her to the Indian agent because at that time they were stealing the children. My grandmother took my mom to be baptized when she was 4 or 5 and a report was put in by the church to the police. They came to kidnap her and all her siblings that came behind her and put her in the Dumas/Thunder Bird residential school. They kept her there till she aged out at 16 years of age. She tried to run away from school but was deceived by farmers who offered to feed them, just to be picked up by RCMP and taken back to school. She ran because a priest tried to rape her. She ran only to be returned to the very priest who attempted to rape her and actually beat her unconscious where others were made to watch and bear witness.

I brought my mother home to die amongst family rather than in a hospital or care facility. One day, I bathed my mother before she passed on and when I rolled her over, I saw the scars on her buttocks that the priest gave her at residential school for attempting to run away. The pain, hurt and suffering she went through which was most likely the reason why she married my white father. She was no longer an Indian that anyone can do anything to. She went back and took all her younger siblings out of residential school, all four of them. Now the next challenge mother had to face was not losing her children into the child welfare system. It is just like a cow and the butchers. As soon as the baby cow drops, they scoop it, cut it up and sell it. In essence, that is what they do to native people and their children in child services.

My mom was beaten for speaking Cree. Yet, now in 2018, I am sitting on the city transit bus, with a lot of people from other countries and they were speaking their language freely. I sat on the bus and cried because I don't even know my own tongue. They don't know how lucky or blessed they are to be able to come here as free citizens while native peoples are not in their own country.

I got arrested. I believe and I will go to my death saying this: it was really highly politically charged then and it still is. In the end, I got sentenced to life, 25. The other man who stood trial with me, and who had all the evidence against him stood trial with me. Same court room, same jury, same evidence – the jury came back with second degree on him and first degree on me. He got life, 10 and I got life, 25. All circumstantial evidence other than a witness statement by my own cousin who made many different statements and whom the Crown got her to say just what they did. Just for the sake of mentioning, there were at least three other murder case convictions, none for first degree though, Lighting case, Blue Horn Case and Omeasso Case – all over turned because they found their one eyewitness in all these cases came forward after saying they were being manipulated by Crown to give evidence as they had. I made history first, first degree-conviction of a native woman. I lost hope in my witness ever coming forward to clear me as she is dead now.

There were statements made in court like "these people, they are not like us." Those were the exact words they said. He turned around and said "Yvonne has had a lifetime of sexual abuse, therefore she took it upon herself to become a vigilante and slay a man she believed was a child molester." I never knew this man to be a child molester. The police did and my other co-accused did. I never knew for fact until I actually had a victim reconciliation and I heard it from their voice. A confirmation that I had to sit in prison 25 years for.

I got sentenced on March 20, 1991. I sat for 30 days to launch an appeal, and eventually, I was denied an appeal. I was sent to Prison for Women (P4W). I tried to stay in the province because that's where my kids were. My request to stay in Province was denied. A Placement Officer said, "The only place you are going is Kingston Prison for Women. This is the only place you will be housed because of the severity of your crime. I have your file right here." He opened it and all that was there were newspaper clippings of my conviction, a transfer warrant, and pen placement order for P4W. He also said, "you are sentenced to life and life you shall serve till you die," and this does happen as I saw women die of cancer in there. I hit there April 25, 1991. That's where it took me a while to get my groundings to try and fight for an appeal. I never did make it to the Supreme Court because they were saying I was in P4W and not eligible for representation of a lawyer in Alberta via Alberta Legal Aid. I was now officially a resident in Ontario. When I tried to get a lawyer and get legal aid to pay for a lawyer in Ontario, I couldn't find one that was legally entitled to work in Alberta. I knew that was it. I definitely got officially screwed again. I let my lawyer go as I felt he did not represent me to the fullest he was capable of as he failed at trial and again at the appeal.

A lot of things were happening in the prison at the time. There were repercussions from the large numbers of suicides and the riot as well as the taking of CSC to court over the deaths and everything going on within the prison. There was a mention of closing P4W and replacing it with five regional female prisons across Canada. I affiliated with the Native Women's Association of Canada (NWAC) at that time. We sat down with Sharon McIvor, Kim Pate and Patricia Monture at that time and we fought for the new prisons to be built across Canada. At this time, the Commission headed by Justice Louise Arbor was under way as well. Then the first and only Native Women's Healing Lodge was built which would become a federal prison in Saskatchewan along with five others across Canada. That is when I first met Bev. Bev became the chairperson of the NWAC. There were a lot of things happening but basically the justice system is flawed. More than flawed if you read the results of Arbour's Commission Report. There was a call for a total revamping of both native and mainstream justice penal systems for women, or so I was led to believe. You will see the victims that say, "there is no justice for the victims," and then you see the so-called offenders saying "well, the justice is not working. It is warped." If you have everybody on all sides saying the system isn't working or balancing out, then I say go back to the way the native people did it. When I was in court, I wanted so much to get up there and tell them exactly what happened in my perspective. That couldn't be done in court of law the way that it was done.

The question is why are we there and why are we expendable? We are not all hateful, crooked and spiteful. But we will stand to fight. We will fight for a helpless child or a helpless woman when there is nobody there to protect them. How many murdered and missing women do they have to take? Most of our men are in prison because of fighting on the streets.

After my book was published,[15] the same people that got me incarcerated came at me again. They used me to abolish the 15-year review and to press the law that says people who are convicted with an offence are no longer allowed to talk about it or to share it even if it may bring good change to things. Scott Newark showed up at a place where Kim Pate was and walked up to Kim and said, "Yvonne Johnson is never going to get out of prison." He said they were going to be there in the courtroom showing full force. I had to go back to the court in which I was sentenced under. I had to go back to the same judge, the same racist area of Wetaskiwin, and under the same conservative stronghold. I knew that if I walked into that court I might as well walk out and throw myself back at the prison. One thing they were not expecting was that I got a change of venue and it was sent to Edmonton. One of the reasons I was granted a change in venue was because I would have been denied the possibility of a fair and unbiased court proceeding in Wetaskiwin.

The Crown did not want any one on my jury that had any knowledge of my book or had bias against the 15-year review or were racist or bias against native peoples. One jury member was excused because of her hate towards native peoples and was very angry when dismissed. Her final words were "that is ok there are lots more on that jury who also hate Indians." The jury themselves also excused a person who they overheard talking hate while waiting to be called in to the courtroom for possible jury selection. I was blown away by that. When the court was done, the jury unanimously said I could apply for parole. Even though I was granted the possibility to apply for parole did not mean I was actually going to get it granted within this system of Corrections Canada, which is not the same as a court of law.

I was about to get my 15-year parole review. Even the National Parole Board was staffed against me. At that time, I fought for Elders to sit at the parole hearing. They pulled back all the Elders. I fought to have Circle Talks at parole hearings. They pulled that back on me. They stomped all over it. It was a mess. By the time

15 Rudy Wiebe and Yvonne Johnston, *Stolen Life: The Journey of a Cree Woman* (Toronto: First Vintage Canada, 1999).

they left it was called an inquisition. I was granted my 15-year review where I could apply for parole. I was granted possible parole eligibility at my 17th year of sentence but I did not receive day parole for and up to the 20-year mark of my sentence. They kept me in one form or another for 25 years. Twenty years in the main prison system and then another four plus within the halfway house system. In fact, I felt like I served the whole 25-year sentence before I was granted my full parole. Even though I am now out on full parole, I am still serving a life sentence of parole until I literally die. So in all actuality, I am a current serving inmate but doing it in the public sector release with the least amount of security under law. So me and the law are married, I guess, til death do us part. The government shall run DNA testing and fingerprinting on me to make sure I am who I am at death, the government will be the first one to kick the dirt in my grave to make sure I am there. They keep my file active for years afterwards just in case I pop up actually alive somewhere.

When the system started carrying the drum, they were trying to say that native women cannot sit at the drum. In P4W back then, we had a few strong people and leaders like Joey Twins who were there prior to me going there. She taught me strong women songs and many other songs. She taught me how to be strong. She suffered a lot in there but they never broke her. The problem was, with me, they couldn't nail me. Couldn't pin me down. Couldn't segregate me because I would stay 24/7 alone and in my own room. I did not associate with anybody. I did not talk to anybody. I had a few friends that I was around with during sisterhood gatherings.

Joey Twins

I'd like to acknowledge our higher power, the Creator and our sacred medicines our sacred fire, that water, the beautiful water that gives us life, and also acknowledge all the Elders across Turtle Island for all their hard work and accomplishments and all our powerful leaders. I'd like to acknowledge Yvonne, Bev, Myrna and each and every one of you in this room and your families as well. I pray that everything will be good today. It will be an awesome day.

My name is Joey. My Indian name is "Firestone Woman Who Holds The Fire." To translate that in Cree, I wouldn't even know how to begin. No fault of my own. I come from a reserve and back in the 1950s I spoke Cree fluently as that was our main language. After I was 6, I was put in a residential school right on the reserve. I stayed there for two and a half years and then I became part of the '60s scoop into a non-native community in the town of Wrigley, Alberta. From there, I moved to Grande Cache, Alberta. I lived there for a while and then I started running away when I was 13 years old. I went to BC. I started learning that hustle – how to survive as a 13-year-old kid. I didn't feel that I belonged in that home. Even though I had one brother with me, I still didn't belong there.

My mother was murdered when I was seven years old, and to this day nobody has come to justice for that. Why? Because she was a native woman. I come from Cree, Scottish and French ancestry. I acknowledge that Scottish and French descent too because that is who I am. It took me a long time to speak for myself, but I had to because of our sacred laws. I stepped into that prison on June 13, 1979. There was only one women's prison across Canada and that was in Kingston. I came from Alberta. I was only 18 years old and I got life, 10. My circumstances are the result of the injustice of the legal system. I've had two constables that basically wrote all statements against me and because of my past, you know the old school code that you just don't rat out nobody and that in being a snitch you won't survive on the street or inside. So, I stood tall. I was a little kid, 112 pounds, and I went to prison with women. I was scared.

We flew from Edmonton right to P4W in Kingston and then the guards from Kingston Penitentiary (KP) came there and led us up with guns and then marched us in these body belts and shackles. We had to walk like this. You cannot move. I would be like one of the sisters that took their own lives in P4W. I believed that we had to suffer to become strong. I could've been one of those sisters to take my life, but I didn't. I wasn't a cutter. I didn't have a tattoo. I didn't have a cut in my arm. But I learned that behavior inside prison because that's what is the common thing to do. There were 175 cells and wings. If you behave yourself, you can go down to the South Wing and North Wing which had 25 rooms on each side and you had your own key. I'd never been there. Maybe once and then was out that day.

In 1981, I escaped from P4W and I lasted two weeks. I was caught in Saskatoon, Saskatchewan, and I thought, "I am doing a life sentence for something I didn't do. So, I am going to enjoy myself and go out there," and that is what I did. I partied for two weeks because I was going to be doing a life sentence anyway so I thought that I might as well have a good time.

In 1983, I started getting angry emotions. I thought, "Why me?" Then, I thought that I needed to be tough. I needed to be tough to survive. So, I changed my way of thinking and made my spirit to be hard and cold. The guards treated us like garbage so why not act like one. I got very notorious in prison. I did things that I am ashamed of today. But it was all for a reason, for a justifiable cause and, as I was speaking earlier, "harm with harm." I didn't come into prison to harm people. But after being kicked down and kicked around by guards you begin to learn to stand up and defend yourself. I had enough kicks. That's what I felt. I started gaining some weight and muscle, smoking cigarettes, and dipping into drugs to cope. I was never exposed to prisons in my life. I had never done time before. I got life, 10. Being a little kid on the block, I met Shaggy. She was a good friend of mine and still is a good friend. I've never forgotten her or the other sisters. I always acknowledge everyone when I speak because they are a part of my transition to become strong.

In 1984–1985, I took a guard hostage. They put a woman with a charge of killing her child in general population down in a wing. That is unacceptable. I have a hard time with that. I have been violated and molested as a child. To this day, I don't tolerate that kind of behaviour from anyone. Children are defenceless. We cannot defend ourselves when we are children. That's an old school code. When you were charged with killing a child or molesting a child you go to protective custody (PC). That was where Karla Homolka was. But you know what? When I once was speaking out about that, somebody said, "We are all PC – protective of the creator." It took me a long time to process that in my thinking and my spiritual and emotional mind because of the old school code. We didn't talk to the guards and they didn't talk to us. You always have to watch your business. See no evil, speak no evil and hear no evil. Just do your own time and that is the only way you will survive.

When I got into taking the hostage, I was left out there by myself and I had to pull it off myself. I grabbed one guard and told her to listen and that I was not going to hurt her. I grabbed her and pulled her down and told her to sit on the floor. I knew that they had guns and if something like this happened they could shoot me. I told her to sit there and do as I say. It lasted 20–25 minutes (if that). I turned my back to talk to somebody who was in the cell because they were locked up and it was just me and that guard. When you put your word into something you have to follow through with it. That's your word that's all you have in life. That's the way I thought and that's the way I think. As I turned my back, she started running towards the other guards and then all of these guards rushed my way. I thought I was going to get the shit kicked out of me. They came down and all I remember is getting crunched in the head and I thought that I needed to do something for myself. I was overpowered and I knew that so I let the pain take over. They dragged me into segregation and I stayed there for a year. I got a year in segregation back to back, 18 months for forcible confinement and three months for possession of a concealed weapon. My weapon was just a little stick. There was no blade. I told the guard it was a stick and I wasn't going to hurt her just do as I say. That was to exchange the PC women from the wing for her. It was an exchange thing but it didn't happen. During that year I was in segregation, after about six to nine months of being in the hole, with no doors but only bars, the bars started moving. During that time, I was working on reading and writing. I got my education in segregation and I walked into prison with a grade 9 education. Today, I have college. I did it inside in a maximum-security prison and now I am a paralegal.

In 1994, there was a riot. There were eight of us. At that time, my friend Ellen Young was getting medication from the medication line. I was doing crafts that afternoon. I used to do a lot of leather crafts. I didn't think anything of it. I put my little scissors in the back of my pocket and then I heard commotion in the medication line. I peeked over through the little window between the A and B range and I see Ellen. She had cut herself. The guards are trying to take her to segregation and the guards smacked her down on the floor. I thought, "No, this isn't going to happen!" She was traumatized already and going through emotional stuff, so why are they taking her to the hole? That is what I was thinking. I had to do what I thought was right. I went running and people followed me. I don't remember the exact words but the guards were telling me to get away. But, I said no! I told them that she is lashing out and cutting and asked why they were taking her to the hole. They are going to put her in segregation because she was cutting herself. Do you think that is right? I don't. Everybody started fighting with the guards. The guards were fighting back with us. It was like a free for all on the range. We kicked their asses. I remember this guard named Gerry. He was a 6-foot guy and managed the whole institution. He had a hard time coming up the stairs because he was so big. He called my name and I turned and he sprayed mace right in my face. That stuff burns. I have been tear-gassed before and didn't think it would hurt but it did and it burnt my face. I started running down the range. I didn't know where to go. I went into this one cell and saw my friends and told them that I needed to hide in the cell. There were these metal trunks in there and I told them that I can't fit and to move the trunk and push it back and then I got in there. All I remember is the guards saying, "Lock down! Lock down!" They locked the cells down and I am in the one cell. They were coming around with some guards upstairs. My friend in the cell who is from up north on the reservation said, "The guards are coming!" I said, "I know. I can smell them." Am I scared? Yes, I am scared. I didn't know where anybody was out of those women they were fighting. They brought the dogs in to sniff us out. They came to cell 16, where I was. Through the two bars I can see the dog and I thought "Oh no!" but I wasn't going to give up. They were 6-foot muscle built men all dressed in black and they said, "Joey Twins! Get out of the cell now," like robots. I thought if I should do it or not but it didn't matter anyways. I don't feel nothing. I don't care. I had that mentality. They opened the cell and came in and I see their big combat boots and the dog was right there. So, I thought ok I will come out.

I called out but they didn't give me a chance to get out. The one guard put his knees on my back. They were really cruel and brutal and I knew that. I knew they weren't going to be nice to me or anyone of us because of what we did with the guards. After that, they had me handcuffed. My arms were hurting with my hands up like this and my feet weren't even touching the ground. One female guard came in and said we are going to do a strip search and I said, "Fuck you!" I hear the rest of my comrades coming in. I don't know who was all involved. All I know was that I was there. There were seven of us involved. We were locked up in segregation. I asked for toilet paper, but they wouldn't give any to me. They turned off our water on the taps and toilet. It was cold because they opened the windows.

I am sitting on the bed. I am still hyped from this. My adrenaline was high and they finally came in and he said strip search and I said, "Alright I'll make this easy." They told me to get on the ground on my knees and to face the wall. That is what I did. They patted me down and got me up and told me to strip. That is what I did. I wanted toilet paper and I wanted water. I asked for blankets and he said no. The other women, I heard them asking for a pad or tampon. These were women on their moontime and they were denied their rights. It's an honorable time when you are on your time especially as a woman. We were treated as garbage. We were given a cup of water once in a while. I was eventually given six of those little sheets of toilet paper and horse blankets.

After about three days, the construction workers came in. I remember seeing the warden. There is a video on this. They came in my cell first. I was sleeping.

The beds are bolted into the wall. I was so mad I had this rage. I didn't know I could do that. I pulled the bed right out of the wall I was so angry. If you see that video you can see the two legs sticking out from when I was sleeping when they came in. They marched me out into the hall and I had no clothes on. I told the women to do what they say because they are going to hurt you. All these construction workers went into my cell, took the bed out, and then were going into other cells to do the same thing. I couldn't believe it. All the stuff I have done in my past and I have never been treated like that. Humiliated. Degraded. I didn't expect any better but not this. We had pajamas but mine I cut down to here and I had a bandana and armband. When they came in, they cut our clothes down.

I try to make humour out of the most degrading, humiliating and saddest times. Not that I think it was funny. A couple days later, at midnight, I was taken to KP. We stayed there for about six to nine months. That's were Kim Pate and everybody came to visit us. We were at a men's institution and it was a protective custody place. All pedophiles, rapists, you name it. The most disgusting men you could hear about. So, here we are, being housed in a big range and we are on a 22–24 hour lockdown. My lawyer, Chip O'Connell, came to see me and I told him I was happy to see him. He asked me what happened. I told him that I don't want to talk too much because the walls have ears, but there is a tape out there of them doing this to us. I explained as much as I could. He took CSC to court to release that tape because they were not going to release that videotape. We filed an injunction in Kingston. Correction Services of Canada is the most corrupt organization in Canada. I say that with pride because I know. They released the video but it was a video when we were being transferred to KP. I told Chip that it was not the video and that there is a video of them treating us this way with the strip searches down the hall and everything with women screaming. It was a really crazy time. They went back to court and finally released that tape. We viewed it and at that time and I didn't realize everything that was happening. It was a very traumatic experience. After that, we spent nine months in the hole. We wanted to transfer back to P4W. They wouldn't take us. So, we had to take them to court again to release us from KP and back to P4W. We won our court challenge and got to go back. After that, a parole officer came and told me what management was saying, "If you agree to plead guilty of all your institutional charges, you will all be released from segregation." I have three assaults on guards and possession with concealed weapon for the scissors I had in my pocket. I was allowed to have them and I had a permit for them. Not realizing that I had them in my pocket, I got additional time for that. The life sentence, 10, I got the first time, I ended up doing 36 years inside. Not because I was an angel, but I did it for a reason.

All of us native women, we did proposals to advocate on our own behalf – to make change. When I think about it and why I did what I did, it is because we wanted to be heard. We had to suffer and go through all that stuff. I didn't say, "We are going to riot and beat up the guards today." It wasn't like that. There had to be an action to a reaction – that is what happened. We had a reaction after the action.

In 1998, the prison permanently closed because of the Arbour commission. We had to do four phases and I sat on all of them because they needed a recommendation to close that place down. The women can go to prison closer to their homes. If you are from out West you can go to Edmonton, BC or wherever. The recommendations that myself and our sisters made it a better place for us so we can cook and be treated like the civilized human beings that we are. Also, I knew that having a heart and compassion enabled me to walk out with integrity. I have done sweats, ceremonies and fasts. All of that. I was not always like that. I was a hard ass because I had to hold down the ship. You cannot be weak here, here, or in your spirits or you will be walked on. Don't be too humble because somebody is going to walk all over you.

I got out in 2012 and I am now in a halfway house in Brampton, Ontario, where we have a sweat lodge and a teepee. I am so grateful. It is a stepping stone to full parole and I should be on full parole in June 2019.

I believe in our Creator and the Seven Grandfather Teachings because that is what was put into my path when I was a little kid. I believe and live that and breathe it every day because that is how I walk in this life. *Miigwech.* Thank you.

Considering some of the issues

Learning about the life experiences of Yvonne and Joey, you can see the many deeply layered, complex and well-articulated issues presented about how the colonial corrections system needs to change. Some of the issues include support to the women, acknowledging the intergenerational traumas, including all types of violence against Indigenous women and their children, and finally, solutions to change the system. I argue that there has to be a complete transition and transformative change to a complete abolition of the prison systems for Indigenous women.

First, I would like to address the link that both Yvonne and Joey made regarding intergenerational traumas and all of the types of violence that has occurred against Indigenous women and that has resulted in the overrepresentation of Indigenous women in federal and provincial prisons. The Missing and Murdered Indigenous Women and Girls Inquiry (MMIWG National Inquiry) called the violence against Indigenous women *genocide*,[16] and I totally agree. Some have identified this as femicide[17] and epistemicide.[18] However the violence has been

16 National Inquiry into Missing and Murdered Indigenous Women and Girls, "Reclaiming Power and Place: The Final Report of the National Inquiry into Missing and Murdered Indigenous Women and Girls. Volume 1b" (2019), online: <https://mmiwg-ffada.ca/wp-content/uploads/2019/06/Final_Report_Vol_1b.pdf> [MMIWG Inquiry Report Volume 1b].

17 The term *femicide* has been used most often in Latin America to describe the killings of Indigenous women and girls. See Katharine Ruhl, "Guatemala's Femicides and the Ongoing Struggle for Women's Human Rights: Update to CGRS's 2005 Report Getting Away with Murder" (2007) 18 *Hastings Women's LJ* 199.

18 Dr. Alex Wilson highlighted the term *epistemicide*, which means the killing of knowledge systems and which she described as the deliberate disconnection of land knowledge. This

described, Indigenous women, girls and two-spirited Indigenous peoples have taken the brunt of colonial state and systemic violence. The MMIWG National Inquiry notes:

> As the evidence demonstrates, human rights and Indigenous rights abuses and violations committed and condoned by the Canadian state represent genocide against Indigenous women, girls, and 2SLGBTQQIA people. These abuses and violations have resulted in the denial of safety, security, and human dignity. They are the root causes of the violence against Indigenous women, girls, and 2SLGBTQQIA people that generate and maintain a world within which Indigenous women, girls, and 2SLGBTQQIA people are forced to confront violence on a daily basis, and where perpetrators act with impunity.[19]

I believe Canada and its institutions (i.e. Corrections Canada) are perpetrators acting with impunity.

We had highlighted this issue of impunity through NWAC's Sisters in Spirit research reports and found that of the numbers of murders of Indigenous women and girls that were included in the study, nearly half of the murder cases involving Indigenous women and girls remain unsolved and that no charges were laid in about 40% of the cases.[20] Although these figures were contested by the RCMP[21] in its report[22] on MMIWG, it was noted by the MMIWG National Inquiry's interim report that

> the most significant issue our partners identified is the role that police forces and the criminal justice system play in perpetrating violence against Indigenous women and girls. There is an overall lack of trust in the justice

---

occurs every time an Indigenous woman is murdered. See Alex Wilson and Marie Laing, "Queering Indigenous Education" in Linda Tuhiwai Smith, Eve Tuck & K. Wayne Yang, eds., *Indigenous and Decolonizing Studies in Education: Mapping the Long View* (New York: Routledge, 2018) at 133.

19 MMIWG Inquiry Report Volume 1b, *supra* note 16 at 167.

20 Native Women's Association of Canada, *What Their Stories Tell Us: Research Findings from the Sisters in Spirit Initiative* (Ottawa: Native Women's Association of Canada, 2010) at 27, online: <www.nwac.ca/wp-content/uploads/2015/07/2010-What-Their-Stories-Tell-Us-Research-Findings-SIS-initiative.pdf>.

21 I must note here that while I was consultant and advisor to Amnesty International on its Stolen Sisters report [Amnesty International Canada, *Stolen Sisters: A Human Rights Response to Discrimination and Violence against Indigenous Women in Canada* (Ottawa: Amnesty International Canada, 2004)] and during my two terms as president of NWAC from 2004–2009, we approached all policing services at that time to assist in the research and there was no response or cooperation by any police services at that time to assist with any of the ongoing research.

22 Royal Canadian Mounted Police, "Missing and Murdered Aboriginal Women: A National Operational Overview" (2014), online: <www.rcmp-grc.gc.ca/wam/media/460/original/0cbc8968a049aa0b44d343e76b4a9478.pdf>.

> system – including the police, courts, coroners, and corrections – and a belief that women and families are not receiving the justice they deserve.[23]

I must note here that I, along with many Indigenous and non-Indigenous lawyers, academics, organizations and activists, participated in a Legal Strategy Coalition on Violence Against Indigenous Women (LSC) to prepare for the MMIWG National Inquiry. The LSC researched, reviewed and analyzed 58 reports that were prepared by federal, provincial and territorial governments and government agencies, national Aboriginal organizations, international human rights organizations and Canadian civil society organizations over the 20 years concerning violence against Indigenous women in Canada.[24] A Master List of Report Recommendations organized by theme was compiled with approximately 700 recommendations reviewed.[25] Specifically, Theme 13 focused on community-based justice and made reference to six reports dating back to 2001 up to the most recent report by the Inter-American Commission on Human Rights in 2015.[26] The recommendations in these reports focused on safety and security of Indigenous women, funding for preventative and proactive community justice, restorative justice and services that are culturally and community based. Although some of these recommendations might be implemented in some communities, any positive results have not been reflected in the reduction of the numbers of Indigenous women in federal and provincial prisons.

The MMIWG Inquiry provided 231 Calls for Justice "directed at governments, institutions, social service providers, industries and all Canadians"[27] which were described as "legal imperatives" and

> arise from international and domestic human and Indigenous rights laws, including the *Charter*, the *Constitution*, and the Honour of the Crown. As such, Canada has a legal obligation to fully implement these Calls for Justice and to ensure Indigenous women, girls, and 2SLGBTQQIA people live in dignity.[28]

23 National Inquiry into Missing and Murdered Indigenous Women and Girls, "Our Women and Girls Are Sacred. Interim Report" (2019), online: <www.mmiwg-ffada.ca/wp-content/uploads/2018/04/ni-mmiwg-interim-report-revised.pdf>.

24 Legal Strategy Coalition on Violence Against Indigenous Women, "Review of Reports and Recommendations on Violence against Indigenous Women in Canada, Analysis of Implementation by Theme" (2015), online: <www.leaf.ca/wp-content/uploads/2015/02/Analusis-of-Implementation.pdf>.

25 Pippa Feinstein and Megan Pearce, Legal Strategy Coalition on Violence against Indigenous Women, "Review of Reports and Recommendations on Violence against Indigenous Women in Canada, Master List of Report Recommendations Organized by Theme" (2015), online: <www.leaf.ca/cp-content/uploads/2015/02/Master-List-of-Recommendations.pdf>.

26 *Ibid.* at 89.

27 National Inquiry into Missing and Murdered Indigenous Women and Girls, "Final Report" (2019), online: <https://mmiwg-ffada.ca/final-report>.

28 MMIWG Inquiry Report Volume 1b, *supra* note 16 at 168.

We continue to wait for implementation of these Calls for Action as well as the 700 other recommendations made in the 58 reports mentioned above as well as the many Commission and Inquiry recommendations, including the Truth and Reconciliation Commission (TRC) recommendations further noted below.

In my former life as president of NWAC, we partnered with the former executive director of the Canadian Association of Elizabeth Fry Societies and now Senator, Kim Pate, and the Strength in Sisterhood to complete a report called *Human Rights in Action* (HRIA).[29] All of us were "committed to working to decrease the use of prison and to developing release strategies."[30] We traveled to all of the federal prisons for women and had Circle Talks with women inside to advise of the work we were to embark upon. This was when I met Joey Twins and Yvonne Johnson. Part of this work was to do prison advocacy training for the women inside to:

- Create advocacy teams made of current prisoners, ex-prisoners, and community people.
- Have federally sentenced women out of prison by their eligibility dates.
- Reduce the number of Aboriginal women in the federal system by 10%.
- Enable all women to stay out of prison once they are released.
- Participate in coalitions that support human rights principles and goals at the local, regional and national levels.[31]

During this work, we knew that there were human rights violations occurring inside. We were also very well aware of the intergenerational traumas and the circumstances that Indigenous women faced prior to them entering the criminal legal system. NWAC and Justice for Girls found:

> The state has effectively trained many aboriginal women to believe they are on their own in circumstances where they face violence. . . . when women are forced to meet violence with violence, the travesty is they are then susceptible to facing criminal charges.[32]

We continued to be disappointed that the system and the state continued to abuse and violate the women. A large number of Indigenous women and girls are criminalized because of the intergenerational traumas, historical traumas and current traumas that they have lived and survived.[33] As noted by Alysa Holmes,

29 Canadian Association of Elizabeth Fry Societies (CAEFS), Native Women's Association of Canada (NWAC) and Strength in Sisterhood (SIS), *Human Rights in Action: Handbook for Women Serving Federal Sentences* (Ottawa: Canadian Association of Elizabeth Fry Societies, 2008).

30 *Ibid.* at 5.

31 *Ibid.*

32 Native Women's Association of Canada and Justice for Girls (2012) *Arrest the Legacy Circles.*

33 Alysa Holmes, "The Overrepresentation of Aboriginal Women in Prisons: A Cycle of Victimization, Discrimination and Incarceration" (2017) *Sociology Undergraduate Journal* 2.

"colonial victimization of Aboriginal women should be considered a significant factor in their overrepresentation in prisons."[34] As a result, there is not only an overpopulation of Indigenous women and young women in prison but there are outstanding questions as to whether they should even be in there suffering in the first place. We learned this from the voices of Yvonne and Joey here. The corrections system is a colluding partner in upholding ongoing colonial violence.

There have been many recommendations for change to the corrections systems made by many organizations including Canadian Association of Elizabeth Fry Societies (CAEFS), NWAC, Amnesty International, and the Office of the Correctional Investigator. The Office was established in 1973 under the *Inquiries Act* as a direct result of a commission of inquiry's recommendation for an external grievance body to independently review offender complaints.[35] The Correctional Investigator has been providing recommendations for change since that time. There have been reports and inquiries with hundreds of recommendations for reform of the broader criminal legal system that might include some specific recommendations of the corrections systems. The 1996 Royal Commission on Aboriginal Peoples (RCAP) stated:

> Reform of the existing system has been the focus of many inquiries preceding ours. . . . During its research phase, the Alberta task force on the criminal justice system assembled a list of 708 recommendations for reform from all the Aboriginal justice reports between 1967 and 1990. In its own 1992 report, *Justice on Trial*, the task force made 340 recommendations of its own. Several hundred additional proposals have been made in other reports, bringing the total to as many as 1800 recommendations for reform. . . . It is clear that the reason is not the lack of sound recommendations but a lack of concrete implementation.[36]

Although there are now thousands of recommendations to reform the whole criminal legal system since RCAP, there are few reports that focus on corrections and federally sentenced Indigenous women. In 1996, The Arbour Commission of Inquiry into Certain Events at the Prison for Women in Kingston provided 14 detailed recommendations specific to women's corrections.[37] What prompted this inquiry was a 1995 special report of the Office of the Special Investigator in which CSC had "closed the book on these events."[38] In 2004, the Systemic Review of Human Rights in Correctional Services for Federally

34 *Ibid.* at 6.

35 Corrections Service Canada, "Office of the Correctional Investigator 1973" online: <www.csc-scc.gc.ca/text/pblct/rht-drt/06-eng.shtml>.

36 Canada. Privy Council Office, *Royal Commission on Aboriginal Peoples: Bridging the Cultural Divide: A Report on Aboriginal People and Criminal Justice in Canada* (Ottawa: Royal Commission on Aboriginal Peoples, 1996).

37 Commission of Inquiry into Certain Events at the Prison for Women in Kingston *Report of the Commission of Inquiry into Certain Events at the Prison for Women in Kingston* (Ottawa: Public Works and Government Services Canada, 1996).

38 *Ibid.* at xi.

Sentenced Women provided 19 recommendations for action "to ensure that the treatment of federally sentenced women is consistent with human rights law."[39] What prompted this review by the Canadian Human Rights Commission was the result of CAEFS, NWAC, the Canadian Bar Association and the National Association of Women and the Law and others bringing attention to the "human rights situation of federally sentenced women, particularly Aboriginal women and women with disabilities."[40]

In 2015, the Truth and Reconciliation Commission made Calls to Action to all federal, provincial, territorial and Aboriginal governments that address corrections and the criminal legal system, specifically, which are from Numbers 30 to 42. Number 30 and 38 specifically related to the overrepresentation of Aboriginal people and Aboriginal youth in prison and Number 31 specifically related to realistic alternatives to imprisonment:

> 30) We call upon federal, provincial, and territorial governments to commit to eliminating the overrepresentation of Aboriginal people in custody over the next decade, and to issue detailed annual reports that monitor and evaluate progress in doing so.
> 38) We call upon the federal, provincial, territorial, and Aboriginal governments to commit to eliminating the overrepresentation of Aboriginal youth in custody over the next decade.
> 31) We call upon the federal, provincial, and territorial governments to provide sufficient and stable funding to implement and evaluate community sanctions that will provide realistic alternatives to imprisonment for Aboriginal offenders and respond to the underlying causes of offending.

Although the TRC did not address specific gendered recommendations (i.e. the overrepresentation of Indigenous women, specifically), the calls to action to address the overall general overrepresentation of Aboriginal peoples and youth were highlighted.

Most recently, in June 2018, the House of Commons Standing Committee on the Status of Women did a "study on Indigenous Women in the Federal Justice and Correctional Systems."[41] There is a total of 96 recommendations, most of which refer to the implementation of previous recommendations of other reports and inquiries as well as the TRC Calls to Action.

Conclusion

Despite all of these recommendations, nothing has changed for Indigenous women in federal prisons. In fact, the over-representation of federally sentenced

39 Canadian Human Rights Commission, *Protecting Their Rights: A Systemic Review of Human Rights in Correctional Services for Federally Sentenced Women* (Ottawa: Public Works and Government Services Canada, 2003).

40 *Ibid.* at preface.

41 *Supra* note 3.

Indigenous women and young girls is horribly worse now than ever.[42] The recommendations made since 1990 have not made a difference. The studies and inquiries and the millions, maybe billions of dollars over the last 30 years to prepare these reports are not making a difference. As noted in the TRC report:

> It is assumed that locking up offenders makes communities safer, but there is no evidence to demonstrate that this is indeed the case.[43]

I would argue that locking up Indigenous women and young girls does not make a community safer and in fact, causes more harm than good.

So, in my humble opinion, there is only one answer to decolonizing corrections, and that is to completely abolish the prison systems.[44] This is not a novel idea, as many organizations and advocates have been fighting for this for a long time. Justice for Girls is an organization that supports the abolishment of prison for girls, as noted by Amber Dean:

> Abolishment of girls' imprisonment represents an important step towards achieving the broader social justice, dignity, and equality that girls are entitled to under Canada's *Charter of Rights and Freedoms.* However, substantial changes in social attitudes and structural inequalities are also urgently needed: instead of investing significant economic resources into forcible means of protection or behaviour change, we need to begin to directly address the circumstances that compromise girls' safety (such as substance abuse and sexual exploitation) and invest in voluntary programs and supports that facilitate girls' development.[45]

The movement towards prevention and empowerment along with the abolishment of prisons will provide a better future for Indigenous women and girls. As noted earlier, there were no prison systems prior to colonization. Indigenous peoples knew how to address conflict. Individuals who caused harm to someone else were accountable to everyone, including their own family and to the family of the person they caused harm to. The *United Nations Declaration on the Rights of Indigenous Peoples* affirms in article 5 that

> Indigenous peoples have the right to maintain and strengthen their distinct political, legal, economic, social and cultural institutions, while retaining

42 The MMIWG National Inquiry acknowledged this in its Interim Report. *Supra* note 23 at 9.

43 The Truth and Reconciliation Commission of Canada, *Honouring the Truth, Reconciling for the Future: Summary of the Final Report of the Truth and Reconciliation Commission of Canada* (Canada: Truth and Reconciliation Commission of Canada, 2015) at 218.

44 Amber Richelle Dean, *Locking Them Up To Keep Them 'Safe': Criminalized Girls in British Columbia: A Systemic Advocacy Project Conducted For Justice for Girls* (Vancouver: Justice for Girls, 2005).

45 *Ibid.* at abstract.

> their right to participate fully, if they so choose, in the political, economic, social and cultural life of the State.[46]

It is thus a right of Indigenous peoples to maintain and strengthen their own Indigenous legal orders to resolve conflict. And it is time to end the current archaic and brutal colonial prison system. As noted in her conclusion of the Arbour Inquiry, the Honourable Louise Arbour stated:

> Section 3 of the *CCRA* asserts that the purpose of the federal correctional system is to contribute to the maintenance of a just, peaceful and safe society. . . . The society in which many women offenders live is neither peaceful nor safe. By the time they go to prison, they should be entitled to expect that it will be just.[47]

There is no *just* in federal prisons for Indigenous women.

46 United Nations General Assembly, *United Nations Declaration on the Rights of Indigenous Peoples: Resolution / Adopted by the General Assembly* (2 October 2007), A/RES/61/295, <www.refworld.org/docid/471355a82.html>.

47 *Supra* note 23 at 248.

12 (Re)bundling *nêhiyaw âskiy*

Nêhiyaw constitutionalism through land stories

Darcy Lindberg

Peyak (one): knowing the spirit of *nêhiyaw âskiy* through *acimowina*

It is said that our stories have social lives too, when they are not being shared – either around the fire, in ceremonies, or casually amongst our kin – they can also live lonely lives without us.[1] They nourish, teach, and sustain us. Our stories also constitute us. They teach us of our relationships with *âskiy* (land) and *nipîy* (water), legal principles outlining our obligations to *miyo wîcêhtowin* (good relations) stitched within their narratives. Consider our *âcimowin* (story) of *paskwamostos sakihikan* (Buffalo Lake). I offer one version of the story here:[2]

Kayas (a long time ago), there was a time when a group of *nêhiyawak* (Plains Cree peoples) were struggling to find food. This was around the time when *paskwâwi-mostos* (buffalo) were disappearing from the prairies. One hunter, knowing he would need assistance to find buffalo, went into ceremony to seek guidance towards a successful hunt. He engaged in ceremony for four days. Finally in the fourth evening, he dreamt about a place where he would find a buffalo. The next morning, he set off with another hunter. After travelling another four days they came upon the hill, and faithful to his dream, they found a buffalo on the other side. With care, the hunter approached and was able to pierce the animal with an arrow. The buffalo sprang away, leaving a trail of blood across the prairies.

They followed this blood trail for another four days. Finally, they came to a spot where the buffalo had finally succumbed to its injury. Pulling the arrow from the buffalo, the two men were surprised to see water springing from the wound, rather than blood. They watched this for some time. The water formed a puddle, then a small pool, and then eventually a pond.

1 Attributed to Muskego storyteller Louis Bird, as shared by Val Napoleon and Hadley Friedland at Indigenous Law Research Unit Gathering in Tsartlip First Nation, January 2016.

2 As an example of the versatility of our stories, I have employed this story in a similar manner to describe potentials for how we treat corporate separateness when corporations create environmental harms. See Darcy Lindberg, "Wahkotowin and Restoring Humane Relationality within the Transnational Corporation" in Oonagh Fitzgerald, ed., *Corporate Citizen: New Perspectives on the Globalized Rule of Law* (Montreal: McGill-Queens Press, 2020).

The hunter who dreamt the buffalo left to gather the rest of the people. This took another four days. When he returned with them, they were surprised to see that the pond had turned into a large lake, in the shape of a buffalo. Understanding that the lake was gift from *kisê-manitow* (the kind creator), the people understood that this would be a place of abundance for them. And the lake provided for generations – it brought all sorts of animals, including buffalo, from the prairies to its banks. It allowed large grasses, shrubs, and trees to form at its shores. Because of these events, the lake became a place of abundance, and nourished the people for many years.

But this is not where the story ends:

One winter, years later, the people were crossing the lake to visit relatives who had settled on the other shore. While they were crossing, a young boy came across a buffalo horn sticking through the ice. You see, the people used to run buffalo into the shallows of the lake for a more successful hunt. They must have hunted so much that year, that this one slipped through their attention, and floated to the center of the lake. The young boy wanted the horn, and he begged his *mosôm* (grandfather) for it. Understanding that it would be a transgression to take it, the mosôm said no. But, as young ones have a special gift for, he was able to work at the tenderness all *mosômak* (grandfathers) hold for their grandchildren, until the grandfather finally relented. Taking his hatchet, he hit the horn to retrieve it. Instead of it coming free, the ice cracked all around them. While some were able to scramble across the ice to the other side and others back to the shore they came from, some were lost in the water.

My oldest brother told this story to me when I was seven or eight years old. He finished the story with this warning: if you go to the shores of Buffalo Lake at night, you can still here the people crying as they fell into the water. The fantastical elements are what captured and froze – like the lake itself – the story in my memory for years. As I grew older, I came to contemplate and understand the lifeworld below the surface within the story, the constitutional and legal principles that were embedded within it. Engaging in the constitutive elements of the story requires a deep contemplation and immersion in the legal knowledge it preserves and transmits from speaker to listener. As I have previously noted about this story:

> At its base, this story cause[s] me to recognize the *inspirited* nature of the land, and how we are obligated to reckon with the autonomy *of those who are inspirited* (animals, plants and other non-human beings and things) in our laws when we hunt.[3]

Among the wealth of legal knowledge in the story, Buffalo Lake also provides lessons on our conceptions of the ecological world, and the language we use – even in law – in describing it. We have words in *nêhiyawewin*, the Plains Cree

3 *Ibid.* at 34.

language, to describe the results of our transgressions towards the natural world. *Ohcinêwin* describes retribution for harmful interactions with the environment. Just like the transgression in the story where the people lose track of the buffalo in the lake (causing the harm at the end of the story), ohcinêwin arises when we lose consideration of law in our interactions with the ecological world.[4] Further, there is an obligation within nêhiyaw law that we *speak* properly about the environment (*ohcinêmowin*).[5] To tell the story in a different way – perhaps to categorize our buffalo kin as commodity or subservient to humans – brings retribution as well. These concepts can be transposed in present-day contexts and guide us in an alternative to the colonial language of the Canadian common law, and counteract the resulting attitudes towards lands, waters, animals, and other non-human beings. Ohcinêwin and ohcinêmowin caution us against commoditizing and enclosing nêhiyaw âskiy (Plains Cree territoriality) without contemplation to our *wahkotowin* (the laws that govern our relationships). At the very least, it calls us to remember the kinship we have with ecological world and to consider these obligations, even in our economic practices.

Constituting ourselves on the land through story

And as I grew, I began to understand that many of our *kayas acimowina* (long-ago stories) and *atayohkewin* (sacred stories) are constitutional. It is not the only story that gives us such legal and constitutional knowledge. Just northeast of *paskwaw-mostos sakihikanihk* lie the Neutral Hills, where according to its origin story, the creator grew the land into hills in the middle of the night to separate the nêhiyaw and *niitsitapi* (Blackfoot peoples) to teach them loving-kindness in sharing the land.[6] Westward is the town of Wetaskiwin, where upon sharing a pipe – another constitutional bundle for nêhiyawak peoples[7] – the nêhiyaw and niitsitapi were able to form a similar treaty based on shared understandings of the sacredness and significance of tobacco.[8] Further east is *Mistasiniy* (or the big stone), a large stone that our stories tell us was once a boy who shifted his form between human and buffalo. Lost by his human family as a child, he was taken in and raised by buffalo peoples. Upon learning of his human roots later in life,

4 Sylvia McAdam, *Nationhood Interrupted: Revitalizing Nehiyaw Legal Systems* (Saskatoon: Purich, 2015) at 44.

5 Pauline Johnson, “E-kawôtiniket 1876: Reclaiming Nêhiyaw Governance in the Territory of Maskwacîs through Wâhkôtowin (Kinship)” (PhD dissertation, University of Western Ontario Graduate Program in Anthropology, 2017) [unpublished] at 155.

6 See the story of the Neutral Hills, in Anne Speight, *The Shadows of the Neutrals and Open Memory's Door* (Coronation, AB: Old Timer's Centennial Book Committee, 1967) at 1–3.

7 As Pauline Johnson notes, “[o]ur [c]onstitution lies in our [o]spwâkan.” See Johnson, *supra* note 5 at 152.

8 Tobacco has traditionally been a necessary gift offered by *nêhiyaw* peoples in inter-societal agreements. See *ibid.* at 125.

he chose to turn himself to stone to avoid having to hunt his own kin.[9] The site of the Mistasiniy, on the elbow of the *kisiskaciwani-sipiy* (the swift flowing, or South Saskatchewan River) was long a ceremonial gathering place for many prairie Indigenous nations.[10] This is not surprising considering the legal principles that the account of *mistasiny* teaches.

And so on. If you were to run your finger across a map of nêhiyaw âskiy, you will find similar constitutive and legal events written into the land through story. Thus land not only shelters and nurtures, but also teaches law. It becomes *constitutionally animated* as it nourishes us through the stories of its creation, when we choose to listen.

Nêhiyaw narrative cycles and traditions are not alone in their constitutive qualities. The decentralized political and legal structure of the nêhiyawak means that other institutions (rather than central enactments and proclamations) have historically been instrumental in carrying out and teaching constitutive principles.[11] Beyond written texts[12] or customary practices,[13] the epistemological and ontological underpinnings of constitutional principles lay within narratives,[14] songs,[15] artistic renderings,[16] ceremonies,[17] spiritual and place names,[18] kinship models,[19]

9 Cree Neal McLeod, *Cree Narrative Memory: From Treaties to Contemporary Times* (Saskatoon: Purich Publishing, 2007) at 23.

10 The mistasiny was submerged in the damming of the South Saskatchewan River in 1967, and currently sits beneath Lake Diefenbaker.

11 See Val Napoleon, "Thinking about Indigenous Legal Orders" in René Provost & Colleen Sheppard, eds., *Dialogues on Human Rights and Legal Pluralism* (New York: Springer, 2013) at 234.

12 For example, the Samson Cree Nation has affirmed in writing its constitutive principles of pimohciwin (Cree way of life), wahkotowin (kinship), sakitowin (love), and tapwewin (honesty) as directive teachings on how their leadership governs. Online: Samson Cree Nation <http://samsoncree.com/aboutus>.

13 Protocols surrounding ceremonial practices are examples of customary norms in Plains Cree societies. A good philosophical exploration of the importance of these protocols to the legal practice of ceremonies is found in Claire Poirer, "Drawing Lines in the Museum: Plains Cree Ontology as Political Practice" (2011) 53 *Anthropologica* 291 at 294.

14 See Shalene Jobin, "Cree Economic Relationships, Governance, and Critical Indigenous Political Economy in Resistance to Settler Colonial Logics" (PhD dissertation, Department of Political Science and Faculty of Native Studies, University of Alberta, 2014) [unpublished] at 78–79.

15 Wahpimaskwasis (Little White Bear) Janice Makokis, "nehiyaw iskwew kiskinowâtasinahikewina – paminisowin namôya tipeyimisowin: Cree Women Learning Self Determination through Sacred Teachings of the Creator" (MA thesis, University of Alberta, 2005) [unpublished] at 10 [Makokis].

16 See the work of Plains Cree artist George Littlechild in George Littlechild et al., *In Honour of Our Grandmothers* (Penticton: Theytus Books, 1994).

17 Makokis, *supra* note 15 at 10.

18 *Ibid.* at 2.

19 Rob Alexander Innes, *Elder Brother and the Law of the People: Contemporary Kinship and Cowessess First Nation* (Winnipeg: University of Manitoba Press, 2013) at 73–76.

bundles,[20] and language.[21] Like all polities, there are differences in opinion on the nature of nêhiyaw constitutionalism, and what belongs within its constitutive tradition.[22] Aside from normative constitutional practices, nêhiyaw peoples and societies are also adept at formal constitutionalism, relying upon written texts[23] as well as entrenched legal processes (such as ceremony) to guide constitutive practices.

These social institutions within nêhiyaw societies provide normative material for the constitutive fabric of *nêhiyaw pimatisiwin* (Plains Cree way of living) to be weaved from. I am using constitutive in a broad, normative sense here. Nêhiyaw constitutionalism encapsulates the totality of the set of ideals, principles, and aspirations arising out of the ontologies and epistemologies that further a shared understanding of what it means to be nêhiyaw.[24] This totality is held collectively and can neither be fully understood nor directed by an individual. It is also never fixed; as social and legal norms continue to be transformed through contestation and shifting agreements amongst society members, so does nêhiyaw constitutionalism. While nêhiyaw constitutionalism has its own proponents of 'originalism'[25] (like those that emerge in the constitutional debates in other societies), the transformative nature and traditions displayed by many of the institutions that hold and teach Plains Cree law give evidence of a dynamic, growing, interpretative constitution.[26]

Niso (two): colonial interventions of abstraction

With the introduction and subsequent asserted supremacy of the common law on the Canadian prairies, nêhiyaw constitutionalism has faced immense intervention

20 Kiera Ladner, "(Re)creating Good Governance, Creating Honourable Governance: Renewing Indigenous Constitutional Orders" Paper presented at the Annual Conference of the Canadian Political Science Association (Ottawa, May 2009), online: <www.cpsa-acsp.ca/papers-2009/Ladner1.pdf> at 4.

21 Makokis, *supra* note 15 at 3.

22 Both the Canadian and American dialogues on constitutional interpretation have had to deal with (and have settled in different manners) the tensions between originalist and 'living-tree' approaches to their respective constitutions. See John Borrows, *Freedom and Indigenous Constitutionalism* (Toronto: University of Toronto Press, 2016) at 129–36 [Borrows, *Freedom*].

23 See Johnson, *supra* note 5 at 141.

24 For other examples of Indigenous constitutionalisms, see Borrows, *Freedom*, *supra* note 23. Aaron Mills, "The Lifeworlds of Indigenous Law: On Revitalizing Indigenous Legal Orders Today" (2016) 61:4 *McGill LJ* 847. Mills' full contribution is instructive to what I am seeking to express here, as he impresses the importance of Anishnaabeg lifeworld to inform what we think of as a constitution. Mills states that "any constitutional order . . . reflects an understanding of what a person is and what community is, and pursues a vision of freedom determined by these understandings for its members. It's only against a shared set of understandings that law comes into the world." *Ibid.* at 855.

25 See McAdam, *supra* note 4.

26 For a sustained exploration of the concept of originalism as it relates to Indigenous peoples in Canada, see John Borrows, "(Ab)Originalism and Canada's Constitution" in Borrows, *Freedom*, *supra* note 22 at 129–60.

and suppression by the Canadian-state. This was not always so. For hundreds of years prior to the making of Treaty 4 (1874) and 6 (1871),[27] *witaskew-osihcikewin* (living together in peace) was the general state of relations between nêhiyaw and *moniyaw*[28] (settler) peoples. The *moniyawak* (settlers) were reliant upon fair and healthy relationships with Indigenous peoples for survival and growth of their societies. The 19th century saw a political and attitudinal shift towards Indigenous nations.[29] Interdependence was replaced with paternalism.[30] The rapid settlement of the prairies after Treaty 4 and 6 significantly changed the demography of nêhiyaw âskiy.[31] Guided by moniyaw-dominated Canadian constitutionalism, the introduction of the *Indian Act* and parallel colonial policies further disenfranchised nêhiyaw peoples from their historical roles in governing nêhiyaw âskiy. As a result, the nêhiyawak were denied the same benefits like title to land, voting rights, and the freedom of mobility that settlers were provided.[32] Further, the reserve system, the pass system, severalty, and peasant farming policies limited nêhiyaw inclusions into reformed social and economic communities.[33] Aside from the individual terrors perpetrated within the schools, the residential school system had devastating effects on the political economy of the nêhiyawak. It deprived nêhiyaw children from teachings on nêhiyaw pimatisiwin, while at the same time reinforcing negative beliefs about their continued practice.

This period fashioned the supremacy of the common and civil laws (in relation to Indigenous legal orders) within Canadian constitutionalism, a hierarchal relationship still largely in place today. This enables common-law relationships to the land – namely the propertization and enclosure of lands – to propagate with little influence by nêhiyaw constitutional and legal principles. Contrasting

27 I use these treaties as a base here, as they deal with lands within Plains Cree territory.

28 Plains Cree for settlers, or more specifically people from the Montreal (Mount Royal) area. I use the term here not in any pejorative sense, but to better identify moniyaw settlers on the prairies, in relation to the term 'settler' which has adopted a broader use presently.

29 See John J. Borrows & Leonard I. Rotman, eds., *Aboriginal Legal Issues: Cases, Materials & Commentary*, 4th ed. (Markham, ON: Lexis Nexis, 2012) at 23; John Borrows, "Wampum at Niagara: The Royal Proclamation, Canadian Legal History and Self-Government" in Michael Asch, ed., *Aboriginal and Treaty Rights in Canada: Essays on Law, Equality and Respect for Difference* (Vancouver: UBC Press, 1997) 155 at 161–165, 168–169 [Borrows, *Wampum*].

30 See Mark D. Walters, "Promise and Paradox: The Emergence of Indigenous Rights Law in Canada" in Benjamin Richardson et al., eds., *Indigenous Peoples and the Law: Comparative and Critical Perspectives* (Portland, OR: Hart, 2009) at 21–50.

31 For example, Saskatchewan's population alone grew over 1,100% between 1891 and 1911. See Randy William Widdis, "Saskatchewan Bound: Migration to a New Canadian Frontier" (1992) 12 *Great Plains Quarterly* 254 at 257.

32 See Sheelah Maclean, "We Built a Life from Nothing: While Settler Colonialism and the Myth of Meritocracy" (2018), online: Canadian Center for Policy Alternatives <www.policyalternatives.ca/sites/default/files/uploads/publications/National%20Office/2017/12/McLean.pdf>; Darcy Lindberg, "The Myth of the Wheat King and the Killing of Colten Boushie" (2018), online: The Conversation Canada <http://theconversation.com/the-myth-of-the-wheat-king-and-the-killing-of-colten-boushie-92398>.

33 Lindberg, *supra* note 32.

nêhiyaw concepts of relationality,[34] this period signals the rapid commoditization and industrialization of lands, with little regard to the autonomy and sovereignty of lands, waters, animals, and other non-human beings.

To highlight the use of enclosure strategies by the Canadian dominion to affect the livelihood of nêhiyaw peoples by disrupting nêhiyaw social and political orders, I will explore the situation George Rain faced in the early 20th century. Rain drew his treaty annuity as part of Samson's band, a primarily nêhiyaw community.[35] Like the majority of Indigenous peoples in Saskatchewan and Alberta (the author's family included), Rain took to farming for a livelihood post–Treaty 6.[36] Homesteading off reserve, Rain's Indian status created a peculiar legal problem: as a status Indian, he was not eligible for a homestead allotment in the same way a moniyaw individual would be.[37] Despite his homestead being on shared traditional territories of the *Pwatak* (Stoney) and nêhiyawak near Pigeon Lake, he was a squatter according to the dominion government at the time.

As a result, Rain faced a difficult but all too common decision of that era for a status Indian: in order to just be eligible to apply for a homestead, he had to seek a surrender of his treaty rights from the Department of Indian Affairs. As you read, perhaps the absurdities of this situation may have already begun to arise for you. Foremost is Rain's categorization as a squatter despite residing on his traditional territory and living on that particular area for over a decade.[38] The second absurdity, while perhaps dulled by its normalcy, is the requirement that Rain renounce one way of being in order to be eligible gain legal effect of

34 Art Napoleon, "Key Terms and Concepts for Exploring Nihiyaw Tapisinowin in the Cree Worldview" (Master's thesis, Faculty of Humanities, University of Victoria, 2014) [unpublished] at 86 [*Key Terms*].

35 Though he was part of a Plains Cree band, Rain is identified as Stoney in the correspondence. Such multi-culturalism was and is a common place within Plains Cree First Nations. See Library and Archives Canada, Black Series, R216–245–8-E. "General Correspondence Regarding Admission to and Discharge From Treaty in the Hobbema Agency" MIKAN no. 2058964, Microfilm reel C-10203, online: Collections Canada <http://collectionscanada.gc.ca/pam_archives/index.php?fuseaction=genitem.displayItem&rec_nbr=2058964&lang=eng&rec_nbr_list=2061389,2061880,2059264,2058964,2059726,2058935,2059266,2059027,2058011,2061802> items 66 to 84 [*Rain Correspondence*].

36 As Sarah Carter notes, the success or failure of Indigenous agriculture on the prairies post-treaty is often misunderstood as a challenge of adaptability by Indigenous peoples, when in reality success or failure was generally a product of the mixture of ecological conditions and Canadian-state intervention. See Sarah Carter, *Lost Harvests: Prairie Indian Reserve Farmers and Government Policy* (Montreal: McGill-Queen's University Press, 1990) at 129–136 [Carter, *Lost Harvests*].

37 Section 126 of the *Indian Act* in 1904 made status and non-status Indians ineligible to homestead land in the prairies.

38 As Rob Innes notes, the inter-societal sharing and kinship was facilitated by the Iron Confederacy. See Rob Innes, "Multicultural Bands on the Northern Plains and the Notion of 'Tribal' Histories" in Robin Jarvis Brownlie & Valerie J. Korinek, eds., *Finding a Way to the Heart: Feminist Writings on Aboriginal and Women's History in Canada* (Winnipeg: University of Manitoba Press, 2012).

another. As the Indian Agent who advocated for Rain's homestead application at the time notes:

> From the report of our Agent it certainly appears that [Rain] is not leading what is regarded as the Indian mode of life. When he hunts and fishes he hunts and fishes as a white man. He works at the saw-mill and does freighting. He is settled on land outside of a reserve, has broken ground and put up fencing. He owns horses and cattle, and other property.[39]

The need for the local Indian agent to advocate for George Rain's *whiteness* is symptomatic of Canadian-state policy at the time. Despite a general ability to adapt to Euro-Canadian modes of livelihood and economics historically (nêhiyaw people were integral in the fur trade, and willingly took up and were successful farmers) Indigenous peoples on the prairies were met with policy that hindered their integration into farming lifestyles. Depriving status-Indians of the same privileges under the *Dominion Lands Act* as moniyaw peoples is just one example. Renouncing treaty was not enough. Thus, the *Gradual Civilization Act* of 1857 required a status-Indian to become 'enfranchised' to be a candidate for a homestead.[40] Enfranchisement required a status Indian to speak English or French proficiently, to have a school-based education, and be deemed of 'good moral character.' Or in essence, sufficiently adapted to a Euro-Canadian mode of living. Thus, enfranchisement not only meant that communities lost members from their geographic sphere (as it meant they would live off reserve), but also socio-political positions within Plains Cree societies.

George Rain's circumstance was not only a normative challenge but a strict textual one as well. In a series of subsequent letters between the local Indian agent, the regional office, and the federal Department of Indian Affairs, officials struggle to find a legal justification to unencumber Rain from the strictures of the Indian Act. As the Department of Indian Affairs asserted at the time:

> Section 126 of the Indian Act makes every Indian and non-treaty Indian ineligible to homestead or pre-empt land in Manitoba or the North West Territories. Now unless a discharge from treaty makes an Indian cease to be an Indian or non-treaty Indian, it would under that section be impossible to protect George Rain in his occupation of the land upon which he has squatted.[41]

As I read these correspondences, it is clear that the local Indian agent is a strong advocate for Rain, while the regional and national offices are seemingly indifferent

39 In correspondence dated 4 November 1904. *Rain Correspondence*, *supra* note 35.

40 *Gradual Civilization Act (An Act to encourage the gradual Civilization of Indian Tribes in this Province, and to amend the Laws relating to Indians)*, 3rd Sess, 5th Parl, 1857.

41 In correspondence dated 30 May 30 1904, *Rain Correspondence*, *supra* note 35.

to the danger of Rain surrendering his treaty rights.[42] The position Rain was forced into – to abandon his connection to Indigenous cultural, legal, and social norms – was common with Indigenous peoples on the prairies have been forced to make these kinds of decisions for the past 150 years. For example, when the Maskwacis reserves were created in Central Alberta in the late 19th century, there were internal debates on whether it was better stay in treaty and be subjugated to the *Indian Act* or to take scrip as a 'halfbreed' and live off the reserve. Proponents of taking scrip understood the paternalistic pressures that those who lived on reserve would likely face, or as an Inspector for Indian Affairs reported at the time: "those who have already taken discharges take every opportunity of taunting those who are apparently contented to remain Indians by calling them slaves and saying every thing you have belongs to the Government."[43]

While the correspondence (nor my subsequent research of the homestead records of the Pigeon Lake area) does not reveal whether Rain is successful in gaining a homestead allotment, the letters capture the ambition of Indian Affairs to use Rain's predicament to further their strategies of reserve land surrender during the period. On March 13, 1907, the secretary of the Department of the Interior wrote:

> If it is of the opinion that entry should be granted to the Messrs. Rain for the lands in question if they are enfranchised, and time ripe for the formation of a precedent for their introduction by proclamation of the Governor in Council into the Province of Alberta and other of the younger provinces, also [consider] whether he would think it desirable to give these two men a portion of the reserve (which would be a fundamental necessity of their enfranchisement) in addition to the proposed homestead.

Such land surrenders during this period – the one above an example of *allotment in severalty* – were a common strategy taken by Indian Affairs to resolve "the Indian problem."[44] In her study of land surrenders from reserves in the prairies between 1896 and 1911, Peggy Martin-McGuire found that "21 per cent of the land reserved to prairie First Nations were surrendered to the Crown to make way for western expansion and influx of immigrants."[45] Surrender strategies included the improper inducement of First Nations by officials, faulty or dubious voting practices, the use of procedures that violated the surrender provisions of the *Indian Act*, and the amendment of law to allow easier surrenders.[46] The

42 *Ibid.*

43 See *Montana Band v. Canada*, 2006 FC 261 (CanLII), <http://canlii.ca/t/1mp5m> at para 155.

44 As Duncan Campbell Scott stated he wanted "to get rid of the Indian problem" by continuing assimilative policies "until there is not a single Indian in Canada that has not been absorbed into the body politic." See National Archives of Canada, Record Group 10, vol. 6810, file 470–2–3, vol. 7, 55 (L-3) and 63 (N-3).

45 Peggy Martin-McGuire, "First Nation Land Surrenders on the Prairies, 1896–1991 Executive Summary" (1998), online: Indian Claims Commission <http://publications.gc.ca/collections/collection_2017/trp-sct/RC31-93-1998-1-eng.pdf> at xiii.

46 *Ibid.* at xxi–xxiii.

conditions proposed to attach to Rain's enfranchisement displays the cravings of Ottawa at the time to diminish reserve lands.

The abstracting nature of private real property

George Rain's story exemplifies the dual avenues that prairie governance, at the behest of Canadian constitutionalism, turned away from nêhiyaw relationality. It pragmatically subjects the land to a different legal praxis while simultaneously attempting to change those who practice this relationality. Enclosed and commoditized in this manner, the land loses the multitude of wealth it holds within a nêhiyaw gift-obligation praxis, transformed into a more abstracted value as a product.[47] Forced to adopt Canadian-state law to continue to live upon the âskiy he homesteaded on for over a decade, Rain has to adopt *common-law storytelling* about the land. He describes it in numbers only (Section 12, Township 47, Range 2 in the 5th Meridian). His working of the land is deemed an 'improvement'. It abstracts from describing the spiritedness of the land. It is far from acknowledging the autonomy of non-human agents on the land.

Rain's success in gaining moniyaw homesteading rights would mean he would enter into the further abstracted logic of the Torrens land registration system, one means of enclosing Indigenous lands and lifeworlds. Other strategies enacted by the Canadian state that aided these enclosures were the destruction of buffalo populations,[48] the control of food to subdue Indigenous governance practices and systems,[49] and the implementation of the reserve system generally. *Allotment in severalty* policies that removed portions of reserve lands to grant to successful enfranchisement applicants as homesteads,[50] and *peasant farming* policies where Indigenous agriculturalists were provided rudimentary tools to ostensibly teach them the value of 'independent labour'[51] further ensured a separation of Indigenous and moniyaw lifeworlds by essentially creating two different agricultural communities. Finally, the residential school system, as an enclosure practice alone has had horrific and longstanding effects on Indigenous citizenries.

As I have noted previously, the enclosure strategies employed towards Indigenous peoples on the prairies post-treaty targeted not only Indigenous lands but lifeworlds as well. As I wrote:

> While many of these enclosure policies may seem contradictory (some isolate Indigenous peoples away from interactions with the settler, while others seek

47 See Alan Pottage, "The Originality of Registration" (1995) 15 *Oxford J. of Legal Studies* 371. Pottage links the development of a 'logic of registration' in modern real property law to the continuing abstraction away from actual possession.

48 Scott Taylor, "Buffalo Hunt: International Trade and the Virtual Extinction of the North American Bison" (2007) 101:7 *American Economic Review* 3162.

49 For example, the control of rations was used as a tool to deter Indigenous resistance and rebellion against colonial policies. See James Daschuk, *Clearing the Plains: Disease, Politics, Starvation, and the Loss of Aboriginal Life* (Regina: University of Regina Press, 2013) at 185.

50 Carter, *Lost Harvest*, *supra* note 36 at 194–195.

51 *Ibid.* at 193.

> their assimilation into settler lifeworlds) there were two main strategies at play. The first was *tutelage*, informed by a belief that with proper instruction, the Plains Cree peoples would move away from their constitutive social and legal norms and assimilate to settler-colonial legal and social orders. Enfranchisement, severalty, and the residential schools sought to 'teach' the Plains Cree of European practices. The second was *isolation*. The Plains Cree, a people whose history involved movement and who were accustomed to such transitions, were stopped from continuing mobile and transitional practices.[52] Enclosure was integral to both strategies.[53]

The isolation and tutelage of nêhiyaw peoples post-treaty abstracted how we perceived the inspirited nature of non-human beings and things, and in turn our obligations towards them. As George Rain's situation shows, common law land tenure furthers this abstraction. Brenna Bhandar notes:

> The commodity logic of abstraction obliterates pre-existing relations to the land, and pre-existing conceptualizations of land as something other than a commodity. The legal form renders invisible (and severely constrains) the ways in which people live, act, (re)produce the conditions of their existence, and relate to one another in ways not confined.[54]

As George Rain's predicament shows, the "logic of registration" – where registration is held as the ultimate form of proof of land ownership and governance, rendering historical relationships and uses of the land inferior – has had devastating effects for Indigenous communities. The development of the Torrens system in South Australia in the 18th century was a vital development to the practice of registration logic, and it resulted in the dispossession of Indigenous lands and territories.[55]

Despite its historical role in dispossessing Indigenous peoples, the legal tools and concepts that employ such 'abstraction logic' are most often viewed as positive developments. Bhandar argues that this is the "cunning of abstraction," where registration "congeals multiple forms of use value, the various types of

52 As John Borrows notes, there are traditions of mobility, both physically and philosophically, practiced by many Indigenous communities, that colonization has significantly hampered. Canadian jurisprudence has particularly affected Indigenous conceptions on the freedom of physical and philosophical mobility. See John Borrows, "Physical Philosophy: Mobility and Indigenous Freedom" in *Freedom & Indigenous Constitutionalism* (Toronto: University of Toronto Press, 2016) [Borrows, *Freedom*].

53 Darcy Lindberg, "Transforming Buffalo: 'Plains Cree Constitutionalism and Food Sovereignty'" in Heather McLeod-Kilmurray, Angela Lee & Nathalie Chalifour, eds., *Food Law and Policy in Canada* (Toronto: Carswell, 2019) at 46.

54 Brenna Bhandar, *Colonial Lives of Property: Law, Land, and Racial Regimes of Ownership* (Durham: Duke University Press, 2018) at 98–99.

55 *Ibid.*

labour involved in producing, cultivating" and "tending to the land."[56] Abstraction mediates the devastations historically caused by rapid commoditization, often felt disproportionally by Indigenous peoples. I note that such turns in our land relationships were always contemplated as abstractions by nêhiyaw peoples. For example, our term for reserves – askîhkân – acknowledges this, as its literal translation is 'fake territory.'

Nisto (three): re-opening our bundle to recognize the *ahcâhk*[57]

How do we respond to the growing gulf between the common-law (and neoliberalism in general) tendencies towards abstraction and nêhiyaw legal principles that foundationally require unmediated relationships with lands, waters, and non-human beings? As the story at the beginning of this chapter suggests, key to this resistance are nêhiyaw epistemological beliefs of the non-human ahcâhk, or the inspirited nature of the ecological world. While commodity logics flatten the relationship between lands and humans towards one defined by property law,[58] the recognition of the *inspirited* nature of non-human beings (and non-beings) ensures relational thinking in the transformation of law.[59] Ahcâhk is a significant concept to the relationship between humans, other living beings, and the inanimate world. While gifted from a larger creative force during our gestations before birth, the ahcâhk resides in the body.[60] For humans, it is linked to our intellectual aspects, as it requires "intelligence and brainpower" to serve its purpose in the physical world.[61] As Danny Musqua explains:

> Prior to birth the spirit knew everything about the spiritual universe from where it came. When the spiritual doorway is shut Ahcahk has to go in the same state as the body that it has adopted. Its human vehicle is childlike and the spirit also becomes childlike. The spirit can fulfill its purpose and mission

56 *Ibid.* at 264. As Bhandar notes the words of Toscano describing Marx's notion of real abstraction: "from [a] fundamentally intellectualist notion of abstraction . . . to a vision of abstraction that, rather than depicting it as a structure of illusion, recognizes it as a social, historical, and trans-individual phenomenon." See A. Toscano, "The Open Secret of Real Abstraction" (2008) 20 *Rethinking Marxism: J. of Economics, Culture and Society* 273 at 275.

57 See Lindberg, *supra* note 2 at 36–37, on how I similarly connect these beliefs on the ahcâhk to the concept of wâhkôtowin.

58 As David Harvey notes, the abstraction of property law erases the "social bond" that is "presupposed" between an owner and their property. See David Harvey, *Seven Contradictions and the End of Capitalism* (Oxford: Oxford University Press, 2014) at 39.

59 I use the word *inspirited* here to describe those things that are viewed to have a spirit or ahcâhk within nêhiyaw epistemology. Inspired by the writing and thinking of Robin Wall Kimmerer in Robin Wall Kimmerer, *Braiding Sweetgrass: Indigenous Wisdom, Scientific Knowledge and the Teachings of Plants* (Minneapolis, MN: Milkweed Editions, 2013).

60 Blair Stonechild, *The Knowledge Seeker: Embracing Indigenous Spirituality* (Regina: University of Regina Press, 2016) at 55.

61 *Ibid.* at 55.

in this earthly life only through the physical body. . . . So gradually the body responds to its purposes in life.[62]

Musqua describes the purpose of the ahcâhk is to gather wisdom through the physical world by experiencing choices and return to the *manitow iskotew* (creator's flame).[63] Blair Stonechild explains, "entering the physical world creates another phenomenon: separation into individual entities, each with an artificial sense of self."[64] Legal norms are an important part of our ahcâhk's journey as in order to work back to an understanding of the inter-relatedness of our respective ahcâhk, "we take guidance from the paths followed by others, in particular from the ways of our family, kinship practices, and our ceremonies."[65] There is even a specific concept for the link between intellectualism and spirituality within the language because of this: *ahcâhkomâmitonihcikan*, or the spirit-mind.[66]

Recalling the story of the creation of Buffalo Lake I shared at the start of this chapter, you can begin to see that within nêhiyaw ways of knowing, ahcâhk is not limited to human beings. It is a foundational belief that everything in creation is animated by some form of ahcâhk.[67] While there are beliefs that some species have a collective ahcâhk,[68] it is a common understanding that plants and animals, like humans, have individual ahcâhk.[69] Recognizing the ahcâhk held by other humans impresses an idea of equality amongst peoples within nêhiyaw constitutionalism. As the creation of our inspirited living comes from the same source, there is an inherent equality to our existence. Acknowledging the ahcâhk of plants, animals, lands, and waters implies a similar equality for the ecological world. It calls for a consideration of the autonomy and sovereignty of beings who are subject to an ahcâhk. As Jerry Saddleback notes, the ahcâhk of âskiy and nipîy require that "we take of . . . Âskiy . . . in the same compassionate manner that she takes care of us" where "[l]aw states that there should always be a conscientious effort in continuity of taking care of the interlinked balance" with âskiy "for our required sustenance and livelihood."[70]

62 Danny Musqua, as reported in Stonechild, *ibid.* at 51.
63 *Ibid.* at 52.
64 *Ibid.*
65 *Ibid.*
66 Napoleon, *supra* note 34 at 26.
67 Johnson, *supra* note 5 at 172.
68 See Stonechild, *supra* note 60 at 63.
69 For example, the Rock Cree of Northern Manitoba believe that animals existed before humans in a state of *ahcahkowiwin*, where animal nations lived out their own cultural values and practices. See Robert Brightman, *Grateful Prey: Rock Cree Human-Animal Relationships* (Regina: University of Regina Press, 1993).
70 See Jerry Saddleback, "Cree Testimony on Water Published in International Organization of Indigenous Resource Development (IOIRD) Stakeholder Communication to the Office of the High Commissioner for Human Rights on Request further to Decision 2/104 on Human Rights and Access to Water, United Nations Human Rights Council", online: United Nations Human Rights Council <www2.ohchr.org/english/issues/water/contributions/civilsociety/IOIRD_Alberta.pdf> at 11.

While acknowledging the ahcâhk resident in non-human beings and things according to nêhiyaw legal thought, it is important to not misidentify this ethic of relationality within the same theoretical bounds as *earth jurisprudence*. Earth jurisprudence is focused on recognizing the rights of the ecological world by developing laws and constitutions that provide 'personhood' rights to non-human actors in our ecological lifeworlds.[71] While similarly relational (and perhaps anti-neoliberal), the recognition of the ahcâhk in non-human beings is not a call to give inspirited beings and things personhood rights, but is a call to recognize the autonomy and sovereignty of ahcâhk-possessing beings. Instead of providing personhood rights to the ecological world, it implies that nêhiyaw peoples rely upon nêhiyaw legal processes to seek consent when human action intervenes with the non-human sovereignty of lands, waters, animals, and plants. Returning to the story of Buffalo Lake, ceremonialism serves as one legal process. The hunter engages in four days of ceremonies to gain consent for the infringement on the sovereignty of the Buffalo peoples. As a teacher of legal process, the gift of the lake (and all the sustenance that comes with it) is a strong persuasive example of the correctness of seeking such consent.

This leads to questions of how we re-bundle Canadian constitutionalism with nêhiyaw constitutive principles and elements. A starting point is to acknowledge the respective normative natures of Canadian constitutionalism and nêhiyaw constitutionalism. As I have previously noted, "borrowing largely from UK constitutional traditions of parliamentary structuralism and unwritten norms,[72] Canadian constitutionalism is tangle-rooted."[73] Canadian constitutionalism is tangle-rooted. As John Borrows states, the Canadian constitution is

> an open ended – perpetual work in progress, a living tree. It is comprised of various written texts, an assortment of established conventions, and a diverse array of oral traditions. It is an open-ended marriage, polyandrous in many ways, allowing for multiple partners. It even has rules that contemplate divorce. In many respects, Canada's constitution is a fluid arrangement, and many people seem to like it that way.[74]

Canadian jurisprudence often overlooks "the broader social function of Canadian law" by unmooring legal reasoning from "their cultural contexts," thus providing the false notion that Canadian law exists almost primarily within a positivistic,

71 See David Humphreys, "Rights of Pachamama: The Emergence of an Earth Jurisprudence in the Americas" (2017) 20:3 *Journal of International Relations and Development* 459 at 459–460; Eleanor Ainge Roy, "New Zealand River Granted Same Legal Rights as Human Being" (16 March 2017) *The Guardian*, online: The Guardian <www.theguardian.com/world/2017/mar/16/new-zealand-river-granted-same-legal-rights-as-human-being>; Clare Kendall, "A New Law of Nature" (24 September 2008) *The Guardian*, online: The Guardian <www.theguardian.com/environment/2008/sep/24/equador.conservation>.

72 Borrows, *Freedom*, *supra* note 22 at 105–106.

73 Lindberg, *supra* 2 note at 42.

74 Borrows, *Freedom*, *supra* note 22 at *105*.

declarative field.[75] Such favoring obscures law not sourced from positivist proclamations or deliberation over other origins.[76] The hyper-centering of constitutional authority in Canada (and the consolidation of law-making and constitution-amending powers within governments) has also had pedagogical consequences as well, as legal ordering that occurs in a decentered or constellating manner[77] is often disregarded as being merely culture or custom, or overlooked altogether. This tendency provides an additional tension from Indigenous scholars and lawyers alike in producing work that is cognizable by a non-Indigenous public but also is faithful to their nations' understanding of constitutions, law, and culture. Aside from positivistic proclamations that say 'this is law!', the clear demarcations between what is 'law' and 'culture' in some instances requires close analysis, and at others is so intertwined that is hard to extract one apart from the other. Art Napoleon notes that

> the nîhiyaw holistic paradigm does not clearly distinguish between values, principles, ethics and wiyasowîwina, 'the laws'. Based on the language there is no distinct boundary between nîhiyaw philosophy, worldview, ontology or knowledge. From a language perspective there is overlap in meaning between nîhiyawîwin words like pimâtisowin 'life or culture', sihcikîwina 'ways of doing things', and nîhiyawâtisowin 'Creeness'. There is not a clear separation between the earthly plane and the spirit world.[78]

The further formal democratization of Indigenous nations has relied upon structures that have centralized and placed more authority unto elected or recognized leaders. For example, the Nipisihkopahk (Samson Cree Nation) is currently developing a detailed constitutional document that will textualize some of its unwritten constitutional and legal norms.[79] It addresses the tension between the normative development of constitutional and legal principles and codifying nêhiyaw *wiyasiwêwina* (laws).[80] The draft document acknowledges the normative foundations of nêhiyaw wiyasiwêwina as it states:

> Kisê-manitow Wiyinikêwina [Creator's laws] have been in existence since time immemorial and are acknowledged through our constitution held in the spiritual and cultural teachings of our, ospwâkan, the pipe . . . the following laws are living documents that through time and practice will change and reflect the interests and values of the people of Maskwacîs but remain rooted in the echoes of our ancestors and upheld by our Elders.[81]

75 John Borrows, *Canada's Indigenous Constitution* (Toronto: University of Toronto Press, 2010) at 109.

76 See Eve Darian-Smith, "Producing Legal Knowledge" in Eve Darian-Smith, ed., *Laws and Societies in Global Contexts* (Cambridge: Cambridge University Press, 2013) at 97.

77 A metaphoric concept from earlier, where I view nêhiyaw legal ordering to occur through micro-centering of legal and constitutive institutions.

78 Napoleon, *supra* note 34 at 51.

79 Johnson, *supra* note 5 at 162–174.

80 *Ibid.* at 162–174.

81 *Ibid.* at 162–163.

It also acknowledges nêhiyaw constitutionalism exists within a constitutional plurality:

> We offer the ability to create a bridge of understanding that combines our Nêhiyaw way of life within the Western Society we find ourselves a part of. We therefore, present our laws in written text but must state, these written laws are not stronger than the oral teachings and narratives from our Kêhtê-ayak.[82]

Or to put it another way, in order to provide the nourishment to decolonize law without losing nêhiyaw legal and constitutional processing, we must always leave enough unwritten that it will be able to nourish us in other seasons. We will always need constitutional material from our lifeworlds to braid law. Acimowina is one institution that continues to provide the strands for our braid, the elements to our bundles.

Neyo (four): conclusion – listening to our stories in constitutional dialogues

Despite the present-day constitutive grip of nêhiyaw âskiy by the Canadian state, the above highlights the possibilities that Indigenous constitutionalisms offer to prairie governance. John Borrows suggests that the Canadian-state should reject "constitutional originalism" by using legal tools already at our disposal to inject Indigenous laws within Canada's "living tree" constitutionalism.[83] Heidi Stark adds that our treaty relationships must be broad enough that they are shaped less by the transactional 'rights-based' frame that current Indigenous-Canadian-state treaty interpretation takes on, and more towards the original "spirit and intent" of treaties within "the larger framework of Indigenous governance and legal traditions that give meaning" to our treaty-making processes.[84] The renewed commitments to the United Nations Declaration on the Rights of Indigenous Peoples provides another avenue for nêhiyaw governance to inform prairie governance. Brenda Gunn suggests that UNDRIP offers an opportunity for the Canadian state to retire the "central and integral to the distinctive culture" approach that has developed in section 35 jurisprudence, to open section 35 towards greater constitutional cooperation between the Canadian-state and Indigenous nations.[85]

82 *Ibid.* at 163.

83 See John Borrows, "Revitalizing Canada's Indigenous Constitution: Two Challenges" (2017) in CIGI. *UNDRIP Implementation: Braiding International, Domestic and Indigenous Laws*, online: Center for International Governance Innovation: <www.cigionline.org/publications/undrip-implementation-more-reflections-braiding-international-domestic-and-indigenous> at 20–27.

84 Heidi Stark, "Changing the Treaty Question" in John Borrows & Michael Coyle, eds., *The Right Relationship: Reimagining the Implementation of Historical Treaties* (Toronto: University of Toronto Press, 2017) at 274.

85 See Brenda Gunn, "Beyond Van der Peet: Bringing Together International, Indigenous and Constitutional Law" in *UNDRIP Implementation: Braiding International, Domestic and Indigenous Laws*, online: Center for International Governance Innovation <www.cigionline.

Similarly, Kiera Ladner notes that section 35 of the *Canadian Constitution Act, 1982* be interpreted to offer a cooperative federalism model for Indigenous/ Canadian state relations.[86] Finally, commitments to decolonization by non-state individuals and organizations can be concrete in returning lands and waters to Indigenous peoples and nations.[87] While a reader may find this act of decolonization as the least realistic, it is perhaps the easiest practically, as it is as simple as transferring title to Indigenous nations who have lost these lands through enclosure strategies.[88]

Short of large constitutional amendment or monumental acts of decolonization, reclaiming an inspirited view of lands and waters within our legal practices is also occurring incrementally. Coming full circle to where this chapter began, I offer a consideration of nêhiyaw storytelling and nêhiyaw ceremonialism as revolutionary actions towards such decolonization. As you recall in the story I shared at the start of this chapter, the hunter engaged in ceremony in order to foster his relationship with the animal relations (buffalo) that he would require for nourishment. Ceremony brings us physically closer to the earth. It also reaffirms our reliance on other inspirited beings and things for survival; it teaches us that our survival is a gift received from the kind-heartedness of other beings, and from lands and waters themselves.

I also reflect on the refrain from Arsene Arcand, that those who remain close to the land will be protected. I often thought about this in a broad and even metaphorical sense, that if we kept our understandings of our kinship and wahkotowin with *kikâwînaw âskiy* (mother earth) in our intellectual journeys, we would be protected from certain hardships in the future. Considering the harms that our commodity logics have done to lands and waters generally, I have started to consider this refrain more literally. And nêhiyaw law provides an antidote. There is a legal principle within nêhiyaw pimatisiwin that is so simple on its face that we often overlook it as law. It is *kiyokewin*, or as it translates into, *to visit.* I consider our ability to visit the spaces within nêhiyaw âskiy, to relate once again to our âskiy acimowina, to reclaim our kinship with the inspirited around us as a high act of high law, a reconstituting practice. And in the end, it will be understood to be quietly revolutionary. *Ekosi.*

---

org/publications/undrip-implementation-more-reflections-braiding-international-domestic-and-indigenous> at 29–38.

86 See Kiera Ladner, "Take 35: Reconciling Constitutional Orders" in A. M. Timpson, ed., *First Nations, First Thoughts* (Vancouver: UBC Press, 2009).

87 Eve Tuck & Wayne Wang, "Decolonization Is Not a Metaphor" (2012) 1:1 *Decolonization: Indigeneity, Education & Society* 1.

88 For example, Kenneth Linde transferred 130 hectares to the Esk'etemc Nation in 2017. See CBC, "'Reconciliation in Its Best Form': B.C. Rancher Gives Land Back to His First Nation Neighbours" online: CBC <www.cbc.ca/radio/asithappens/as-it-happens-friday-edition-1.4112585/reconciliation-in-its-best-form-b-c-rancher-gives-land-back-to-his-first-nation-neighbours-1.4112589>.

13 Conducting research from an Indigenous lens

Valarie Waboose

This Anishinabe[1] teaching, referred to as the Seventh Fire Prophecy,[2] has been passed down from generation to generation for hundreds of years:

> The seventh prophet that came to the people long ago was said to be different from the other prophets. He was young and had a strange light in his eyes. He said, "In the time of the Seventh Fire an Osh-ki-bi-ma-di-zeeg (New People)[3] will emerge. They will retrace their steps to find what was left by the trail.
>
> Their steps will take them to the Elders who they ask to guide them on their journey. But many of the Elders will have fallen asleep. They will awaken to this new time with nothing to offer. Some of the Elders will be silent out of fear. Some of the Elders will be silent because no one will ask anything of them. The New People will have to be careful in how they approach the Elders. The task of the New People will not be easy.
>
> If the New People will remain strong in their quest, the Waterdrum of the Midewiwin Lodge will again sound its *voice* [emphasis added]".[4]

1 *Anishinabe* in the Ojibway language is composed of *Ani* (From Whence), *Nishina* (Lowered), *Abe* (The Male of the Species or also known as Original Man). For more information, see Benton-Banai, *infra* note 4 at 3. It should also be noted that this chapter is written by Anishinabe Kwe (woman), therefore the word Anishinabe will be used when referring specifically to the Anishinabe culture.

2 The Seventh Fire Prophecy is one of seven prophecies that have been shared generation to generation since the beginning of time. The Anishinabe are not the only First Nation that have prophecies, other Indigenous Nations across Canada have similar prophecies. The phrase *Seven Fire Prophecies* is capitalized here to illustrate the importance of this prophecy to the subject of the chapter. For more information on the Seven Fires Prophecies see Benton-Banai, *infra* note 4 at Chapter 13.

3 In this chapter, *New People* is capitalized because of the importance they have to this topic of discussion.

4 Edward Benton-Banai, *The Mishomis Book* (Minneapolis: University of Minnesota Press, 2010) [Benton-Banai].

Since the beginning of time, the Anishinabe have transferred Indigenous knowledge,[5] such as stories, legends, teachings and prophecies (also known as Indigenous legal traditions, or ILT)[6] to the young to ensure their cultural survivance.[7] Gifted storytellers, mentored by Elders,[8] were passed the responsibility of transmitting stories, legends, teachings and prophecies onto subsequent generations. The above quote is an example of one such teaching. This prophecy is one of seven prophecies of the Anishinabe also known as the Seven Fires teachings.[9] This teaching, along with many, provided the foundation upon which Anishinabe children were socialized before introduction to colonial society.

After contact, the socialization of Indigenous[10] children changed considerably. During the 1800s, Indigenous children were removed from their homes and sent to Indian Residential Schools[11] (IRS) for long periods of time. While attending these schools, children were taught that their parents were pagan and their cultural ways were evil. Due to the fact that children lived far from home, they no longer heard the teachings and Elders were no longer able to transmit the teachings to subsequent generations. This time was predicted in the Sixth Fire Prophecy.[12] It has been told that during this time, a group of visionaries brought a message to the Anishinabe that the Midewiwin way of life was in danger. Upon hearing this, the ceremonies went underground, the sacred bundles and sacred scrolls were hidden,[13] and the stories, legends, teachings and prophecies were rarely shared.

The secrecy surrounding Anishinabe ceremonies continued for years until a cultural revitalization began in the 1980s amongst Indigenous people across Canada. The younger generation started searching for Elders who remembered the original teachings of the ancestors. This era is known as the time of the Seventh Fire

5 Indigenous knowledge can be found in teachings, stories, legends and prophecies of the original peoples of a specific territory. "Indigenous knowledge" will be used when speaking generally about any Indigenous group of people. It should also be noted that Indigenous knowledge and Indigenous legal traditions are one and the same, even though scholars may use different terms to describe this knowledge.

6 Indigenous legal traditions are discussed in detail in text by John Borrows text: *Canada's Indigenous Constitution* (Toronto: University of Toronto Press, 2010) [Borrows].

7 Survivance is a critical term used Anishinabe scholar Gerald Vizenor. There he explains that "Survivance is an active sense of presence, the continuance of native stories, not a mere reaction, or a survivable name. Native survivance stories are renunciations of dominance, tragedy and victimry." See *Manifest Manners: Narratives on Postindian Survivance* (Lincoln: Nebraska, 1999) at vii [*Manifest Manners*].

8 In Anishinabe culture Elders are those that acquired Indigenous knowledge throughout their lifetime.

9 To read all seven teachings of the Seven Fires teachings of the Anishinabe see Benton-Banai, *supra* note 4 at Chapter 13.

10 I use the term Indigenous here to illustrate that not only Anishinabe children were impacted after contact. Every Indigenous Nation, whether it be Cree, Mohawk, Blackfoot or Squamish, whose children attended an Indian residential school were impacted.

11 There were approximately 130 Indian residential schools in Canada during the Indian residential school era.

12 The Sixth Prophecy can be found in Benton-Banai, *supra* note 4 at 91.

13 *Ibid.*

Prophecy.[14] This prophecy states: "if the New People will remain strong in their quest, the Waterdrum of the Midewiwin Lodge will sound its *voice* again".

After the cultural revitalization movement began, many Anishinabe went back to practice the original teachings and started living their life accordingly. Today, the momentum that began 30 years ago continues. During this time of change, struggle and resistance, the Indigenous people of Canada were able to negotiate spaces for themselves within local, regional and national institutions and organizations. Although change was slow, it is important to note here because the struggles, occupations and resistance demonstrated by Indigenous people across Turtle Island[15] exemplified a need for change. Even institutions of higher learning were experiencing a paradigm shift. As Indigenous people returned to the teachings, completed educational degrees and accepted positions in institutions of higher learning, changes occurred. Indigenous scholars began writing and conducting research within these spaces, incorporating their stories, legends, teachings and prophecies, placing ILT at the forefront of Indigenous scholarship. Thus, a new wave of scholarship emerged; Indigenous scholars are now conducting their research and writing using the cultural lens of their ancestors.[16]

Leading Indigenous scholar Dr. John Borrows[17] shared his thoughts about the future of ILT in a book titled *Canada's Indigenous Constitution*. In this book, he states that ILT flows from many different sources.[18] He further states that although ILT is not prominent in Canada, it has a huge impact upon the lives of Indigenous people.[19] Also diverse in their overall structure and process, Borrows states that ILT can be divided into five distinct areas: sacred law, natural law, deliberative law, positivistic law and customary law.[20] As previously shared stories, legends, teachings and prophecies are a part of ILT.

At this juncture, I want to step back and share some information about this chapter. Firstly, this chapter is one chapter from my PhD dissertation. Secondly, I want to explain the organization of the chapter for the reader. The chapter began with the Anishinabe Seventh Fire Prophecy to provide the context in which this chapter is written. The next section includes a summary of the research topic – IRS and the compensation processes utilized by IRS Survivors. The chapter then moves onto a discussion of how the methodology and theoretical framework

14 The Seventh Prophecy can be found in Benton-Banai, *supra* note 4 at 91.

15 To many Indigenous Nations across Canada and the United States, the North American continent is known as Turtle Island.

16 Many Indigenous scholars are utilizing their respective Indigenous lens to write within the academy. For more insight into writing from an Indigenous lens see the works of various Indigenous authors, such as Val Napoleon, Shawn Wilson, Margaret Kovach, Leeanne Simpson, Kathleen E. Absolon, Heidi Kiiwetinepinesiik Stark, Aimée Craft, Jeffrey G. Hewitt, Beverley Jacobs, Sylvia McAdam, Sakej Henderson and Leroy Little Bear.

17 Dr. John Borrows is the Canada Research Chair in Indigenous Law at the University of Victoria Law School in British Columbia.

18 Borrows, *supra* note 6 at 23.

19 *Ibid.*

20 *Ibid.* at 24–55.

transpired. The following section continues with a discussion about the interrelatedness of the research topic and the sacred teachings of the Seven Fire Prophecies. The conclusion ends with some thoughts about the future direction of Indigenous scholarship within Canada.

Indian residential school legacy

My research examined the compensation processes utilized by IRS Survivors[21] as outlined in the Indian Residential School Settlement Agreement (IRSSA). The residential school legacy is one of the darkest chapters in Canadian history. From the mid-1850s to 1996, thousands of Aboriginal children were taken from their homelands and placed in IRS. Taken against their will, many dreaded attending these schools. Some children attended for as long as 10 to 15 years, only to be strangers in their own communities upon their return. In the past 30 years, Survivors began disclosing the loneliness, confusion, fear, punishment and humiliation they suffered within these institutions and reported traumatic incidents of sexual, physical or emotional abuse. These childhood traumas still haunt them today.

Since the last IRS closed, Survivors were able to negotiate the IRSSA. The IRSSA provided an Alternative Dispute Resolution system called the Independent Assessment Process for physical and sexual abuses, a Common Experience Payment process which compensated every Survivor that attended an IRS using the 10 + 3 formula.[22] The IRSSA also included the development of a Truth and Reconciliation Commission of Canada (TRC), which archived the stories of thousands of Survivors across the country.

Methodology

I begin this section by sharing how my cultural values and beliefs supported the completion of my dissertation. It is not known whether other Indigenous researchers know before starting their study that they will utilize an Indigenous methodology in their research – I can only share my personal experience. At the onset, I must admit that using an Anishinabe methodology did not come automatically. Reflecting upon this time reminds me of how I, as an Indigenous student, became immersed and reliant upon Western academic thought. Although I am an Anishinabe Kwe who studied in an Indigenous Knowledge program, my initial thoughts about the methodology I would use in my work only included Western methodologies; never did I think otherwise. I was trained as a lawyer to think black- and white-letter law. Therefore, when asked by my supervisor to think of an Indigenous theoretical framework to use, I was perplexed. I didn't

21 In this chapter, *Residential School Survivors* and *Survivors* are used interchangeably. The Survivors referred to are of either Aboriginal, Métis or Inuit descent. Further, the word *Survivors* is capitalized to illustrate the significance of these people to the story that unfolds.

22 The 10 + 3 formula used by the Federal Government to compensate Survivors included $10,000 for the first year and $3,000 for each additional year any survivor that attended an IRS.

know what a theoretical framework was because this was not taught in law school. So, I queried my supervisor – I needed an example to understand what was being asked of me. I thought long and hard and even frantically searched the dictionary to understand the term. I spent a good portion of my time at one writing retreat focusing on a theoretical framework to explain my work. Finally, after much thought about the stories of IRS Survivors, the teaching of the Seventh Fire Prophecy and the *voice* within the Waterdrum, I was struck by the similarities of the Survivors sounding their *voices* by telling their IRS stories and the sounding of the Waterdrum (*voice*) as they returned to the teachings and ceremonies. At that second, a vision of the Little Boy Waterdrum came to me. I was overjoyed. As I envisioned the Waterdrum teachings further, I was convinced this would be the framework for my work. The feelings that ran through my body assured me I was on the right path.

However, I was still reluctant to use this sacred object and teachings as my methodology and theoretical framework. I needed something more to settle my fear, therefore, I conducted a literature review of Indigenous research methodologies to satisfy this reluctance. Reading how other scholars were using Indigenous methodologies in their work put me at ease. According to Wilson, Indigenous methodologies are now being used in the research of Indigenous scholars throughout the world. He states:

> Within the past decade though, research and researchers have begun to change. More is being done to bring Indigenous communities into the research process, and the usefulness of the research is becoming more visible and beneficial to communities. A precursor for this change has been the growing number of Indigenous people who have excelled in academia and who focus their study on their own peoples. These new Indigenous scholars have introduced Indigenous beliefs, values and customs into the research process and this in turn has helped research to become much more culturally sensitive to Indigenous peoples.[23]

By using research methodologies that are culturally relevant and sensitive to Indigenous people, Indigenous researchers can use their stories as theoretical frameworks within which they can interpret other stories, teachings and experiences.[24] Margaret Kovach explains:

> Conceptual frameworks make visible the way we see the world. Within research, these frameworks are either transparent (i.e. through form) or not, yet always present. The rationale for explicit representation of one's conceptual framework is that it provides insight into a researcher's beliefs about knowledge

23 Shawn Wilson, *Research Is Ceremony: Indigenous Research Methods* (Halifax: Fernwood, 2008) at 15 [Wilson].

24 Leanne Simpson, *Dancing on Our Turtle's Back: Stories of Nishnaabeg Re-creation, Resurgence and a New Emergence* (Winnipeg: Arbeiter Ring, 2011) at 32 [Simpson].

> production, in general, and how those beliefs will impact the research project. The content and form of the conceptual framework itself assists in illustrating the researcher's standpoint, thus giving the reader insight into the interpretative lens that influences the research.[25]

Kathleen Absolon further states:

> The past, present and future intersect and much of our research is about searching for truth, freedom, emancipation and ultimately finding our way home. Finding our way home means searching to return to our roots and finding the dignity and humanity intended by the Creator.[26]

Wilson, Kovach and Absolon state that using our own theoretical framework helps Indigenous researchers such as me, to better understand Western research practices. Kovach further states that

> we carry our framework, which is not inherently good or bad, around with us and it is through this framework that we view the data.[27]

After this review, I understood what an Indigenous theoretical framework encompassed. In addition, I was assured that by using elements of Anishinabe sacred law in my work, I would not be exploiting my culture. Pondering this reluctance, I realize my cultural teachings as an Anishinabe Kwe, Second-Degree Midewiwin member of the Midewiwin Society made me fearful of exploiting the teachings and that is something that I could not do. However, I understood what I had to do. My heart was first and foremost Anishinabe, therefore I must use my lens to tell this story.

As I look back upon the vision that appeared to me, I recall how quickly the IRS story began unravelling before my eyes; all the visions that I experienced during my working hours showed me how the story was meant to be told and the manner in which it must be shared. I was emotionally and spiritually moved by the vision of the Waterdrum and the Seven Fires Prophecies. Never did I think that someday the teachings that I had heard many times before in the Midewiwin Lodge would lead to the completion of my PhD dissertation.

Interconnectedness

Everything in Creation is interconnected. Just like a spider that spins its web interconnecting each strand to another, all living things in Creation are

25 Margaret Kovach, *Indigenous Methodologies: Characteristics, Conversations and Contexts* (Toronto: University of Toronto Press, 2009) at 41 [Kovach].

26 Kathleen Absolon, *Kaandossiwin: How We Come to Know* (Halifax: Fernwood, 2011) at 55 [Absolon].

27 Borrows, *supra* note 6 at 24–55.

interconnected as well. The aim of this section is to illustrate the connections and interconnectedness between the IRS legacy and the teachings of the Anishinabe, while demonstrating how an Indigenous lens shaped this dissertation.

The Seven Fires Prophecies

The heart of my story about the IRS, previously stated, lies within the teachings of the Seven Fire Prophecies and the Waterdrum. As the story unfolds one chapter at a time,[28] the journey of the IRS Survivors travels through a timeline of over a hundred years. Although the prophecies spoke of the path that IRS Survivors (New People) would take in the future, in all fairness, they probably never knew the path they were travelling was such a significant one.

The voice *within the Waterdrum*

At the early stages of the interview process, it became very clear the methodology would have to reflect the Survivors' responses word per word. During a conversation with one Survivor, I was told point-blank not to change any of the words he shared with me as other researchers had done to him in the past. What he wanted was for the story he shared with me to be in his words – his *voice*. In my view, his concerns were valid, so I decided then that I would not change any words spoken by the Survivors. Little did I know then, this conversation would become one of the driving forces of the study. Not only did this conversation lead to the methodology used in this study but it also led to the theoretical framework. As I contemplated writing in the *voice* of the Survivors, I remembered the prophecy teaching: "If the New People will remain strong in their quest, the Waterdrum of the Midewiwin Lodge will again sound its *voice*".[29] In that instant, I understood the connection between the Survivors and the Waterdrum: Survivors were not only sounding the *voice* of the Waterdrum – they were also demanding their *voices* be heard. As I thought about the Survivors and the path that led them to the IRSSA, I envisioned the Waterdrum awakening the spirits of the Survivors. One by one, they recognized the sound of the Waterdrum and as they were awakened, they felt a profound strength as they stood up to tell their stories of the IRS. After years of having their *voice* silenced, they were finally being heard across the land. This is such a beautiful story of IRS Survivors demonstrated amazing resilience and courage and demanding resolution to the wrongs that were committed against them.

28 As previously stated, this chapter is one chapter from my dissertation. Because not all seven chapters are reviewed here, the reader will not be able to see how my dissertation unfolds. To view the total manuscript, see: "Re-living the Residential School Experience: An Anishinabe Kwe's Examination of the Compensation Processes for Residential School Survivors" (Thesis and PhD dissertations, Trent University), online: <https://digitalcollections.trentu.ca>.

29 Benton-Banai, *supra* note 4 at 93.

The Waterdrum

The Anishinabe use two different types of Waterdrums in the Midewiwin Lodge: the Grandfather Drum and the Little Boy Waterdrum.[30] The Grandfather drum can be recognized by the hoop placed at the top of the drum, while the Little Boy Waterdrum is tied together with seven small, round stones. In this dissertation, when referring to the Waterdrum, it is the Little Boy Waterdrum being referenced.

The Waterdrum is constructed using various elements taken from Mother Earth. The elements required to assemble a Waterdrum include a hollowed tree, a piece of deer hide, seven round stones, approximately six feet of leather lace, a wooden plug and water. Once the various parts are assembled, they are placed on the Drumkeeper's altar[31] in preparation for dressing. Putting the pieces of the Waterdrum together is referred to as 'dressing the Little Boy'.

In this chapter, the dressing of the Little Boy can be compared to preparing for a research project to begin. When constructing a Waterdrum, the builder must search for a tree that will be used to construct the drum. Not just any tree will suffice; it must be a tree which can perform the duties required of a Waterdrum. Similarly, before a research project begins, the author will search for the appropriate methodology and framework that suits the research project. In this dissertation, both Anishinabe and qualitative methodologies are used. In the following pages, the methodology and theoretical framework are shared to impart an understanding of the preparations that went into this dissertation.

The Anishinabe conceptual framework of the Waterdrum includes six elements that are required to dress the Little Boy: the tree, the stones, the deer hide, the

30 *Ibid.* at 71.

31 The Drumkeeper's altar is the place where the sacred objects used in a ceremony are placed. Normally the sacred objects are placed on a cloth or animal hide, but the type of altar a Drumkeeper uses is their choice.

deer hide lacing, the water and the wooden plug. Below are various research elements used to illustrate how the Waterdrum was used metaphorically to put the pieces together.

Tree – Anishinabe conceptual framework

The hollowed tree stump carved into the Waterdrum is the conceptual framework employed for this dissertation. This framework is borrowed from the teachings of the Waterdrum transmitted in the Midewiwin Lodge.

The drum is the heartbeat of Mother Earth. As long as the heart continues to beat, the life of the Anishinabe people will remain. The powerful and beautiful *voice* of the Anishinabe is the being that accompanies the sounding of the Waterdrum. The importance of the Waterdrum should never be underestimated, for it is the *voice* of the Anishinabe. Without the appealing sound of the Waterdrum and the beautiful *voice* of the Anishinabe people, the Eighth and Final Fire[32] will never be lit.

Stones – methodological principles

The stones tied around the Waterdrum are used to illustrate the various methodological principles required to undertake this study. To illustrate these principles, this section is divided into subsections to represent the stones used to tie the Waterdrum. In the circle of stones that fastens the deer hide to the base of the drum, no stone is more important than the other. Each stone is important to the overall construction of the Waterdrum as are the methodological principles of a dissertation.

32 To read more about the Eighth and Final Fire Prophecy see Benton-Banai, *supra* note 4 at 93.

Stone 1: relationality

In Anishinabe society, as well as other Indigenous societies, relationships are extremely important to the peaceful coexistence of the community. Relationships not only exist within the human realm but also within the spiritual and physical realms as well.[33] According to Anishinabe teachings, all living things within the universe are interconnected; therefore, relationships are crucial to the survival of humankind and the universe.

Before commencing interviews with residential school Survivors, a plan had to be developed. To capture a broad cross-section of residential school Survivors from across Canada, it was decided that interviews would take place in Ontario, Manitoba and British Columbia. Manitoba was chosen because it is a central province; British Columbia was selected because a previous research project identified a large number or residential school survivor litigants residing in this province; and Ontario was chosen because it is my home territory.

Even though well planned, the interview process did not roll out as expected. Contact people were needed to locate and identify residential school Survivors to interview. I began by thinking of relationships established with various people in Manitoba and British Columbia. One of my best friends (Pauline Terbasket) lives in British Columbia, so that was easy; however, I knew very few people in Manitoba.

Shortly thereafter, I attended a residential school conference held in Winnipeg, Manitoba, and was fortunate enough to meet Jennifer Wood, the coordinator for the Residential School Survivors program at the Assembly of Manitoba Chiefs office. She agreed to be my contact person in Manitoba. Susie Jones, a resident school survivor, was my contact person in Ontario.

Absolon describes relationships in this way:

> Community relationships are another common strength of Indigenous methodologies. Consistently, conscious Indigenous re-searchers agree that our searches be purposeful and beneficial to community (whatever that community is and represents). My re-search community is comprised of a diverse representation and includes Indigenous educators, scholars and searchers. I also have my traditional community, geographic community and nation community. I have a clan family and a circle of people who I choose to be in relationship with and who lovingly support me. Some searchers may interpret community to be their reserve, their First Nation, Indigenous peoples generally, their land base, either cultural orientation or their lifestyle. Community is determined and defined with respect to the searcher.[34]

In this case, the community relationships consisted of those involved in the residential school issue – family, friends, those of Anishinabe ancestry and others that worked with residential school Survivors.

33 Absolon, *supra* note 26 at 125.
34 *Ibid.* at 127.

Another important relationship fundamental to the success of this dissertation was my friendship with Elder Shirley Williams, professor emeritus of Trent University. Shirley was a residential school survivor and a role model for the Aboriginal Healing Foundation. Also, Shirley was a previous professor of mine at Trent University; therefore, I knew Shirley, but not as well as I would in the months that followed entry into the PhD program. Together, we developed and taught a university course on residential schools for two years while I completed my residency requirements at Trent. We travelled to residential school conferences together and met regularly for breakfast, lunch or supper. Due to the fact that she is knowledgeable of the residential school legacy, she was invited to be a committee member on this dissertation journey.

Stone 2: outsider/insider – respecting local protocols

Another consideration requiring prior thought and consideration was how to enter the community without offending community members. Going into an Aboriginal community without prior contact or a contact person would be a grave mistake because community members do not think favourably of research conducted within their community by outsiders. Therefore, as an outsider I would need someone to introduce me to the community in Manitoba and British Columbia. According to Linda Smith:

> Most research methodologies assume that the researcher is an outsider able to observe without being implicated in the scene. This is related to positivism and notions of objectivity and neutrality. . . . Indigenous research approaches problematize the insider model in different ways because there are multiple ways of both being an insider and an outsider in indigenous contexts. The critical issue with insider research is the constant need for reflexivity.[35]

Although outsiders are useful in some instances, it is important not to offend Survivors in their own community. Therefore, I eased myself into the urban community of Winnipeg and into the Okanagan Nation in two very different ways.

In Winnipeg, my contact person Jennifer Wood made the initial contacts with the people that were interviewed, and she set up the interviews at the Assembly of Manitoba Chiefs offices. Since she made the initial contact, she acted as the gatekeeper between the survivor and myself. She knew most of the residential school Survivors in the Winnipeg area and they knew and trusted her; so, they were open to being interviewed.

In the Okanagan Nation territory, I was fortunate to be in the area when several residential school survivor gatherings were scheduled in Penticton and the Lower Similkameen Indian Band. My contact person took me to these gatherings and introduced me to many of the Survivors. While in the area, it was possible to also

35 Linda Smith, *Decolonizing Methodologies* (Dunedin: University of Otago Press, 1999) at 137 [Smith].

attend several other community social events such as wedding anniversaries and baseball and basketball games. Attending these gatherings proved to be an excellent opportunity to meet a lot of residential school Survivors. Therefore, when it came time to start interviews, people in the community were familiar with me, which made interviewing easier.

The interviews conducted on Walpole Island First Nation introduced a set of different variables because this was my home territory. Although viewed as an insider, my relationship with the community triggered a different set of expectations. As stated by Smith:

> Insiders have to live with the consequences of their processes on a day-to-day basis forever more, and so do their families and communities. For this reason, insider researchers need to build particular sorts of research-based support systems and relationships with their communities. They have to be skilled at defining clear research goals and "like . . . . Of relating" which are specific to the project and somewhat different from their own family networks.[36]

As an insider researcher, there is still the requirement to be ethical and respectful, as reflexive and critical as an outsider[37] while being humble at the same time. Smith states that one of the difficult risks insider researchers take is to "test" their own taken-for-granted views about their community. It is a risk because it can unsettle beliefs, values, relations and the knowledge of different histories within the community.[38]

On Walpole Island, the residential school Survivors have been meeting for the last 5 to 10 years on a regular basis. My mother was a part of this group before she passed away in 2007. I had attended several meetings with her, so the group members were aware of my interest in the subject. When it came time to interview members of this group, I contacted the group's organizer to inform her of my research and to ask for her guidance. She arranged for me to introduce my research at a Residential School Survivors meeting scheduled in February 2009. After the presentation, 10 people indicated that they were interested in being interviewed.

Stone 3: ethical considerations

There were many ethical considerations to contemplate before undertaking this research. My past experience working with residential school Survivors gave me insight into the type of questions that could be asked and those that could do potential harm during the interview process. Some of the ethical considerations to be considered prior to interviews include, but are not limited to, what to do if a person disclosed a physical or sexual assault they had never disclosed to anyone

36 *Ibid.* at 137.
37 *Ibid.* at 139.
38 *Ibid.*

else; what to do if the person went into a fit of rage; how to respond if the person cried uncontrollably; what to do if the person fled the room.

Every possible situation that could arise had to be examined and a response plan considered beforehand. It was also necessary to have contact information for the local police, counsellors and other support people in the event a disclosure or negative outburst occurred. As each hypothetical scenario was pondered, a response had to be prepared.

Stone 4: creating the time and the place

Another consideration decided beforehand was the place where the interview would be conducted and the time required. Every residential school survivor interviewed was given the opportunity to name the location where they would be interviewed, either in the comfort of their home, in a community hall, in a hotel room or at an Aboriginal organization with which they were familiar. To ensure they felt safe and comfortable, each survivor was able to state the time they would be interviewed. Safety was one of the most important aspects of the interview process; therefore, every survivor was accommodated to the best of my ability.

Stone 5: reciprocity

Reciprocity in Aboriginal communities is taught when children are very young. For everything a person takes from Creation, something must be given back. This notion is reflected in the work of Bagele Chilisa, as shared here:

> Third and fourth-world communities have resisted intrusion into their lives since the colonial period. The resistance has been largely ignored because, in essence, it questions the validity of the colonial research-built theories. Once they brought tobacco, Ellis and Earley (2006) report, key informants responded positively to the request for the interview saying "You have shown respect for our ways by offering tobacco and smudging, your intentions seem to be good ones, let's see how we can help you".[39]

The practice of offering tobacco is important to Aboriginal people in many areas of Turtle Island; therefore, upon entering Okanagan, Saulteaux and Cree territory, tobacco was offered. In Anishinabe society, tobacco is offered to give thanks for the knowledge gained from the interview.

In this exchange as a doctoral student, what I learned had to be given back to the community in some manner. Giving back can take many shapes and forms. In this instance I give back not only to my immediate family, but to my community, the Anishinabe people and the Aboriginal people of Canada. By undertaking this study, the words of the Survivors are shared regarding their experiences with the

39 Bagele Chilisa, *Indigenous Research Methodologies* (Los Angeles: Sage, 2012) at 115 [Chilisa].

processes. By sharing with those who are interested, I give back what has been learned to every reader. In a research context Kovach states:

> They say that we traditionally knew about portal, the doorway, how to get knowledge and that it was brought to the people by sharing, by community forums, by sitting in circles, by engaging in ceremony, by honouring your relationship to the spirit. When we do that, the spirit will reciprocate and we will be given what we are needed.[40]

The belief in reciprocity and doing things in the right manner ensures that researchers will be given what we need to complete our research while respecting those interviewed.

Stone 6: the interview questions and process

The interview involved 10 questions. Eight of the 10 questions dealt with the process utilized for the compensation payments; the other two questions concerned the Truth and Reconciliation Commission. A list of the questions can be found in the Appendix 12 of the manuscript found in the Trent University archives.[41] The interview process began by explaining the interview process, signing the Informed Consent Form[42] and reading the Information Sheet[43] and the Feedback Form.[44] Each survivor who participated could expect at least one hour for the interview; however, some interviews were as short as 15 minutes. The majority of the interviews were conducted beginning in February until November 2009, with the exception of one, which was conducted the summer of August 2010.

The interviews were recorded and later transcribed by myself using a digital recorder and laptop computer. The recorder and laptop were both required to have secured passwords so no one could access the files unless given the password.

Stone 7: cultural protocols

When conducting research in an Aboriginal community, cultural protocols are important to consider when planning the research strategy. With familiarity of my own community, very little preparation was needed. However, learning proper protocol for British Columbia and Manitoba was extremely important

40 Kovach, *supra* note 25 at 154.

41 See *supra* note 28 where PhD manuscript can be found – Trent University, online: <https://digitalcollections.trentu.ca/>.

42 *Ibid.* at Appendix 2.

43 *Ibid.* at Appendix 1.

44 *Ibid.* at Appendix 3.

for conducting the research in a respectful manner, for I knew very little of the cultural protocol of these two regions. Each of the contact people in these two provinces provided invaluable guidance to the correct protocol in each region. In Aboriginal society, it is common practice when approaching Elders for knowledge that a gift of tobacco is offered. Simpson states:

> When we put our tobacco down and ask for help to solve a problem, to come up with a strategy or so that the Stone we threw ripples through the world in a positive way, we are asking the implicate order to visit our action.[45]

However, during the residential school era, the cultural practices within many communities were lost and many Elders and residential school Survivors converted to Christianity and did not practice their traditions any longer. For this reason, direction from the contact people on how to approach the Survivors to be interviewed was critical, for they knew their community members. On their advice, it was decided to offer either tobacco pouches or gifts to those interviewed based upon the recommendations made by the contact person.

Deer hide – positionality and self-care

The deer hide used to create the Waterdrum represents my positionality within the research. During the interview process, it was quickly learned how emotionally demanding the topic of the research was for both me and those interviewed. For this reason, it was crucial to my well-being not to take on the negative emotions of those who were interviewed, should they surface. I had to learn to shake the negativity whenever it began weighing me down, for my own self-care.

45 Simpson, *supra* note 24 at 146.

At times, a call to Elder Shirley Williams for support was needed. At one particular time in Winnipeg, a Survivor's reactions took me by total surprise. Settled into a secluded space at the Assembly of Manitoba Chiefs office, the Survivor was welcomed when he walked in. He began by stating he was not going to participate in the interview, and he thought this research was not right. He continued on for about half an hour. Then he smiled and left the room. Astounded and almost in tears, I went to Jennifer's office and told her what happened. At that point in the research process I began to doubt myself and wanted to drop all things and run home. Instead I called Elder Shirley Williams who reaffirmed there would always be someone that would disagree with what I was doing and to think about all the positive experiences and move forward with this important research. This example demonstrates the importance of having a support person to assist through the rough times so work can continue.

Deer hide lacing – important considerations

The lacing securing the deer hide over the top of the drum is seen as the considerations taken into account before conducting the research. Before the interview process started, the implications of the research had to be considered from many different angles for both myself and those who would be interviewed. Before the interview process began, every stone would have to be turned over and thought through to ensure no preventable harm would come to the Survivors.

Support systems

Undertaking a research project that involved interviewing residential school Survivors was an incredible responsibility, more than ever imagined. One very important aspect of the interview process was finding support networks in the area. The support person identified was contacted before scheduled interviews to ensure they would be available during or after the interview. The name of a traditional person or Elder was also identified in the event the person being interviewed asked for this person.

The support person was selected based on previous experience, profession or traditional experience and recommendation of my contact person in that province. When interviews were arranged, each Survivor was asked whether they wanted a support person with them when they were interviewed. Participants were also given the option of having a family member, friend or Elder of their choice with them when they were being interviewed.

Water – people (the participants of this research)

The water poured into the Waterdrum represents the residential school Survivors interviewed – the life-force of the study. Therefore, choosing who to interview had to be considered. The final decision regarding selection of people to interview was made with the assistance of the contact person in each of the locations. The contact person provided a list of residential school Survivors that they felt would be a "good candidate" to interview. By a "good candidate" meant a person that would be less likely to be traumatized by the experience and someone who would be able to provide valuable information. It was particularly difficult to determine who to interview in Manitoba and British Columbia; I had to trust my contact person, and for the most part, those recommended were perfect candidates who provided rich and valuable information.

From the interviews conducted, approximately 35% of those interviewed were from Ontario, 30% from Manitoba and 35% from British Columbia. This in my view is a good cross section of residential school Survivors from three different provinces.

The total number of residential school Survivors interviewed was 24. The following information provides a profile of those interviewed:

> In Ontario, a total of nine were interviewed: six were women and three were men. In Manitoba, a total of six were interviewed: two were women and

four were men. In British Columbia, a total of nine were interviewed: three were women and six were men.

The 11 women interviewed ranged from 50 to 75 years of age.
The average age of the women interviewed was 67 years of age.
The 13 men interviewed ranged from 53 to 80 years of age.
The average age of the men interviewed was 63 years of age.

Another interesting fact learned was the youngest child sent to residential school in this group was four and a half years of age and was from Walpole Island First Nation, in Ontario. Of the residential school Survivors interviewed, only one man and one woman were placed in more than one residential school. The woman was placed in two different schools, while the man was placed in three different schools.

Another observation was that the longest amount of time spent in a residential school was 12 years. In Canada, the average time spent at a residential school was seven years. The average time spent in residential schools in Ontario was six years; the average time for those in Manitoba was eight and a half years; and the average of those from British Columbia was 10 years.[46]

The wooden plug – my word/the promise I gave

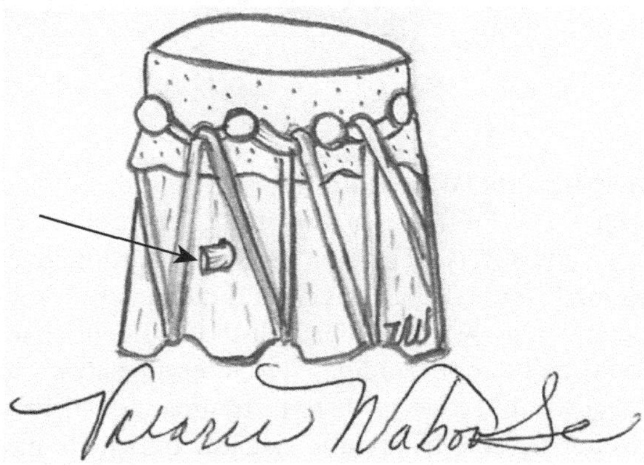

The wooden plug that secures the water in the Waterdrum represents the promise made to Survivors interviewed. As previously stated while being interviewed, several survivors spoke adamantly about not being quoted properly or their story not being told accurately in other research studies they had participated in. Their statements were deeply disturbing, and as a result, I gave them my word that they would not be misquoted. For many, the process was intimidating and difficult. For some, being interviewed yet again was unwarranted and seen as another exercise of being misunderstood or misinterpreted.

46 Benton-Banai, *supra* note 4 at 93.

One of the main reasons a qualitative methodology was selected was to ensure that the *voice* of the survivors would be heard. The methodology had to tell their story and their experiences with the compensation processes from their perspective and not my own. While this may have seemed an unrealistic expectation at the time, I gave my "word"; therefore, I am bound by this promise.[47]

Conclusion

The purpose of this chapter was twofold: firstly, to share my research journey illustrating how an Indigenous scholar utilized an Indigenous lens to write a PhD dissertation; and secondly, to provide a space for IRS Survivors' *voice* to be heard. Although I never intended to write about my personal research journey, I felt it necessary to do so. I wanted the reader to fully understand how a colonized Indigenous legal scholar struggled to write from an Indigenous lens at the onset. After writing in this manner for the last 10 years, I can honestly say that my research and writing has taken on a whole new meaning for me. I can now use my cultural knowledge and personal experience as an Anishinabe Kwe to share my deepest thoughts and understanding of current issues using the teachings of the Elders. Writing within this context provides me with an opportunity to drift into deep thought and concentration about the meanings behind the teachings and ceremonies. Thinking about this, I am reminded of Shawn Wilson's book title: *Research is Ceremony*. The title of his book rings so true – researching from an Indigenous paradigm teaches so much, not only about the research topic but also about self, the teachings of the ancestors and our interconnection to all living things. It is an experience that I will cherish forever and one which I believe all Indigenous scholars should undertake.

I want to end by sharing some closing thoughts about being an Indigenous legal scholar. I take the responsibility of teaching young lawyers very seriously. As more and more students learn about Indigenous history and issues that we face, I believe we are moving one step closer to reconciliation in Canada. I also believe as more Indigenous scholars utilize methodologies from their respective Nations, the more cultural awareness will be raised. The time for Indigenous scholars to utilize the spaces within educational institutions to further educate society is upon us. The time to speak our truth is now. Our *voice* was silenced during the IRS era. As second and third-generation survivors of the IRS legacy, we must continue sounding our *voice* to honour our ancestors and ensure that we are never silenced again.

47 In Aboriginal society, when one gives their word that they will do something for another person, their word is generally accepted as a given. This would be comparable to two Western society individuals using a handshake to close a deal. For Aboriginal people, giving your word is a sacred covenant. This is especially true since I was speaking to Elders who understand and still practice these sacred ways. Therefore, when I gave my word to the Survivors, I made a commitment to them to share the truth as they spoke it.

I want to end this chapter by sharing the Eighth and Final Fire Prophecy. The prophecy states:

> It is at this time that the Light-skinned Race will be given a choice between two roads. If they choose the right road, then the Seventh Fire will light the Eighth and Final Fire – an eternal Fire of peace, love, brotherhood and sisterhood.[48]

48 This prophecy sends a beautiful message about how we as citizens of this Universe must reconcile our differences so we can live in everlasting peace. I share this prophecy so that those reading this chapter will understand the Indigenous worldview, especially the Anishinabe worldview that is shared in this chapter, and begin meaningful conversations about how our Nations can move towards reconciliation. Reconciliation is a huge undertaking that the Canadian government has promised to implement in its entirety. Although I would love to share more about this subject, but I don't want to take away from this chapter, so I'll leave it for another day.

Notes on contributors

Paola Andrea Acosta-Alvarado has a PhD and an MAS in international law and international relations from the Instituto Ortega y Gasset and the Universidad Complutense de Madrid (Spain), a master's degree in public law from Universidad Externado (Colombia) and a postgraduate diploma in human rights and democratization processes from the Universidad de Chile (Chile). She is Associate Professor at the School of Law of the Universidad Externado (Colombia). Her research focuses on the relations between international law and domestic law, international legal education and international human rights law. She is a founding member of the REDIAL project.

Amaya Álvez Marín is Associate Professor at Universidad de Concepción (Chile). She has a PhD in law from the University of York (Canada), an LLM from the University of Toronto (Canada), an MAS from the Université de Liège (Belgium) and a degree in law and social sciences from the Universidad de Concepción (Chile). Her work focuses on constitutional law, Indigenous People's rights and water resources. She also works as a lawyer at the law firm Colectiva Justicia en Derechos Humanos as a member of the Mapuche People.

Courtney Arseneau recently completed her PhD in community psychology at Wilfrid Laurier University. Her doctoral research focused on processes of consultation and free, prior and informed consent (FPIC) in proposed development on Indigenous territories in northern Ontario. During her graduate studies, she worked with the Laurier Indigenous Rights and Resource Governance Research Group, where she explored ways to share information about the UNDRIP and the right to FPIC at the community level.

José Aylwin is a human rights lawyer. With legal studies at the University of Chile in Santiago (1981) and at the University of British Columbia (Canada), where he obtained a master in laws degree (1999), he has researched and published on human rights, ethnic and cultural diversity, environmental rights, and on business and human rights. He teaches Indigenous Peoples' rights at the School of Law of the Universidad Austral de Chile. He currently acts as Coordinator of the Globalization and Human Rights Program of the

Observatorio Ciudadano (Citizens' Watch), a non-governmental organization aimed at documenting and promoting human rights. (Email: jaylwin@ obervatorio.cl)

Reem Bahdi is an associate professor at the Faculty of Law, University of Windsor. Her research focuses on access to justice in Canada, especially as it relates to Arab and Muslim communities, and on access to justice and development in Palestine. She created and directed, along with Dr. Mudar Kassis of Birzeit University (Palestine), the Karamah judicial education initiative. She has taught courses about access to justice, human dignity, torts, torture and national security, legal theory, and Arabs, Muslims and the law.

Maria Bargh (Te Arawa, Ngāti Awa) is Associate Professor in Te Kawa a Māui, Māori Studies, Victoria University of Wellington. Her research is in the areas of Māori politics and resource management.

Laura Betancur-Restrepo is Associate Professor at the School of Law and Director of the Masters in Peace Building at Universidad de los Andes (Colombia). She holds degrees in law and philosophy, a masters degree in International Law and International Organizations and a PhD in law. Her research focuses on international legal theory, education on international law in Latin America and the relation between international law and domestic peace building. She is a founding member of the REDIAL project and of the Editorial Collective of Third World Approaches to International Law Review (TWAILR.com).

Amar Bhatia is an associate professor at Osgoode Hall Law School, York University, Canada. His research focuses on transnational migration in a settler colonial context and the intersection of immigration and refugee law, Aboriginal law, treaty relations and Indigenous laws. He has also co-edited the Journal of Law Social Policy and been a member of the Third World Approaches to International Law Review's editorial collective. At Osgoode, he has taught property law, refugee law, globalization and the law (focused on migrant work), and co-directed the Intensive Program in Indigenous Lands, Resources and Governments.

Aimée Craft is an associate professor at the Faculty Law, University of Ottawa, and an Indigenous (Anishinaabe-Métis) lawyer from Manitoba. She is an internationally recognized leader in the area of Indigenous laws, treaties and water. She prioritizes Indigenous-led and interdisciplinary research, including visual arts and film, co-leads a series of major research grants on decolonizing water governance and works with many Indigenous nations and communities on Indigenous relationships with and responsibilities to *nibi* (water). She plays an active role in international collaborations relating to transformative memory in colonial contexts and relating to the reclamation of Indigenous birthing practices as expressions of territorial sovereignty.

Assis da Costa Oliveira is a professor of human rights at the Federal University of Pará, Brazil. He is a lawyer and PhD at the University of Brasília Faculty of Law, Brazil.

Mary Eberts received her legal education at Western University and Harvard Law School. She has appeared as counsel to parties and interveners in the Supreme Court of Canada, Courts of Appeal and Superior Courts in Ontario and other provinces, the Federal Court and Court of Appeal, and before administrative tribunals and inquests across Canada. She was instrumental in securing the present language of section 15 of the Charter and was one of the founders of the Women's Legal Education and Action Fund (LEAF). Since 1991, she has been litigation counsel to the Native Women's Association of Canada (NWAC). She has been a faculty member at the Faculty of Law, University of Toronto, and has held the Gordon Henderson Chair in Human Rights at the University of Ottawa and the Ariel Sallows Chair in Human Rights at the College of Law, University of Saskatchewan, where she taught courses in test case litigation. She is an Officer of the Order of Canada, and has received the Law Society Medal, the Governor-General's Award in Honour of the Persons' Case, the Queen's Diamond Jubilee Medal and several honorary degrees.

Fabia Fernandes Carvalho Veçoso is a postdoctoral fellow with the Laureate Program in International Law at Melbourne Law School. Her research project focuses on the emergence and circulation of the principle of non-intervention in Latin America in the twentieth century. Before joining Melbourne Law School, Fabia was an assistant professor of International Relations at the Federal University of São Paulo. Her research and teaching interests are focused on the theory and history of international law, regionalism and Latin America, and international human rights law. Fabia earned her LLB and LLM from the University of São Paulo Law School, where she also completed her doctorate in international law. Fabia was a Doctoral Visiting Research Fellow at the Erik Castrén Institute of International Law and Human Rights at the University of Helsinki. She is a founding member of the REDIAL Project.

Jeffery G. Hewitt (Cree) is an assistant professor at the Osgoode Hall Law School, York University. His research interests include Indigenous legal orders and governance, constitutional and administrative law, human rights and remedies, business law, art and law. Since 2002, he has served as general counsel to Rama First Nation during which time the General Counsel's office received a 2011 Canadian General Counsel Award for Social Responsibility for work with First Nation Elders and youth. He holds an LLB and LLM from Osgoode Hall Law School and is called to the Bar in the Province of Ontario (since 1998).

Tatsuhiko Inatani is an associate professor of law at Kyoto University and a visiting researcher at RIKEN AIP. He also serves as a member of research committee for a governance innovation at the METI in Japan. His academic works has focused on criminal justice from comparative law perspective, legal methodology, and law and technology.

Marta Infantino is Associate Professor of Comparative Law, IUSLIT Department, University of Trieste. She has held visiting professorships at the Scuola Normale Superiore in Italy, at the Université de Montréal in Canada, at the Los Andes University in Colombia, and at the Université d'été of the Fondation pour le droit continental in France. She has written books and articles on comparative contract law, comparative tort law, methodologies of comparative law and global indicators.

Beverley Jacobs, CM (Member of the Order of Canada), LLB (1994, University of Windsor), LLM (2000, University of Calgary), PhD (2018, University of Calgary) is a member of the Bear Clan, Mohawk Nation of the Haudenosaunee Confederacy. She is Associate Professor and Associate Dean (Academic) at the Faculty of Law, University of Windsor, and she practices law part-time in her home community of Six Nations of the Grand River Territory. She is also a consultant/researcher/writer/public speaker. Her work centers around ending gendered colonial violence against Indigenous people and restoring Indigenous laws, beliefs, values and traditions.

Yvonne Johnson, member of the Cree Nation of Treaty Six Territory, Red Pheasant First Nations, daughter of Cecilia, great-granddaughter of Chief Big Bear, grandmother and survivor of the colonial legal system.

Mudar Kassis is Associate Professor of Philosophy and Director of the Muwatin Institute for Democracy and Human Rights at Birzeit University in Palestine. His research interests include law and society, democracy, human rights, decolonization, the concept of dignity, the everyday, research ethics, political corruption and populism. He founded and directed, with Professor Reem Bahdi, the Karamah judicial education initiative.

Estella Libardi de Souza is a lawyer, a public servant at the Nacional Foundation of Indigenous People and a doctoral candidate at the Federal University of Pará Faculty of Law, Brazil.

Darcy Lindberg is an assistant professor with the University of Alberta's Faculty of Law, where he teaches courses on constitutional law, Indigenous legal orders, treaties and Indigenous environmental laws. He is mixed-rooted Plains Cree, with his relations coming from Samson Cree Nation in Alberta and the Battleford area in Saskatchewan. His research focuses on the constitutional and legal theory of Plains Cree peoples in relation to lands, waters and animals.

Deborah McGregor holds a Canada Research Chair cross-appointed with Osgoode Hall Law School and the Faculty of Environmental Studies, York University. She has been at the forefront of Indigenous environmental justice and Indigenous research theory and practice. Over the years, she has achieved international recognition through her creative and innovative approach using digital and social media to reach Indigenous communities and the public. Her work has been shared through the IEJ project website (https://iejproject.

info.yorku.ca/) and UKRI International Collaboration on Indigenous research (www.indigenous.ncrm.ac.uk/).

Terry Mitchell is a professor in the Balsillie School of International Affairs. She is a community psychologist and a registered clinical psychologist with a focus on colonial trauma, self-determination and resource governance. Her research focuses on collaborations with Indigenous communities and interdisciplinary teams of scholars to study the implementation of the UNDRIP and the right to FPIC in land and resource governance. She advances the curating and dissemination of academic and community accessible resources on the right to FPIC through her mobile-friendly site (www.fpic.info).

Usha Natarajan, PhD, MA, LLB, BA, is Edward W. Said Fellow at Columbia University, Global South Visiting Scholar at University of British Columbia, and Senior Fellow at Melbourne Law School. Her research is interdisciplinary, utilizing postcolonial and third world approaches to international law to provide an interrelated understanding of development, environment, migration and conflict. Her research is recognized by global awards and grants in the fields of international environmental law, migration and refugee law, and postcolonialism. Previously, she was a tenured associate professor of international law at the American University in Cairo and worked with international organizations including UNDP and UNESCO.

Ogamauh annag qwe (Sue Chiblow) is Crane Clan from Garden River First Nation. As a PhD candidate at York University, her work focuses on N'bi G'giikendaaswinmin (water knowledge) exploring humanity's relationship to N'bi and how improving this relationship can support the well-being for N'bi and all life. Sue is the recipient of the Vanier Graduate Scholarship and is in the Pre-doctoral Fellowship in American Indian and Indigenous Studies Program at Michigan State University. She has worked extensively with First Nation Peoples and is a volunteer for the Traditional Ecological Knowledge Elders of the Robinson Huron Treaty territory.

Enrique Prieto-Ríos has a Phd in Law from Birkbeck – University of London, MA in International Law The London College UCK and Attorney at Law – Universidad del Rosario Bogotá. Enrique's research focuses on International Economic Law, International Investment Law and Business and Human Rights, and Law and Education. Enrique is currently Director of the Research Group of International Law, Research Director and Associate Professor at the Faculty of Law – Universidad del Rosario. Enrique is Commissioner at the Advisory Commission on Peace and Human Rights that was created by the 2016 Peace Accord. Enrique has been a visiting lecturer at the School of Law – Universidad de los Andes, a visiting fellow at Osgoode the School of Law – University of York, a visiting fellow at the School of Law – University of Warwick and a sessional lecturer at the School of Law – Birkbeck University of London. Enrique has been the Director of the British and Colombian

Lawyers Association – BRICOL, intern at the International Bar Association – IBA and a consultant for law firms in Bogotá and in London.

Daniel Rivas-Ramírez is Managing Editor of the *Latin American Law Review*, edited by Universidad de los Andes (Colombia) and CIDE (Mexico). His research focuses on constitutional law, the relationship between international law and domestic law, and international legal education. He studied a bachelor of laws at Universidad Externado (Colombia).

Rayanna Seymour-Hourie is Bear Clan from Anishinaabeg of Naongashiing in Treaty 3 Territory (Northwestern Ontario). She is a staff lawyer at West Coast Environmental Law, and Manager of the RELAW Program (Revitalizing Indigenous Law for Land, Air and Water). She is just beginning her career as a lawyer, with work and volunteer experience in advocacy for Indigenous peoples (specifically youth), the land and water for close to a decade.

Dr. Darren Thomas is Bear Clan and member of the Seneca Nation from the Grand River Territory of the Haudenosaunee. He is an assistant professor at Laurier Brantford in the Indigenous Studies program. His research interests are in Indigenous community development, strengthening Indigenous health and well-being, Indigenous law and Indigenous rights.

Joey Twins is a Cree Woman from Maskwacis also known as Hobbema. She is a survivor of the prison system.

Estair Van Wagner is an Associate professor at Osgoode Hall Law School at York University. She researches and teaches in the areas of land use planning, natural resource and property law and is Co-director of Osgoode's Environmental Justice and Sustainability Clinic. She is currently involved in a project examining government consultation with Maori under New Zealand mining law and is the PI of a project exploring the relationship between Aboriginal title, Indigenous property, and privately-owned land.

Valarie Waboose is Assistant Professor at University of Windsor, Faculty of Law and teaches Aboriginal Law, Indigenous Legal Orders, Reconciliation and the Residential School Legacy and Anishinabe Law Camp. Before completing her doctoral degree, she obtained a BA from Trent University, an LLB from Windsor Law and an LLM from Osgoode Hall. Additionally, she worked as in-house legal counsel for Walpole Island First Nation and owned and operated a consultant business specializing in strategic planning, policy development and program planning and evaluation. Her research interests include Indigenous legal orders and traditions, Indigenous methodologies, child welfare, reconciliation and Indian residential schools.

Sujith Xavier (LLB, LLM, PhD) is an associate professor at the Faculty of Law, University of Windsor. His research spans domestic and international legal theory, including Third World Approaches to International Law (TWAIL), constitutions and administrations, global governance, international law and transitional justice. He is one of the co-editors of *Third World Approaches to International Law: On Praxis and the Intellectual* and is a founding member of the Editorial Collective of Third World Approaches to International Law Review (TWAILR.com). He has significant experience working with grassroots organizations in Sri Lanka. He is a member of the Law Society of Ontario and has appeared before the Supreme Court of Canada and the Canadian Federal Court and Federal Court of Appeal.

Index

Page numbers in *italics* indicate a figure and page numbers in **bold** indicate a table on the corresponding page. Page numbers followed by 'n' indicate a note.